D1491405

BEYOND BIAS AND BARRIERS

FULFILLING THE POTENTIAL OF WOMEN IN ACADEMIC SCIENCE AND ENGINEERING

Committee on Maximizing the Potential of Women in
Academic Science and Engineering

Committee on Science, Engineering, and Public Policy

NATIONAL ACADEMY OF SCIENCES,
NATIONAL ACADEMY OF ENGINEERING, AND
INSTITUTE OF MEDICINE
OF THE NATIONAL ACADEMIES

THE NATIONAL ACADEMIES PRESS
Washington, D.C.
www.nap.edu

THE NATIONAL ACADEMIES PRESS 500 Fifth Street NW Washington, DC 20001

NOTICE: The project that is the subject of this report was approved by the Governing Board of the National Research Council, whose members are drawn from the Councils of the National Academy of Sciences, the National Academy of Engineering, and the Institute of Medicine. The members of the committee responsible for the report were chosen for their special competences and with regard for appropriate balance.

Support for this project was provided by the National Academies; the National Institutes of Health Office for Research on Women's Health under Contract 1-OD-4-2137, Task Order 166; Eli Lilly Company; the National Science Foundation award SBE-0536999; and the Ford Foundation. Eli Lilly funds were used only to support project research. Any opinions, findings, conclusions, or recommendations expressed in this publication are those of the authors and do not necessarily reflect the views of the organizations or agencies that provided support for the project.

Library of Congress Cataloging-in-Publication Data

Committee on Maximizing the Potential of Women in Academic Science and Engineering (U.S.)
    Beyond bias and barriers : fulfilling the potential of women in academic science and engineering / Committee on Maximizing the Potential of Women in Academic Science and Engineering, Committee on Science, Engineering, and Public Policy.
    p. cm.
    Includes bibliographical references and index.
    ISBN-13: 978-0-309-10042-7 (hardback)
    ISBN-10: 0-309-10042-9 (hardback)
    ISBN-13: 978-0-309-65454-8 (pdf)
    ISBN-10: 0-309-65454-8 (pdf)
    1. Women in science—United States. 2. Women in engineering—United States. 3. Science—Study and teaching—United States. 4. Engineering—Study and teaching—United States. 5. Women—Education—United States. 6. Vocational interests—United States. I. Committee on Science, Engineering, and Public Policy (U.S.) II. Title.
    Q130.C65 2006
    500.82'0973—dc22
                                        2006036337

Committee on Science, Engineering, and Public Policy, 500 Fifth Street NW, Washington, DC 20001; 202-334-2807; Internet, http://www.nationalacademies.org/cosepup.

Additional copies of this workshop summary are available from the National Academies Press, 500 Fifth Street NW, Lockbox 285, Washington, DC 20055; (800) 624-6242 or (202) 334-3313 (in the Washington metropolitan area); Internet, http://www.nap.edu.

Copyright 2007 by the National Academy of Sciences. All rights reserved.

Printed in the United States of America

THE NATIONAL ACADEMIES
Advisers to the Nation on Science, Engineering, and Medicine

The **National Academy of Sciences** is a private, nonprofit, self-perpetuating society of distinguished scholars engaged in scientific and engineering research, dedicated to the furtherance of science and technology and to their use for the general welfare. Upon the authority of the charter granted to it by the Congress in 1863, the Academy has a mandate that requires it to advise the federal government on scientific and technical matters. Dr. Ralph J. Cicerone is president of the National Academy of Sciences.

The **National Academy of Engineering** was established in 1964, under the charter of the National Academy of Sciences, as a parallel organization of outstanding engineers. It is autonomous in its administration and in the selection of its members, sharing with the National Academy of Sciences the responsibility for advising the federal government. The National Academy of Engineering also sponsors engineering programs aimed at meeting national needs, encourages education and research, and recognizes the superior achievements of engineers. Dr. Wm. A. Wulf is president of the National Academy of Engineering.

The **Institute of Medicine** was established in 1970 by the National Academy of Sciences to secure the services of eminent members of appropriate professions in the examination of policy matters pertaining to the health of the public. The Institute acts under the responsibility given to the National Academy of Sciences by its congressional charter to be an adviser to the federal government and, upon its own initiative, to identify issues of medical care, research, and education. Dr. Harvey V. Fineberg is president of the Institute of Medicine.

The **National Research Council** was organized by the National Academy of Sciences in 1916 to associate the broad community of science and technology with the Academy's purposes of furthering knowledge and advising the federal government. Functioning in accordance with general policies determined by the Academy, the Council has become the principal operating agency of both the National Academy of Sciences and the National Academy of Engineering in providing services to the government, the public, and the scientific and engineering communities. The Council is administered jointly by both Academies and the Institute of Medicine. Dr. Ralph J. Cicerone and Dr. Wm. A. Wulf are chair and vice chair, respectively, of the National Research Council.

www.national-academies.org

Denice Dee Denton, 1959-2006

A valued member of this committee, Denice Denton was an extraordinarily talented scholar, educational leader, and relentless voice for progress. She helped shape the direction of our nation's science and engineering enterprise through her research, teaching, technology development, service, leadership, mentoring, public communication of science and engineering, initiatives to promote diversity and inclusion, and outreach to our schools.

She was bigger than life. She opened doors, and stood in them to let others through. She mentored young scholars and students. Her enthusiasm for science was clear and infectious.

She was a force—a magnificent force. She pushed the institutions she inhabited to be better than they wanted to be.

With her tragic death we lost a friend, a colleague, and a champion. We proudly dedicate this report to her.

We will miss her.

Donna E. Shalala
Chair, Committee on Maximizing the Potential
of Women in Academic Science and Engineering

COMMITTEE ON MAXIMIZING THE POTENTIAL OF WOMEN IN ACADEMIC SCIENCE AND ENGINEERING

DONNA E. SHALALA [IOM] (*Chair*), President, University of Miami, Miami, Florida

ALICE M. AGOGINO [NAE], Roscoe and Elizabeth Hughes Professor of Mechanical Engineering, University of California, Berkeley, California

LOTTE BAILYN, Professor of Management, Sloan School of Management, Massachusetts Institute of Technology, Cambridge, Massachusetts

ROBERT J. BIRGENEAU [NAS], Chancellor, University of California, Berkeley, California

ANA MARI CAUCE, Executive Vice Provost and Earl R. Carlson Professor of Psychology, University of Washington, Seattle, Washington

CATHERINE D. DEANGELIS [IOM], Editor-in-Chief, Journal of the American Medical Association, Chicago, Illinois

DENICE DEE DENTON,* Chancellor, University of California, Santa Cruz, California

BARBARA J. GROSZ, Higgins Professor of Natural Sciences, Division of Engineering and Applied Sciences, and Dean of Science, Radcliffe Institute for Advanced Study, Harvard University, Cambridge, Massachusetts

JO HANDELSMAN, Howard Hughes Medical Institute Professor, Department of Plant Pathology, University of Wisconsin, Madison, Wisconsin

NANNERL O. KEOHANE, President Emerita, Duke University, Durham, North Carolina

SHIRLEY MALCOM [NAS], Head, Directorate for Education and Human Resources Programs, American Association for the Advancement of Science, Washington, DC

GERALDINE RICHMOND, Richard M. and Patricia H. Noyes Professor, Department of Chemistry, University of Oregon, Eugene, Oregon

ALICE M. RIVLIN, Senior Fellow, Brookings Institution, Washington, DC

RUTH SIMMONS, President, Brown University, Providence, Rhode Island

ELIZABETH SPELKE [NAS], Berkman Professor of Psychology, Harvard University, Cambridge, Massachusetts

JOAN STEITZ [NAS/IOM], Sterling Professor of Molecular Biophysics and Biochemistry, Howard Hughes Medical Institute, Yale University School of Medicine, New Haven, Connecticut

ELAINE WEYUKER [NAE], Fellow, AT&T Laboratories, Florham Park, New Jersey

MARIA T. ZUBER [NAS], E. A. Griswold Professor of Geophysics, Massachusetts Institute of Technology, Cambridge, Massachusetts

Principal Project Staff

LAUREL L. HAAK, Study Director

JOHN SISLIN, Program Officer

NORMAN GROSSBLATT, Senior Editor

JUDY GOSS, Senior Program Assistant

IAN CHRISTENSEN, Christine Mirzayan Science and Technology Policy Graduate Fellow

ERIN FRY, Christine Mirzayan Science and Technology Policy Graduate Fellow

JENNIFER HOBIN, Christine Mirzayan Science and Technology Policy Graduate Fellow

MARGARET HORTON, Christine Mirzayan Science and Technology Policy Graduate Fellow

RACHAEL SCHOLZ, Christine Mirzayan Science and Technology Policy Graduate Fellow

---

*Served from September 2005 to June 2006.

COMMITTEE ON SCIENCE, ENGINEERING, AND PUBLIC POLICY

GEORGE WHITESIDES (*Chair*), Woodford L. and Ann A. Flowers University Professor, Harvard University, Boston, Massachusetts

UMA CHOWDHRY, Vice President, Central Research and Development, DuPont Company, Wilmington, Delaware

RALPH J. CICERONE (Ex officio), President, National Academy of Sciences, Washington, DC

R. JAMES COOK, Interim Dean, College of Agriculture and Home Economics, Washington State University, Pullman, Washington

HAILE DEBAS, Executive Director, University of California at San Francisco Global Health Sciences, Maurice Galante Distinguished Professor of Surgery, San Francisco, California

HARVEY FINEBERG (Ex officio), President, Institute of Medicine, Washington, DC

MARYE ANNE FOX (Ex officio), Chancellor, University of California, San Diego, California

ELSA GARMIRE, Sydney E. Junkins Professor of Engineering, Dartmouth College, Hanover, New Hampshire

M.R.C. GREENWOOD (Ex officio), Professor of Nutrition and Internal Medicine, University of California, Davis, California

NANCY HOPKINS, Amgen Professor of Biology, Massachusetts Institute of Technology, Cambridge, Massachusetts

MARY-CLAIRE KING, American Cancer Society Professor of Medicine and Genetics, University of Washington, Seattle, Washington

W. CARL LINEBERGER, Professor of Chemistry, Joint Institute for Laboratory Astrophysics, University of Colorado, Boulder, Colorado

RICHARD A. MESERVE, President, Carnegie Institution of Washington, Washington, DC

ROBERT M. NEREM, Parker H. Petit Professor and Director, Institute for Bioengineering and Bioscience, Georgia Institute of Technology, Atlanta, Georgia

LAWRENCE T. PAPAY, Retired Sector Vice President for Integrated Solutions, Science Applications International Corporation, La Jolla, California

ANNE PETERSEN, Professor, University of Michigan and President, Global Philanthropic Alliance, Kalamazoo, Michigan

CECIL PICKETT, President, Schering-Plough Research Institute, Kenilworth, New Jersey

EDWARD H. SHORTLIFFE, Professor and Chair, Department of Biomedical Informatics, Columbia University Medical Center, New York, New York

HUGO SONNENSCHEIN, Charles L. Hutchinson Distinguished Service Professor, Department of Economics, University of Chicago, Chicago, Illinois

LYDIA THOMAS, President and Chief Executive Officer, Mitretek Systems, Inc., Falls Church, Virginia

SHEILA E. WIDNALL, Abby Rockefeller Mauze Professor of Aeronautics, Massachusetts Institute of Technology, Cambridge, Massachusetts

WM. A. WULF (Ex officio), President, National Academy of Engineering, Washington, DC

MARY LOU ZOBACK, Senior Research Scientist, Earthquake Hazards Team, US Geological Survey, Menlo Park, California

Staff

RICHARD BISSELL, Executive Director
DEBORAH STINE, Associate Director
LAUREL HAAK, Program Officer
MARION RAMSEY, Administrative Coordinator

Preface

When I started graduate school at Syracuse University in the late sixties, the chair of my department informed me that I would not be eligible for fellowships, because I was a woman. Pulling out a page of statistics, he pointed to the data indicating that women didn't finish PhD programs, and if they did, they interrupted their academic careers for marriage and children and therefore didn't go back to catch up with their peers. They were, he concluded, "a bad investment" for the department and the university.

Needless to say, with assistance from the Dean and other more progressive members of the faculty, I did finish my PhD. Then I went to New York to begin my academic career at the City University. At the end of my second semester of teaching, the department chair called me in for an evaluation. After pointing out that I was an excellent teacher and had published more than all of the other professors in the department put together, he said that he felt it necessary to be candid with me. "We have never tenured a woman, and never will; a bad investment," he said. I immediately called a department chair at Columbia University who had been trying to recruit me and moved over there.

Overt gender discrimination is now very rare, but it is still an issue. There has been considerable progress since I started my career, but it has been painfully slow, especially in science and engineering. The playing field is still not level. Growing numbers of women have earned undergraduate, graduate, and professional degrees. More and more of these well-qualified scientists and engineers have sought to pursue their calling in both academic and nonacademic settings. However, although women have risen to the challenge of scientific, medical, and technical study and research, the nation's academic institutions have not hired them for their faculties. The academy has a disappointing record. Institutional policies for attaining tenure are still based on a rigid apprentice system that assumes that a total commitment to an academic career is possible throughout one's life. Women—and sometimes men who shoulder significant care-giving responsibilities—are still perceived to be "a bad investment." Women also must deal with lifelong questioning of their ability in science and mathematics and their commitment to a career. As a result, women are underrepresented in science and engineering, particularly in the higher faculty ranks and leadership positions. Women scientists and engineers with minority racial and ethnic backgrounds are virtually absent from the nation's leading science and engineering departments.

This needless waste of the nation's scientific talent must end. In addition to considerations of equity that govern employment in other sectors of the nation's workforce, the United States now faces stiffening science and engineering competition from other nations. We urgently need to make full use of all of our talent to maintain our nation's leadership. Affording women scientists and engineers the academic career opportunities merited by their educational and professional achievements must be given a high priority by our nation.

The Committee on Science, Engineering, and Public Policy formed our Committee on Maximizing the Potential of Women in Academic Science and Engineering and charged it to recommend methods for achieving that goal. The committee's mandate was to gather and analyze the best available information on the status of women in academic science and engineering and to propose ways of putting their abilities to the best use.

Specifically, our committee was charged

• To review and assess the research on gender issues in science and engineering, including innate differences in cognition, implicit bias, and faculty diversity.
• To examine institutional culture and the practices in academic institutions that contribute to and discourage talented individuals from realizing their full potential as scientists and engineers.
• To determine effective practices to ensure that women who receive their doctorates in science and engineering have access to a wide array of career opportunities in the academy and in other research settings.
• To determine effective practices for recruiting women scientists and engineers to faculty positions and retaining them in these positions.
• To develop findings and provide recommendations based on these data and other information to guide faculty, deans, department chairs, and

other university leaders; scientific and professional societies; funding organizations; and government agencies in maximizing the potential of women
in science and engineering careers.

Our committee, composed of distinguished scientists and engineers who
have attained outstanding careers in academic research and university governance, undertook its task with enthusiasm and dedication. As people who
have held major administrative positions, committee members were able to
put gender issues into the broadest context. In fulfillment of its mandate,
the committee met in Washington, DC, on three occasions to examine
evidence and consult with leading experts. We also conferred by conference
call on numerous other occasions.

In December 2005, we hosted a public convocation with outstanding
researchers to explore the impact of sex and gender on the cognitive and
intellectual abilities of men and women and on the attitudes and social
institutions that affect the education, recruitment, hiring, promotion, and
retention of academic science and engineering faculty. Over 150 interested
people from academe, government, private funding agencies, and other
organizations listened to the presentations, enriched the discussion with
questions and comments, and presented their research in a poster session.

The convocation speakers discussed a number of crucial and, in some
cases, controversial questions in light of the latest research findings. What
does sex-difference research tell us about capability, achievement, and behavior? What are the effects of socialization and social roles on career
development? What role do gender attitudes and stereotypes play in evaluation of people, their work, and their potential? What institutional features
promote or deter the success of female scientists and engineers? What are
the overlapping issues of sex, race, and ethnicity? What else do we need to
know, and what key research is needed? The convocation informed the
thinking and research that underlie the committee's final report; the proceedings with invited papers and poster abstracts have been collected into a
workshop report, *Biological, Social, and Organizational Components of
Success for Women in Academic Science and Engineering*, published by the
National Academies Press.

During the committee's February 2006 meeting, the committee heard
presentations by nationally recognized experts on topics ranging from recent developments in employment discrimination law to programs and strategies used by universities and other employers to advance the careers of
women scientists and engineers. At its March meeting, the committee reviewed and refined the report's findings and recommendations. Throughout the spring, multiple meetings by teleconference permitted our committee to exchange views and information and to prepare our final findings
and recommendations.

At all those sessions and throughout the months-long process of examining the evidence and developing this exhaustive report, in addition to data and opinions supplied by experts, committee members brought their own substantial expertise, insights, energy, and dedication to bear on this project and its goals. We have tried to carry out our task with great rigor, understanding the extraordinary impact that answering these questions and developing strategies can have on the next generation of women in science and engineering. It is our hope that in the future women in science and engineering will not face attitudes and institutional structures that denigrate their work and careers as "questionable" investments. Instead, our work will help ensure that women scientists and engineers take their unquestioned place as full, valued, and vital members of the nation's academic community.

We have no doubt that a combination of leadership, resources, peer pressure, law enforcement, and public outcry can fundamentally change the culture and opportunities at our research universities. We need look no further than our playing fields for evidence that the academy is capable of cultural and behavioral change when faced with a national imperative. It is time—our time—for a peaceful, thoughtful revolution.

Donna E. Shalala, Chair
Committee on Maximizing the Potential of Women
in Academic Science and Engineering

Acknowledgments

The Committee on Science, Engineering, and Public Policy (COSEPUP) appreciates the support of the standing National Academies Committee on Women in Science and Engineering (CWSE), which is represented on the guidance group, on the study committee, and on project staff.

This report is the result of the efforts of many people. We would like to thank those who spoke at our convocation and our committee meetings. They were (in alphabetical order)

MAHZARIN RUSTUM BANAJI, Department of Psychology, Harvard University, and Radcliffe Institute for Advanced Study, Cambridge, Massachusetts

FRANK DOBBIN, Department of Sociology, Harvard University, Cambridge, Massachusetts

ROBERT DRAGO, Department of Labor Studies and Industrial Relations and Department of Women's Studies, Pennsylvania State University, State College, Pennsylvania

SUSAN FISKE, Department of Psychology, Princeton University, Princeton, New Jersey

JAY GIEDD, National Institute of Mental Health, National Institutes of Health, Bethesda, Maryland

DONNA GINTHER, Department of Economics, University of Kansas, Lawrence, Kansas

MARCIA GREENBERGER, National Women's Law Center, Washington, DC
DIANE HALPERN, Berger Institute for Work, Family, and Children, Claremont McKenna College, Claremont, California
ELIZABETH HIRSH, Department of Sociology, University of Washington, Seattle, Washington
JANET HYDE, Department of Psychology, University of Wisconsin, Madison, Wisconsin
JOANNE MARTIN, Graduate School of Business, Stanford University, Stanford, California
BRUCE MCEWEN [NAS/IOM], Rockefeller University, New York, New York
KELLEE NOONAN, Technical Career Path, Hewlett Packard, Sunnyvale, California
JOAN REEDE, Harvard Medical School, Cambridge, Massachusetts
SUE ROSSER, Ivan Allen College, Georgia Institute of Technology, Atlanta, Georgia
JOCELYN SAMUELS, National Women's Law Center, Washington, DC
TONI SCHMADER, Department of Psychology, University of Arizona
ANGELICA STACY, Department of Chemistry, University of California, Berkeley, California
SARAH WARBELOW, American Association of University Women Legal Advocacy Fund, Washington, DC
JOAN WILLIAMS, Center for WorkLife Law, University of California, Hastings College of the Law, San Francisco, California
YU XIE, Department of Sociology, University of Michigan, Ann Arbor, Michigan

The committee thanks the researchers and consultants who have contributed to the report: Joan Burelli, Frank Dobbin, Donna Ginther, Marc Goulden, Marcia Greenberger, Valerie Kuck, and Mark Regets.

Next, we thank the reviewers of the report. This report has been reviewed in draft form by people selected for their knowledge, expertise, and wide range of perspectives in accordance with the procedures approved by the National Research Council's Report Review Committee. The purpose of this independent review is to provide candid and critical comments that will assist the institution in making the published report as sound as possible and to ensure that the report meets institutional standards of objectivity, evidence, and responsiveness to the study charge. The review comments and draft manuscript remain confidential to protect the integrity of the deliberative process. We thank the following for their participation in the review of this report:

KENNETH ARROW [NAS/IOM], Professor of Economics and
Operations Research, Emeritus, Stanford University

DAVID BALTIMORE [NAS/IOM], President, California Institute of
Technology

SUZANNE BRAINARD, Director, Center for Women in Science and
Engineering, University of Washington

ALICIA CARRIQUIRY, Associate Provost and Professor of Statistics,
Iowa State University

FRANK DOBBIN, Professor of Sociology, Harvard University

RON EHRENBERG, Professor of Industrial and Labor Relations and
Director, Cornell Higher Education Research Institute, Cornell
University

CLAUDIA GOLDIN [NAS], Henry Lee Professor of Economics, Harvard
University

MARC GOULDEN, Principal Research Analyst, Graduate Division,
University of California, Berkeley

EVELYNN HAMMONDS, Senior Vice Provost for Faculty Development
and Diversity, Harvard University

SOPHIA HUYER, Executive Director, Women and Global Science and
Technology, Brighton, Ontario

MARC W. KIRSCHNER [NAS], Professor and Chairman, Department of
Systems Biology, Harvard Medical School

MARIA KLAWE, President, Harvey Mudd College

WILLIAM MILLER [NAS], Distinguished Professor, Department of
Chemistry, University of California, Berkeley

WILLIE PEARSON, JR., Chair, School of History, Technology, and
Society, Ivan Allen College, Georgia Institute of Technology

ABIGAIL STEWART, Associate Dean for Academic Affairs, University of
Michigan

SHIRLEY TILGHMAN [NAS/IOM], President, Princeton University

C. MEGAN URRY, Director, Center for Astronomy and Astrophysics,
Yale University

SHELDON WEINBAUM [NAS/NAE/IOM], CUNY Distinguished
Professor of Biomedical and Mechanical Engineering, City College of
the City University of New York

RICHARD ZARE [NAS], Marguerite Blake Wilbur Professor in Natural
Science and Chair, Chemistry Department, Stanford University

Although the reviewers had many constructive comments and suggestions about the report, they were not asked to endorse the findings and recommendations of the report, nor did they see a final draft of the report before its release. The report review was overseen by May Berenbaum [NAS], Professor and Head of the Department of Entomology at the University of Illinois Urbana-Champaign, and MRC Greenwood [IOM], Professor of Nutrition and Internal Medicine at the University of California at Davis, appointed by the Report Review Committee, who were responsible for making certain that an independent examination of this report was carried out in accordance with institutional procedures and that all review comments were carefully considered. Responsibility for the final content of this report rests entirely with the author committee and the institution.

In addition, we thank the guidance group that oversaw this project:

NANCY HOPKINS [NAS/IOM] (*Guidance Group Chair*), Amgen Professor of Biology, Massachusetts Institute of Technology, Cambridge, Massachusetts

ELSA GARMIRE [NAE], Sydney E. Junkins Professor of Engineering, Dartmouth College, Hanover, New Hampshire

W. CARL LINEBERGER [NAS], Professor of Chemistry, Joint Institute for Laboratory Astrophysics, University of Colorado, Boulder, Colorado

ANNE PETERSEN [IOM], President, Global Philanthropic Alliance, Kalamazoo, Michigan

MAXINE SINGER [NAS/IOM], President Emerita, Carnegie Institution of Washington, Washington, DC

HUGO SONNENSCHEIN [NAS], Charles L. Hutchinson Distinguished Service Professor, Department of Economics, University of Chicago, Chicago, Illinois

LILLIAN SHIAO-YEN WU, Director of University Relations, International Business Machines, New York, New York

MARY LOU ZOBACK [NAS], Senior Research Scientist, Earthquake Hazards Team, US Geological Survey, Menlo Park, California

Finally, we thank the staff of this project for their guidance, including Laurel Haak, program officer with COSEPUP and study director, who managed the project; John Sislin, the collaborating program officer with CWSE; Beryl Benderly, science writer; Norman Grossblatt, report editor; Rita Johnson, managing editor of reports; Judy Goss, who provided research, writing, and project support; Christine Mirzayan Science and Technology Graduate Policy Fellows Ian Christensen, Erin Fry, Jennifer Hobin, Margaret Horton, and Rachael Scholz, who provided research and analytical support; Jong-On Hahm, former director of CWSE; Peter Henderson, acting director of CWSE; Mary Mattis, former senior program officer, National Academy of Engineering; Richard Bissell, executive director, and Charlotte Kuh, deputy executive director of the Policy and Global Affairs Division; and Deborah Stine, associate director of COSEPUP.

Contents

APPENDIXES

Figures, Tables, and Boxes

FIGURES

TABLES

BOXES

Controversies

Defining the Issues

Focus on Research

Experiments and Strategies

Tracking and Evaluation

Summary

The U.S. economy relies on the productivity, entrepreneurship, and creativity of its people. To maintain its scientific and engineering leadership amid increasing economic and educational globalization, the United States must aggressively pursue the innovative capacity of *all* of its people—women and men. Women make up an increasing proportion of science and engineering majors at all institutions, including top programs such as those at the Massachusetts Institute of Technology where women make up 51% of its science undergraduates and 35% of its engineering undergraduates. For women to participate to their full potential across all science and engineering fields, they must see a career path that allows them to reach their full intellectual potential. Much remains to be done to achieve that goal.

Women are a small portion of the science and engineering faculty members at research universities, and they typically receive fewer resources and less support than their male colleagues. The representation of women in leadership positions in our academic institutions, scientific and professional societies, and honorary organizations is low relative to the numbers of women qualified to hold these positions. It is not lack of talent, but unintentional biases and outmoded institutional structures that are hindering the access and advancement of women. Neither our academic institutions nor our nation can afford such underuse of precious human capital in science and engineering. The time to take action is now.

The National Academies, under the oversight of the Committee on Science, Engineering, and Public Policy, created the Committee on Maximizing the Potential of Women in Academic Science and Engineering to develop specific recommendations on how to make the fullest possible use of a large source of our nation's talent: women in academic science and engineering. This report presents the consensus views and judgment of the committee members, who include five university presidents and chancellors, provosts and named professors, former top government officials, leading policy analysts, and outstanding scientists and engineers—nine of whom are members of the National Academy of Sciences, National Academy of Engineering, or the Institute of Medicine, and many of whom have dedicated great thought and action to the advancement of women in science and engineering. The committee's recommendations—if implemented and coordinated across educational, professional, and government sectors—will transform our institutions, improve the working environment for women and men, and profoundly enhance our nation's talent pool.

FINDINGS

1. Women have the ability and drive to succeed in science and engineering. Studies of brain structure and function, of hormonal modulation of performance, of human cognitive development, and of human evolution have not found any significant biological differences between men and women in performing science and mathematics that can account for the lower representation of women in academic faculty and scientific leadership positions in these fields. The drive and motivation of women scientists and engineers is demonstrated by those women who persist in academic careers despite barriers that disproportionately disadvantage them.

2. Women who are interested in science and engineering careers are lost at every educational transition. With each step up the academic ladder, from high school on through full professorships, the representation of women in science and engineering drops substantially. As they move from high school to college, more women than men who have expressed an interest in science or engineering decide to major in something else; in the transition to graduate school, more women than men with science and engineering degrees opt into other fields of study; from doctorate to first position, there are proportionately fewer women than men in the applicant pool for tenure-track positions; active recruiting can overcome this deficit.

3. The problem is not simply the pipeline. In several fields, the pipeline has reached gender parity. For over 30 years, women have made up over 30% of the doctorates in social sciences and behavioral sciences and over 20% in the life sciences. Yet, at the top research institutions, only 15.4% of the full professors in the social and behavioral sciences and 14.8% in the life sciences are women—and these are the only fields in science and engineering where the proportion of women reaches into the double digits.

Women from minority racial and ethnic backgrounds are virtually absent from the nation's leading science and engineering departments.

4. Women are very likely to face discrimination in every field of science and engineering. Considerable research has shown the barriers limiting the appointment, retention, and advancement of women faculty. Overall, scientists and engineers who are women or members of racial or ethnic minority groups have had to function in environments that favor—sometimes deliberately but often inadvertently—the men who have traditionally dominated science and engineering. Well-qualified and highly productive women scientists have also had to contend with continuing questioning of their own abilities in science and mathematics and their commitment to an academic career. Minority-group women are subject to dual discrimination and face even more barriers to success. As a result, throughout their careers, women have not received the opportunities and encouragement provided to men to develop their interests and abilities to the fullest; this accumulation of disadvantage becomes acute in more senior positions.

These barriers have differential impact by field and by career stage. Some fields, such as physics and engineering, have a low proportion of women bachelor's and doctorates, but hiring into faculty positions appears to match the available pool. In other fields, including chemistry and biological sciences, the proportion of women remains high through bachelor's and doctorate degrees, but hiring into faculty positions is well below the available pool.

5. A substantial body of evidence establishes that most people—men and women—hold implicit biases. Decades of cognitive psychology research reveals that most of us carry prejudices of which we are unaware but that nonetheless play a large role in our evaluations of people and their work. An impressive body of controlled experimental studies and examination of decision-making processes in real life show that, on the average, people are less likely to hire a woman than a man with identical qualifications, are less likely to ascribe credit to a woman than to a man for identical accomplishments, and, when information is scarce, will far more often give the benefit of the doubt to a man than to a woman. Although most scientists and engineers believe that they are objective and intend to be fair, research shows that they are not exempt from those tendencies.

6. Evaluation criteria contain arbitrary and subjective components that disadvantage women. Women faculty are paid less, are promoted more slowly, receive fewer honors, and hold fewer leadership positions than men. These discrepancies do not appear to be based on productivity, the significance of their work, or any other measure of performance. Progress in academic careers depends on evaluation of accomplishments by more senior scientists, a process widely believed to be objective. Yet measures of success underlying the current "meritocratic" system are often arbitrary and applied in a biased manner (usually unintentionally). Characteristics that are often selected for and are believed, on the basis of little evidence, to relate to scientific creativity—namely assertiveness and single-mindedness—are given greater weight than other characteristics such as flexibility, diplomacy, curiosity, motivation, and dedication, which may be more vital to success in science and engineering. At the same time assertiveness and single-mindedness are stereotyped as socially unacceptable traits for women.

7. **Academic organizational structures and rules contribute significantly to the underuse of women in academic science and engineering.** Rules that appear quite neutral may function in a way that leads to differential treatment or produces differential outcomes for men and women. Structural constraints and expectations built into academic institutions assume that faculty members have substantial spousal support. The evidence demonstrates that anyone lacking the work and family support traditionally provided by a "wife" is at a serious disadvantage in academe. However, the majority of faculty no longer have such support. About 90% of the spouses of women science and engineering faculty are employed full-time; close to half the spouses of male faculty also work full-time.

8. **The consequences of *not* acting will be detrimental to the nation's competitiveness.** Women and minority-group members make up an increasing proportion of the labor force. They also are an increasing proportion of postsecondary students. To capture and capitalize on this talent will require revising policies adopted when the workplace was more homogeneous and creating new organizational structures that manage a diverse workforce effectively. Effective programs have three key components: commitment to take corrective action, analysis and utilization of data for organizational change, and a campus framework for monitoring progress.

To facilitate clear, evidence-based discussion of the issues, the committee compiled a list of commonly held beliefs concerning women in science and engineering (Table S-1). Each is discussed and analyzed in detail in the text of the report.

CONCLUSIONS

The United States can no longer afford the underperformance of our academic institutions in attracting the best and brightest minds to the science and engineering enterprise. Nor can it afford to devalue the contributions of some members of that workforce through gender inequities and discrimination. It is essential that our academic institutions promote the educational and professional success of all people without regard for sex, race, or ethnicity. So that our scientists and engineers can realize their greatest potential, our academic institutions must be held accountable and provide evidence that women and men receive equitable opportunities, resources, and support. Institutional policies and practices must move from

TABLE S-1 Evidence Refuting Commonly Held Beliefs About Women in Science and Engineering

Belief	Evidence	Where Discussed
(1) Women are not as good in mathematics as men.	Female performance in high school mathematics now matches that of males.	Chapter 2
(2) The matter of "under-representation" on faculties is only a matter of time; it is a function of how many women are qualified to enter these positions.	Women's representation decreases with each step up the tenure-track and academic leadership hierarchy, even in fields that have had a large proportion of women doctorates for 30 years.	Chapter 3
(3) Women are not as competitive as men. Women don't want jobs in academe.	Similar proportions of men and women science and engineering doctorates plan to enter postdoctoral study or academic employment.	Chapter 3
(4) Behavioral research is qualitative; why pay attention to the data in this report?	The data are from multiple sources, were obtained using well-recognized techniques, and have been replicated in several settings.	Chapters 2-5
(5) Women and minorities are recipients of favoritism through affirmative-action programs.	Affirmative action is meant to broaden searches to include more women and minority-group members, but not to select candidates on the basis of race or sex, which is illegal.	Chapter 4
(6) Academe is a meritocracy.	Although scientists like to believe that they "choose the best" based on objective criteria, decisions are influenced by factors—including biases about race, sex, geographic location of a university, and age—that have nothing to do with the quality of the person or work being evaluated.	Chapter 4
(7) Changing the rules means that standards of excellence will be deleteriously affected.	Throughout a scientific career, advancement depends upon judgments of one's performance by more senior scientists and engineers. This process does not optimally select and advance the best scientists and engineers, because of implicit bias and disproportionate weighting of qualities that are stereotypically male. Reducing these sources of bias will foster excellence in science and engineering fields.	Chapter 4

continued

TABLE S-1 Continued

Belief	Evidence	Where Discussed
(8) Women faculty are less productive than men.	The publication productivity of women science and engineering faculty has increased over the last 30 years and is now comparable to men's. The critical factor affecting publication productivity is access to institutional resources; marriage, children, and elder care responsibilities have minimal effects.	Chapter 4
(9) Women are more interested in family than in careers.	Many women scientists and engineers persist in their pursuit of academic careers despite severe conflicts between their roles as parents and as scientists and engineers. These efforts, however, are often not recognized as representing the high level of dedication to their careers they represent.	Chapter 5
(10) Women take more time off due to childbearing, so they are a bad investment.	On the average, women take more time off during their early careers to meet their caregiving responsibilities, which fall disproportionately to women. But, by middle age, a man is likely to take more sick leave than a woman.	Chapter 5
(11) The system as currently configured has worked well in producing great science; why change it?	The global competitive balance has changed in ways that undermine America's traditional science and engineering advantages. Career impediments based on gender or racial or ethnic bias deprive the nation of talented and accomplished researchers.	Chapter 6

the traditional model to an inclusive model with provisions for equitable and unbiased evaluation of accomplishment, equitable allocations of support and resources, pay equity, and gender-equal family leave policies. Otherwise, a large number of the people trained in and capable of doing the very best science and engineering will not participate as they should in scientific and engineering professions.

RECOMMENDATIONS

Career impediments for women deprive the nation of an important source of talented and accomplished scientists and engineers who could contribute to our nation's competitiveness. Transforming institutional structures and procedures to eliminate gender bias is a major national task that will require strong leadership and continuous attention, evaluation, and accountability. Because those obstacles are both substantial and systemic, there are no easy fixes; however, many practices developed in the last decade by universities and funding agencies have proven effective in increasing both the participation of women on faculties and their appointment to leadership positions. In part, the challenge is to use such strategies more widely and evaluate them more broadly to ensure we are accessing the entire talent pool to find truly the best people for our faculties. We need to think creatively about opportunities for substantial and overarching reform of the academic enterprise—its structure, incentives, and accountability—to change outcomes and achieve equity.

The committee's recommendations are large-scale and interdependent, requiring the interaction of university leaders and faculties, scientific and professional societies, funding agencies, federal agencies, and Congress.

A. Universities

A1. *Trustees, university presidents, and provosts* should provide clear leadership in changing the culture and structure of their institutions to recruit, retain, and promote women—including minority women—into faculty and leadership positions.

(a) University leaders should *incorporate into campus strategic plans goals of counteracting bias against women in hiring, promotion, and treatment.* This includes working with an inter-institution monitoring organization (see below) to perform annual reviews of the composition of their student body and faculty ranks, publicizing progress toward the goals annually, and providing a detailed annual briefing to the board of trustees.

(b) University leaders should *take action immediately to remedy inequities in hiring, promotion, and treatment.*

(c) University leaders should as part of their *mandatory overall management efforts hold leadership workshops for deans, department heads, search committee chairs, and other faculty with personnel management responsibilities that include an integrated component on diversity and strategies to overcome bias and gender schemas* and strategies for encouraging fair treatment of all people. It is crucial that these workshops are integrated into the fabric of the management of universities and departments.

(d) University leaders should *require evidence of a fair, broad, and aggressive search before approving appointments and hold departments accountable for the equity of their search process and outcomes* even if it means canceling a search or withholding a faculty position.

(e) University leaders should *develop and implement hiring, tenure, and promotion policies that take into account the flexibility that faculty need* across the life course, allowing integration of family, work, and community responsibilities. They should provide uniform policies and central funding for faculty and staff on leave and should visibly and vigorously support campus programs that help faculty with children or other caregiving responsibilities to maintain productive careers. These programs should, at a minimum, include provisions for paid parental leave for faculty, staff, postdoctoral scholars, and graduate students; facilities and subsidies for on-site and community-based child care; dissertation defense and tenure clock extensions; and family-friendly scheduling of critical meetings.

A2. ***Deans and department chairs and their tenured faculty*** should take responsibility for creating a productive environment and immediately implement programs and strategies shown to be successful in minimizing the effect of biases in recruiting, hiring, promotion, and tenure.

(a) Faculties and their senates should initiate a *full faculty discussion of climate issues*.

(b) Deans, department chairs, and their tenured faculty should *develop and implement programs that educate all faculty members and students in their departments on unexamined bias and effective evaluation*; these programs should be *integrated into* departmental meetings and retreats, and professional development and teacher-training courses. For example, such programs can be incorporated into research ethics and laboratory management courses for graduate students, postdoctoral scholars, and research staff; and can be part of management leadership workshops for faculty, deans, and department chairs.

(c) Deans, department chairs and their tenured faculty should *expand their faculty recruitment efforts* to ensure that they reach adequately and proactively into the existing and ever-increasing pool of women candidates.

(d) Faculties and their senates should immediately *review their tenure processes and timelines* to ensure that hiring, tenure, and promotion policies take into account the flexibility that faculty need across the life course and do not sacrifice quality in the process of meeting rigid timelines.

A3. *University leaders should work with their faculties and department chairs* to *examine evaluation practices* to focus on the quality of contributions and their impact.

B. Professional societies and higher education organizations have a responsibility to play a leading role in promoting equal treatment of women and men and to demonstrate a commitment to it in their practices.

B1. Together, *higher education organizations* should *consider forming an inter-institution monitoring organization.* This body could act as an intermediary between academic institutions and federal agencies in recommending norms and measures, in collecting data, and in cross-institution tracking of compliance and accountability. Just as the opening of athletics programs to girls and women required strong and consistent inter-institutional cooperation, eliminating gender bias in faculty recruitment, retention, and promotion processes requires continuous inter-institutional cooperation, including data-gathering and analysis, and oversight and evaluation of progress.

    (a) As an initial step, the committee recommends that the American Council on Education, an umbrella organization encompassing all of higher education, convene national higher education organizations, including the Association of American Universities, the National Association of State Universities and Land Grant Colleges, and others to consider the creation of a cross-university monitoring body.

    (b) A primary focus of the discussion should be on defining the scope and structure of data collection. The committee recommends that data be collected at the department level by sex and race or ethnicity and include the numbers of students majoring in science and engineering disciplines; the numbers of students graduating with bachelor's or master's degrees in science and engineering fields; post-graduation plans; first salary; graduate school enrollment, attrition, and completion; postdoctoral plans; numbers of postdoctoral scholars; and data on faculty recruitment, hiring, tenure, promotion, attrition, salary, and allocation of institutional resources. The committee has developed a scorecard that can be used for this purpose (Chapter 6).

B2. *Scientific and professional societies* should
    (a) *Serve in helping to set professional and equity standards,* collect and disseminate field-wide education and workforce data, and provide professional development training for members that includes a component on bias in evaluation.

(b) Develop and enforce guidelines to *ensure that keynote and other invited speakers* at *society-sponsored events reflect the diverse membership of the society.*

(c) Ensure *reasonable representation of women on editorial boards and in other significant leadership positions.*

(d) Work to ensure that women are recognized for their contributions to the nation's scientific and engineering enterprise through *nominations for awards and leadership* positions.

(e) Provide *child-care and elder-care grants or subsidies* so that their members can attend work-related conferences and meetings.

B3. *Honorary societies* should *review their nomination and election processes* to address the underrepresentation of women in their memberships.

B4. *Journals* should *examine their entire review process,* including the mechanisms by which decisions are made to send a submission to review, and take steps to minimize gender bias, such as blinded reviews.

C. Federal funding agencies and foundations should ensure that their practices—including rules and regulations—support the full participation of women and do not reinforce a culture that fundamentally discriminates against women. All research funding agencies should

C1. *Provide workshops to minimize gender bias.* Federal funding agencies and foundations should work with scientific and professional societies to host mandatory national meetings that educate members of review panels, university department chairs, and agency program officers about methods that minimize the effects of gender bias in evaluation. The meetings should be held every 2 years for each major discipline and should include data and research presentations on subtle biases and discrimination, department climate surveys, and interactive discussions or role-modeling. Program effectiveness should be evaluated on an ongoing basis.

C2. *Collect, store, and publish composite information* on demographics, field, award type and budget request, review score, and funding outcome for all funding applications.

C3. *Make it possible to use grant monies for dependent care expenses* necessary to engage in off-site or after-hours research-related activities or to attend work-related conferences and meetings.

C4. *Create additional funding mechanisms* to provide for interim technical or administrative support during a leave of absence related to caregiving.

C5. *Establish policies for extending grant support* for researchers who take a leave of absence due to caregiving responsibilities.

C6. *Expand support for research* on the efficacy of organizational programs designed to reduce gender bias, and for research on bias, prejudice, and stereotype threat, and the role of leadership in achieving gender equity.

D. Federal agencies should lay out clear guidelines, leverage their resources, and rigorously enforce existing laws to increase the science and engineering talent developed in this country.

D1. Even without additional resources, federal agencies should *move immediately to enforce the federal anti-discrimination laws* at universities and other higher education institutions through regular compliance reviews and prompt and thorough investigation of discrimination complaints.[1] Federal enforcement agencies should ensure that the range of their enforcement efforts covers the full scope of activities involving science and engineering that are governed by the anti-discrimination laws. If violations are found, the full range of remedies for violation of the anti-discrimination laws should be sought.

D2. Federal enforcement efforts should *evaluate whether universities have engaged in any of the types of discrimination* banned under the anti-discrimination laws, including: intentional discrimination, sexual harassment, retaliation, disparate impact discrimination, and failure to maintain required policies and procedures.

D3. Federal compliance review efforts should *encompass a sufficiently broad number and range of institutions* of higher education to secure a substantial change in policies and practices nationwide. Types of institutions that should be included in compliance reviews include 2-year and 4-year institutions; institutions of undergraduate education; institutions that grant graduate degrees; state universities; private colleges; and educational enterprises, including national laboratories and independent research institutes, which may not be affiliated with universities.

D4. Federal enforcement agencies, including the Equal Employment Opportunity Commission, the Department of Justice, the Department of La-

---

[1]Applicable laws include Title VI, Title VII, and Title IX of the Civil Rights Act; Executive Order 11246; the Equal Protection clause of the Constitution; the Equal Pay Act; the Pregnancy Discrimination Act; and the Family Medical Leave Act. Each of these statutes is discussed in detail in Chapter 5.

bor, the Department of Education, and individual federal granting agencies' Offices of Civil Rights should *encourage and provide technical assistance* on how to achieve diversity in university programs and employment. Possible activities include providing technical assistance to educational institutions to help them to comply with the anti-discrimination laws, creating a clearinghouse for dissemination of strategies that have been proven effective, and providing awards and recognition for model university programs.

E. Congress should take steps necessary to encourage adequate enforcement of anti-discrimination laws, including *regular oversight hearings* to investigate the enforcement activities of the Department of Education, the Equal Employment Opportunity Commission, the Department of Labor, and the science granting agencies—including the National Institutes of Health, the National Science Foundation, the Department of Defense, the Department of Agriculture, the Department of Energy, the National Institute of Standards and Technology, and the National Aeronautics and Space Administration.

CALL TO ACTION

The fact that women are capable of contributing to the nation's scientific and engineering enterprise but are impeded in doing so because of gender and racial/ethnic bias and outmoded "rules" governing academic success is deeply troubling and embarrassing. It is also a *call to action.* Faculty, university leaders, professional and scientific societies, federal agencies, and the federal government must unite to ensure that all our nation's people are welcomed and encouraged to excel in science and engineering in our research universities. Our nation's future depends on it.

1

Introduction

Science and engineering education and research are increasingly global endeavors. As described in the recent National Academies report *Rising Above the Gathering Storm*, globalization has already begun to challenge the longstanding scientific pre-eminence of the United States and, therefore, its economic leadership. Identifying the best, brightest, and most innovative science and engineering talent will be crucial if the nation's industries and the nation itself are to maintain their competitive edge.

> Major American businesses have made clear that the skills needed in today's increasingly global marketplace can only be developed through exposure to widely diverse people, cultures, ideas, and viewpoints.
>
> —Sandra Day O'Connor[1]

In the last 30 years, the numbers and proportion of women obtaining science and engineering bachelor's, master's, and doctoral degrees have increased dramatically. Women's presence has grown across the sciences (Figure 1-1). In the life sciences, women outnumber men in both under-

---

[1]*Opinion of the court.* Grutter v. Bollinger 539 US 306, 2003. *http://www.law.cornell.edu/supct/pdf/02-241P.ZO.*

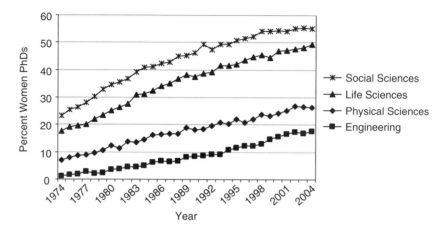

FIGURE 1-1 Percentage of science and engineering PhDs awarded to women, 1974-2004.

SOURCE: National Science Foundation (2006). Survey of Earned Doctorates, 1974-2004. Arlington, VA.

graduate and graduate programs.[2] Women now earn one-third of the PhDs granted by the 50 leading departments in chemistry, 27% in mathematics and statistics, and one-fourth in physics and astronomy. Even in engineering, historically the field with the fewest female participants, women now constitute one-fifth of undergraduate and graduate students.[3] In the top 50 engineering departments, women earn one-fourth of the PhDs granted in chemical engineering and 15% in engineering overall.[4]

In counterpoint to that dramatic educational progress, women, who constitute about half of the total workforce in the United States and half of the degree recipients in a number of scientific fields, still make up only one-fifth of the nation's scientific and technical workers. As shown in Chapter 3, at every academic career milestone the proportion of women in science and engineering declines. These declines are evident even in 2003, the most recent year for which data are available. In examining the transition into academic positions (Figure 1-2), the declines are greatest in fields requiring

---

[2]Government Accountability Office (2004). *Gender Issues: Women's Participation in the Sciences Has Increased, but Agencies Need to Do More to Ensure Compliance with Title IX* (GAO-04-639). Washington, DC: US Government Accountability Office.
[3]GAO (2004), ibid.
[4]Handelsman J, N Cantor, M Carnes, D Denton, E Fine, B Grosz, V Hinshaw, C Marrett, S Rosser, D Shalala, and J Sheridan (2005). More women in science. *Science* 309:1190-1191 *http://www.sciencemag.org/cgi/content/full/309/5738/1190.*

a period of postdoctoral study, namely life sciences, chemistry, and mathematics. It is interesting that in psychology, which like life sciences and chemistry is a field with a high proportion of women undergraduate and graduate students, there is a substantial decline in the proportion of women with increasing faculty rank. In comparison, in fields with a low proportion of women undergraduate and graduate students such as computer science and physical sciences, these proportions remain fairly constant with increasing faculty rank (Figure 1-2).

The situation is especially severe for minority-group women in sciences and engineering,[5] who are subject to dual discrimination and are required to overcome more barriers to achieve success. The bottom line is that minority-group women doctorates are less likely to be in tenure positions than men of any racial group or white women. The data on women faculty of color are discouraging (Box 1-1).

RECOGNIZING OBSTACLES

Women continue to face impediments to academic careers that do not confront men of comparable ability and training. Those barriers cause substantial waste of scientific and engineering talent and training. Several reports issued in the last 3 years have examined the barriers that women interested in science and engineering encounter at various stages of their career development. Some reports, including those by the Congressional Commission on the Advancement of Women and Minorities in Science, Engineering, and Technology (CAWMSET) and the Building Engineering and Science Talent (BEST) Initiative (Box 1-2) have focused on broad pipeline issues. Others, including RAND's *Gender Differences in Major Federal External Grant Programs* and the Government Accountability Office's *Women's Participation in the Sciences Has Increased, but Agencies Need to Do More to Ensure Compliance with Title IX*, have focused on the role of funding agencies. A number of university task forces have also issued reports on the institutional climate for women faculty,[6] including Harvard

---

[5]Ethnic and racial minority groups are defined using the current nomenclature of the US Census Bureau: African American, Hispanic, Native American (which includes Alaskan Natives and American Indians), and Asian American and Pacific Islanders. While the definition of underrepresented minorities varies by federal agency and between grant programs within agencies, by university, and between scientific and engineering disciplines, in this report by underrepresented minority we mean African American, Hispanic American, and Native American.

[6]For a listing of University reports, see the National Academies' Committee on Women in Science and Engineering Web page, *Gender Faculty Studies at Research I Institutions, http://www7.nationalacademies.org/cwse/gender_faculty_links.html.*

A: Postdoctoral Scholars and Assistant Professors

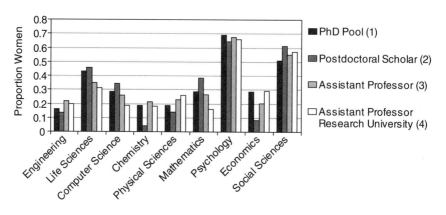

B: Associate Professors

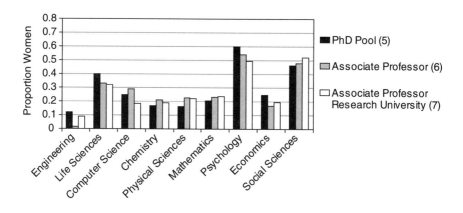

FIGURE 1-2 Comparison of the proportion of women in PhD pools with those in tenure-track or tenured professor positions in 2003, by field.

C: Full Professors

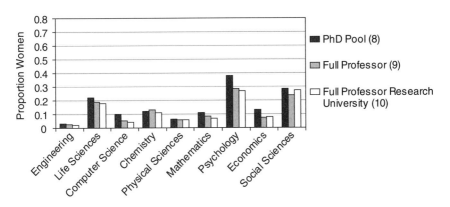

FIGURE 1-2 Continued.

NOTES: The Survey of Doctoral Recipients includes only those who earned doctorates in the United States and may underrepresent the actual number of postdoctoral scholars and tenure-track and tenured professors, particularly in those fields such as life sciences where there are a substantial number of international postdoctoral scholars and engineering where there are substantial number of international professors.[7] *Engineering* includes aeronautics, civil, electrical, environmental, industrial, mechanical, and other engineering fields; *Life Sciences* includes agricultural and biological sciences; *Chemistry* includes chemical engineering and chemistry fields; *Physical Sciences* includes geosciences, physics, and other physical science fields; *Social Sciences* includes political science, sociology and anthropology, and other social science fields. (1) The PhD pool for assistant professors was derived from a sum of all PhDs earned 0-6 years before 2003. (2) Includes those in postdoctoral positions who earned doctorate 0-6 years before 2003. (3) Includes those in assistant professor positions who earned doctorate 0-6 years before 2003. (4) Includes those in assistant professor positions at research universities who earned doctorate 0-6 years before 2003. Research Universities include those with undergraduate and graduate programs, as denoted by the former Carnegie classifications Doctorate 1 and 2 and Research 1 and 2. (5) The PhD pool for associate professors was derived from a sum of all PhDs earned 7-15 years before 2003. (6) Includes those in associate professor positions who earned doctorate 7-15 years before 2003. (7) See note 4. (8) The PhD pool for full professors was derived from a sum of all PhDs earned 16 or more years before 2003. (9) Includes those in full professor positions who earned doctorate 16 or more years before 2003. (10) See note 4.

SOURCE: National Science Foundation (2006). Survey of Doctoral Recipients, 2003. Arlington, VA: National Science Foundation.

---

[7]See NAS/NAE/IOM (2005). *Policy Implications of International Graduate Students and Postdoctoral Scholars in the United States.* Washington, DC: The National Academies Press.

DEFINING THE ISSUES

BOX 1-1 Diversity among Women

Discrimination in the post-Civil Rights era is less a function of conscious antipathy and increasingly a byproduct of longstanding social structures, interaction patterns, and unexamined stereotypes that systematically disadvantage minority groups.[a] These may include negative stereotypes of a group's scientific or academic ability, the lack of influential mentors, and exclusion from social networks that facilitate career advancement.[b]

The historical experiences and cultural practices and values of America's various ethnic communities differ widely from one another as well as from American culture at large. So do the stereotypes that the culture at large imposes on them. Because of the diversity of cultural patterns, the experience and expectations of women vary by race and ethnicity.[c] The additional challenges that girls and women in ethnic and racial minority groups face in attaining scientific and engineering careers thus merit specific attention. Underrepresentation of this group of women is especially acute; Donna Nelson reports that "underrepresented minority women faculty are almost nonexistent in science and engineering departments at research universities."[d]

In December 1975, an American Association for the Advancement of Science conference on minority women in science found that both minority-group members (male and female) and women (minority and majority) faced considerable barriers to participation. Being both a woman and a minority-group member meant facing the barriers of both groups—a "double bind."[e]

Thirty years later seemingly little has changed. Cathy Trower and Richard Chait note that "despite earning doctorates in ever increasing numbers, many women and persons of color are eschewing academic careers altogether or exiting the academy prior to the tenure decision because both groups experience social isolation, a chilly environment, bias, and hostility."[f] The situation is worse if one is both a woman and a minority-group member. The numbers paint a bleak picture for minority women:

- Most African Americans who earn science and engineering doctorates are women, and yet these women are less represented in academic faculties than are African American men.[g]

University's task forces on *Women Faculty* and *Women in Science and Engineering* (Box 1-2).

The National Academies, under the oversight of the Committee on Science, Engineering, and Public Policy, formed the Committee on Maximizing the Potential of Women in Academic Science and Engineering to provide a synthesis of the existing reports and basic research and to examine the implicit and explicit obstacles to educational and academic career advancement of women scientists and engineers, and the effects of race and sex in academic science and engineering careers.

- The proportion of tenured minority-group women declined from 1989 to 1997.[h]
- In 2002, there were no African American, Hispanic, or Native American women in tenured or tenure-track faculty positions in the nation's "top 50" computer science departments.[i]
- In 2002, Native American women held no full professor positions in physical sciences or engineering; there was only one African American woman full professor in the "top 50" physical sciences and engineering departments.[j]

---

[a]WT Bielby (2000). Minimizing workplace gender and racial bias. *Contemporary Sociology* (29) 12-129; B Reskin (2000). The proximate causes of employment discrimination. *Contemporary Sociology* 29:319-328; S Strum (2001). Second generation employment discrimination: A structural approach. *Columbia Law Review* 101(3):458-568.

[b]CM Steele (1997). A threat in the air: How stereotypes shape intellectual identity and performance. *American Psychologist* 52:613-629; J Lach (1999). Minority women hit concrete ceiling. *American Demographics* 21(9):18-19.

[c]DS Davenport and JM Yurich (1991). Multicultural gender issues. *Journal of Counseling and Development* 70(1):64-71; SA Hill (2002). Teaching and doing gender in African American families. *Sex Roles* 47(11-12):493-506; GM Combs (2003). The duality of race and gender for managerial African American women: Implications of informal social networks on career advancement.

[d]DJ Nelson (2005). *A National Analysis of Diversity in Science and Engineering Faculties at Research Universities.* http://cheminfo.chem.ou.edu/~djn/diversity/briefings/Diversity%20Report%20Final.pdf.

[e]S Malcom, P Hall, and J Brown (1976). *The Double Bind: The Price of Being a Minority Woman in Science.* (AAAS Publication 76-R-S). Washington, DC: American Association for the Advancement of Science.

[f]C Trower and R Chait (2002). Faculty diversity: Too little for too long. *Harvard Magazine* (March-April).

[g]SL Myers and CS Turner (2004). The effects of PhD supply on minority faculty representation. *The American Economic Review* 94(2):296-301.

[h]Trower and Chait (2002), ibid.

[i]Nelson (2005), ibid.

[j]Nelson (2005), ibid.

The committee was aided in fulfilling its charge by the National Academies' Committee on Women in Science and Engineering, which during the same time was working on two reports on related subjects, *To Recruit and Advance Women Students and Faculty in US Science and Engineering*, and *Gender Differences in the Careers of Science, Engineering, and Mathematics Faculty* (Box 1-3). The Committee on Maximizing the Potential of Women in Academic Science and Engineering also benefited from the expertise of the outside panelists and other participants in its convocation, held on December 9, 2005, in Washington, DC. A workshop report, *Bio-*

DEFINING THE ISSUES

BOX 1-2 Building Engineering and Science Talent: The CAWMSET and BEST Projects

The innovation economy is a major factor in job growth in the United States; jobs in this economy require some technical or scientific knowledge. Women, African-Americans, Hispanics, Native Americans, and persons with disabilities make up two-thirds of the overall workforce but hold only about one-fourth of the scientific and technical jobs.[a]

The **Congressional Commission on the Advancement of Women and Minorities in Science, Engineering, and Technology (CAWMSET) Development** was established in 1998 to examine the "barriers that exist for women, underrepresented minorities and persons with disabilities at different stages of the science, engineering, and technology (SET) pipeline."[b] In September 2000 the Commission issued its report, *Land of Plenty: Diversity as America's Competitive Edge in Science, Engineering, and Technology.*

Finding	*Recommendation*
• Inadequacies in precollege education prevent access to high-quality science and mathematics education for minorities. A lack of role models and well-qualified teachers acts to discourage interest in SET careers.	• Develop, implement, and adopt high-quality state-level math and science curricula and teacher-quality standards.
• There are significant problems of access to higher education for underrepresented groups. These include lack of preparation, lack of encouragement, cost of attendance, and poor integration between 2- and 4-year colleges.	• Develop aggressive intervention programs focused on the transition from high school to college. • Expand federal and state financial investment in the undergraduate and graduate education of under-represented groups.
• The US workplace culture does not value underrepresented groups.	• Hold employers accountable for the career development and advancement of all employees, including members of underrepresented groups.
• The public image of scientists and engineers is inaccurate and derogatory. Women in particular do not receive adequate and accurate portrayal.	• Establish a body to coordinate actions to transform the public image of SET careers.

To build upon the recommendations of CAWMSET, the **Building Engineering and Science Talent (BEST) Initiative** was launched in September 2001. The objective of BEST was to "convene the nation's respected practitioners, researchers and policy makers, and identify what's working across the country to develop the technical talent of under-represented groups in pre-K through 12, higher education, and the workplace."[c] BEST produced three reports:

- What it Takes: Pre-K-12 Design Principles to Broaden Participation in Science, Technology, Engineering and Mathematics[d]
- A Bridge for All: Higher Education Design Principles to Broaden Participation in Science, Technology, Engineering and Mathematics[e]
- The Talent Imperative: Diversifying America's Science and Engineering Workforce[f]

The BEST report, *The Talent Imperative: Diversifying America's Science and Engineering Workforce*, focused on identifying principles and factors that underlie effective programs "developed to broaden the participation of women, underrepresented minorities and persons with disabilities in science, engineering, and technology." It identifies several principles and best practices in K-12 education, higher education, and the workforce, including:

Higher Education

- Institutional leadership. *Leadership matters in creating successful programs. A commitment by administration and senior faculty helps to ensure that increasing participation is an essential part of successful higher education programs.*
- Targeted recruitment. *Establishing and sustaining a feeder system can play an important role in increasing participation of underrepresented groups.*
- Engaged faculty. *Faculty members should be engaged in diversifying student talent. Successful student outcomes are a measure of faculty performance.*
- Bridging to the next level. *Successful programs build the relationships and skills needed for students to move through the educational system and on to career achievements.*
- Continuous evaluation. *Successful programs continually evaluate their processes and outcomes.*

Workforce

- Sustained commitment to change. *Successful workforce programs seek lasting change in organizations through comprehensive efforts at all levels.*
- Integrated organizational strategy. *Stand-alone activities do not succeed. Successful programs are able to make diversity initiatives a seamless part of the organization's operation.*
- Managerial accountability. *Successful programs hold managers at all levels accountable for achieving diversity goals.*
- Continuous improvement. *Successful programs include metrics to identify what is working and what is not working.*

---

[a]Congressional Commission on the Advancement of Women and Minorities in Science, Engineering, and Technology Development (CAWMSET) (2000). *Land of Plenty: Diversity as America's Competitive Edge in Science, Engineering, and Technology, http://www.nsf.gov/pubs/2000/cawmset0409/cawmset_0409.pdf.*
[b]CAWMSET (2000), ibid.
[c]The BEST Initiative. *http://www.bestworkforce.org/.*
[d]Part 1: *http://www.bestworkforce.org/PDFdocs/BESTPre-K-12Rep_part1_Apr2004.pdf;* Part 2: *http://www.bestworkforce.org/PDFdocs/BESTPre-K-12Rep_part2_Apr2004.pdf.*
[e]*http://www.bestworkforce.org/PDFdocs/BEST_BridgeforAll_HighEdFINAL.pdf.*
[f]*http://www.bestworkforce.org/PDFdocs/BESTTalentImperativeFINAL.pdf.*

FOCUS ON RESEARCH

BOX 1-3 Committee on Women in Science and Engineering:
Gender Differences in the Careers of Science, Engineering, and Mathematics Faculty

In response to a formal mandate from Congress, the Committee on Women in Science and Engineering (CWSE) and the Committee on National Statistics of the National Research Council conducted a study to assess sex differences in the careers of science, engineering, and mathematics faculty, focusing on major research institutions. The study builds on the previous work by CWSE and examines such issues as faculty hiring, promotion, tenure, and allocation of institutional resources including laboratory space.

The study committee performed departmental surveys and faculty surveys at the 89 Research I institutions.[a] CWSE surveyed 6 fields: biology, chemistry, civil engineering, electrical engineering, mathematics, and physics. In total, they distributed the survey to 492 departments with an 85% response rate, and about 1800 faculty with a 77% response rate. The departmental survey asked questions about department size, recent tenure-track hires, and applications, interviews, and first offers for those positions. It also asked about tenure and promotion. The faculty survey collected demographic information and asked about career milestones, productivity, professional activities, and institutional resources. In addition, the committee has collected and posted information on faculty and climate surveys performed at academic institutions across the United States.[b]

Because of timing, the Committee on Maximizing the Potential of Women in Academic Science and Engineering did not have an opportunity to review these survey results. Footnotes have been added in the text of this report to indicate where the forthcoming CWSE report may shed additional light on issues discussed.

---

[a]*Research I (R1) university* was a category formerly used by the Carnegie Classification of Institutions of Higher Education to indicate those universities in the United States that received the highest amounts of federal science research funding. The category is, since 2000, obsolete, but the term is still widely used.
[b]See *http://www7.nationalacademies.org/cwse/gender_faculty_links.html*.

---

logical, Social, and Organizational Components of Success for Women in Academic Science and Engineering (*http://books.nap.edu/catalog/11766. html*), published by the National Academies Press, details the proceedings of that event.

DEFINING THE ISSUES

This report is organized according to the major themes of the committee's charge. **Chapter 2** examines the research on learning and performance to answer the question of whether cognitive differences between men and women exist and, if so, whether they form a basis for the differential success of men and women in science and engineering careers. **Chapter 3** follows the education and career trajectory of scientists and engineers and examines the persistence and attrition of men and women from high school graduation through hiring to tenure as science and engineering faculty members. **Chapter 4** examines how success is defined and evaluated in science and engineering and how gender schemas and discriminatory practices can affect evaluation of success. **Chapter 5** examines academic institutions and how apparently gender-neutral policies interact with systematic constraints to disproportionately hinder the career progression of women scientists and engineers. **Chapter 6** draws together the findings and shows why and what action should be taken to improve the career progression of women in science and engineering and concludes with a call to action.

Throughout the report, quotations, figures, tables, and boxes provide vignettes and additional data to illustrate the main points. Where possible, the committee broke out data by sex and by race or ethnicity. The boxes are organized into five categories: *Controversies, Defining the Issues, Experiments and Strategies, Focus on Research,* and *Tracking and Evaluation.* To assist universities in their efforts to remove the barriers that limit women's participation in academic science and engineering, the committee has developed a scorecard that universities can use to evaluate their progress. It appears as a box in Chapter 6. Appendixes provide information on the committee and its charge and reprint a chapter discussing theories of discrimination from a 2005 National Academies report entitled *Measuring Racial Discrimination.*

As the committee's deliberations progressed, it became increasingly clear that various cultural stereotypes and commonly held but unproven beliefs play major, frequently unacknowledged roles in the perception and treatment of women and their work in the scientific and engineering community. Those beliefs have often been cited as arguments against taking steps to improve the position of women in science and engineering or as reasons why such efforts are unnecessary, futile, or even harmful. To facilitate clear, evidence-based discussion of the issues, the committee compiled a list of commonly-held beliefs concerning women in science and engineering (Table S-1). Each is discussed and analyzed in detail in the text of the report.

The committee hopes that each of the actors involved in determining institutional culture and implementing relevant policies—universities, professional societies and higher education organizations, journals, federal funding agencies and foundations, federal agencies, and Congress—will give careful consideration to the extensive evidence supporting its findings and recommendations.

2

Learning and Performance

CHAPTER HIGHLIGHTS

Do cognitive differences between the sexes influence their differential success in science and engineering? A large body of research has probed the existence and nature of cognitive sex differences. Attempts to marshal the findings to answer that question have been hampered by three features of the public discussion of women in science.

First, the discussion has drawn on research in a highly selective way, emphasizing a small number of measures that show sex differences and de-emphasizing both the overlap between men and women on the measures and the large number of measures by which sex differences are small or nonexistent.[1] Second, most studies of sex differences in average abilities for mathematics and science focus on measures that were designed to predict academic success in high school or college mathematics or science, such as the quantitative portion of the Scholastic Aptitude Test (SAT-M). Because the academic success of girls now equals or exceeds that of boys at the high school and college levels, however, there is no

---

[1]JS Hyde (2005). The gender similarities hypothesis. *American Psychologist* 60:581-592; ES Spelke (2005). Sex differences in intrinsic aptitude for mathematics and science? A critical review. *American Psychologist* 60(9):950-958.

longer a gender gap for the studies to explain. Third, most studies of cognitive sex differences at the highest levels of mathematical and scientific ability also focus on measures that predict success in high school and college. These measures, however, have not proved to be predictive of success in later science careers.[2] Thus, we cannot look to cognitive sex differences to explain the differential success of men and women scientists and engineers.

FINDINGS

2-1. A large body of research has probed the existence and nature of cognitive sex differences.

2-2. Most discussions of cognitive sex differences emphasize a small number of measures showing sex differences and de-emphasize the overlap between men and women on those measures as well as the large number of measures by which sex differences are small, nonexistent, or favor women.

2-3. Studies of brain structure and function, of hormonal modulation of performance, of human cognitive development, and of human evolution have not revealed significant biological differences between men and women in performing science and mathematics that can account for the lower representation of women in these fields.

2-4. The academic success of girls now equals or exceeds that of boys at the high school and college levels, rendering moot all discussions of the biological and social factors that once produced sex differences in achievement at these levels.

2-5. Measures of aptitude for high school and college science have not proved to be predictive of success in later science and engineering careers. Notably, it is not just the top SAT scorers who continue on to successful careers; of the college-educated professional workforce in mathematics, science, and engineering, fewer than one-third of the men had SAT-M scores above 650, the lower end of the threshold typically presumed to be required for success in these fields.

2-6. The differing social pressures and influences on boys and girls appear to have more influence than their underlying abilities on their motivations and preferences.

---

[2] Y Xie and KA Shauman (2003). *Women in Science: Career Processes and Outcomes.* Cambridge, MA: Harvard University Press.

2-7. Activation of negative stereotypes can have a detrimental effect on women's interest and performance in domains relevant to success in academic science and engineering.

2-8. The present situation of women in scientific and engineering professions clearly results from the interplay of many individual, institutional, social, and cultural factors. If systematic differences between male and female scientific and mathematical aptitude and ability do exist, it is clear that they cannot account for women's underrepresentation in academic science and engineering.

RECOMMENDATION

2-1. Continued research is needed in elucidating the role of sex and gender in performance, including research on motivation, stereotype threat, and educational programs for improving performance in science and engineering fields.

RESEARCH APPROACHES

Researchers in a variety of disciplines and with a variety of perspectives—including neuroscience, cognitive psychology, evolutionary biology, and developmental and educational psychology—have sought to explore, measure, and explain whether boys and girls, and the men and women they become, differ from or resemble one another in various aptitudes, skills, behaviors, and decisions. Studies have examined such features as brain organization, hormonal influences on cognitive performance, genetics, and gender roles and socialization. In addition, researchers have performed meta-analyses of various bodies of research; this technique combines data from a number of studies to increase statistical power and give a clearer picture of results (Box 2-1).

Scientists are people of very dissimilar temperaments doing different things in very different ways. Among scientists are collectors, classifiers, and compulsive tidiers-up; many are detectives by temperament and many are explorers; some are artists and others artisans. There are poet-scientists and philosopher-scientists and even a few mystics. What sort of mind or temperament can all these people be supposed to have in common? Obligative scientists must be very rare, and most people who are in fact scientists could easily have been something else instead.

—Peter Medewar, The Art of the Soluble (1967)

FOCUS ON RESEARCH

BOX 2-1 Meta-analysis

Hundreds of studies examine gender differences in performance. Rather than conduct an additional study, one can synthesize the existing studies to find an overall outcome. *Meta-analysis* refers simply to the application of quantitative or statistical methods to combine evidence from numerous studies. Meta-analysis can tell us, when we aggregate over all the available studies, whether there really is a gender difference in mathematical ability. It can tell us the direction of the difference: do males score higher on average or do females? And it can also tell us the magnitude of any gender difference.

The *d* statistic, or effect size, is used to measure the gender difference. To obtain *d*, the mean score of females is subtracted from the mean score of males in a particular study, and the result is divided by the pooled within-gender standard deviation. Essentially, *d* tells us how far apart the means for males and females are in standardized units. *d* can have positive or negative values. A positive value means that males score higher, and a negative value means that females score higher. To give a tangible example, the gender difference in throwing distance is + 1.98.

In a meta-analysis, *d* is computed for each study, and then *d*s are averaged across all studies. Because meta-analysis aggregates over numerous studies, a meta-analysis typically represents the testing of tens of thousands, sometimes even millions of participants. Thus, the results should be far more reliable than those from any individual study.

How do we know when a *d*, an effect size, is small or large? The statistician Jacob Cohen provided the guideline that a *d* of 0.20 is small, 0.50 is moderate, and 0.80 is large.[a]

---

[a]J Cohen (1988). *Statistical Power Analysis for the Behavioral Sciences.* 2nd ed., Hillsdale, NJ: Erlbaum.

Average differences in ability or performance on various intellectual or cognitive tasks have appeared in many studies. That statistically significant differences among groups can be identified, however, does not indicate that they have practical consequences. A generation ago, boys tended to outperform girls in high school and college mathematics and science, and the findings of these studies were invoked to explain differential representation in math and science professions. Now this gender gap in school achievement has disappeared and the relevance of average sex differences as predictors of success in real-world academic science and engineering is debatable.

In cognitive studies comparing boys and men with girls and women, the overlap between the sexes is generally large—usually much larger than the purported differences. Moreover, systematic sex differences do not exist in most cognitive functions.[3] For the variables that do show statistically significant sex differences, some observers argue that small effect sizes indicate that the variable is not important for future success. Means drawn from comparing large groups may provide little insight into the abilities and choices of the relatively small number of people who pursue advanced studies in science or engineering and seek academic careers in those fields. Others argue, however, that small sex differences can accumulate over time and lead to substantial differences in career success (Box 6-1).[4]

That differences exist in abilities, skills, or brain organization does not indicate that they are immutable, nor that they are related to the underrepresentation of women in science and engineering. Biological, social, and psychological factors interact.[5] Genetics and sex hormones are known to influence performance in a number of ways, but experience also influences brain function in both children and adults. Research over the past 25 years indicates that complex interactions, between biological and sociocultural influences, together with the purely personal happenstance of individual lives, explain the constellation of abilities that any particular person possesses.

COGNITION

A great deal of research has centered on comparing male and female cognitive abilities in domains presumed to be related to success in science and engineering. Broadly speaking, *cognition* refers to the mental processes that underlie information processing, including object perception, learning, memory, language acquisition, and problem solving.[6] Research into sex differences in scientific and engineering ability has emphasized comparisons of mathematical, spatial, and verbal abilities.

Cognitive studies use a number of strategies. Some examine the performance of large numbers of people—from elementary school children through adult college students—on standardized pencil-and-paper tests such as the SAT or the National Assessment of Educational Progress (NAEP). Others use controlled laboratory experiments to measure performance on such tasks as solving mathematical problems, performing spatial rotations, or comprehending or reproducing linguistic passages. Some research probes

---

[3]JS Hyde (2005). The gender similarities hypothesis. *American Psychologist* 60(6):581-592.

[4]R Rosenthal, RL Rosnow, and DB Rubin (2000). *Contrasts and Effect Sizes in Behavioral Research: A Correlational Approach.* Cambridge, UK: Cambridge University Press.

[5]DF Halpern and U Tan (2001). Stereotypes and steroids: Using a psychobiosocial model to understand cognitive sex differences. *Brain and Cognition* 45:392-414.

[6]MRW Dawson and DA Medler (1999). *Dictionary of Cognitive Science, http://www.bcp.psych. ualberta.ca/~mike/Pearl_Street/Dictionary/contents/C/cognitive_psychology. html.*

the neurobiological correlates of cognition, using such techniques as functional magnetic resonance imaging while subjects carry out various mental tasks. Some compare levels of sex hormones with performance on a variety of tests. Meta-analyses combine the data from multiple studies to obtain increased statistical power.

> Some researchers object to the study of sex differences because they fear that it promotes false stereotypes and prejudice. There is nothing inherently sexist in a list of cognitive sex differences; prejudice is not intrinsic in data, but can be seen in the way people misuse data to promote a particular viewpoint or agenda. Prejudice also exists in the absence of data. Research is the only way to separate myth from empirically supported findings.
>
> —Diane F Halpern, Professor of Psychology and Director of the Berger Institute for Work, Family, and Children, Claremont McKenna College (2006)[7]

Mathematical and Spatial Performance

Mathematics plays such a central role in science that the question of whether there are sex differences in mathematical aptitude or ability has been a major focus of research.[8] Evidence shows that boys' and girls' aptitude is similar in early childhood, as are the developmental stages at which they integrate various components of mathematics ability.[9] Girls do as well as if not better than boys in high school mathematics and science classes,[10] and by 1998, girls were as likely as boys to take advanced mathematics and science classes.[11]

From 1990-2003, scores on the NAEP revealed no performance gap

---

[7]DF Halpern (2006). Biopsychosocial contributions to cognitive performance. In: *Biological, Social, and Organizational Contributions to Science and Engineering Success*. Washington, DC: The National Academies Press.

[8]DF Halpern (2005). Sex, brains, hands: Gender differences in cognitive abilities. *Limbic Nutrition, http://www.limibicnutrition.com/blog/archives/028860.html*; S Pinker (2005). The science of gender and science: A debate. *Edge: The Third Culture, http://www.edge.org/3rd_culture/debate05/debate05_index.html*.

[9]ES Spelke (2005). Sex differences in intrinsic aptitude for mathematics and science? A critical review. *American Psychologist* 60(9):950-958.

[10]National Center for Education Statistics (2004). *Trends in Educational Equity of Girls and Women: 2004* (NCES 2005-016). Washington, DC: US Department of Education; B Bridgeman and C Wendler (1991). Gender differences in predictors of college mathematics performance and in college mathematics course grades. *Journal of Educational Psychology* 83(2):275-284; Y Xie and KA Shauman (2003). *Women in Science: Career Processes and*

between boys and girls among 4th, 8th, and 12th grade students.[12] Scores on the SAT-M show a somewhat different picture, however, with the average score for boys consistently above that for girls.[13] Because SAT-M scores underpredict the mathematics performance of college women relative to men,[14] the relevance of the difference is not clear. Many studies suggest that differences in spatial ability may underlie differential mathematics performance. Some spatial tasks show sex differences favoring girls, others show differences favoring boys, and disagreement exists on the relevance and predictive power of each set of tasks.[15] Sex differences favoring boys are concentrated in particular tasks, specifically those requiring visuospatial transformation and unconventional mathematical knowledge.[16] Girls, in contrast, excel in mathematical tasks that involve language processing.[17] Men appear to use spatial strategies more often than women, and such strategic choices may account for a male advantage among high

---

Outcomes. Cambridge, MA: Harvard University Press; AM Gallagher and JC Kaufman (2005). *Gender Differences in Mathematics.* New York: Cambridge University Press.

[11]National Science Board (2004). *Science and Engineering Indicators, 2004* (NSB 04-01). Arlington, VA: National Science Foundation, Chapter 1.

[12]National Center for Education Statistics (2004), ibid.

[13]JS Hyde, E Fennema, and JS Lamon (1990). Gender differences in mathematics performance: A meta-analysis. *Psychological Bulletin* 107(2):139-155; MB Casey, RL Nuttall, E Pezaris, and CP Benbow (1995). The influence of spatial ability differences in mathematics college entrance scores across diverse samples. *Developmental Psychology* 31(4):697-705; LV Hedges and A Nowell (1995). Sex differences in mental test scores, variability, and numbers of high-scoring individuals. *Science* 269:41-45.

[14]Gallagher and Kaufman (2005), ibid.

[15]MB Casey, RL Nuttall, E Pezaris, and CP Benbow (1995), ibid; MB Casey, RL Nuttall, and E Pezaris (1997). Mediators of gender differences in mathematics college entrance test scores: A comparison of spatial skills with internalized beliefs and anxieties. *Developmental Psychology* 33(4):669-680; DC Geary, SJ Saults, F Liu, and MK Hoard (2000), ibid; MC Linn and AC Petersen (1985). Emergence and characterization of sex differences in spatial ability: A meta-analysis. *Child Development* 56:1479-1498; D Voyer, S Voyer, and MP Bryden (1995). Magnitude of sex differences in spatial abilities: A meta-analysis and consideration of critical variables. *Psychological Bulletin* 117(2):250-270.

[16]DF Halpern (2000). *Sex Differences in Cognitive Abilities (3rd ed.).* Mahway, NJ: Erlbaum; E Spelke (2005), ibid; A Gallagher, JY Levin, and C Cahalan (2002). *Cognitive Patterns of Gender Differences on Mathematics Admissions Tests* (GRE Board Professional Report No. 96-17P). Washington, DC: Educational Testing Service; DC Geary, SJ Saults, F Liu, and MK Hoard (2000). Sex differences in spatial cognition, computational fluency, and arithmetical reasoning. *Journal of Experimental Child Psychology* 77:337-353; Linn and Petersen (1985), ibid; Voyer, Voyer, and Bryden (1995), ibid; DC Geary (2001). Sex differences in spatial abilities among adults from the United States and China: Implications for evolutionary theory. *Evolution and Cognition* 7(2):172-177; DW Collins and D Kimura (1997). A large sex difference on a two-dimensional mental rotation task. *Behavioral Neuroscience* 111(4):845-849.

[17]A Gallagher, JY Levin, and C Cahalan (2002), ibid; Pinker (2005), ibid; Spelke (2005), ibid.

performers on tests of mathematical reasoning.[18] When all students are encouraged to use spatial strategies, the gender gap in performance narrows.[19] If sex differences on speeded tests result from strategy choices rather than ability differences, the equal performance of men and women in college mathematics courses may be more significant than the small differences between their average scores on speeded tests such as the SAT-M.

One of the most robust cognitive sex differences concerns the ability to imagine an object at different orientations in space (the "mental rotation" task).[20] Boys and men perform consistently faster and more accurately on this task, and some argue that this difference gives them an advantage in science, mathematics, and technology.[21] Evidence indicates that the difference between men and women on this task may be largely due to stereotype threat (Box 2-4).[22] Furthermore, mental rotation and similar measures of spatial ability have been found to be less effective than verbal skills in predicting achievement in mathematics and science.[23] People with strong spatial skills are less likely than those with high verbal skills or high overall intelligence to have earned credentials at every academic level and more likely to work in blue-collar occupations that do not require advanced education.[24]

Another sex difference has to do with variability: there are more men at both the high and low ends of many cognitive performance distributions.[25]

---

[18]DC Geary (1996). Sexual selection and sex differences in mathematical abilities. *Behavioral and Brain Sciences* 19:229-284; A Gallagher, JY Levin, and C Cahalan (2002), ibid; A Gallagher, R De Lisi, PC Holst, AV McGillicuddy-De Lisi, M Morely, and C Cahalan (2000) Gender differences in advanced mathematical problem solving. *Journal of Experimental Child Psychology* 75:165-190.

[19]Geary (1996), ibid.

[20]RN Shepard and J Metzler (1971). Mental rotation of three-dimensional objects. *Science* 171(972):701-703; see review by J Huttenlocher, S Levine, and J Vevea (1998). Environmental input and cognitive growth: A study using time-period comparisons. *Child Development* 69:1012-1029.

[21]S Pinker (2002). *The Blank Slate: The Modern Denial of Human Nature.* New York: Viking; DC Geary (1996). Sexual selection and sex differences in mathematical abilities. *Behavioral and Brain Sciences* 19:229-284.

[22]MS McGlone and J Aronson (2006). Stereotype threat, identity salience, and spatial reasoning. *Journal of Applied Developmental Psychology* (in press).

[23]AM Gallagher and JC Kaufman (2005). *Gender Differences in Mathematics.* New York: Cambridge University Press.

[24]LG Humphreys, D Lubinski, and G Yao (1993). Utility of predicting group membership and the role of spatial visualization in becoming an engineer, physical scientist, or artist. *Journal of Applied Psychology* 78(2):250-261.

[25]CP Benbow and JC Stanley (1980). Sex differences in mathematical ability: fact or artifact? *Science* 210:1262-1264; CP Benbow and JC Stanley (1988). Sex differences in mathematical reasoning ability: more facts. *Science* 222:1029-1031; LV Hedges and A Nowell (1995). Sex differences in mental test scores, variability, and numbers of high-scoring individuals. *Science* 269:41-45.

Some argue that variability differences may be more important than average differences in accounting for the preponderance of men scientists; however, this is based on the assumption that only those in the extreme upper tail of the performance distribution go on to successful careers in science and engineering. Recent data bring this assumption into question: the differences in sex distribution at the tails is decreasing,[26] and scientists and engineers may be drawn from a wider range of the distribution, not just the tails (Box 2-2).

Verbal and Written Performance

The data on verbal skills generally show women outperforming men. Although one early meta-analysis found the effect sizes too small to have practical meaning,[27] a variety of tests done over several decades have found girls outscoring boys, on the average, in a number of tasks involving reading, writing, vocabulary, and spelling.[28] In particular, girls and women perform better on tasks involving writing and comprehending complex prose; rapid access to and use of phonological, semantic, and episodic information in long term memory;[29] and speech articulation and fine motor tasks.[30] In 1988-1996, the US Department of Education reports that girls consistently and substantially outperformed boys in writing achievement at the 4th, 8th, and 11th grade levels.[31] Researchers and the mass

---

[25]Benbow and Stanley (1980), ibid; Benbow and Stanley (1983), ibid; LV Hedges and A Nowell (1995). Sex differences in mental test scores, variability, and numbers of high-scoring individuals. *Science* 269:41-45.

[26]LE Brody and CJ Mills (2005). Talent search research: What have we learned? *High Ability Studies* 16(1):97-111.

[27]Hyde and Linn (1988), ibid.

[28]A Feingold (1988), ibid; Nowell A and LV Hedges (1998). Trends in gender differences in academic achievement from 1960 to 1994: an analysis of differences in mean, variance and extreme scores, *Sex Roles: A Journal of Research* (39):21-43; Campbell, Hombo, and Mazzeo (2000), ibid; National Center for Education Statistics (2004), ibid; EM Weiss, G Kemmler, EA Deisenhammer, W Fleischhacker, and M Delazer (2003). Sex differences in cognitive functions. *Personality and Individual Differences* 35(4):863-875; Halpern (2005), ibid.

[29]A Herlitz, L-G Nilsson, and L Baeckman (1997). Gender differences in episodic memory. *Memory and Cognition* 25:801-811; LJ Levy, RS Astur, and KM Frick (2005). Men and women differ in object memory but not performance of a virtual radial maze. *Behavioral Neuroscience* 119:853-862.

[30]For example, see MW O'Boyle, EJ Hoff, and HS Gill (1995). The influence of mirror reversals on male and female performance in spatial tasks: A componential look. *Personality and Individual Differences* 18:693-699.

[31]National Center for Education Statistics (2000). *Trends in Educational Equity of Girls and Women: 2000* (NCES 2000-030). Washington, DC: US Department of Education.

media alike have called the sex difference in writing so large as to be "alarming" or a "crisis."[32] A more recent study shows consistent improvement among boys, and stresses that the predominant issues are race and class, not sex.[33] The female advantage in writing may be one reason why girls get higher grades in school, on average. Any assessment that relies on writing provides an advantage to women and girls.

Researchers have asked whether cognitive differences have changed over the years, especially as gender roles and expectations in society have changed in recent decades. Meta-analyses and examinations of data from several national standardized tests have found the gap in mathematical performance narrowing[34] while gaps in verbal performance, visuospatial rotation, and SAT-M scores have held steady.[35] Perhaps more salient are international comparisons. Most countries participating in the Programme for International Student Assessment (PISA)[36] showed significantly higher scores for girls than boys in reading literacy. Another international test found no sex difference among 8th-graders in science scores and a small but significant sex difference in mathematics favoring boys.[37] Perhaps most interesting is that girls in Taiwan and Japan dramatically outscore US boys in mathematics—a finding that supports the idea that the cultural values attached to mathematics, in particular attitudes about the importance of ability as opposed to effort, can substantially affect performance.[38]

[32]Hedges and Nowell (1995), ibid; P Tyre (2006). The trouble with boys. *Newsweek* 147(5):44-52 (January 30).

[33]Education Sector (2006). *The Truth About Boys and Girls*. Washington, DC: Education Sector.

[34]JS Hyde, E Fennema, and JS Lammon (1990), ibid; Feingold (1988), ibid; JR Campbell, CM Hombo, and J Mazzeo (2000), ibid.

[35]Feingold (1988), ibid; Hedges and Nowell (1995), ibid; Masters MS and Sanders B (1993). Is the gender difference in mental rotation disappearing? *Behavior Genetics* 23: 337-341.

[36]PISA is run by the Organisation for Economic Co-operation and Development. It performs a survey every 3 years of 15-year-olds in the principal industrialized countries to assess mathematics, science, and reading skills. See *http://www.pisa.oecd.org/*.

[37]National Center for Education Statistics (1997). *The Third International Mathematics and Science Study*. Washington, DC: US Department of Education.

[38]M Lummis and HW Stevenson (1990). Gender differences in beliefs and achievement: A cross-cultural study. *Developmental Psychology* 26(2):254-263. Note that researchers using those parts of the SAT-M that produced the largest differencies for US boys and firls, found no gender differences in performance among Chinese or Japanese students. JP Byrnes, H Li, and X Xhaoging (1997). Gender differences on the math subset of the scholastic aptitude test may be culture specific. *Educational Studies in Mathematics* 34:49-66.

DEFINING THE ISSUES

BOX 2-2 The Variability Hypothesis

Mean differences between men and women in scores on mathematics and science achievement tests are not especially large, and mean scores have been converging. Many believe that these trends are largely irrelevant, however, because people who go on to research careers in science, mathematics, and engineering are not drawn from areas near the midpoint of science and mathematics abilities, or the fat part of the bell curve. Instead, the assumption is often made that those who end up in research careers in science, engineering, and mathematics (SEM) are drawn from the top 1-5% of the distribution in mathematics and science talent.[a]

It is precisely at this extreme tail of science and mathematics abilities that sex differences are most evident. For example, in a study of close to 10,000 talented 12- and 14-year-olds who had taken the SAT, the male:female ratio was 2:1 for those with SAT-M scores of at least 500; it was about 12:1 for those with scores of at least 700.[b] Such findings are often viewed as part of a pattern of greater variability in ability and achievement among men than among women. As Steven Pinker has so succinctly stated, when it comes to male abilities and achievement there are "more prodigies, more idiots."[c]

The variability hypothesis has a great deal of face validity and appeal. College-educated SEM professionals make up only 2-3% of the US workforce, so shouldn't they be those in the top 2-3% in science and mathematics abilities? Interestingly, the answer to that question, often assumed, has not been examined until recently. And the answer appears to be no. A recent economic analysis by Weinberger examined characteristics of the college-educated SEM workforce and found that fewer than one-third of the white males had SAT-M scores above 650, which is at the low end of the threshold for ability in mathematics typically presumed to be required for success in these fields.[d] In both samples of adolescents followed in the analysis, about one-fourth of the college-educated men and women in the SEM workforce had SAT-M scores below the 75th percentile, and more than half the men (and almost half the women) had scores below the 85th percentile—much closer to the fat part of the curve than anyone had imagined.

Those findings cast serious doubt on the variability hypothesis as the cause for the large discrepancy between the numbers of men and women who go on to SEM careers. It should be noted that the Weinberger study included SEM workforce participants holding bachelors degrees and above, and did not address the subset of those who obtain SEM doctorates.

A further argument against the variability hypothesis stems from its malleability over time. Although the upper tail male:female ratio was about 12:1 in the 1970s, it has declined to 3:1 in more recent samples.[e] This difference obviously cannot be explained by biological factors and suggests that social and cultural changes in the education of men and women have influenced test scores.

Further evidence against the hypothesis that men are biologically predisposed to achievement in mathematics at the highest levels comes from studies of stereotype threat (Box 2-4). Although women and men tend to perform equivalently well on less demanding mathematical material, women tend to underperform when given high-pressure tests with highly demanding problems. Research reveals that cultural factors mediate this drop in women's performance. Because the conditions that favor stereotype threat are just those required for highest performance on the SAT, it is not surprising that among the highest scorers, SAT scores underpredict the academic performance of women relative to men.

Even after controlling for mathematics test scores, less than half as many women as men were found to pursue SEM careers, both among a pool of all college graduates[f] and among a large sample of mathematically gifted youth.[g] Most notably, among youth scoring in the top 1% of mathematics ability as adolescents, men were almost twice as likely as women to obtain degrees in the physical sciences and engineering. Lack of innate mathematics ability could not explain this difference.

---

[a]C Benbow and O Arjmand (1990). Predictors of high academic achievement in mathematically talented students: A longitudinal study. *Journal of Educational Psychology* 82:430-441; LV Hedges and A Nowell (1995). Sex differences in mental test scores, variability, and numbers of high-scoring individuals. *Science* 270:364-365; M Paglin and AM Rufolo (1990). Heterogeneous human capital, occupational choice, and male-female earnings differences. *Journal of Labor Economics* 8(1):123-144; S Pinker (2005). The science of difference: Sex ed. *The New Republic,* February 14.

[b]CP Benbow (1988). Sex differences in mathematical reasoning ability in intellectually talented preadolescents: Their nature, effects, and possible causes. *Behavioral and Brain Sciences* 11:169-232.

[c]Pinker (2005), ibid.

[d]CJ Weinberger (2005). *Is the Science and Engineering Workforce Drawn from the Far Upper Tail of the Math Ability Distribution?* Working Paper. Institute for Social, Behavioral and Economic Research and Department of Economics, University of California at Santa Barbara.

[e]LE Brody and CJ Mills (2005). Talent search research: What have we learned? *High Ability Studies* 16(1):97-111.

[f]CJ Weinberger (2005), ibid.

[g]CP Benbow, D Lubinski, DL Shea, and H Eftekhari-Sanjani (2000). Sex differences in mathematical reasoning ability at age 13: Their status 20 years later. *Psychological Science* 11(6):474-480.

TABLE 2-1 The Magnitude ("d") of Sex Differences in Mathematics Performance, by Age and Test Cognitive Level

	Cognitive Level		
Age Group	Computation	Concepts	Problem Solving
5-10	−0.20	−0.02	0.00
11-14	−0.22	−0.06	−0.02
15-18	0.00	0.07	0.29
19-25	N/A	N/A	0.32

NOTES: Ages were grouped roughly into elementary school (ages 5-10 years), middle school (11-14), high school (15-18), and college age (19-25). Cognitive level of the test was coded as assessing either simple computation (requires the use of only memorized mathematics facts, such as $7 \times 8 = 56$), conceptual (involves analysis or comprehension of mathematical ideas), problem solving (involves extending knowledge or applying it to new situations), or mixed. Conventionally, a negative number indicates a female advantage, and a positive number a male advantage. N/A = not available.

SOURCE: JS Hyde, E Fennema, and SJ Lamon (1990). Gender differences in mathematics performance: A meta-analysis. *Psychological Bulletin* 107:139-155.

Longitudinal Manifestation of Cognitive Differences

This broad assessment of the magnitude of sex differences is probably less useful than an analysis by both age and cognitive level. Meta-analyses show that sex differences in verbal performance do not change much with age.[39] However, some aspects of mathematics performance show striking age dependence (Table 2-1). Elementary and middle school girls outperform boys by a small margin in computation; there is no sex difference in high school. For understanding of mathematical concepts, there is no sex difference at any age level. For problem solving there is no sex difference in elementary or middle school, but one favoring boys and men emerges in high school and the college years. Problem solving performance deserves attention because problem solving is essential to success in science and engineering occupations.

Hyde suggests that differences in problem solving may result from course choice, that is, the tendency of girls and boys to select optional advanced mathematics and science courses in high school.[40] As described

---

[39]LV Hedges and A Nowell (1995). Sex differences in mental test scores, variability, and numbers of high-scoring individuals. *Science* 269:41-45; JS Hyde and MC Linn (1988). Gender differences in verbal ability: A meta-analysis. *Psychological Bulletin* 104:53-69.

[40]JS Hyde (2005). The gender similarities hypothesis. *American Psychologist* 60:581-592.

in Chapter 3, differences in mathematics course taking has narrowed over the last decade, so that by 1998 girls were as likely as boys to have taken advanced mathematics courses. Girls also are as likely as boys to take advanced biology, but they are less likely to take advanced chemistry and physics classes.[41] If problem solving is related to course choice, then it is possible that these differences have substantially narrowed during the last 15 years.

BIOLOGY

Four types of studies have been used to suggest a biological basis for the differing career outcomes of men and women: brain structure and function, hormonal influences on cognitive performance, psychological development in infancy, and evolutionary psychology.

Brain Structure and Function

The brains of human men and women show highly similar structure and organization at all points in development. Indeed, human brains are so similar that the explosively growing field of human functional brain imaging uses a single template to map the structures and functions of the brains of both sexes. Despite the overall similarity, however, a body of research has found sex differences in aspects of brain organization and the size and activity level during relevant tasks of different regions of the cerebral cortex.[42] The onset, symptomology, and prevalence of psychiatric disorders show marked sex differences. Lateralization of language functions (e.g., the extent to which functions appear primarily in one side of the brain instead of being represented in both hemispheres) may or may not be correlated with sex.[43] A relationship between handedness (preference for using the right or left hand) and cognitive abilities provides a useful avenue for

---

[41]National Science Board (2004). *Science and Engineering Indicators, 2004* (NSF 04-01). Arlington, VA: National Science Foundation.

[42]SF Witelson (1991). Neural sexual mosaicism: Sexual differentiation of the human temporo-parietal region for function asymmetry. *Psychoneuroendocrinology* 16(1-3):131-153; SF Witelson, II Glezer, and DL Kigaar (1995). Women have greater density of neurons in the posterior temporal cortex. *The Journal of Neuroscience* 15(5):3418-3428.

[43]BA Shaywitz, SE Shaywitz, KR Pugh, RT Constable, P Skudlarski, RK Fulbright, RA Bronen, JM Fletcher, DP Shankweler, L Katz, and JC Gore (1995). Sex differences in the functional organization of the brain for language. *Nature* 373:607-609; JA Frost, JR Binder, JA Springer, TA Hammeke, PSF Bellgowan, SM Rao, and RB Cox (1999). Language processing is strongly lateralized in both sexes. *Brain* 122(2):199-208; IEC Sommer, A Aleman, A Bouma, and RS Kahn (2004). Do women really have more bilateral language representation than men? A meta-analysis of functional imaging studies. *Brain* 127(8):1845-1852.

investigating neurological differences.[44] In right-handed people and half of left-handers, the brain's left hemisphere dominates in verbal tasks, and the right hemisphere dominates in nonlinguistic spatial tasks. The remaining left-handers show either the reverse pattern or equal representation of tasks between the hemispheres. Left-handed men are more likely to show mathematical talent but also to suffer from dyslexia, stuttering, and mental retardation. Left-handed women have been found to exceed men in spatial tasks.

Hormonal Influences on Cognitive Performance

Hormones have received considerable attention as a possible source of sex differences in cognition and behavior. The findings are complex because of failure to replicate numerous reported effects and because hormones can influence both cognitive abilities and their manifestation in performance. The influences can be either direct or indirect. Influences on the neural substrates of cognition are direct. The individual preferences that lead to culture-specific experiences that enhance particular abilities are indirect.[45]

The presumed masculinizing effect of androgens on spatial ability and personal preferences has attracted particular interest.[46] Studies have cited androgen effects on brain development including a greater preference for male-typical toys, as well as superior spatial ability and lower interest in language tasks; these findings are based on research in girls affected by congenital adrenal hyperplasia, a condition resulting in overproduction of testosterone during fetal development.[47] That the condition causes girls to have masculinized genitalia raises the possibility that differences in preference or behavior may have a societal component resulting from the belief, by the girls themselves or their parents, that they are more masculine or less

---

[44]Halpern (2005), ibid.

[45]D Geary (1996). Sexual selection and sex differences in mathematical abilities. *Behavioral and Brain Sciences* 19:229-284.

[46]CCC Cohen-Bendahan, C van de Beek, and SA Berenbaum (2005). Prenatal sex hormone effects on child and adult sex-typed behavior: Methods and findings. *Neuroscience and Biobehavioral Reviews* 29:353-384.

[47]VL Pasterski, ME Geffner, C Brain, P Hindmarsh, B Charles, and M Hines (2005). Prenatal hormones and postnatal socialization by parents as determinants of male-typical toy-play in girls with congenital adrenal hyperplasia. *Child Development* 76:264-278; M Hines, BA Fane, VL Pasterski, GA Mathews, GS Conway, and C Brook (2003). Spatial abilities following prenatal androgen abnormality: Targeting and mental rotations performance in individuals with congenital adrenal hyperplasia. *Psychoneuroendocrinology* 28:1010-1026; SM Resnick, SA Berenbaum, II Gottesman, and TJ Bouchard (1986). Early hormonal influences on cognitive functioning in congenital adrenal hyperplasia. *Developmental Psychology* 22(2):191-198; Hines et al. (2003), ibid; Resnick et al. (1986), ibid.

feminine than other girls. That might encourage them to act in less stereotypically feminine ways.[48]

Research into the relationship between variations in fetal hormones in normal children and later behaviors considered typical of one sex or the other has produced mixed results. The amount of eye contact that boys make with their parents, for example, appears to correlate negatively with measures of fetal testosterone, possibly suggesting a role of the hormone in social development.[49] In addition, one study indicated that levels of fetal testosterone appear to be correlated positively with girls' ability to do mental rotation tasks.[50] Another study has found testosterone levels to be correlated negatively with counting and number facts. Levels of sex hormones are correlated with spatial ability in adults, some evidence shows. According to one study, testosterone strongly improved the ability of women, and impaired that of men, to do mental rotation, and estradiol impaired women's mental rotation ability.[51] Another study, however, found sex differences in spatial and verbal abilities but showed that different levels of testosterone, estradiol, or progesterone had no effect.[52] Where impairments are found, their sources could be either cognitive or motivational and social. Motivational and social influences on cognitive test performance are discussed below.

Psychological Development in Infancy

The last 30 years have brought an explosion of research on the cognitive abilities of human infants. In the vast majority of studies, male and female infants have shown equal abilities to perceive and represent objects, space, and number.[53] When sex differences in those abilities are found,

---

[48]M Hines (2003). Sex steroids and human behavior: Prenatal androgen exposure and sex-typical play behavior in children. *Annals of the New York Academy of Sciences* 1007:272-282; CCC Cohen-Bendahan et al. (2005), ibid; Pasterski et al. (2005), ibid.

[49]S Luchtmaya, S Baron-Cohen, and P Raggatt (2002). Foetal testosterone and eye contact in 12-month-old human infants. *Infant Behavior and Development* 25:327-335.

[50]Luchtmaya et al. (2002), ibid.

[51]M Hausmann, D Slabbekoorn, SHM Van Goozen, PT Cohen-Kettenis, and O Güntürkün (2000). Sex hormones affect spatial abilities during the menstrual cycle. *Behavioral Neuroscience* 114(6):1245-1250.

[52]R Halari, M Hines, V Kumari, R Mehrotra, M Wheeler, V Ng, and T Sharma (2005). Sex differences in individual differences in cognitive performance and their relationship to endogenous gonadal hormones and gonadatropins. *Behavioral Neuroscience* 119(1):104-117.

[53]ES Spelke (2005). Sex differences in intrinsic aptitude for mathematics and science? A critical review. *American Psychologist* 60(9):950-958; DC Geary (1996). Sexual selection and sex differences in mathematical abilities. *Behavioral and Brain Sciences* 19:229-284.

they tend to favor girls and to be transitory;[54] such results are consistent with findings that girl infants develop somewhat more rapidly than boys across the board.

Some investigators have proposed that sex differences in mathematics and science abilities stem from innate predispositions to learn about different things, with infant boys more oriented to objects and infant girls to people.[55] With the exception of one study whose methods have been criticized for inadequate controls,[56] a large body of research fails to support that hypothesis, showing instead that infant girls and boys show equally strong interests in people and in objects.[57] Along similar lines, some researchers cite children's preferences for stereotypically masculine or feminine toys—trucks and blocks vs. dolls, for example—as evidence of innate biological differences in the preferences of the two sexes.[58] Children do not begin to show such toy preferences until the age of 18 months, however, and such differences are inconsistent even later in development.[59] Moreover, the basis of those sex differences has not been investigated. It is possible that features of the toys that are irrelevant to their representational significance, such as color, may account for the observed preferences. It is consistent with the latter interpretation that vervet monkeys have been reported to show the same sex differences in toy preferences as human children, even though monkeys fail to engage in the "cultural learning" that

------

[54]R Baillargeon, L Kotovksy, and A Needham (1995). The acquisition of physical knowledge in infancy. In eds. D Sperber and D Premack, *Causal Cognition: A Multidisciplinary Debate* (pp. 79-116). New York: Clarendon Press. Oxford University Press; K van Marle (2004). *Infants' understanding of number: The relationship between discrete and continuous quantity.* Doctoral dissertation, Yale University.

[55]S Baron-Cohen (2002). *The Essential Difference: The Truth about the Male and the Female Brain.* New York: Basic Books; KR Browne (2002). *Biology at Work.* New Brunswick, NJ: Rutgers University Press.

[56]J Connellan, S Baron-Cohen, S Wheelwright, A Batki, and J Ahluwalia (2000). Sex differences in human neonatal social perception. *Infant Behavior and Development* 23:113-118.

[57]EE Maccoby and CN Jacklin (1974). *Psychology of Sex Differences.* Stanford, CA: Stanford University Press; ES Spelke (2005). Sex differences in intrinsic aptitude for mathematics and science? A critical review. *American Psychologist* 60(9):950-958.

[58]A Nordenström, A Servin, G Bohlin, A Larsson, and A Wedell (2002). Sex-typed toy play behavior correlates with the degree of prenatal androgen exposure assessed by CYP 21 genotype in girls with congenital adrenal hyperplasia. *Journal of Clinical Endocrinology and Metabolism* 87(11):5119-5124; VL Pasterski, ME Geffner, C Brain, P Hindmarsh, B Charles, and M Hines (2005). Prenatal hormones and post-natal socialization by parents as determinants of male-typical toy play in girls with congenital adrenal hyperplasia. *Child Development* 76(1):264-278.

[59]LA Serbin, D Poulin-Dubois, KA Colburne, MG Sen, and JA Y Eichstedt (2001). Gender stereotyping in infancy: Visual preferences for and knowledge of gender stereotyped toys in the second year. *International Journal of Behavioral Development* 25:7-15.

leads human children to treat toys as representations of real objects.[60] The existence of equivalent sex differences in the object preferences of male and female children and monkeys suggests that the preferences are not mediated by differences in cognitive interests or abilities.

Evolutionary Psychology

If biologically based differences in mathematics, science, or related abilities do separate the sexes, some scholars argue they probably have origins in human evolution.[61] Such explanations are exceedingly difficult to evaluate, because humans' paleolithic ancestors did not practice science or formal mathematics. Some investigators argue that humans and their ancestors were hunter-gatherers for countless generations and that natural selection would have favored men who had strong spatial skills useful in traveling long distances to locate game and then felling it with spears or arrows. Others argue that because both global and local spatial cues are important for navigation, women, whose food gathering required detailed geographic knowledge and possibly extensive travel, would also have needed to have good spatial ability to find and remember good food sources.[62] Some call into question whether hunting and gathering were sex-typed activities.[63] In addition to sex differences in cognition, some researchers argue that motivation has clear evolutionary links (Box 2-3).

In summary, studies of brain structure and function, of hormonal influences on cognitive performance, of psychological development in infancy, and of human evolution provide no clear evidence that men are biologically advantaged in learning and performing mathematics and science. That makes sense in light of the fact that most of the studies focus on average abilities and on structures and functions that are ingredients to success in

---

[60]M Tomasello and J Call (1997). *Primate Cognition.* New York: Oxford University Press.

[61]DC Geary (1998). *Male, Female: The Evolution of Human Sex Differences.* Washington, DC: American Psychological Association; S Baron-Cohen (2002). *The Essential Difference: The Truth about the Male and Female Brain.* New York: Basic Books; S Pinker (2002). *The Blank Slate: The Modern Denial of Human Nature.* New York: Viking; KR Browne (2002). *Biology at Work: Rethinking Sexual Equality.* New Brunswick, NJ: Rutgers University Press.

[62]D Geary (1996). Sexual selection and sex differences in mathematical abilities. *Behavioral and Brain Sciences,* 19:229-284; S Hrdy (1997). Raising Darwin's consciousness: Female sexuality and the prehominid origins of patriarchy. *Human Nature* 8(1):1-49; K Cheng (2005). Reflections on geometry and navigation. *Connection Science* 17(1-2):5-21; NS Newcombe and J Huttenlocher (2006). Development of spatial cognition. In *Handbook of Child Psychology: Vol. 2. Cognition, Perception, and Language* (6th ed.). Eds. D Kuhn and R.S Siegler, New York: Wiley.

[63]Hrdy (1997), ibid.

CONTROVERSIES

BOX 2-3 The Evolution of Motivation

The main evolutionary psychology argument focuses not on a cognitive difference but rather on a motivational one: men are said to be more competitive, and competitiveness is said to be good for science and engineering. The claim that men are more competitive is controversial: some researchers argue that women are just as competitive but express their competitiveness in different ways. And, it is far from clear that greater competitiveness makes for more effective science. A mistake that is often made in considering the aptitude of a minority group for a given discipline is to conclude, from the fact that the characteristics of the majority group predominate in the discipline, that the majority traits are required for success in the discipline. Examples of that error are easy to see when one looks to the past. In the 1930s to 1950s, there were no Jews in academic psychology. EG Boring, one of the fathers of experimental psychology, argued that Jews were unfit to be experimental psychologists because of the "defects of their race." Specifically, he argued that all the successful psychologists had qualities of Christian temperance. Today, we would say that Christianity was a typical characteristic of the experimental psychologists of Boring's day for social reasons, not because it gave a biological advantage for successful science. Similarly, today's scientists and engineers have a whole array of typically male characteristics that may or may not enhance the quality of their science.

high school and college mathematics and science. Because men and women do not differ in their average abilities and because they have now achieved equal academic success in science through the college level, there is no sex performance difference for the biological studies and theories to explain.

SOCIETY AND CULTURE

As members of a highly social species, humans do not exist solely as biological entities. We live within complex interpersonal networks and cultural frameworks that strongly mold our development, behavior, opportunities, and choices. The abilities that people exhibit and the skills that they possess therefore result not only from their biological endowment but also from the social and cultural influences that begin at the moment of their birth and continue to the end of their lives. Those influences and their results can vary markedly among cultures. In Iceland, for example, adolescent girls outscore boys in mathematical reasoning;[64] in the United States,

---

[64]US Department of Education (2004). *International Outcomes of Learning in Mathematics Literacy and Problem Solving: PISA 2003 Results from the US Perspective: Highlights* (NCES 2005–003). Washington, DC: US Department of Education.

a higher proportion of African American women than white women pursue degrees in science and engineering (Table 3-2).[65]

Socialization of Infants and Children

Societies have quite specific stereotypes about male and female characteristics and behaviors and generally begin applying them in earliest infancy. Evidence indicates that parents and others interpret baby boys' and girls' characteristics and behavior—even when they are identical—as reflecting qualities consistent with traditional gender roles.[66] During childhood, many parents encourage sex differences in behavior and experience—and therefore possibly in neurobiology—by treating boys and girls differently, and also by estimating their abilities differently, again in line with gender stereotypes.[67]

Such treatment can powerfully affect children's own concepts of gender and influence their view of their own talents, especially regarding gender stereotyped endeavors, such as social relations, sports, mathematics, and science, the last of which, according to one study, parents believe boys find easier and more interesting than do girls.[68] However, another study found that children with less traditional views of gender roles expressed stronger interest in mathematics. According to a meta-analysis, the effect sizes of the influence of parents' gender beliefs diminished after the mid-1980s, possibly indicating a decrease in gender stereotyping.[69] Moreover, the equal

---

[65]National Science Foundation (2004). *Women, Minorities and Persons with Disabilities in Science and Engineering 2004*. Arlington, VA: National Science Foundation.

[66]SM Condry and JC Condry (1976). Sex differences: A study of the eye of the beholder. *Child Development* 47:812-819; SM Condry, JC Condry, and LW Pogatshnik (1983). Sex differences: A study of the ear of the beholder. *Sex Roles: A Journal of Research* 9(6):697-705.

[67]Geary (1996), ibid; Valian (1998), ibid; JE Jacobs and JS Eccles (1992). The impact of mothers' gender-role stereotypic beliefs on mothers' and children's ability perceptions. *Journal of Personality and Social Psychology* 63(6):932-944.

[68]Jacobs and Eccles (1992), ibid; HR Tenenbaum and C Leaper (2003a). Are parents' gender schemas related to their children's gender-related cognitions? A meta-analysis. *Developmental Psychology* 38(4):615-630; JE Jacobs, P Davis-Kean, M Bleeker, JS Eccles, and O Malanchuk (2005). "I can, but I don't want to": The impact of parents, interests, and activities on gender differences in math. In *Gender Differences in Mathematics: An Integrative Psychological Approach.*, eds. AM Gallagher and JC Kaufman, New York: Cambridge University Press (pp. 246-263); HR Tenenbaum and C Leaper (2003b). Parent-child conversations about science: The socialization of gender inequities. *Developmental Psychology* 39(1):34-47; K Crowley, MA Callanan, HR Tenenbaum, and E Allen (2001). Parents explain more often to boys than to girls during shared scientific thinking. *Psychological Science* 12(3):258-261.

[69]C Leaper, KJ Anderson, and P Sanders (1998). Moderators of gender effects on parents' talk to their children: A meta-analysis. *Developmental Psychology* 34(1):3-27.

performance of boys and girls in high school and college mathematics suggests either that the gender stereotypes have waned or that they are not powerful enough to prevent girls' academic success.

Education

Throughout the school years many parents respond differently to their sons and daughters as they study science and mathematics, generally engaging more with and showing more encouragement to the boys. Some data indicate that parents' interest and engagement in these subjects predicts the grades that children earn later in school careers.[70] Other studies, however, found more mixed effects.[71] Still, negative gender stereotyping of abilities can do more than deprive people of encouragement to pursue a field or of the expectation that they can succeed. In addition to parents, teachers and their stereotypes also strongly influence children's conceptions of what they can achieve.[72]

As children progress through school and begin to consider possible adult careers, studies have shown the ambitions of boys and girls begin to diverge. Girls tend to show more interest in languages, literature, music, and drama than equally bright boys, who are likelier to focus on physical science and mathematics and history.[73] Other studies found little difference between college men's and women's attitudes toward mathematics, but a lower likelihood that women would have mathematics-related career goals.[74] Many of the data showing those preferences date from the 1970s and 1980s, but more recent work finds the same tendencies among students in the 21st century. Neither the subjects that individuals studied nor their levels of mathematics achievement accounted for these differences inasmuch as girls not only took as many mathematics and science courses as boys, but earned better grades.[75]

---

[70]Tenenbaum and Leaper (2003b), ibid; Crowley et al. (2001), ibid; Jacobs and Eccles (1992), ibid.

[71]H Lytton and DM Romney (1991). Parents' differential socialization of boys and girls: A meta-analysis. *Psychological Bulletin* 109(2):267-296.

[72]CM Steele (1997). A threat in the air: How stereotypes shape intellectual identity and performance. *American Psychologist* 52(6):613-629.

[73]JS Eccles (1994). Women's educational and occupational choices. *Psychology of Women Quarterly* 18:585-609.

[74]JS Hyde, E Fennema, M Ryan, LA Frost, and C Hopp (1990). Gender comparisons of mathematics attitudes and affect: A meta-analysis. *Psychology of Women Quarterly* 14:299-324; JM Singer and JE Stake (1986). Mathematics and self-esteem: Implications for women's career choice. *Psychology of Women Quarterly* 10:339-352.

[75]ME Evans, H Schweingruber, and HW Stevenson (2002). Gender differences in interest and knowledge acquisition: The United States, Taiwan, and Japan. *Sex Roles: A Journal of*

In summary, the different social pressures on boys and girls appear to have more influence on their motivations and preferences than their underlying abilities. Some of that influence may stem from misconceptions of the nature of work in SEM, including the idea that it is suited to isolated, asocial people. Some of the influence may stem from mistaking the characteristics that are *typical* of current scientists, engineers, and mathematicians for characteristics that are necessary ingredients of success in SEM careers. Because most current scientists, engineers, and mathematicians are male, the typical characteristics of "success" more likely resemble those of male rather than of female students. This may deter some young women from viewing SEM careers as appropriate. To the extent that these forces account for the underlying sex difference in students' expressed interests in SEM, they may wane as the numbers of women in graduate school and in postdoctoral and faculty positions continue to rise.

> Minority students must be freed from lowered expectations that dampen drive and achievement as well as from exalted expectations of those few who earn advanced degrees. As is true for all populations, from a large pool the elite stars will emerge. The challenge to all of us, then, is to create an environment... in which the intellectual talents of all Americans can be developed and applied. There are no simple formulas or clever insights to do this—just hard, committed work and support.
>
> -Carlos Guiterrez, Professor of Chemistry, California State University, Los Angeles (2001)[76]

Social Effects on Women's Cognitive Performance

If men and women have equal average capacity for science, why do they perform differently on some speeded tests of mathematical and scientific reasoning? In addition to sex differences in the use of spatial and linguistic problem solving strategies discussed above, research in social psychology provides evidence that women's awareness of negative stereotypes of women in science can undermine their performance in high-stakes, speeded tests of scientific and mathematics aptitude. *Stereotype threat* re-

---

Research 47(3-4):153-167; C Morgan, JD Isaac, and C Sansone (2001). The role of interest in understanding the career choices of female and male college students. *Sex Roles: A Journal of Research* 44(5-6):295-320; Y Xie and KA Shauman (2003). *Women in Science: Career Processes and Outcomes.* Cambridge, MA: Harvard University Press.

[76]C Gutierrez (2001). Who will do chemistry? *Chemical and Engineering News* 79(21):5.

FOCUS ON RESEARCH

BOX 2-4 Stereotype Threat

In 1995, Claude Steele and Josh Aronson published an influential article in which they demonstrated a phenomenon they called *stereotype threat.*[a] Stereotype threat occurs when people feel that they might be judged in terms of a negative stereotype or that they might do something that might inadvertently confirm a stereotype of their group.

When any of us find ourselves in a difficult performance situation, especially one that has time pressure involved, we might recognize that if we do poorly, others could think badly about our own individual abilities. But if you are a woman or minority-group student trying to excel in science or engineering, there is the added worry that poor performance could be taken as confirmation that group stereotypes are valid.

Stereotype threat has been shown to apply to women performing a difficult mathematics test. Women tend to do more poorly than men, not on the average questions, but only on the high-level questions and only when their gender has been commented upon.[b] When stereotype threat is at work, fewer women will have high scores, and their scores will under-predict their achievement.

A series of studies by Toni Schmader and colleagues suggests that women's performance can be improved by acknowledging stereotype threat, as shown in Figure B2-4. In one condition, one group of men and women was given a set of word problems and told that it was a problem-solving exercise, with no mention of a test, mathematics, or ability. In this condition ("Problem Solving"), women's performance on the test was not different from that of their male peers, regardless of whether differences in SAT were controlled for. In a second condition, a different group of men and women was given the same set of word problems and told that their task would yield a diagnostic measure of mathematics ability that would be used to compare men's and women's scores; in this condition ("Math Test"), there was a gender gap similar to that seen in SAT-M scores.

In a third condition, a third group of men and women was told that the test they were taking—the same set of word problems as used in condition one and two—was a diagnostic measure of mathematics ability, and that their performance would be used to compare men's and women's scores. These are the same conditions that led to performance decrements in the second group. However, they were also informed about stereotype threat and reminded that if they were feeling anxious while taking the test, it might be a result of external stereotypes and not a

fers to the "experience of being in a situation where one faces judgment based on societal stereotypes about one's group" (Box 2-4).[77] For example, women perform worse than men on difficult but not easy math tests if gender stereotypes are made salient or if they are told that the tests have sex differences in performance. But, when women are told that there are no sex

---

[77]SJ Spencer, CM Steele, and DM Quinn (1999). Stereotype threat and women's math performance. *Journal of Experimental and Social Psychology* 35:4-28.

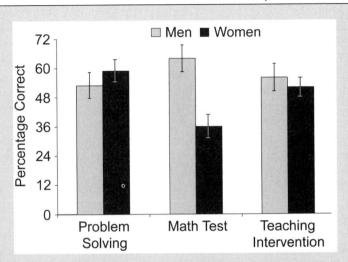

FIGURE B2-4 Teaching about stereotype threat inoculates against its effects.
ADAPTED FROM: M Johns, T Schmader, and A Martens (2005). Knowing is half the battle: Teaching stereotype threat as a means of improving women's math performance. *Psychological Science* 16:175-179.

reflection of their ability to do well. Under those conditions ("Teaching Intervention"), women's performance was significantly increased and not significantly different from that of their male peers.[c]

---

[a]CM Steele and J Aronson (1995). Stereotype threat and the intellectual test performance of African Americans. *Journal of Personality and Social Psychology* 69:797-811.

[b]SJ Spencer, CM Steele, and DQ Quinn (1999). Stereotype threat and women's math performance. *Journal of Experimental Social Psychology* 35:4-28.

[c]Similar targeted interventions have been proven to improve performance among minority-group middle-school students (GL Cohen, J Garcia, N Apfel, and A Master (2006). Reducing the racial acheivement gap: A social-psychological intervention. *Science* 313:1307-1310) and women college students (MS McGlone and J Aronson (2006). Stereotype threat, identity salience, and spatial reasoning. *Journal of Applied Developmental Psychology* (in press).

differences in test performance[78] or that tests are not diagnostic of ability[79] they perform just as well as men. That effect has been replicated in highly selected and less-highly selected samples of women.[80]

---

[78]Spencer, Steele, and Quinn (1999), ibid.

[79]PG Davies, SJ Spencer, DM Quinn, and R Gerhardstein (2002). Consuming images: How television commercials that elicit stereotype threat can restrain women academically and professionally. *Personality and Social Psychology Bulletin* 28(12):1615-1628.

[80]Spencer, Steele, and Quinn (1999), ibid.

Making sex salient can further degrade women's performance on speeded tests of mathematics. For example, women's mathematics performance decreases as the number of men present during testing increases.[81] Schmader shows that linking sex to math performance has a negative effect on performance only for women who have a high level of gender identity and only if test performance is linked to sex.[82] Additionally, women with stronger gender identities, including those who have selected mathematics-intensive majors, hold more negative attitudes toward mathematics and identify less with mathematics.[83] Notably, Asian women performed better on a mathematics test when their Asian identity was made salient but worse when their female identity was made salient.[84]

Quinn and Spencer find that stereotype threat exerts its effects on women's mathematics performance by diminishing their ability to formulate problem solving strategies.[85] As evidence, women underperformed compared to men on mathematics word problems but not when the problems were converted to their numerical equivalents. An analysis of the problem-solving strategies of women in high and low stereotype threat conditions revealed that women in the high-threat condition formulated fewer problem-solving strategies than women in the low-threat condition. Moreover, women in the high-threat condition were less likely than men to be able to strategize.

Davies and colleagues found that television commercials that evoked gender stereotypes caused women to underperform compared with men.[86] The effect was more pronounced in women for whom the commercials resulted in greater activation of the stereotype. It is important that exposure to gender stereotypic commercials also caused women to avoid answering mathematics questions in favor of verbal questions on a subsequent aptitude test. A control group of women exposed to gender-neutral commercials, like men, attempted to answer more mathematics than verbal questions.

---

[81]M Inzlicht and T Ben-Zeev (2000). A threatening intellectual environment: Why females are susceptible to experiencing problem-solving deficits in the presence of males. *Psychological Science* 11(5):365-371.

[82]T Schmader (2002). Gender identification moderates stereotype threat effects on women's math performance. *Journal of Experimental Social Psychology* 38:194-201.

[83]Nosek, BA, MR Banaji, and AG Greenwald (2002). Math = Male, Me = Female, Therefore Math ≠ Me. *Journal of Personality and Social Psychology* 83:44-59.

[84]M Shih, TL Pittinsky, and N Ambady (1999). Stereotype susceptibility: Identity salience and shifts in quantitative performance. *Psychological Science* 10(1):80-83.

[85]DM Quinn and SJ Spencer (2001). The interference of stereotype threat with women's generation of mathematical problem-solving strategies. *Journal of Social Issues* 57(1):55-71.

[86]Davies, Spencer, Quinn, and Gerhardstein (2002), ibid.

The negative effect of stereotype threat on women is not limited to mathematics performance. Women exposed to gender stereotypic commercials expressed less interest in academic and vocational domains in which they risked being negatively stereotyped, such as mathematics and engineering; they expressed more interest in neutral domains, such as creative writing and linguistics. Kray and colleagues showed that women's ability to negotiate was undermined by stereotype threat.[87] When participants were told that a test was diagnostic of negotiating ability, men expected to perform better and made more extreme opening offers than women. When traits that are stereotypical of men were experimentally linked to effective negotiators and traits that are stereotypical of women were linked to ineffective negotiators, men performed better than women in negotiations. Taken together, the findings show that activation of negative stereotypes can have a detrimental effect on women's interest and performance in domains relevant to success in academic science and engineering.

CONCLUSION

The present situation of women in scientific and engineering professions clearly results from the interplay of many individual, institutional, social, and cultural factors. Research shows that the measured cognitive and performance differences between men and women are small and in many cases nonexistent. There is no demonstrated connection between these small differences and performance or success in science and engineering professions. Furthermore, measurements of mathematics- and science-related skills are strongly affected by cultural factors, and the effects of these factors can be eliminated by appropriate mitigation strategies, such as those used to reduce the effects of stereotype threat.

Because sex differences in cognitive and neurological functions do not account for women's underrepresentation in academic science and engineering, efforts to maximize the potential of the best scientists and engineers should focus on understanding and mitigating cultural biases and institutional structures that affect the participation of women. These issues and successful strategies to enhance the recruitment and retention of women in science and engineering are discussed in the following chapters.

---

[87]LJ Kray, L Thompson, and A Galinsky (2001). Battle of the sexes: Gender stereotype confirmation and reactance in negotiations. *Journal of Personality and Social Psychology* 80(6):942-958.

3

Examining Persistence and Attrition

CHAPTER HIGHLIGHTS

Women who start out on the path toward a career in academic science and engineering leave it for other fields at higher rates than their male counterparts. While there are field differences in pattern of attrition, more women than men leave at nearly every stage of the career trajectory. Fewer high school senior girls than boys state a desire to major in science or engineering in college. Girls who state such an intention are likelier than comparable boys to change their plans before arriving at college. Once in college, women and men show a similar persistence to degree, but women science and engineering majors are less likely than men to enter graduate school.

Women who enter graduate school in science and engineering are as likely as men to earn doctorates, but give a poorer rating to faculty-student interactions and publish fewer research papers than men. Many women graduate students report feelings of isolation. More women than men report plans to seek postdoctoral positions. Among postdoctoral scholars, women report lower satisfaction with the experience, and women are proportionately underrepresented in the applicant pools for tenure-track faculty positions.

It appears that women and men faculty in most fields who are reviewed receive tenure at similar rates. There is substantial faculty mobility prior to the tenure case, when some tenure-track ladder faculty move between institutions and others leave academe. Mo-

bility patterns differ between women and men; men who move prior to tenure tend to leave academe, while women tend to enter adjunct positions. For women faculty members, feelings of isolation, lack of respect of colleagues, and difficulty in integrating family and professional responsibilities are major factors in attrition from university careers. For universities, faculty attrition presents a serious loss both economically and in morale.

FINDINGS

3-1. There is substantial attrition of both men and women along the science and engineering educational pathway to first academic position. The major differences between the patterns of attrition are at the transition points: fewer high school girls intend to major in science and engineering fields, more alter their intentions to major in science and engineering between high school and college, fewer women science and engineering graduates continue on to graduate school, and fewer women science and engineering PhDs are recruited into the applicant pools for tenure-track faculty positions.

3-2. Productivity does not differ between men and women science and engineering faculty, but it does between men and women graduate students and postdoctoral scholars. Differences in numbers of papers published, meetings attended, and grants written reflect the quality of faculty-student interactions.

3-3. There is substantial faculty mobility between initial appointment and tenure case. Faculty at Research I universities are half as likely as the overall population of faculty to move to other types of academic institutions. Men and women hired into tenure-track positions had a similar likelihood of changing jobs, but men were twice as likely to move from academia to other employment sectors (15.3% of men and 8.5% of women) and women were 40% more likely to move to an adjunct position (9.2% of men and 12.7% of women).

3-4. Overall, men and women science and engineering faculty who come up for tenure appear to receive it at similar rates. Differences in the rate at which men and women receive tenure vary substantially by field and by race or ethnicity. For example, in social sciences women are about 10% less likely than men to be awarded tenure. African American women science and engineering faculty were 10% less likely than men of all ethnicities to be awarded tenure.

3-5. As faculty move up in rank, differences between men and women become apparent in promotions, awards, and salary.

3-6. No organization addresses the concerns of minority-group women; scientific and professional society committees address either women or minorities; most data are collected and analyzed by sex *or* by race or ethnicity.

3-7 Policy analyses of the education, training, and employment of scientists and engineers are hampered by data collection inadequacies, including lack of data, inability to compare data among surveys, difficulty in constructing longitudinal cohorts, difficulty in examining sex *and* race or ethnicity, and lags in the reporting of data.

RECOMMENDATIONS

3-1. Efforts to increase the number of women in science and engineering should be focused on both recruiting and retention. Professional societies should work to recruit high school students to science and engineering careers. Colleges and universities should work to recruit women and minority students to science and engineering majors, to graduate school, and to faculty positions. University leaders and faculties need to work together to identify and remedy issues that address faculty retention.

3-2. Recruiting for faculty positions needs to be an active process that consciously develops and reaches out to women and minority-group scientists. Deans and department chairs and their tenured faculty should expand their faculty recruitment efforts to ensure that they reach adequately and proactively into the existing and ever-increasing pool of women candidates.

3-3. We need to understand more about faculty turnover. Universities should collect department data and scientific and professional societies should track discipline-wide turnover; the data should be collected annually and shared so that turnover dynamics can be understood and appropriate policies can be developed to retain faculty.

3-4. Changes should be made in the type of data that are collected on minority-group women and efforts should be made to ensure that the data are comparable across surveys and studies. Specifically, the National Science Foundation (NSF) *Survey of Doctorate Recipients* needs to be made more robust to allow for analysis of the small numbers of women of color. Other national surveys must collect data in a way that permits multiple demographic comparisons. Federal agencies and professional societies must report data so that the particular experiences of minority-group women can be understood and tracked and appropriate policies can be developed.

3-5. Universities should collect data annually on education and employment of scientists and engineers by sex and race or ethnicity using a standard scorecard format (Box 6-8). Data should include the number of students majoring in science and engineering disciplines; the number of students graduating with a bachelor's or master's degree in science and engineering fields; postgraduation plans; graduate school enrollment, attrition, and completion; postdoctoral plans; number of postdoctoral scholars; and data on faculty recruitment, hiring, turnover, tenure, promotion, salary, and allocation of institutional resources. The data should be made publicly available.

3-6. Scientific and professional societies should collect and disseminate field-wide education and workforce data with a similar scorecard.

Women who start on the path toward a career in academic science leave that path in favor of other fields at a higher rate than their male colleagues. In this chapter, we will analyze sex differences in science and engineering education and career trajectories and rates of departure from the academic science track in favor of careers in other sectors. The decision to pursue a particular career path is a choice, but certainly not an arbitrary one. Forces other than individual preference or scholastic aptitude and preparation affect choices about career paths and appear to be driving women into careers outside of academic research.

Not everyone who pursues a scientific education wants to be an academic scientist; 59% of science and mathematics, 55% of social science, and 28% of engineering graduate students say that they are preparing to become college or university faculty members or to seek postdoctoral research or academic appointments.[1] In the United States, fewer than half of all people with PhDs in science and engineering are employed in the academic sector (Figure 3-1).

As discussed in Chapter 2, social expectations and stereotypes regarding what it means to be a scientist or engineer influence career choices. Men benefit from a series of accumulated advantages: the implicit assumption that men can be academic scientists and engineers, the encouragement they

---

[1]MT Nettles and CM Millett (2006). *Three Magic Letters: Getting to PhD*. Baltimore, MD: Johns Hopkins University Press. This study followed a sample of 9,036 graduate students from 21 of the major US doctorate-producing institutions from 1996 to 2001.

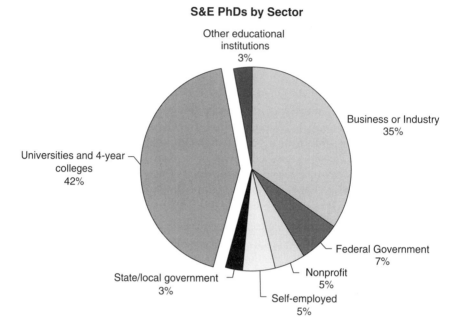

FIGURE 3-1 Occupations of science and engineering PhDs by sector, 2002.

SOURCE: National Science Foundation (2004). *Women, Minorities, and Persons with Disabilities in Science and Engineering, 2004.* Arlington, VA: National Science Foundation.

receive to pursue academic careers, and role models provided by men who have successful academic careers. Women often suffer from a series of accumulated disadvantages, so when they make career choices, they choose from a set of options different from that of their male counterparts.[2] Research shows that the more ways in which a person differs from the norm, the more social interactions affect choices; thus, the interlocking effects of

---

[2]V Valian (1998). *Why So Slow? The Advancement of Women.* Cambridge, MA: MIT Press; MA Mason and M Goulden (2004). Marriage and baby blues: Redefining gender equity in the academy. *Annals of the American Academy of Political and Social Science* 596 (1):86-103; D Ginther (2006). The economics of gender differences in employment outcomes in academia. In *Biological, Social, and Organizational Components of Success for Women in Academic Science and Engineering.* Washington, DC: The National Academies Press.

sex and race can further restrict career options.[3] An analysis by the Education Trust[4] found that 93 of every 100 white kindergartners would graduate from high school, 65 would complete some college, and 33 would obtain a bachelor's degree. The corresponding numbers for black kindergartners were 87, 50, and 18, respectively. Of 100 Hispanic and Native American kindergartners, only 11 and 7, respectively, would earn a bachelor's degree.

> There is no linear path to a degree. The default 'pipeline' metaphor . . . is wholly inadequate to describe student behavior [which] moves in starts and stops, sideways, down one path to another and perhaps circling back. Liquids move in pipes; people don't.
>
> —Cliff Adelman, in The Toolbox Revisited: Paths to Degree Completion From High School Through College (2006)[5]

The question is where are differences in decision making manifested between men and women? The cohort of high school graduates who are now of an age to be assistant professors (assuming a direct educational path and no stop-outs) would have been seniors in the mid-1980s (Box 3-1 for a description of lagged cohort analysis). For this cohort, specific differences exist between the rates at which men and women chose and persevered in science and engineering education and careers.[6] In 1982, high school senior girls were half as likely as boys to plan a science or engineering major in college. This difference was compounded by girls' rate—2.4 times higher than that of boys—of attrition from the science and engineering educational trajectory during the transition from high school to college. During college, women and men showed similar perseverance to degrees in science and engineering fields. The other substantial difference in education and career attrition or perseverance between men and women in the cohort occurred during the transition from graduate school to tenure-track positions (Figure 1-2).

---

[3]CSV Turner (2002). Women of color in academe: Living with multiple marginality. *Journal of Higher* Education 73(1):74-93.

[4]Education Trust, Inc. (2002). *The Condition of Education, 2002*. Data were from surveys conducted by the US Department of Education and the US Department of Commerce Bureau of the Census, March Current Population Surveys, 1971-2001.

[5]Available from the US Department of Education at *http://www.ed.gov/rschstat/research/pubs/toolboxrevisit/toolbox.pdf*.

[6]Y Xie and KA Shauman (2003). *Women in Science: Career Processes and Outcomes*. Cambridge, MA: Harvard University Press.

CONTROVERSIES

BOX 3-1 Models of Faculty Representation

Most analyses of career trajectories of women scientists and engineers use a pipeline analogy, positing that women are underrepresented at senior levels of academe because they are disproportionately "lost" along the journey from interested high school student to tenured faculty. However, analyses must take into account the number of years it takes for a person to progress from a newly attained PhD to a tenured faculty position. There is a lag between earning a degree and advancing to the next level and "without considering lag time, we are left with erroneous conclusions about what the distribution of women faculty *should* be without enough information about what the available pool of women is."[a]

Senior-level academics attained their PhDs a number of years before reaching the level of full professor. One study reports that in 2002 the middle 50% of full professors in physics earned their doctorates in 1967-1980.[b] Therefore, in considering the representation of women in this faculty rank, it is most appropriate to consider that representation in terms of the cohort of PhDs granted in 1967-1980. Similarly for associate professors the appropriate cohort (again using the example of physics) is 1984-1991 and for assistant professors (the "entry level" of the professoriate) it is 1991-1997. That is what is meant by considering "lag time." Although the specific length of the lag time may vary from field to field (based on such factors as number of postdoctoral fellowships required before receiving a faculty appointment), the general principle applies in fields other than physics.

When lag time is considered, one notices that when the current cohort of senior faculty received their doctorates there were fewer women in the pool than there are now. In some fields, that almost completely explains the low numbers of women in senior faculty positions. For instance in physics, in 2005 5% of full professors were women; in 1967-1980 (when the current cohort of full physics professors would have attained their PhDs) an average of 4% of PhDs were awarded to women. At the associate professor level, 11% were women in 2005; and in 1984-1991 (the appropriate year range for this cadre) 9% of PhDs went to women. At the assistant professor level, 16% were women in 2005; and in 1991-1997 (the appropriate year range for this cadre) 12% of PhDs went to women.[c] Similar findings are not confined to the discipline of physics. Using a similar type of analysis a National Research Council panel reported, in a general non-discipline-specific finding, that "much, but not all, of the difference in men and women in their success in becoming faculty is due to differences in the stage of their career."[d] The panel predicted, in the coming decades, increases in the percentages of female faculty.

However, other work presents an alternative view. Nelson, in a study of faculty representation at "top 50" science and engineering schools, reports that "in most science disciplines studied, the percentage of women among recent PhD recipi-

---

[a]R Ivie and KN Ray (2005). *Women in Physics and Astronomy, 2005.* College Park, MD: American Institute of Physics, *http://www.aip.org/statistics/trends/reports/women05.pdf.*
[b]Ivie and Ray (2005), ibid.
[c]Ivie and Ray (2005), ibid.
[d]National Research Council (2001). *From Scarcity to Visibility: Gender Differences in the Careers of Doctoral Scientists and Engineers.* Washington, DC: National Academy Press.

ents is much higher than their percentage among assistant professors, the typical rank of recently hired faculty."[e] Nelson finds further, that even in fields where women earn more PhDs than men (such as biology), "white males maintain their hold on the vast majority of assistant professor positions."[f] Similar findings were reported by Myers and Turner, who found the disparity between the number of female PhD recipients and the number of female assistant professors to be especially acute for underrepresented minority groups.[g] Such findings indicate that qualified female candidates exist, but in many fields they are not being recruited into the tenure-track applicant pool in proportion to their presence in the PhD pool and suggest that the lag model is insufficient to account for the current underrepresentation of female faculty.

The usefulness of the lag model discussed above depends on the validity of the pipeline model itself, a validity that has been questioned by some. The traditional pipeline model assumes a one-way flow in career progression, suggesting that once a person leaves science it is not possible to return. Work by Xie and Shauman challenges this paradigm, arguing that "exit, entry and reentry are real possibilities. Many persons, especially women, become scientists through complicated processes rather than by just staying in the pipeline."[h] Others, including the Building Engineering and Science Talent (BEST) Initiative (Box 1-2) and the Human Frontier Science Program, have developed new paradigms for education, training, and career paths in the natural sciences.[i] Women may be more likely to pursue career paths that are not accounted for in traditional models of representation. Efforts should be made to be cognizant and supportive of those different career paths, and, in considering faculty representation, it is important to consider pathways beyond the pipeline paradigm. Xie and Shauman argue that the underrepresentation of women in science and engineering is "a complex social phenomenon that defies any attempt at simplistic explanation." They note the "complex and multifaceted nature of women scientists' career processes and outcomes" and suggest that increasing "women's representation in science/engineering requires many social, cultural and economic changes that are large-scale and independent." Clearly the pipeline model is important but, by itself, it is not sufficient to address underrepresentation.

A National Research Council panel[j] found that, "while the most important

---

[e]DJ Nelson (2005). *A National Analysis of Diversity in Science and Engineering Faculties at Research Universities.* Available at: *http://cheminfo.chem.ou.edu/%7Edjn/diversity/briefings/Diversity%20Report%20Final.pdf.*

[f]Nelson (2005), ibid.

[g]SL Myers and CS Turner (2004). The effects of PhD supply on minority faculty representation. *American Economic Review* 94(2):296-301.

[h]Xie and Shauman (2003). *Women in Science: Career Processes and Outcomes.* Cambridge: Harvard University Press.

[i]The BEST Initiative (2004). *The Talent Imperative: Diversifying America's Science and Engineering Workforce.* Available at *http://www.bestworkforce.org/PDFdocs/BEST TalentImperativeFINAL.pdf;* European Science Foundation (2002). Towards a new paradigm for education, training, and career paths in the natural sciences. *European Science Foundation Policy Briefing* 16, *http://www.esf.org/publication/139/ESPB16.pdf#search=%22Torsten%20Wiesel%20training%20paradigm%22.*

[j]National Research Council (2001), ibid.

continued

BOX 3-1 Continued

factor affecting gender differences in faculty status is the age of a scientist or engineer, there are important differences related to field, type of institution, and other variables." A study by Kuck and colleagues highlights one of the other factors: the significance of the institution from which a person received their PhD as a factor in women's likelihood of attaining a tenure-track position in chemistry. Kuck and colleagues examined hiring patterns in the 50 top-rated chemistry departments. They found that among the 50 departments, 10 schools supplied 60% of the younger faculty members, while only 32% of the faculty came from the other 40 schools.[k] The 10 top faculty-supplying schools were, with a few exceptions, also the top-rated graduate schools. In other words, "a small group of schools contributed a disproportionate number of younger faculty." Postdoctoral placements also play a role in attaining tenure-track positions. Kuck and colleagues report that hiring of chemistry faculty by the top 50 universities is tracking the growth of women in postdoctoral appointments. Those who hold appointments at the top five suppliers of faculty are more likely to be preferentially hired by a top-50 department.

Such findings demonstrate the influence of the PhD or postdoctoral institution on future career prospects and suggest that, when looking at faculty representation, it may be important to look at the pool of doctorates and postdoctorates from only a select subset of research universities.

---

[k]VJ Kuck et al. (2004). Analysis by gender of the doctoral and postdoctoral institutions of faculty members at the top-fifty ranked chemistry departments. *Journal of Chemical Education* 81(3):356-363.

That type of analysis is useful for broad-brush policy development, but very specific differences by field must be acknowledged. Over the past decade, there have been significant changes, including increases in the numbers and proportion of girls taking high-level science and mathematics classes in high school and increases in graduate school enrollments and degrees. Research on underrepresentation in science and engineering focuses on the two categories of sex and race or ethnicity in large part because the data are collected by sex or race or ethnicity. As a consequence, minority-group women tend to disappear in analyses.[7] Where possible, in the analysis of persistence and attrition in science and engineering education

---

[7]See, for example, CB Leggon (2006). Women in science: Racial and ethnic differences and the differences they make. *Journal of Technology Transfer* 31:325-333.

and academic careers, this report includes data on minority-group women broken out by race and ethnicity.[8]

COURSE SELECTION IN HIGH SCHOOL

Rigorous study in high school is the best predictor of persistence to a degree in college.[9] Advanced mathematics study appears to be an additional important factor in preparing students for college and can substantially narrow differences between racial and ethnic groups.[10] The gender gap in science and mathematics courses taken in high school has narrowed over the last decade (Table 3-1). Since 1994, girls have been as likely as boys to complete advanced mathematics courses, including Advanced Placement or International Baccalaureate calculus.[11] Also since 1994, girls have been more likely than boys to take advanced biology and chemistry. Physics is the only advanced science subject in which boys continue to complete courses at higher rates than girls, although the difference is small. African Americans and Hispanics were less likely than whites to complete advanced mathematics and science courses in high school.

In an analysis of the National Educational Longitudinal Survey, Hanson found variability in attitudes toward science among women.[12] For ex-

---

[8]The committee acknowledges that there are different experiences within racial and ethnic groups. These are addressed in more detail in the National Science Foundation's *Women, Minorities, and Persons with Disabilities in S&E* reports, *http://www.nsf.gov/statistics/wmpd/*; BEST reports, *http://www.bestworkforce.org*; NAS/NAE/IOM (2006). *Biological, Social, and Organizational Components of Success for Women in Academic Science and Engineering*. Washington, DC: The National Academies Press; G Campbell, R Denes, and C Morrison (1999). *Access Denied: Race, Ethnicity and the Scientific Enterprise*, New York: Oxford University Press; National Research Council (1992). *Science and Engineering Programs: On Target for Women?* Washington, DC: National Academy Press; National Research Council (1991). *Women in Science and Engineering: Increasing Their Numbers in the 1990s: A Statement on Policy and Strategy*. Washington, DC: National Academy Press; National Research Council (1989). *Everybody Counts: A Report to the Nation on the Future of Mathematics Education*. Washington, DC: National Academy Press.

[9]LJ Horn and L Kojaku (2001). *High School Academic Curriculum and the Persistence Path Through College: Persistence and Transfer Behavior of Undergraduates 3 Years after Entering 4-Year Institutions* (NCES 2001-163). Washington, DC: US Department of Education.

[10]C Adelman (1999). *Answers in the Toolbox: Academic Intensity, Attendance Patterns, and Bachelor's Degree Attainment* (PLLI 1999-8021). Washington, DC: US Department of Education; G Orfield (2005). *Dropouts in America: Confronting the Graduation Rate Crisis.* Cambridge, MA: Harvard Education Press.

[11]National Science Board (2006). *Science and Engineering Indicators, 2006*. Arlington, VA: National Science Foundation, Appendix Table 1-17.

[12]SL Hanson (2004). African American women in science: Experiences from high school through the post-secondary years and beyond. *NWSA Journal* 16(1):96.

TABLE 3-1 Percentage of High School Graduates Completing Advanced Coursework in Mathematics and Science, by Sex and Year of Graduation

Subject	1990		1994		1998		2000	
	Men	Women	Men	Women	Men	Women	Men	Women
Mathematics								
• Trigonometry/Algebra III	20.6	20.9	23.0	24.9	19.4	22.5	17.9	21.1
• Precalculus/Analysis	14.4	13.0	16.3	18.4	23.1	22.9	25.4	27.9
• Statistics and probability	1.2	0.8	2.0	2.1	3.4	4.0	5.8	5.6
• Calculus	8.3	6.2	10.3	10.1	12.0	11.6	13.3	12.0
Science								
• Advanced biology	25.7	29.2	31.5	37.8	33.8	40.8	31.5	40.5
• Chemistry	43.8	46.1	47.5	53.3	53.3	59.2	58.1	66.8
• Physics	24.9	18.3	26.7	22.5	31.0	26.6	35.6	31.5

SOURCES: US Department of Education, National Center for Education Statistics, National Assessment of Educational Progress, 1990, 1994, 1998, and 2000 High School Transcript Studies. Based on Table 1-8 in National Science Board (2006). *Science and Engineering Indicators, 2006.* Arlington, VA: National Science Foundation.

ample, African American girls expressed a greater interest in science than did white girls in both the 8th and 10th grades.

COLLEGE-GOING AND MAJORS

In the mid-1980s, about half of high school graduates enrolled in college immediately on graduation. In 2003, 65% of high school graduates enrolled in college on graduation, with 43% at 4-year colleges and 22% at 2-year colleges. The proportion entering college was higher among white students than among African American or Hispanic students. In addition, the rate of increase was higher among women than men at both 4- and 2-year colleges.[13]

A larger proportion of women than men high school seniors indicate an expectation to attend and complete college, but men are about 60% more likely to indicate an expectation to major in a science and engineering field.[14] For at least 20 years, about one-third of all first-year college students have planned to study science and engineering.[15] The proportion is similar among most racial and ethnic groups and, similar to high school intentions, is higher among men than women in many fields (Table 3-2). It should be noted that the percentages of Asian, African American, and Hispanic first-year college students who intend to pursue a science or engineering major are higher than that of their white counterparts.

Undergraduate Persistence to Degree

Women undergraduates have outnumbered men since 1982, and in 2002 they earned 58% of all bachelor's degrees. The share and number of science and engineering bachelor's degrees awarded to women and minority-group members has increased over the last 20 years, and women have earned at least half of all bachelor's degrees in science and engineering since 2000.[16] Much of the increase among minorities was fueled by an increase in science and engineering degrees awarded to women. A recent study[17]

---

[13]National Science Board (2006). *Science and Engineering Indicators, 2006.* Arlington, VA: National Science Foundation, Figures 1-28 and 1-29.

[14]Y Xie and KA Shauman (2003). *Women in Science: Career Processes and Outcomes.* Cambridge, MA: Harvard University Press, Chapter 2.

[15]HS Astin (2005). *Annual Survey of the American Freshman, National Norms.* Los Angeles, CA: Higher Education Research Institute.

[16]National Science Board (2006), ibid.

[17]C Goldin, LF Katz, and I Kuziemko (2006). *The Homecoming of American College Women: The Reversal of the College Gender Gap* (NBER Working Paper No. 12139). Cambridge, MA: National Bureau of Economic Research.

TABLE 3-2 Percentages of First-Year College Students Intending to Major in Science and Engineering, by Sex and Race or Ethnicity, 2004

	Overall		African American	
	Men	Women	Men	Women
Physical sciences	2.9	1.9	1.7	1.9
Life sciences	7.4	9.0	7.5	10.9
Mathematics	1.0	0.6	0.6	0.4
Computer sciences	4.1	0.4	6.2	1.5
Social and behavioral sciences	7.5	11.5	7.1	14.3
Engineering	17.9	2.9	15.1	2.9
Total	40.8	26.3	38.2	31.9

NOTES: *Physical sciences* include earth, atmospheric, and ocean sciences; *life sciences* include agricultural sciences and biological sciences; and *social and behavioral sciences* includes psychology. The *Hispanic American* category includes Latinos; *Native American* includes Alaskan Natives and American Indians; and *Asian American* includes Pacific Islanders. Students with unknown race or ethnicity and those who are temporary residents are not included.

suggests that those trends result from much longer term shifts in which women saw higher education as a way to gain entrance into the skilled labor market.

There are substantial variations in the demographics of degree recipients by field, sex, and race or ethnicity (Table 3-3). A larger proportion of Asian Americans earn science and engineering bachelor's degrees than that of any other racial or ethnic group. African American women earn more science bachelor's degrees than African American men. In all racial or ethnic categories, men earn more engineering bachelor's degrees than women. It is also interesting to note that, although one-third of all first-year college students plan to study science and engineering, only half that proportion graduate with degrees in science and engineering. The most important factor for completing a bachelor's degree for both men and women appears to be rigorous preparation in high school.[18]

---

[18]C Adelman (2006). *The Toolbox Revisited: Paths to Degree Completion from High School through College.* Washington, DC: US Department of Education, *http://www.ed.gov/rschstat/research/pubs/toolboxrevisit/toolbox.pdf.*

Hispanic		Native American		Asian American		White	
Men	Women	Men	Women	Men	Women	Men	Women
2.1	1.3	3.2	2.1	2.6	2.0	3.0	1.9
7.9	10.4	8.2	9.0	14.1	18.0	6.4	7.7
0.8	0.7	0.7	0.5	1.0	0.8	1.0	0.7
4.5	0.6	4.7	0.5	4.1	0.6	3.9	0.3
8.7	15.6	8.7	14.4	6.7	10.6	7.4	10.6
21.0	3.1	15.2	2.9	25.8	5.6	17.0	2.7
45.0	31.7	40.7	29.4	54.3	25.8	38.7	23.9

SOURCE: National Science Board (2006). *Science and Engineering Indicators, 2006.* Arlington, VA: National Science Foundation, Appendix Table 2-6. Data compiled from HS Astin (2005). *Survey of the American Freshman: National Norms.* Higher Education Research Institute, University of California at Los Angeles.

Social Factors Influencing Undergraduate Attrition

Many students who enter college intending to obtain a science and engineering bachelor's degree abandon their goal along the way. As shown above and in numerous other studies, it is not poor high school preparation, ability, or effort, but rather the educational climate of science and engineering departments that correlates with the high proportion of undergraduates who opt out of science and engineering.[19] Although the gap between intention and attainment is large for all students, research shows that a lower proportion of women realize their high school intentions.[20] In

---

[19]E Seymour and NM Hewitt (1997). *Talking about Leaving.* Boulder, CO: Westview Press; S Laurich-McIntyre and SG Brainard (1995). Retaining Women Freshmen in Engineering and Science: A Success Story. *Women in Engineering Conference Proceedings: Is Systemic Change Happening?* Washington, DC, pp. 227-232; A Ginorio (1995). *Warming the Climate for Women in Academic Science.* Washington, DC: Association of American Colleges and Universities.

[20]SE Berryman (1983). *Who Will Do Science? Minority and Female Attainment of Science and Mathematics Degrees: Trends and Causes.* New York: Rockefeller Foundation; TL Hilton and VE Lee (1988). Student interest and persistence in science. *Journal of Higher Education*

TABLE 3-3 Number of Bachelor's Degrees in Science and Engineering, by Sex and Race or Ethnicity, 2001

	Overall		African American	
	Men	Women	Men	Women
Physical sciences	10,598	7,533	530	604
Life sciences	33,981	45,575	2,053	3,628
Mathematics	5,958	5,497	330	451
Computer sciences	31,284	11,900	1,628	1,989
Social and behavioral sciences	68,458	120,164	5,146	13,629
Engineering	47,344	11,914	3,054	1,026
Total	197,623 (15.7)	202,583 (16.1)	12,741 (11.9)	21,327 (20.0)

NOTES: The numbers in parentheses indicate the percent of total bachelor's degrees awarded represented by science and engineering degrees for that racial or ethnic category. For example, 15.7 of all bachelor's degrees awarded are in science and engineering fields; for African American women 20% of all bachelor's degrees awarded are in science and engineering fields. *Physical sciences* include earth, atmospheric, and ocean sciences; *life sciences* includes agricultural sciences and biological sciences; and *social and behavioral sciences* includes psychology. *Native American* includes Alaskan Natives and American Indians; and *Asian Ameri-*

addition, more men college students make the transition into science and engineering fields from other fields.[21]

Data indicate that these climate issues affect decision making early on; once students enroll in college, the probability of completing a science and engineering major is similar for men and women. Xie and Shauman report that, for students who declare a major in science and engineering, 60% of

59(5):510-526; J Oakes (1990). Opportunities, achievement, and choice: Women and minority students in science and mathematics. *Review of Research in Education* 16:153-222; Y Xie (1996). A demographic approach to studying the process of becoming a scientist/engineer. In: *Careers in Science and Technology: An International Perspective.* Washington, DC: National Academy Press; E Seymour and NM Hewitt (1997). *Talking about Leaving.* Boulder, CO: Westview Press.
[21]Xie and Shauman (2003), ibid.

Hispanic		Native American		Asian American		White	
Men	Women	Men	Women	Men	Women	Men	Women
448	497	59	59	730	700	8,046	5,202
1,493	3,101	312	334	3,356	4,536	24,868	31,407
357	295	28	23	482	434	4,245	3,928
2,302	726	193	78	4,280	2,046	19,043	5,448
5,505	9,999	534	930	4,786	8,023	47,272	79,622
1,858	962	192	64	5,341	1,684	31,710	7,057
11,963 (13.3)	15,580 (17.3)	1,318 (15.2)	1,478 (17.1)	18,975 (25.1)	17,423 (23.0)	135,184 (15.2)	132,664 (14.9)

can includes Pacific Islanders. Students with unknown race or ethnicity and those who are temporary residents are not included.

SOURCE: National Science Foundation, Division of Science Resource Statistics, special tabulations of US Department of Education, National Center for Education Statistics, Integrated Postsecondary Education Data System, Completions Survey. Arlington, VA: National Science Foundation. Data available at *http://www.nsf.gov/statistics/wmpd/tables/tabc-15.xls*.

women and 57% of men complete the major.[22] Students' expectations of their social roles strongly influence their educational and career goals. Applying Eagly and Karau's *role congruity theory* to women in science suggests an incongruity between stereotypical female characteristics and the attributes that are thought to be required for success in academic science and engineering.[23]

Women and men appear to enter science and engineering majors for different reasons. Seymour and Hewitt suggest that women were almost twice as likely as men to have chosen a science and engineering major through the active influence of someone important to them, such as a

[22]Xie and Shauman (2003), ibid.
[23]Eagly and Karau (2002), ibid.

relative, teacher, or close friend. In contrast, men were twice as likely as women to cite being good at mathematics or science in high school as a reason for declaring the major (whether or not they were actually better prepared than women).[24] That suggests that more young men than women had the confidence to take higher-level mathematics and science courses in college.

Women and men also appear to leave science and engineering majors for different reasons (Table 3-4). Similar proportions of men and women cited losing interest in science, engineering, and mathematics (SEM) majors, poor teaching, and shifting to more appealing career options. More women felt that they could get a better education in a non-SEM major, rejected SEM careers and lifestyles, and felt that advising was inadequate. Men more frequently cited course overload, loss of confidence, financial problems, and issues with competition. A study on the retention of science and engineering undergraduates at the University of Washington also indicates that advising and a supportive community are important factors in the retention of women in SEM majors.[25]

The University of Washington study looked only at women who entered college with an interest in pursuing a science or engineering major. The sequencing of science and engineering courses is often strict, so it can be difficult to enter a science or engineering major from a nonscience or nonengineering field. Even so, men are twice as likely as women to move from a nonscience field into a science field during their first 2 years.[26] Universities can institute programs to increase enrollment and reduce attrition (Box 3-2).

COLLEGE TO GRADUATE SCHOOL

A larger percentage of men than women who major in science and engineering enroll in graduate school in science and engineering fields (about 15% of men and 10% of women). An additional 8% of men and 12% of women enter graduate school in a nonscience or nonengineering field, and nearly 75% of those who earn science and engineering bachelor's degrees enter the workforce directly.[27]

---

[24]Seymour and Hewitt (1997), ibid.

[25]SG Brainard and L Carlin (1997). *A Longitudinal Study of Undergraduate Women in Engineering and Science, http://fie.engrng.pitt.edu/fie97/papers/1252.pdf.*

[26]Xie and Shauman (2003). *Women in Science: Career Processes and Outcomes.* Cambridge, MA: Harvard University Press.

[27]Xie and Shauman (2003), ibid.

TABLE 3-4 Top Reasons for Leaving Science, Engineering, or Mathematics Undergraduate Degree Program, by Sex

Reason for Switching to Non-SEM Major	Women		Men	
	%	Rank	%	Rank
Non-SEM major offers better education	**46**	1	35	5
Lack/loss of interest in SEM	43	2	42	1
Rejection of SEM careers and associated lifestyles	**38**	3	20	11
Poor teaching by SEM faculty	33	4	39	3
Inadequate advising or help with academic problems	**29**	5	20	10
Curriculum overload	29	6	**42**	2
SEM career options not worth the effort	27	7	**36**	4
Shift to more appealing non-SEM career option	27	8	27	6
Loss of confidence due to low grades	19	9	**27**	7
Financial problems	11	14	**24**	9
Morale undermined by competition	4	19	**26**	8

NOTE: Percentages in bold face indicate where differences between men and women were significant.

SOURCE: E Seymour and NM Hewitt (1997). *Talking about Leaving.* Boulder, CO: Westview Press.

The proportion of women varies by field and personal factors:[28]

•   Women bachelor's degree recipients in the physical sciences are more likely than men to attend graduate school in a non-science and engineering field (19% compared to 5%).
•   Women with an undergraduate degree in engineering are more likely than men to attend graduate school in engineering (20% compared to 15%). In contrast with science fields, a bachelor's degree in engineering is

---

[28]Xie and Shauman (2003), ibid.

EXPERIMENTS AND STRATEGIES

**BOX 3-2 Carnegie Mellon's Women
in Computer Science Program**

Carnegie Mellon University brought female enrollment in its undergraduate computer science program up from 7% to 40% from 1995 to 2000 and significantly reduced attrition.[a]
Here's what it did:

• **Created the Summer Institute for Advanced Placement Computer Science (CS) Teachers**. With a grant from the NSF, Carnegie Mellon trained 240 Advanced Placement (AP) CS teachers to teach C++ (a major component of the AP exam) and informed the teachers about the gender gap in CS and what they could do about it. *By 2000, 18% of female CS majors had a high school CS teacher who had attended the summer institute (up from 0% in 1995).*
• **Changed admissions criteria**. In addition to demonstrated academic competence, more weight is given to nonacademic factors such as leadership potential and commitment to give back to the community for both admission and financial aid. The admissions office also emphasizes "no prior programming experience necessary."
• **Built a supportive community**. The Women@SCS Advisory Council was created and holds weekly meetings to foster community, address the needs of women in CS, and organize outreach to women and girls with an interest in CS.

------

[a]It should be noted that the proportion of women enrolled in the computer science program at Carnegie Mellon University (CMU) decreased to between 25-30% since 2000, despite continued efforts by CMU. This is still higher than 15%, the average proportion of women in computer science programs at Research I universities.

---

often considered a terminal degree; many engineering graduates find satisfying and well-paying jobs in the private sector. To gain entry to these jobs, employers may require more credentials from women than men.[29]

•   Married women and women with children are far less likely than married men and men with children to attend graduate school.

Graduate School

The number of science and engineering doctoral degrees awarded in the United States has remained fairly constant over the last two decades, fluctu-

------

[29]C Goldin (2002). A *Pollution Theory of Discrimination: Male and Female Differences in Occupations and Earnings* (Working Paper 8985). Cambridge, MA: National Bureau of Economics Research.

ating between 12,000 to 14,000 degrees awarded each year. The major change has been in the percentage of PhD recipients who have been temporary residents, which has risen from 23% in 1966 to 39% in 2003.[30] Among US citizens and permanent residents, the number of white men earning science and engineering PhDs has decreased from a peak of 11,000 in 1975 to about 7,000 in 2003. The number and proportion of science and engineering PhDs awarded to white women and to members of underrepresented minorities have increased over the past two decades; from 1983 to 2003, the number of science and engineering PhDs earned by African Americans, Hispanics, and Native Americans had more than doubled to 1,500, or 5% of all PhDs awarded (Table 3-5).

There are a few key differences in perseverance to degree by sex. In a recent longitudinal study of PhD completion, Nettles and Millett[31] followed a cohort of graduate students to determine the significant factors affecting time to degree and degree completion. They found women and men to have similar completion rates and time to degree. All students ostensibly had access to a faculty adviser, but only a subset of students (69%) indicated they had a mentor.[32]

Research productivity is of concern for women in SEM. When several background and experience factors were adjusted for, men graduate students showed a significant advantage in paper presentations, publishing research articles, and consequently total research productivity. Overall, the most consistent contributions to productivity measures were having a mentor and being supported by a research assistantship during the course of one's studies. Women were as likely as men to have mentors and assistantship support, so other factors besides the conventional departmental indicators underlie the sex differences in productivity. Nettles and Millett point to the sex difference in graduate students' rating of their interactions with faculty. The fact that women gave low ratings to their interactions with

---

[30]R Freeman, E Jin, and C-Y Shen (2004). *Where Do New US-Trained Science-Engineering PhDs Come From?* (NBER Working Paper 10554). Cambridge, MA: National Bureau of Economic Research.

[31]MT Nettles and CM Millett (2006). *Three Magic Letters: Getting to PhD.* Baltimore, MD: Johns Hopkins Press. This study followed 9,036 students who completed their first year of graduate studies in 1996. Data are reported by sex or race or ethnicity; there are no specific data reported on minority women.

[32]In their questionnaire, Nettles and Millet defined mentor as "someone on the faculty to whom students turned for advice, to review a paper, or for general support and encouragement." This definition made it possible for the mentor and adviser to be the same person, but it did give the researchers a chance to examine mentorship separately from advising.

TABLE 3-5 Number of PhD Degrees Awarded In Science and Engineering, by Race or Ethnicity and Sex, 2003

	Overall		African American	
	Men	Women	Men	Women
Physical science	1,726	752	46	28
Life science	2,451	2,071	54	70
Mathematics	364	152	11	5
Computer science	343	97	12	5
Social and behavioral science	2,256	3,292	105	250
Engineering	1,726	437	57	18
Total	8,866	6,801	285	376

NOTES: *Physical science* includes earth, atmospheric, and ocean sciences; *life science* includes agricultural sciences and biological sciences; *mathematics* includes statistics; and *social and behavioral science* includes psychology. *Native American* includes Alaskan Natives and Ameri-

faculty may be a consequence of the predominance of male faculty in science and engineering fields.[33] Minority-group women face additional challenges in navigating student-faculty interactions in graduate school.[34]

---

[33]Nettles and Millett (2006), ibid; BR Sandler (1991). *The Campus Climate Revisited: Chilly Climate for Women Faculty, Administrators, and Graduate Students.* Washington, DC: Association of American Colleges.

[34]Y Moses (1989). *Black Women in Academe: Issues and Strategies.* Washington, DC: Association of American Colleges; B Books (2000). Black and female: Reflections on graduate school. In *Women in Higher Education,* eds. J Glazer-Raymo, EM Bensimon, and BK Townsend, 2nd Ed. Boston, MA: Pearson Publishing; S Nieves-Squires (1991). *Hispanic Women: Making their Presence on Campus Less Tenuous.* Washington, DC: Association of American Colleges.

Hispanic		Native American		Asian American		White	
Men	Women	Men	Women	Men	Women	Men	Women
58	31	2	2	125	81	1,406	575
110	87	6	9	283	261	1,875	1,574
9	7	1	1	27	24	297	110
6	4	2	0	62	17	240	64
113	209	14	24	112	173	1,798	2,494
80	23	9	2	259	80	1,256	300
376	362	34	38	868	636	6,872	5,117

can Indians; in 2003 *Asian American* does not include Pacific Islanders. Students with un-known race or ethnicity and those who are temporary residents are not included.

SOURCE: National Science Foundation (2003). *Survey of Earned Doctorates, 2003*. Arling-ton, VA: National Science Foundation.

> Overall, the finding that men rated student-faculty social interactions higher than women is the most troubling observation, because it implies the continu-ing existence of the "old boys club" and possible sex discrimination.
>
> —Michael Nettles and Catherine Millett (2006)[35]

For minority-group students, it appears that type of graduate funding support, although it does not impact time to degree, can have a significant effect on formation of peer connections, faculty interactions, and research productivity. In the sciences and mathematics, African Americans were more than three times less likely than whites to publish.[36] Science and engineering teaching assistants appear to have fewer opportunities to pub-

---

[35]Nettles and Millett (2006), ibid.
[36]Nettles and Millett (2006), ibid.

lish articles, and those supported on research assistantships reported higher publication rates. Nettles and Millett suggest that fellowship support of minority-group students may separate them from both research obligations and opportunities. Other research supports the finding that type of graduate research support can affect faculty interaction and career outcomes; students on fellowships were less likely to continue in academic science and engineering careers.[37]

It is notable that there are substantial differences by field, sex, and race or ethnicity in the types of graduate research support received (Table 3-6). Biological sciences have a very low proportion of students using personal funds (12.4%) compared with computer science (25.0%) and social and behavioral sciences (41.8%). Teaching assistantships are 2.5 times more prevalent in mathematics (52.5%) than in any other field. Research assistantships are prevalent in physical sciences (47.2%), engineering (43.2%), and biological sciences (35.7%). Engineering and computer science have a higher proportion of students receiving employer assistance than science fields (8.3%, 9.1%, and 2.3%, respectively). More women support their graduate work with personal funds and more men receive employee reimbursement. More African Americans and Hispanics receive fellowship support, more whites receive teaching assistantships, and more Asian Americans receive research assistantships.

Single women without children appear to be equally likely as all men to complete a science and engineering graduate degree.[38] Other research indicates that doctoral students who are married or who have children under the age of 18 years have experiences similar to those of their peers who are not married or do not have children. They report similar peer interactions, social and academic interactions with faculty, and levels of research productivity. The primary difference is that students with children were more likely to temporarily stop out of their graduate program, and, in engineering and social sciences (but not other sciences), students with children took longer to complete their PhDs.[39] In 2006, both Stanford University and Dartmouth College announced specific graduate student childbirth policies to facilitate the retention of women graduate students (Box 6-6).

As discussed in the chemistry case study, one's academic pedigree can affect the likelihood of landing a tenure-track position, particularly in a research university. Most men and women who earn science and engineer-

---

[37]M Gaughan and S Robin (2004). National science training policy and early scientific careers in France and the United States. *Research Policy* 33:569-581.
[38]Xie and Shauman (2003), ibid.
[39]Nettles and Millett (2006), ibid.

TABLE 3-6 Primary Source of Support (Percent) for US Citizen and Permanent Resident Science and Engineering Doctorate Recipients, by Sex and Race or Ethnicity, 1999-2003

Primary Source of Support	All S&E	Men	Women	African American	Hispanic	Native American	Asian American	White
Personal/Family funds	22.9	19.4	27.7	25.1	23.8	30.4	12.6	24.2
Teaching assistantship	15.3	15.7	14.6	9.3	11.3	9.1	13.6	16.2
Research assistantship, traineeship, and internship	29.8	33.1	25.3	15.2	18.7	17.7	40.4	30.1
Fellowship, scholarship, or dissertation grant	23.5	22.4	24.9	40.5	34.4	29.9	24.8	21.7
Employer reimbursement	3.2	4.1	1.9	2.6	3.0	3.1	2.9	3.3

NOTE: Numbers do not add to 100%; the "other" category was not included in table.

SOURCE: National Science Foundation (1999-2003). *Survey of Earned Doctorates*. Arlington, VA: National Science Foundation.

TABLE 3-7 Top 10 US Baccalaureate Institutions of Science and
Engineering Doctorate Recipients, 1999-2003

	Men	Women
Total S&E PhDs	80,516	46,432
1	University of California, Berkeley (957)	University of California, Berkeley (552)
2	Cornell University, all campuses (719)	Cornell University, all campuses (462)
3	University of Illinois, Urbana-Champaign (671)	University of Michigan, Ann Arbor (450)
4	Massachusetts Institute of Technology (650)	University of California, Los Angeles (379)
5	Pennsylvania State University, main campus (591)	University of Wisconsin, Madison (324)
6	Harvard University (558)	Harvard University (321)
7	University of Michigan, Ann Arbor (558)	University of Illinois, Urbana-Champaign (317)
8	Brigham Young University, main campus (524)	University of California, San Diego (311)
9	University of Wisconsin, Madison (510)	University of Texas, Austin (305)
10	University of Texas, Austin (501)	University of California, Davis (501)

SOURCE: National Science Foundation (1999-2003). *Survey of Earned Doctorates.* Arlington, VA: National Science Foundation.

ing doctorates earned their baccalaureate degrees at research universities (Table 3-7); Gaughan and Robin found that obtaining an undergraduate degree at one of the Research I universities is highly predictive of entry into an academic career.[40] There are differences by sex, race, and ethnicity in the baccalaureate origins of science and engineering doctorates.[41] For example, historically black colleges and universities and women's colleges

---

[40]Gaughan and Robin (2004), ibid.

[41]DG Solorzano (1994). The baccalaureate origins of Chicana and Chicano doctorates in the physical, life, and engineering sciences: 1980-1990. *Journal of Women and Minorities in Science and Engineering* 1(4):253-272; NR Sharpe and CH Fuller (1995). Baccalaureate origins of women physical science doctorates: Relationship to institutional gender and science discipline. *Journal of Women and Minorities in Science and Engineering* 2(1):1-15; T Lintner (1996). *The Forgotten Scholars: American Indian Doctorate Receipt, 1980-1990, http://eric.ed.gov/ERICDocs/data/ericdocs2/content_storage_01/0000000b/80/25/be/36.pdf;*   CB Leggon and W Pearson (1997). The baccalaureate origins of African American female PhD scientists. *Journal of Women and Minorities in Science and Engineering* 3(4):213-224.

have played a larger role in producing women African American science PhD students: 75% of the African American women who earned PhDs in biology from 1975-1992 earned their baccalaureate degrees from either Spelman College or Bennett College.[42]

Graduate School Attrition

A number of researchers have examined the factors involved in graduate school attrition. Graduate Record Examination scores and undergraduate grade point averages are poor predictors of PhD attainment rates.[43] The social climate of graduate school plays a large role in whether a woman obtains a PhD in science or engineering.

While in graduate school, students face many challenges, not the least of which is maintaining self-confidence. Some have suggested that women are conditioned to measure the value of their achievements by the amount and nature of the feedback and attention they receive from others, but that men are taught to require little support from others.[44] Those social expectations would make women more vulnerable to losing their self-confidence in situations where little praise is given—a common occurrence in graduate school.[45] Other researchers reported that a loss in self-confidence adversely affected career plans and the determination to carry them out.[46] The integration of students into a community is associated with lower attrition rates.[47]

The isolation that women experience in graduate school has led to a number of adverse consequences, such as reduced opportunities to compare experiences with others, to seek help without the fear of being judged as inadequate or lacking in intelligence, to receive affirmation of their evaluations of situations, to obtain advice on ways of addressing a problem, to

[42]CB Leggon and W Pearson (1997). The baccalaureate origins of African American female PhD scientists. *Journal of Women and Minorities in Science and Engineering* 3:213-224.

[43]National Research Council (1996). *The Path to the PhD*. Washington, DC: National Academy Press.

[44]VJ Kuck, CH Marzabadi, SA Nolan, and J Buckner (2004). Analysis by gender of the doctoral and postdoctoral institutions of faculty members at the top-fifty ranked chemistry departments. *Journal of Chemical Education* 81(3):356-363, *http://www.chem.indiana.edu/ academics/ugrad/Courses/G307/documents/Genderanalysis.pdf.*

[45]CA Trower and JL Bleak (2004). *Study of New Scholars. Gender: Statistical Report* [Universities]. Cambridge, MA: Harvard Graduate School of Education, *http:// www.gse.harvard.edu/~newscholars/newscholars/downloads/genderreport.pdf.*

[46]Kuck et al. (2004), ibid.

[47]BE Lovitts (2001). *Leaving the Ivory Tower: The Causes and Consequences of Departure from Doctoral Study*. Lanham, MD: Rowman and Littlefield.

TABLE 3-8 Location and Type of Planned Postgraduate Study for US
Citizens and Permanent Resident Science and Engineering PhD
Recipients, by Sex, 2003

Location and Type of Postgraduate Activity	All S&E PhD recipients	Women	Men
US PhD recipients	10,863	4,545	6,316
Based in United States	96.4%	96.7%	96.1%
Academic employment	24.0%	26.6%	22.2%
Industry employment	16.6%	11.7%	20.1%
Postdoctoral study	42.9%	45.3%	41.2%
Other[a]	12.8%	13.1%	12.6%
Based abroad	3.3%	3.1%	3.5%
Location unknown	0.3%	0.2%	0.4%

[a] Includes elementary and secondary schools, government, nonprofit, and other or unknown.

SOURCE. National Science Foundation, Division of Science Resource Statistics, *Survey of Earned Doctorates, 2003.* Arlington, VA: National Science Foundation.

gain peer support and encouragement, and to build a professional network.
In group meetings, female students reported that often their remarks were
barely recognized by other group members, while the comments of their
male peers were met with enthusiasm and support. Other studies reiterate
this finding—that women are indeed "left out of informal networks" of
communication.[48]

POSTGRADUATE CAREER PLANS

A majority of students in the sciences and mathematics (59%) and the
social sciences (55%), but only 28% of students in engineering, prepare to
become postdoctoral scholars or college or university faculty. Among all
science and engineering PhD recipients in 2003, more women than men
reported plans to enter postdoctoral study, and substantially more men
than women reported plans to enter industrial employment (Table 3-8).

---

[48]Kuck et al. (2004), ibid.

POSTDOCTORAL APPOINTMENTS

Postdoctoral research is virtually required in the life sciences, and is becoming increasingly common in the physical sciences and engineering. In the life sciences, men and women PhDs obtain postdoctoral appointments at similar rates (70.7% of women and 72.5% of men)—nearly 6,400 women and 10,500 men. In the physical sciences, 42.7% of women and 47.4% of men obtain postdoctoral appointments —1,000 women and 5,100 men.[49]

Professional Development and Productivity

In a recent national survey, Davis[50] reports that postdoctoral scholars with the highest levels of oversight and professional development are more satisfied, give their advisers higher ratings, report fewer conflicts with their advisers, and are more productive than those reporting the lowest levels of oversight. Although salaries and benefits were weakly linked to subjective success and positive adviser relations, higher salaries[51] and increased structured oversight appear to be linked to paper production, both for all peer-reviewed papers and first-author papers. Perhaps most interesting is the role of planning. Davis found that postdoctoral scholars who had crafted explicit plans with their adviser at the outset of their appointments were more satisfied with their experience than those who had not. In addition to subjective measures of success, postdoctoral scholars with written plans submitted papers to peer-reviewed journals at a 23% higher rate, first-author papers at a 30% higher rate, and grant proposals at a 25% higher rate than those without written plans.

Research on the post-PhD employment of scientists and engineers has shown that men employed in the academic sector express significantly greater job satisfaction than women; members of underrepresented minority groups are far less satisfied.[52] Similarly, Davis found that men postdoctoral scholars had higher levels of subjective success than women. Men had higher publication rates, although women submitted grant proposals at a higher rate; this suggests different resource allocation strategies. Underrepresented minority postdoctoral scholars submitted first-author papers at a lower rate than majority postdoctoral scholars. These data may

---

[49]National Science Foundation (2004). *Graduate Students and Postdoctorates in Science and Engineering.* Arlington, VA: National Science Foundation.

[50]G Davis (2005). *Optimizing the Postdoctoral Experience: An Empirical Approach* (Working Paper). Research Triangle Park, NC: Sigma Xi, The Scientific Research Society.

[51]One standard deviation in each (for salary, a 19% difference, or roughly $7,600) corresponds to a 6.5-7% increase in the rate of paper production.

[52]P Moguerou (2002). *Job Satisfaction among US PhDs: The Effects of Gender and Employment Sectors* (Working Paper), *http://www.rennes.inra.fr/jma2002/pdf/moguerou.pdf.*

reflect what has been reported in mentoring studies of graduate students (see above) and junior faculty, where men and women report substantially different mentoring relationships. One institution found that women faculty were less likely than men to have mentors who actively fostered their careers and more likely than male faculty to report having mentors who used the women faculty's work for the mentor's own benefit (Box 6-3).

Funding Source

Overall, postdoctoral funding source does not appear to have a differential effect on career outcome. Certainly, being awarded a prestigious fellowship appears to have a favorable effect on one's chances of landing a tenure-track position,[53] but is not clear whether the fellowships select those who are already destined to land such positions or provide an additional advantage in being hired.

Recognizing that the age at which researchers receive their first independent award has been increasing over the last 20 years, the National Institutes of Health created the Pathway to Independence Award.[54] The award provides an opportunity for promising postdoctoral scientists to receive both mentored and independent research support from the same award. It remains to be seen how this award will affect the proportion of postdoctoral scholars who successfully transition to faculty positions or whether it will increase the proportion of women scientists who continue in academic careers.

Similarly, it is unclear whether there is a differential effect on career progression for women who receive a prestigious award such as the NSF Faculty Early Career Development (CAREER) award. Each year NSF selects nominees for the Presidential Early Career Awards for Scientists and Engineers (PECASE) from among the most meritorious new CAREER awardees. The PECASE program recognizes outstanding scientists and engineers who early in their careers show exceptional potential for leadership at the frontiers of knowledge. PECASE is the highest honor bestowed by the US government on scientists and engineers beginning their independent careers.[55] It is notable that the proportion of women CAREER and PECASE awardees in the last 10 years meets or exceeds the proportion of women in the PhD pool (Figure 3-2).

---

[53]G Pion and M Ionescu-Pioggia (2003). Bridging postdoctoral training and a faculty position: Initial outcomes of the Burroughs Wellcome Fund Career Awards in the Biomedical Sciences. *Academic Medicine* 78(2):177-186.

[54]*http://grants.nih.gov/grants/new_investigators/pathway_independence.htm.*

[55]*http://www.nsf.gov/pubs/2002/nsf02111/nsf02111.htm.*

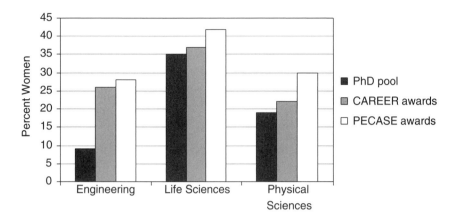

FIGURE 3-2 Proportion of women CAREER and PECASE awardees, 1995-2004.

NOTES: PhD pool was calculated as the average proportion of women earning PhDs in the 5-year period prior to the award. *Physical sciences* include mathematics and computer sciences.

SOURCE: *PhD Pool:* National Science Foundation, *Survey of Earned Doctorates, 1991-1999; CAREER awards* and *PECASE awards* are published by the National Science Foundation and available at *http://www.nsf.gov/awardsearch.* Engineering awards were those made by the ENG directorate, life sciences awards were those made by the BIO directorate, and physical sciences awards were those made by the CSE, GEO and MPS directorates.

FACULTY POSITIONS

Gains in women's representation among bachelor's and doctoral degree recipients have not translated into representation among college and university faculty (Figure 1-2 and Table 3-9). Four times as many men as women with science and engineering doctorates hold full-time faculty positions.[56] Data derived from the Association of American Medical Colleges Faculty Roster show that less than 5% of medical school faculty identify themselves as African American, Hispanic, or Native American.[57] Even though more African American women than African American men earn

---

[56]CPST (2002). *Professional Women and Minorities: A Total Human Resources Data Compendium,* 14th ed. Washington, DC: Commission on Professionals in Science and Technology.

[57]A Palepu, PL Carr, RH Friedman, H Amos, AS Ash, and MA Moskowitz (1998). Minority faculty in academic medicine. *JAMA* 280(9):767-771.

TABLE 3-9 Bachelor's Degree Recipients Compared with Faculty, by Sex and Field, 2002

	Percent Women		Percent Men	
	Students	Faculty	Students	Faculty
Biological sciences	58.4	20.2	41.6	79.8
Chemistry	47.3	12.1	52.7	87.9
Computer science	27.7	10.6	72.3	89.4
Physics	21.4	6.6	78.6	93.4

SOURCE: CB Leggon (2006). Women in science: Racial and ethnic differences and the differences they make. *Journal of Technology Transfer* 31:325-333.

science and engineering degrees, African American women make up less than half of the total African American full-time faculty in colleges and universities.[58] As discussed above, the underrepresentation of women on faculties can contribute to undergraduate and graduate students opting into career paths outside of academe.[59] It can also contribute to feelings of isolation among female faculty.

Hiring New Doctorates into Faculty Positions

No data are available on the total number of science and engineering tenure-track positions available each year. It is well known, however, that there are not nearly enough faculty positions to accommodate the new PhD pool. In physics in 2003, for example, there were 679 new faculty recruitments (including tenured, tenure-track, temporary, and non-tenure-track positions) and 1,197 new PhDs.[60] In mathematics in 2004, there were

[58]WB Harvey (2003). *20th Anniversary Minorities in Higher Education Annual Status Report*. Washington, DC: American Council on Education; K Hamilton (2002). The state of the African American professoriate. *Black Issues in Higher Education* 19(7):30-31.

[59]Discussed in ALW Sears (2003). Image problems deplete the number of women in academic applicant pools. *Journal of Women and Minorities in Science and Engineering* 9:169-181; MF Fox and PE Stephan (2001). Careers of young scientists: Preferences, prospects, and realities by gender and field. *Social Studies of Science* 31(1):109-122.

[60]R Ivie and KN Ray (2005). *Women in Physics and Astronomy, 2005* (AIP Publication Number R-430.02). College Park, MD: American Institute of Physics, *http://www.aip.org/statistics/trends/reports/women05.pdf*.

1,081 doctoral recipients and 232 reported hires in all faculty departments (126 were tenure-track at Research I universities).[61]

Fields vary in the proportion of female faculty relative to the available pool. In physics in 2004, a higher percentage of women were hired as junior faculty than are represented in the recent PhD pool: 18% of new physics hires and 13% of recent physics PhDs.[62] In mathematics in 2004, women made up 31% of doctoral recipients and 28.4% of new faculty hires.[63] Paradoxically, fields with higher proportions of women in the PhD pool have lower proportions of women in the applicant pool (Figure 1-2a, b, and c).[64] The same appears to be true in academic medicine (Box 3-3).

Usual department hiring processes often do not identify exceptional female candidates. That point is brought into sharp focus by a recent report from the Massachusetts Institute of Technology (MIT),[65] in which the number of women science faculty is plotted over time (Figure 3-3).

> The increases in the representation of women and minorities don't just "happen," but result from specific pressures, policies, and positive initiatives designed to increase the hiring of women or minorities; and that when these pressures abate or expire, hiring progress stops or even reverses.
>
> —Nancy Hopkins, Diversification of a University Faculty (2006)

In 2006, there were 36 female faculty and 240 male faculty in the School of Science at MIT. The total number of tenured and untenured women faculty in the MIT science departments rose steeply twice: between 1972 and 1976 and between 1997 and 2000. Those rises do not reflect contemporaneous increases in the size of the faculty. The number of male faculty actually decreased (from 259 to 229) during the rise in female faculty between 1997 and 2000 because of an early retirement program. Instead, the first sharp rise in the number of women science faculty beginning in 1972 was the result of pressures associated with the Civil Rights Act

---

[61]EE Kirkman, JW Maxwell, and CA Rose (2005). 2004 Annual Survey of the Mathematical Sciences. *Notices of the American Mathematical Society, http://www.ams.org/employment/2004Survey-Third-Report.pdf.*

[62]R Ivie and KN Ray (2005). *Women in Physics and Astronomy, 2005.* American Institute of Physics.

[63]Kirkman, Maxwell, and Rose (2005), ibid.

[64]Applications, interviews, and hiring decisions are discussed in the forthcoming report by the National Academies Committee on Women in Science and Engineering (Box 1-3).

[65]Hopkins (2006), ibid. Available at *http://web.mit.edu/fnl/volume/184/hopkins.html.*

DEFINING THE ISSUES

BOX 3-3 Academic Medicine

During the last 30 years the share of women graduating from medical colleges has nearly reached parity with the share of male graduates. However, as shown in Figure B3-1, while the share of women students and faculty members was similar before 1974, since then, increases in the proportion of women medical school graduates have not translated into similar increases in the proportion of women in faculty positions.

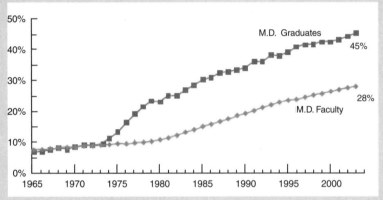

FIGURE B3-1 Representation of women MDs in academic medicine faculty positions, 1965-2004.

ADAPTED FROM: Association of American Medical Colleges (2005). The changing representation of men and women in academic medicine. *AAMC Analysis in Brief* 5(2):1-2, *http://www.aamc.org/data/aib/aibissues/aibvol5_no2.pdf.*

A Snapshot of the Current Situation for Female Faculty Members in Medicine[a]

• The growth trajectories of women students and women faculty are now similar, but the dramatic increase in women students in the years 1974-1980 was not matched by any change in the rate of growth of women faculty (Figure B3-1).

• The proportion of women in senior faculty positions in 2004 matched the proportion of women graduates in 1980 (Figure B3-2).

• Across all levels of seniority, women medical faculty earn significantly lower salaries than male faculty. Minority-group faculty earn less than white faculty.

• Women do not gain in academic rank at a rate that is proportional to their representation in medical school faculties.

---

[a]AS Ash, PL Carr, R Goldstein, and RH Friedman (2004). Compensation and advancement of women in academic medicine: Is there equity? *Annals of Internal Medicine* 141(3):205-212.

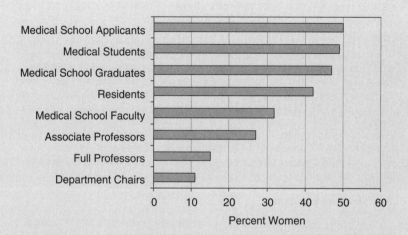

FIGURE B3-2 Proportion of women in academic medicine, by educational stage and rank.

ADAPTED FROM: Association of American Medical Colleges (2005). *Women in US Academic Medicine: Statistics and Medical School Benchmarking, http://www.aamc.org/members/wim/ statistics/stats05/wimstats2005.pdf.*

Reasons for Differences

Brown and colleagues[b] note that a number of factors may contribute to women's slower advancement, but a pipeline problem is not among them. They conclude that the supply of women graduating from medical schools is adequate and that "the **culture of academic medicine**, not the numbers of available women, drives the lopsided numbers." Cultural issues include a lack of high-ranking female role models; gender stereotyping that works to limit opportunities; exclusion from career development opportunities; differences in workplace expectations for men and women; social and professional isolation; and gender differences in the amount of funding, space, and staff support provided. Those factors have been found to adversely affect female faculty members' career satisfaction and advancement. In addition, traditional constructs of reward and hierarchy within departments have been found to impede advancement of women faculty because they are inherently gender-biased. Bickel et al. point out "medicine tends to over-value heroic individualism" with the result that "women will not 'measure up' as easily as men do."[c]

---

[b]A Brown, W Swinyard, and J Ogle (2003). Women in academic medicine: A report of focus groups and questionnaires, with conjoint analysis. *Journal of Women's Health* 12(10):999-1008.

[c]J Bickel, D Wara, BF Atkinson, LS Cohen, M Dunn, S Hostler, TRB Johnson, P Morahan, AH Rubenstein, GF Sheldon, and E Stokes (2002). Increasing women's leadership in academic medicine: Report of the AAMC project implementation committee. *Academic Medicine* 77(10):1043-1061.

continued

BOX 3-3 Continued

A second difficulty is related to **tensions between professional and personal life** which seem to be especially acute for women in academic medicine. Brown et al. report that "the demands of career and personal life [are] each great enough to extract compromise from the other, and, further, that anticipated support from a partner, the community, and medical center was inadequate to make it possible to succeed in multiple roles at once." Bickel and colleagues note that academic medicine tends to "reward unrestricted availability to work (i.e., neglect of personal life)." Furthermore, as in other fields, the pressures of the tenure timeline in academic medicine often coincide with decisions (and associated pressures) to start a family.

Potential Policy Options

Potential policy actions to redress those problems focus on adjusting the institutional environment in a way that improves the experiences of both male and female faculty. Improving the quality of professional development programs for all faculty has proven effective in addressing culture and climate issues[d] (Chapter 4 and Box 6-3). Other suggestions are to:

- Improve department mentoring programs, including providing guidance to male faculty on how to be effective mentors for female faculty.
- Address the tensions between work and personal lives and obligations.
- Identify which institutional practices tend to favor men's over women's professional development and rebalance them to value the institution's goals in a gender-neutral way.
- Recognize models of career success based on quality rather than quantity, so that people can craft careers that both serve the institution's needs and harmonize with their own core values.
- Place more value on accomplishments accruing from collaborative work.
- Provide more flexibility for part-time work.
- Adjust tenure policies.
- Provide options for partner hiring programs and childcare.

---

[d]LP Fried, CA Francomano, SM MacDonald, EM Wagner, EJ Stokes, KM Carbone, WB Bias, MM Newman, and JD Stobo (1996). Career development for women in academic medicine: Multiple interventions in a department of medicine. *Journal of the American Medical Association* 276(11):898-905; S Mark, H Link, PS Morahan, L Pololi, V Reznik, and S Tropez-Sims (2001). Innovative mentoring programs to promote gender equity in academic medicine. *Academic Medicine* 76:39-42.

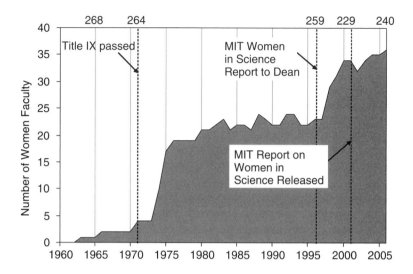

FIGURE 3-3 Number of women faculty in the School of Science at the Massachusetts Institute of Technology, 1963-2006.

NOTES: The numbers of male faculty in several relevant years are shown along the top of the graph.

ADAPTED FROM: N Hopkins (2006). Diversification of a university faculty: Observations on hiring women faculty in the schools of science and engineering at MIT. *MIT Faculty Newsletter* 18(4):1, 16-23. *http://web.mit.edu/fnl/volume/184/hopkins.html.*

and affirmative action regulations. In particular, Secretary of Labor George Schultz in 1971 ordered compliance reviews of hiring policies of women in universities. All institutions receiving federal funding were required to have such plans in effect as of that year. The second sharp rise between 1997 and 2000 resulted directly from the Dean of the School of Science's response to the 1996 MIT *Report on Women Faculty in the School of Science.*

The "Pool"

As discussed in Box 3-1, one of the current controversies is how to define the available pool of talent. Some base their figures on the proportion of women who have recently graduated with a PhD or MD; others suggest it should be based on the average over several years. In some fields where postdoctoral appointments are common, "recent" may be 5 years prior to a search. Others suggest the appropriate pool should be the proportion of women in the postdoctorate pool. Still others argue that the pool should be based on the proportion of women earning PhDs in top-tier institutions. As discussed in Box 3-1, there is currently no consensus on how to measure the "pool" of qualified candidates.

At the University of California, Berkeley, "doctoral pool" is defined in a two-step process. First, the average proportion of US residents earning PhDs in the relevant field in the 5 years prior is obtained from the National Science Foundation Survey of Earned Doctorates, which publishes these figures annually. Second, the pool is narrowed by considering only those PhDs awarded at the 35 institutions producing the most PhDs at top-quartile-rated doctoral programs, based on the National Research Council's *Research Doctorate Programs in the United States: Continuity and Change* report.[66] Indeed, research on hiring shows that faculty at Research I universities received their doctorate degrees from a very select group of institutions,[67] and that narrowing the institutional filter further may provide a more realistic picture of actual hiring practice. This issue is discussed in more detail later in this chapter in the *Chemistry Case Study* section. Perception of career opportunities is another factor affecting the sex distribution of the academic job applicant pool; some research indicates that women mathematics and science graduate students perceive academic careers more negatively than do men.[68]

Applicant data on biology and the health sciences at the University of California, Berkeley, in 2001-2004 show that women made up 47% of recent biology and health sciences doctorates from the top-quartile of graduate schools, but only 29% of applicants for tenure-track faculty positions (Figure 3-4). In physical science, mathematics, computer science, and engineering disciplines, women made up 21% of recent PhDs from those top schools and 15% of applicants (Figure 3-5). Minority-group women, in contrast with white women, are present in the University of California, Berkeley, applicant pool in the same proportion as in the PhD pool, but are not represented proportionately among assistant professors.

---

[66]National Research Council (1995). *Research Doctorate Programs in the United States: Continuity and Change*. Washington, DC: National Academy Press.

[67]For example, see VJ Kuck, CH Marzabadi, SA Nolan, and J Buckner (2004). Analysis by gender of the doctoral and postdoctoral institutions of faculty members at the top-fifty ranked chemistry departments. *Journal of Chemical Education* 81(3):356-363.

[68]ALW Sears (2003). Image problems deplete the number of women in academic applicant pools. *Journal of Women and Minorities in Science and Engineering* 9:169-181; D Barbezat (1992). The market for new PhD economists. *Journal of Economic Education* 23:262-276.

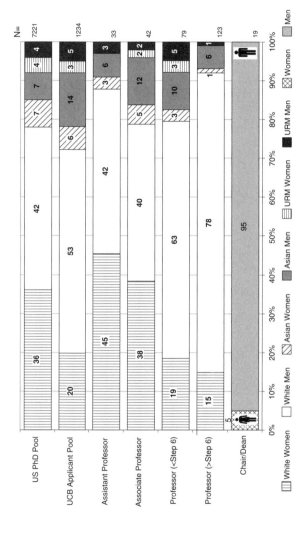

FIGURE 3-4 Biological and health sciences applicant pool and faculty positions at the University of California, Berkeley, 2001-2004.

NOTES: *Underrepresented minority (URM)* includes African American, Hispanic American, and Native American. *Chair/Dean* figures are broken down only by sex because of low counts. The PhD pool is based on PhDs granted to US residents, 1997-2001, at the 35 institutions producing the most PhDs at top-quartile-rated doctoral programs (National Research Council Reputational Ratings).

SOURCE: UC Berkeley Faculty Applicant Pool Database, 2001-2004; UC Berkeley Faculty Personnel Records, 2003; and National Science Foundation Survey of Earned Doctorates.

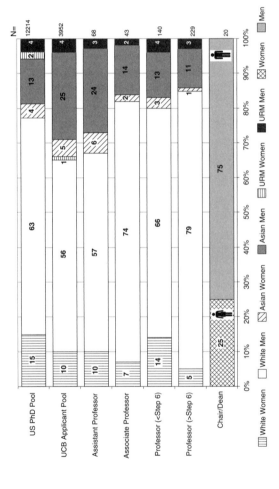

FIGURE 3-5 Physical sciences, mathematics, and engineering applicant pool and faculty positions at the University of California, Berkeley, 2001-2004.

NOTES: *Underrepresented minority (URM)* includes African American, Hispanic American, and Native American. There are no URM women in faculty positions in physical sciences, mathematics, and engineering departments. *Chair/Dean* figures are broken down only by gender because of low counts. The PhD pool is based on PhDs granted to US residents, 1997-2001, at the 35 institutions producing the most PhDs at top-quartile-rated doctoral programs (National Research Council Reputational Ratings).

SOURCE: UC Berkeley Faculty Applicant Pool Database, 2001-2004. UC Berkeley Faculty Personnel Records, 2003; and National Science Foundation Survey of Earned Doctorates.

Faculty Mobility

Estimates of faculty attrition are hard to come by. Most available attrition data are on retirements, not on mobility between universities or other nonretirement attrition. There is very little information available on where faculty go who leave academe. In 1999, about 7.7% of full-time faculty left their positions, 2.2% for retirement and 5.5% for a variety of other reasons.[69] The few sources of data for this type of analysis are the Association of American Medical Colleges (AAMC) Faculty Roster, which collects and reports data on medical college faculty; the American Chemical Society Directory of Graduate Research; and the American Institute of Physics Academic Workforce Survey (Box 3-4).

To better understand faculty turnover and mobility, we used the NSF *Survey of Doctoral Recipients* (SDR), a longitudinal survey of a sample of people who earned doctorates in the United States. We examined the sample of full-time, untenured but tenure-track science, engineering, and social science faculty in 1995 who were also part of the survey 6 years later, in 2001. We found that men and women faculty exhibit different mobility: more men receive tenure or seek positions outside of academe, and more women move to non-tenure-track positions within academe.

- A slightly greater percentage of men than women moved from academe to other sectors of employment in 2001 (8.6% of women and 11.1% of men).
- A greater percentage of women faculty than men were unemployed in 2001 (3.4% of women and 0.8% of men).
- Men and women faculty had a similar likelihood of being employed at the same type of institution in 1995 and 2001 (68.5% of women and 70.1% of men).
- Men and women faculty had a similar likelihood of moving to a different type of institution between 1995 and 2001 (18.7% of women and 17.5% of men).
- Women faculty were significantly more likely than men to change jobs only in the social sciences.
- Of tenure-track faculty in 1995 who were employed in the same type of institution in 2001, more men than women faculty had received tenure (54.5% of women and 59.2% of men).

---

[69]Y Zhou and JF Volkwein (2004). Examining the influences on faculty departure intentions: A comparison of tenured versus nontenured faculty at research universities using NSOPF-99. *Research in Higher Education* 45(2):139-176.

TRACKING AND EVALUATION

BOX 3-4 The Association of American Medical Colleges' Faculty Roster, the American Chemical Society Directory of Graduate Research, and the American Institute of Physics Academic Workforce Survey

The AAMC Faculty Roster was started in 1966 through joint sponsorship of the National Institutes of Health (NIH) and AAMC as an effort to assess and track the intellectual capital of medical education. The Faculty Roster contains, on a voluntary basis, employment, educational, and demographic information on faculty members at accredited US medical schools. Currently the roster contains records on about 113,000 active, full-time faculty and 122,000 inactive faculty.[a]

The Faculty Roster is used for a variety of purposes. Although it was initially conceived to deal with the development of personnel to staff new medical schools, in more recent years it has been used to track the progress of medical schools in increasing the representation of women and minorities in faculty positions. The roster can be used to examine sources of faculty, provide background on faculty training, track inter-institutional movement by faculty, and study reasons behind faculty departure from medical academe.[b] NIH uses the Faculty Roster to inform policy decisions, using its data to study such topics as the growth rate of faculty or the typical age of faculty at the time at which they receive their first professorships. In addition to providing the database to its members for communication and research purposes, AAMC uses it to produce a series of annual reports on US medical school faculty, which present data on the national distribution of full-time faculty, including such information as specialty, department, rank, degree, sex, and race or ethnicity.[c]

The American Institute of Physics conducts a biennial survey on the number of faculty, turnover, retirements, and recruitments at physics degree-granting departments. It also collects information on sex, race, and ethnicity.[d] The American Chemical Society also maintains a faculty database, the Directory of Graduate Research (DGR). The DGR focuses on faculty involved in chemistry research and provides information on faculty research field, academic rank, sex, and contact information. It does not collect information on race or ethnicity. The DGR provides a statistical summary of 665 chemical science departments and listings for nearly 11,000 faculty members.[e]

---

[a]Association of American Medical Colleges. *Faculty Roster, http://www.aamc.org/data/facultyroster/start.htm. Inactive faculty* are those who are no longer faculty at an institution for reasons of leaving for private practice, retirement, or death.

[b]Association of American Medical Colleges. *FAMOUS User's Guide, http://www.aamc.org/data/facultyroster/famous.pdf.* FAMOUS is the on-line administration system used to enter and edit data in the Faculty Roster.

[c]Association of American Medical Colleges. *Reports Available Through Faculty Roster,* http://www.aamc.org/data/facultyroster/reports.htm.

[d]R Ivie, S Guo, and A Carr (2006). *2004 Physics & Astronomy Academic Workforce Report.* College Park, MD: AIP, *http://www.aip.org/statistics/trends/facultytrends.html.*

[e]The American Chemical Society *Directory of Graduate Research* is searchable on-line at *http://dgr.rints.com/.*

Next, we looked at full-time, untenured, tenure-track science, engineering, and social science faculty employed at a Research I institution in 1995. We found that between 1995 and 2001:

• Faculty at Research I universities were half as likely as the overall population of science, engineering, and social sciences faculty to move to other types of higher education institutions.

• Men were almost twice as likely as women to move to jobs outside academe (8.5% of women and 15.3% of men).

• Women who were employed as tenure-track faculty in 1995 were more likely than men not to be employed in 2001 (2.5% of women, 0.6% of men).

• Women tenure-track faculty who were employed at a Research I institution in both 1995 and 2001 cohorts were less likely than men to have received tenure in 2001 than corresponding men (56.3% of women and 61.6% of men).

Exiting the Tenure Track[70]

We did an additional analysis to determine why tenure-track and tenured faculty changed jobs, using the 1995-2003 SDR. To be included in the sample, individuals must have had tenure or have had tenure-track jobs in 1995. Most individuals indicated multiple reasons for job changes. The single most important reason given was pay and promotion—this did not differ by field. Other reasons for changing jobs did differ by field, rank, and sex. Across fields, women faculty consistently ranked working conditions, family, and job location higher than men among their reasons for changing jobs (Table 3-10).[71] Differences were most prevalent in life sciences, particularly among full professors.

---

[70]The research described in this section was commissioned by the committee from Donna Ginther, Associate Professor of Economics, University of Kansas.

[71]This finding corroborates earlier work on faculty intentions to leave. See LLB Barnes, MO Agago, and WT Coombs (1998). Effects of job-related stress on faculty intention to leave academia. *Research in Higher Education* 39(4):457-469; S Kulis, Y Chong, and H Shaw (1999). Discriminatory organizational contexts and black scientists on postsecondary faculties. *Research in Higher Education* 40(2):115-148; Y Zhou and JF Volkwein (2004). Examining the influences on faculty departure intentions: A comparison of tenured versus untenured faculty at research universities using NSOPF-99. *Research in Higher Education* 45(2):139-176; VJ Rosser (2004). Faculty members' intentions to leave: A national study on their worklife and satisfaction. *Research in Higher Education* 45(3):285-309; RR Callister (2006). The impact of gender and department climate on job satisfaction and intentions to quit for faculty in science and engineering fields. *Journal of Technology Transfer* 31:367-375.

TABLE 3-10 Reasons for Job Change by Sex, All Faculty Ranks, All Fields, 1995-2003

Reason for Job Change	Male	Female	P-value
Change in professional interest	0.031	0.043	0.00
Working xonditions	0.035	0.054	0.00
Family-related	0.014	0.024	0.00
Laid off/job terminated	0.010	0.018	0.00
Job location	0.030	0.044	0.00
Pay/promotion	0.070	0.105	0.00
Retirement	0.002	0.001	0.32
School related	0.012	0.026	0.00
Other reason	0.008	0.009	0.45

NOTES: Fields include life sciences, physical sciences, engineering, and social sciences. The means are weighted by sample probability weights. The p-values report the level of significance for a two-sided hypothesis of no significant differences in means.

SOURCE: National Science Foundation, *Survey of Doctoral Recipients, 1995-2003.*

There are sex differences in where women and men land after leaving tenure-track positions. A hazard analysis of the 1973-2001 longitudinal SDR sample shows that across science fields, men were significantly more likely to leave the tenure track for nonacademic employment. The overall hazard rate is 0.830 (p=0.05), which means that about 20% more men than women exited to nonacademic jobs. Where are the women going? Across all fields of science and engineering women are 40% more likely than men to exit the tenure track for an adjunct academic position (p=0.01). In addition to sex, the factors with the strongest correlation to this outcome were race or ethnicity, and employment at a private university or medical school. Women whose primary or secondary responsibility was teaching or those who had government funding were significantly less likely to exit to adjunct positions.

Tenure

Faculty mobility may be pushed by the expectation of a negative tenure decision. At MIT, for example, there is a 50% tenure rate in the science and engineering departments.[72] This is similar to the overall tenure rate at

---

[72]N Hopkins (2006). Diversification of a university faculty: Observations on hiring women faculty in the schools of science and engineering at MIT. *MIT Faculty Newsletter* 18(4):1, 16-23.

Research I universities (see above and footnote 95). Our analysis showed a small 4% difference in tenure rates for men and women; a number of other reports have documented similar differential tenure rates for men and women.[73] Others document differential tenure rates for minority faculty.[74] Some researchers have broken out tenure rates by field;[75] in this finer analysis, between 1973 and 2001, women were between 1-3% less likely than men to get tenure in physical sciences, 2-4% more likely than men to get tenure in life sciences and engineering, and 8% less likely than men to get tenure in social sciences.

In addition to the cohort analysis described above, another way to analyze tenure decisions is by examining faculty who are reviewed for tenure.[76] This analysis excludes faculty who leave the tenure track, and does not address time to tenure. Compared to the cohort analysis, the "review" paradigm yields higher tenure rates that are similar for men and women faculty.[77] For early tenure decisions—those made within 2 years of hiring—tenure rates are 96% to 100% for men, women, and minority faculty. For 4th- and 6th-year tenure review cases, the rates are also similar for men and women in, but are lower for, minority faculty: 85% to 90% of men and women are granted tenure, while 75% to 82% of minority faculty are granted tenure.

Promotion

Women faculty gain promotion more slowly than men and are less likely to reach the highest academic rank, especially in the Research I universities (see Chapter 4). At one university, for example (Figure 3-6), the

---

[3]National Science Foundation (2004). *Gender Differences in the Careers of Academic Scientists and Engineers* (NSF 04-323). Arlington, VA: National Science Foundation; AS Ash, PL Carr, R Goldstein, and RH Friedman (2004). Compensation and advancement of women in academic medicine: Is there equity? *Annals of Internal Medicine* 141(3):205-212; D Ginther (2001). *Does Science Discriminate Against Women? Evidence from Academia* (Working Paper 2001-02). Atlanta, GA: Federal Reserve Bank of Atlanta; National Research Council (2001). *From Scarcity to Visibility: Gender Differences in the Careers of Doctoral Scientists and Engineers*. Washington, DC: National Academy Press.

[74]MJ Dooris and M Guidos (2006). Tenure Achievement Rates at Research Universities. *Presentation at the Annual Forum of the Association for Institutional Research, Chicago, IL, May 2006, http://www.psu.edu/president/pia/planning_research/reports/AIR_Tenure_Flow_Paper_06.pdf.*

[75]D Ginther and S Kahn (2006). *Does Science Promote Women? Evidence from Academia 1973-2001* (NBER SEWP Working Paper). Cambridge, MA: National Bureau of Economics Research, *http://www.nber.org/~sewp/GintherKahn_Sciences_promo_NBER.pdf.*

[76]This type of analysis is used by the National Academies Committee on Women in Science and Engineering in their 2006 workshop report (Box 1-3).

[77]Dooris and Guidos (2006), ibid.

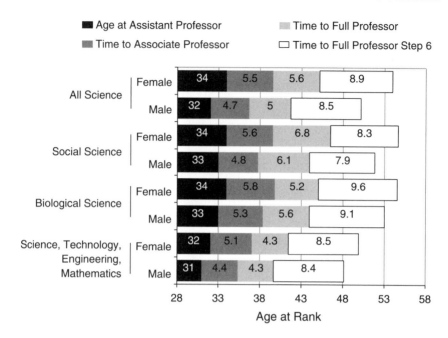

FIGURE 3-6 Advancing through the ranks: University of California, Berkeley, faculty, by sex and field.

NOTES: *Science, technology, engineering, and mathematics* (STEM) departments do not include biology. *All Science* is a composite of STEM, biology, and social science departments. Data are presented for all faculty, whether married, single, or parents. The regular professorial series consists of three ranks: assistant professor, associate professor, and full professor. Each rank is divided into steps. Advancement to full professor step six requires great distinction, recognized nationally or internationally in scholarly achievement or in teaching. See *http://www.ucop.edu/acadadv/acadpers/tenure.html*.

SOURCE: UC Berkeley Faculty Personnel Records, 1980-2003.

most substantial difference between men and women is in the time it takes to reach the associate professor level, although there is also a difference in the timing between tenure and full professor.[78] The pattern is not unique; it has also been shown at Duke University and at MIT, where women faculty are promoted more slowly than men. Race and ethnicity is an additional

---

[78]Additional data on time to promotion is provided by the National Academies Committee on Women in Science and Engineering in their 2006 workshop report (Box 1-3).

factor strongly correlated with reduced probability of promotion to full professor: between 1973 and 2001, African American women were almost 10% less likely than men to be promoted to full professor within 15 years of PhD.[79]

The persistent effect of sex, even after controlling for a number of relevant variables, suggests that there is more to learn about the promotion process. Some researchers suggest that a reasonable explanation of women's slower promotion and longer time in rank is that women are expected to meet higher standards for promotion, especially at Research I institutions.[80] Another possibility is that women, particularly in the transition from achieving tenure to full professorship, are less likely to feel ready to apply. As discussed in Chapter 4, research shows that bias affects the judgments made about women scientists and engineers and often results in their research being less valued than research by men.

Faculty Retention

From a number of reports, projects, and task forces examining factors behind faculty retention and attrition a number of common threads emerge (Box 3-5).[81]

A key factor in retaining faculty of all types is the problem of **differences in salaries** between groups. A task force at the University of Colorado at Boulder (UC-Boulder) found that "non-competitive salaries represent the most-cited factor in faculty retention."[82] That concern was most prevalent among men; senior women faculty expressed more concern over salaries than junior women faculty. Other studies have found, however, that female faculty were less satisfied with their salaries than male faculty[83] and studies

---

[79]D Ginther, research commissioned by the committee.

[80]J Long, P Allison, and R McGinnis (1993). Rank advancement in academic careers: Sex differences and effects of productivity." *American Sociological Review* 58(5):703-722; Ginther (2006), ibid.

[81]See NAS/NAE/IOM (2006). *Biological, Social, and Organizational Components of Success for Women in Science and Engineering.* Washington, DC: The National Academies Press; Gender Faculty Studies at Research I Universities Web site, *http://www7.nationalacademies. org/cwse/gender_faculty_links.html*; and the NSF ADVANCE Web site, *http://www.nsf.gov/ advance.*

[82]University of Colorado at Boulder (2001). *Faculty Recruitment and Retention Task Force Report, http://www.colorado.edu/AcademicAffairs/fac_recruit/fac_ recruit.doc.*

[83]M Hemmasi, LA Graf, and JA Lust (1992). Correlates of pay and benefit satisfaction: The unique case of public university faculty. *Public Personnel Management* 21(4):442-443; CA Trower and JL Bleak (2004). *Study of New Scholars. Gender: Statistical Report* [Universities]. Cambridge, MA: Harvard Graduate School of Education, *http://www.gse.harvard.edu/ ~newscholars/newscholars/downloads/genderreport.pdf.*

DEFINING THE ISSUES

BOX 3-5 Factors Affecting Faculty Attrition

- Tenure policies and practices
- Salary
- Department and workplace environment
- Financial support for teaching activities
- Housing assistance programs
- Staff support
- Administrative burden
- Quality of office and laboratory space
- Professional development programs
- Research support
- Mentoring and collaboration
- Spouse or partner hiring programs
- Child-care options
- Benefits and start-up packages
- Opportunity to serve on important committees

---

at MIT[84] and elsewhere have noted that women faculty are often under-paid relative to men.[85]

An important issue related to salary is how universities structure and explain their **tenure policies and procedures.** Rigid policies for attaining tenure can raise difficulties for women and for junior faculty in general. As discussed above, women are more likely than men to leave the university at early points in their career.[86] Trower and Chait report that both men and women receive little guidance about tenure policies and that junior faculty are likely to view tenure practices as "outmoded."[87] The Study of New Scholars at Harvard University reports significant differences in men and

---

[84]Massachusetts Institute of Technology (1999). *A Study on the Status of Women Faculty in Science at MIT, http://web.mit.edu/fnl/women/women.html.*

[85]RR Callister (2006). The impact of gender and department climate on job satisfaction and intentions to quit for faculty in science and engineering fields. *Journal of Technology Transfer* 31:367-375.

[86]Also see D Teodorescu (2002). *Faculty Gender Equity at Emory: PCSW Study Finds Both Fairness and Imbalances, http://www.emory.edu/ACAD_EXCHANGE/2002/octnov/pcsw.html*; MN Harrigan (1999). *An Analysis of Faculty Turnover at the University of Wisconsin-Madison.* University of Wisconsin-Madison, *http://wiscweb3.wisc.edu/obpa/Faculty Turnover/FacultyTurnover2.html.*

[87]C Trower and R Chait (2002). Faculty diversity: Too little for too long. *Harvard Magazine.* March-April 2002.

women faculty views of the tenure process; men are found to have clearer views of tenure prospects and expectations.[88] Annual reviews and effective mentoring programs have been shown to clarify expectations and improve faculty retention (Box 6-3).

Conflicts between personal and professional life, as in the case of tenure, are often important in retention of junior and women faculty. Several studies show that women faculty are less satisfied than men with the interaction between their personal and professional lives.[89] A task force at Columbia University notes that family responsibilities disproportionately impact women. Women are in their childbearing years at the same time they are developing their careers, and the demands of career and family often conflict.[90] Such policies as child-care options and spousal hiring programs that are cognizant of the conflict can play a significant role in faculty retention. The UC-Boulder task force notes that spouse or partner employment opportunities can be an especially prevalent concern among junior faculty.[91]

Within a given faculty member's professional life **department climate** and the presence or absence of a **supportive work environment** have important influence on attrition and retention. A number of factors commonly cited in faculty retention and attrition studies are related to the environment that faculty encounter in their workplaces.[92] Work done by Callister suggests that department climate is an important factor for universities to consider when attempting to improve faculty job satisfaction and intentions to quit.[93] Callister reports that women faculty tend to be less satisfied than men in their jobs and more likely to quit. In a similar finding, the Study of New Scholars at Harvard reports that women faculty are less satisfied than

---

[88]Trower and Bleak (2004), ibid.

[89]S Bullers (1999). Selection effects in the relationship between women's work/family status and perceived control. *Family Relations: Interdisciplinary Journal of Applied Family Studies* 48(2):181-188; LJ Sax, LS Hagedorn, M Arredondo, and FA Dicrisi (2002). Faculty research productivity: Exploring the role of gender and family-related factors. *Research in Higher Education* 43(4):423-446.

[90]Trower and Bleak (2004), ibid.

[91]University of Colorado at Boulder (2001). *Faculty Recruitment and Retention Task Force Report, http://www.colorado.edu/AcademicAffairs/fac_recruit/fac_recruit.doc.*

[92]SPK Jena (1999). Job, life satisfaction, and occupational stress of women. *Social Science International* 15(1):75-80; JC Holder and A Vaux (1998). African American professionals: Coping with occupational stress in predominantly white environments. *Journal of Vocational Behavior* 53(3):315-333; YF Niemann and JF Dovidio (1998). Relationship of solo status, academic rank, and perceived distinctiveness to job satisfaction of racial/ethic minorities. *Journal of Applied Psychology* 83(1):55-71.

[93]Callister (2006), ibid.

men faculty with their workplace expectations and relationships, including availability of support, mentoring, and collaboration.[94]

The UC-Boulder task force noted a sense of "professional isolation" as the third-most common reason for faculty attrition for women and men faculty. Professional isolation may include a lack of support from colleagues, lack of inclusion in the department community, and rude or unsympathetic students. Furthermore, several studies, including ones at Colorado and Columbia, note that women (and junior faculty members) have fewer opportunities to serve on meaningful department and university committees.[95] The 1999 MIT study expressed concern that women faculty were "excluded from any substantial power within the University."[96]

A final issue related to the workplace environment was uncovered in a recent study at Rutgers University, which suggested that some women faculty's outside offers are less likely than those of men to yield serious responses from university administrators, and it is more likely that those women will move to other universities.[97]

Surveys of female faculty members illuminate specific climate issues. In a national survey of more than 1,000 university faculty members carried out by the Higher Education Research Institute, women were more likely than men to feel that colleagues devalued their research, that they had fewer opportunities to participate in collaborative efforts, and that they were constantly being scrutinized.[98] Other researchers found that men tended to devalue women's contributions to an effort.[99] In another study, exit interviews of faculty women who "voluntarily" left a large university indicated that one of the key reasons for their departure was the lack of respect that they had been given by their colleagues.[100] Preston found that a majority of female professors perceived that because of their sex they had not been respected or treated appropriately.[101] Similarly, in a survey of Professional

---

[94]Trower and Bleak (2004), ibid.

[95]Columbia University (2005). *http://www/cumc.columbia.edu/dept/ps/facultycouncil/docs/ TaskForceonWomen Faculty Final Report 02_24_05.doc.* University of Colorado at Boulder (2001), ibid; MIT (1999), ibid.

[96]Massachusetts Institute of Technology (1999), ibid.

[97]Rutgers University (2001). *A Study of Gender Equity in the Faculty of Arts and Sciences, http://fas.rutgers.edu/onlineforms/gender_report.pdf.*

[98]HS Astin and LJ Sax (1996). Developing scientific talent in undergraduate women. In *The Equity Equation: Fostering the Advancement of Women in the Sciences, Mathematics and Engineering,* eds. CS Davis, AB Ginorio, BB Hollenshead, and PM Rayman. San Francisco: Jossey-Bass Publishers.

[99]L Chliwniak (1997). *ASHE-ERIC Higher Education Report ED 410 847.* Washington, DC: ERIC Clearinghouse.

[100]SA Wenzel and C Hollenshead (1998). *Former Women Faculty: Reasons for Leaving One Research University.* Washington, DC: ERIC Document Service.

[101]AE Preston (2004). *Leaving Science: Occupational Exit from Scientific Careers.* New York: Russell Sage Foundation.

Opportunities for Women in Research and Education grant recipients, women faculty reported that they had limited opportunities to participate in department or decision-making processes, had heard their research trivialized and discounted by other faculty members, had received little guidance about department procedures, and were ill informed about the tenure process.[102] The Yale Women Faculty Forum has developed a specific exit survey and interview process (Box 3-6) that can serve as a model for others; the survey has led to the creation of specific professional development courses for postdoctoral scholars and junior faculty.

When asked why they left academic science and engineering, men overwhelmingly focus on low pay and the lack of career advancement, while women offered three main reasons: desire for more interesting work, lack of mentor or guidance, and difficulty shouldering family and career responsibilities.[103] There is reason to believe that many women (and men) experience those discontents and do not leave the field, which can translate into lack of job satisfaction for more senior employees.

Departments vs. Centers

In light of the findings for faculty employed in university departments, it is interesting to note that participation in academic centers may offer different career opportunities for women scientists and engineers. In a nationally representative dataset on scientists and engineers working in research universities, Corley and Gaughan[104] found that women were as likely as men to join centers and do so at a similar stage in their career. Most of the male-female differences observed in disciplinary settings, such as lower proportions of women in leadership positions, were sustained in centers, but women appeared to have greater research equality. Men and women in centers spend the same amount of time in writing grant proposals, conducting research, supervising graduate students, and administering grants. Corley and Gaughan suggest that centers may potentially serve as a leveling field for men and women academics, but much work remains to be done, particularly at the leadership level (Tables 4-3, 4-4, and 4-5). Women in centers are younger on the average and less likely to be tenured than their male colleagues. There are also fewer women of color in centers than in university departments.

---

[102]SV Rosser (2004). *The Science Glass Ceiling*. New York: Routledge.

[103]AE Preston (2004), ibid. See also P Moguerou (2002). *Job Satisfaction among US PhDs: The Effects of Gender and Employment Sectors* (Working Paper), *http://www.rennes. inra.fr/jma2002/pdf/moguerou.pdf.*

[104]E Corley and M Gaughan (2005). Scientists' participation in university research centers: What are the gender differences? *Journal of Technology Transfer* 30:371-381.

EXPERIMENTS AND STRATEGIES

BOX 3-6 Task Force on the Retention and Promotion of Junior Faculty, Yale Women Faculty Forum[a]

One way to determine the reasons for leaving an academic position is simply to ask. To a certain degree, this is done in the longitudinal Survey of Doctoral Recipients, carried out by the National Science Foundation. However, institutions can gather more detailed information that can help modify existing policies or shape new initiatives focused on faculty retention. One such effort has been spearheaded by the Yale University Women Faculty Forum Task Force on Retention and Promotion of Junior Faculty. The Task Force designed an exit survey and distributed it to those tenure-track ladder faculty who departed in 2004 and 2005.[b] There was a 43% response rate; the task force performed follow-up interviews with many of the respondents.

The task force collected basic demographic information, and asked respondents a series of questions about their employment plans, their experience at Yale, and for their rating of departmental environment. Among the survey questions were:

• Did you come to Yale with a partner or significant other who required employment or desired continuing education? To what extent was Yale helpful in finding an appropriate position for him/her?

• Over the past academic year, what percentage of your time was spent on: scholarship, teaching, advising, administrative, committee work, and professional activities outside Yale?

• Was this departure voluntary or involuntary? If voluntary did you seek a counter-offer?

• When you came to Yale, how did you rate your own chances of obtaining tenure?

• When you came to Yale, to what extent were the expectations you would need to meet to obtain tenure made clear to you?

ECONOMIC IMPACT OF FACULTY ATTRITION

Even while turnover has its benefits in terms of bringing in new talent and ideas, replacing faculty members who leave can represent a substantial cost to universities, so it is worthwhile to invest in policies and practices that encourage faculty retention. Start-up costs associated with hiring new professors are often high. In addition to the costs incurred by a recruitment committee, average start-up costs for a new professor range from about $110,000 for an assistant professor in physics at a public nonresearch university to nearly $1.5 million for a senior faculty member in engineering at a private research institution.[105] The Task Force on Faculty Recruitment

---

[105]RG Ehrenberg, MJ Rizzo, and GH Jakubson (2003). Who bears the growing cost of science at universities? (Working Paper 9627). Cambridge, MA: National Bureau of Economic Research, *http://www.nber.org/papers/w9627*.

- In your opinion, did you receive adequate feedback on whether your performance was meeting expectations?
- To what extent did your experience at Yale enhance your professional development?
- To what extent did your experience provide resources to enhance your teaching skills?
- Did you receive mentoring from faculty inside and/or outside your department? How satisfied are you with the quantity and quality of mentoring you received?
- How do you think your overall experience at Yale compares with that of your graduate school peers who went on to work at other institutions?
- In retrospect, was coming to Yale a good decision?

After collating the survey and interview responses, the task force met with the college and graduate school deans, provosts, and the director of the Office of Institutional Research (OIR). OIR provided statistics on tenure and promotion that previously were not readily available. Following this meeting, the Dean of the Graduate School asked all department chairs to report on their mentoring practices for junior faculty. Since then, Yale has instituted a new position, Deputy Provost for Science and Technology and Faculty Development, to oversee the implementation of a core curriculum for the professional development of postdoctoral scholars and junior faculty. The first series of courses are being developed for the 2006-2007 academic year.

---

[a]P Kavathas, M LaFrance, and S Benhabib, *Task Force on the Retention and Promotion of Junior Faculty, Yale Women Faculty Forum.* For more information or the complete questionnaire contact WFF@yale.edu.

[b]All but six of the over 50 Faculty of Arts and Sciences departments provided names of departing faculty.

and Retention at UC-Boulder reports that in general, replacement costs are much greater than retention costs.[106] It estimates that it costs $200,000-$400,000 to replace a natural sciences or engineering faculty member at a public research university, whereas "only a fraction of these costs would go a long way" in programs to help retain existing faculty.[107] Tables 3-11 and 3-12 provide detailed listings of estimated start-up costs for new faculty hires.

Costs associated with hiring new faculty fall into several categories.

---

[106]University of Colorado at Boulder (2001). *Faculty Recruitment and Retention Task Force Report, http://www.colorado.edu/AcademicAffairs/fac_recruit/fac_recruit.doc.*
[107]University of Colorado at Boulder (2001), ibid.

TABLE 3-11 Average Start-up Packages for Assistant Professors in Selected Fields Starting in 2000-2001 at Public Research I Universities

Field	Start-up Equipment	Other Support[a]	Moving Allowance	Total Startup
Biology	$190,000	$27,000	$4,000	$221,000
Chemical engineering	$225,000	$164,000	$5,000	$394,000
Chemistry/biochemistry	$231,000	$14,000	$5,000	$250,000
Computer science	$51,000	$35,000	$4,000	$90,000
Economics	$6,000	$17,000	$5,000	$28,000
Geology	$119,000	$0	$4,000	$123,000
Physics	$156,000	$20,000	$4,000	$180,000
Political science	$4,000	$5,000	$3,000	$12,000
Psychology	$35,000	$9,000	$3,000	$47,000
Sociology	$5,000	$4,000	$4,000	$13,000

[a]Includes graduate student support ($140,000) and summer salary ($24,000) for chemical engineering; other disciplines also include support for postdoctoral scholars, renovations, and travel, but many schools left off such "other support" in the survey.

SOURCE: University of Colorado at Boulder (2001). *Faculty Recruitment and Retention Task Force Report, http://www.colorado.edu/AcademicAffairs/fac_recruit/fac_recruit.doc.*

There are costs associated with establishing search and recruitment committees and costs associated with relocation allowances, infrastructure, and support (for example, for laboratory renovations, offices, and equipment that might be required in support of new faculty). Those costs are included in the estimates discussed previously (and detailed in Tables 3-11 and 3-12). In addition, there is a substantial secondary cost associated with the loss of faculty and hiring of new faculty: that of research and grant productivity. In many cases, new faculty do not immediately bring the type of research-grant award support that productive, established faculty might. Callister reports that "it can take 10 years for a new faculty member in science or engineering to develop enough of a positive revenue stream from grants and to recoup start-up costs. If a faculty member leaves before start-up costs are recovered, the university loses money and must start over again."[108] In monetary terms, that can be substantial. The UC-Boulder task force estimated that a productive faculty member "may bring about $100K per year" in external support to the university, external support that would take a new faculty member several years to generate.[109]

---

[108]RR Callister (2006). The impact of gender and department climate on job satisfaction and intentions to quit for faculty in science and engineering fields. *Journal of Technology Transfer* 31:367-375.
[109]University of Colorado (2001), ibid.

TABLE 3-12 Start-up Costs Associated with New Professors

		Private Research 1 Average (N)	Private Nonresearch 1 Average (N)	Public Research 1 Average (N)	Public Nonresearch 1 Average (N)
AA	Physics and astronomy	395,746 (9)	147,944 (18)	320,932 (42)	169,491 (56)
AA	Biology	403,071 (14)	199,754 (26)	308,210 (38)	172,582 (55)
AA	Chemistry	489,000 (20)	221,052 (29)	441,155 (43)	210,279 (71)
AA	Engineering	390,237 (19)	152,101 (20)	213,735 (52)	112,875 (46)
HA	Physics and astronomy	563,444 (9)	254,071 (14)	481,176 (41)	248,777 (47)
HA	Biology	437,917 (12)	208,886 (22)	430,270 (37)	217,082 (49)
HA	Chemistry	580,000 (17)	259,348 (23)	584,250 (40)	284,269 (60)
HA	Engineering	416,875 (16)	209,057 (21)	259,494 (50)	146,831 (43)
AP	Physics and astronomy	701,786 (7)	90,000 (2)	740,486 (29)	359,783 (23)
AP	Biology	957,143 (7)	481,458 (12)	651,087 (23)	438,227 (31)
AP	Chemistry	983,929 (14)	532,046 (11)	989,688 (32)	550,349 (33)
AP	Engineering	1,441,667 (9)	326,694 (14)	408,443 (38)	223,292 (23)
HP	Physics and astronomy	1,000,000 (4)	418,333 (3)	1,110,577 (24)	455,882 (17)
HP	Biology	1,575,000 (5)	555,500 (10)	856,250 (16)	709,444 (27)
HP	Chemistry	1,172,222 (9)	575,000 (8)	1,187,115 (26)	648,913 (23)
HP	Engineering	1,807,143 (7)	452,000 (34)	472,086 (34)	254,597 (23)

NOTES: Responses were tabulated from the Cornell Institute of Higher Education Research Institute *Survey of Start-Up Costs and Laboratory Space Allocation Rules* that was mailed to 3-5 chairs of selected biological science, physical science, and engineering departments at each research and doctoral university during the summer of 2002. AA: average start-up costs for new assistant professors. HA: high-end start-up costs for new assistant professors. AP: average start-up costs for senior faculty. HP: high-end start-up costs for senior faculty.

SOURCE: RG Ehrenberg, MJ Rizzo, GH Jakubson (2003). *Who Bears the Growing Cost of Science at Universities?* (Working Paper 9627). Cambridge, MA: National Bureau of Economic Research, *http://www.nber.org/papers/c9627.*

Because science and engineering faculty incur costs continuously, some researchers have suggested that the aggregate costs required by new faculty (and not merely the initial start-up costs) should be considered in analyzing the cost of faculty turnover. Joiner[110] has suggested an economic model for calculating the cost of turnover based on net present value (NPV). This model is commonly used in business to project the value of projects. It views faculty as long-term investments by considering all positive and negative cash flows for faculty members over time. Applying the model to faculty costs allows projections of the yearly costs of faculty salary, fringe and personal benefits, supplies and equipment, facility renovation, and other factors that are typically part of the costs accrued by universities in support of faculty (either new or existing). At the same time, the positive cash flows provided by a faculty member to the university (grant support, clinical revenues, and so on) are estimated. In concert, those two parts of the NPV model yield an estimate of the net cost (or financial yield) of a faculty member to a university.[111]

Using the NPV model, one could estimate the length of time a faculty member must remain at an institution for the institution to see a financial return on its investment. From a strictly economic perspective, if a faculty member leaves an institution prematurely (before the NPV model shows a positive yield), the institution loses money. In essence the NPV model dictates that "a dollar today is worth more than a dollar tomorrow."[112] Existing faculty are likely to have a positive NPV, whereas new faculty are likely to show a negative net cost. Accordingly, this model suggests that it is in the best financial interest of the university to direct efforts at retaining faculty. Some effective retention practices are outlined in Box 3-7.

CASE STUDY: CHEMISTRY[113]

To examine the issue of faculty recruitment in more detail, the committee focused on chemistry, a field with a relatively high proportion of women PhDs. Information on the age, sex, and training of chemistry faculty members was obtained from the American Chemical Society's 2001 DGR. The study was limited to faculties in the departments of chemistry, chemistry and biochemistry, or chemical biology at 86 Research I institutions. Only

---

[110]KA Joiner (2005). A strategy for allocating central funds to support new faculty recruitment. *Academic Medicine* 80(3):218-224.

[111]Joiner (2005), ibid.

[112]Joiner (2005), ibid.

[113]This section is based on research commissioned by the committee from Valerie J Kuck, Visiting Professor, Seton Hall University (Retired, Bell Labs).

EXPERIMENTS AND STRATEGIES

BOX 3-7 The University of Washington Faculty Retention Toolkit[a]

"Faculty retention is critical to the health of a university department both for morale reasons and also for economic reasons . . ."
Recognizing that, the University of Washington has developed a toolkit designed to assist department chairs in retaining faculty of all ranks. The toolkit contains nine specific measures that when applied together act to encourage faculty satisfaction and productivity. The measures are designed to be applied to all faculty in a department but are noted to be "particularly important to women and underutilized minorities." The toolkit contains the following measures:

1. **Monitoring the health and welfare of departments**. Avoid disparities in workload, resources, salary, and recognition. Departments should provide regular state-of-the-department reviews, monitor faculty workload, and establish a process of individual faculty review meetings.
2. **Transparency in operations including fair and open promotion and tenure guidelines**. Encourage open communication in the tenure process. Committee members should rotate, and faculty should have access to the evaluation process.
3. **Creating a welcoming department climate**. Professional isolation is a common reason for faculty attrition. Encourage the development of a common department community, including social activities and professional recognition programs.
4. **Mentoring**. Mentoring can be used as a powerful tool for fostering a sense of community and for professional development, learning, and collaboration.
5. **Valuing diversity in the department**. Not all faculty fit the traditional view of a professor. Criteria of excellence should be expanded to include diverse approaches and values, such as involvement in outreach activities or nontraditional approaches to research.
6. **Supporting career development of pretenure faculty**. New and pretenure faculty are at the highest risk of attrition. Specific efforts should be made to support and retain new and pretenure faculty by providing recognition, mentoring, professional development opportunities, and balanced workloads.
7. **Encouraging midcareer professional development**. Professional development activities should continue for midcareer faculty. They include mentoring, professional recognition, and providing support to encourage creativity.
8. **Faculty development programs, benefits, and resources.** Provide ongoing development programs, such as workshops and seminars, to introduce new faculty to programs on campus and renew and reinvigorate existing faculty.
9. **Flexible and accommodating policies and practices**. Flexible family leave policies, dual career partner hiring programs, and transition support programs can play important roles in faculty productivity and retention.

---

[a]University of Washington (2003). *ADVANCE Center for Institutional Change Faculty Retention Toolkit, http://www.engr.washington.edu/advance/resources/Retention/index.html.*

TABLE 3-13 2001 Chemistry Faculty Members, by
Country of Doctorate

	Total	Men	Women
All	2,476	2,218	261 (10.5%)
Foreign PhD	305	284	21 (6.9%)

SOURCE: American Chemical Society (2001). *Directory of Graduate
Research.* Washington, DC: American Chemical Society.

data on persons holding the rank of assistant, associate, or full professor
were ascertained. Persons for whom there was no biographical information
on training or rank were excluded from the study.[114] The hiring data
clearly show that chemistry faculty who have done their graduate work at
Research I universities are overwhelmingly preferred; in addition, women
faculty are drawn from a smaller pool of institutions than men.

Of the 2,476 faculty members at the Research I institutions, 10.5%
were female (Table 3-13). 12.3% of the faculty members earned their doctorates at a non-US institution; of these 6.9% were women—a smaller
fraction than they were of all the faculty members. The top foreign institutions training the greatest number of future faculty members were Cambridge University, University College of London, and Oxford University.

The median and average age of men faculty members were 49 years and
50 ± 11.8 years, respectively. The women faculty members were on average
younger, with a median age of 42 years and an average age of 44 ± 9.2
years. It should be noted that a number of individuals did not give their date
of birth (20 men and 11 females); therefore, they could not be included in
these calculations.

Since 1981 there has been an increase in the hiring/retention of women.
A comparison of the number of men and women faculty members who
received their doctorates during the same years indicates that the growth in
the number of women faculty members has mirrored that of men who
received their doctorate in the same time interval (Figure 3-7).

In 2001, women held 18.3% of the positions at the rank of assistant
professor and 17.9% of associate professor (Table 3-14) at Research I
universities. A much lower percentage, 6.4%, of the full professor positions
were held by women.

Less than 4% of chemistry doctorates were found to hold faculty

---

[114]The DGR contained the names of about 20 faculty members with no other information
on their training or rank.

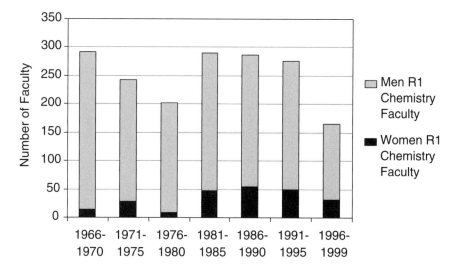

FIGURE 3-7 Comparison of the number of men and women chemistry faculty members at RI institutions.

SOURCE: American Chemical Society (2001). *Directory of Graduate Research*. Washington, DC: American Chemical Society.

positions at Research I institutions. With the exception of the years 1971-1975, a higher percentage of men than women who earned chemistry PhDs ever were employed on Research I university faculties (Table 3-15). It appears that after all the efforts to increase the diversity of faculties, women with doctorates are still lagging behind men in attaining faculty positions at Research I institutions.

There is a strong preference by Research I chemistry departments to hire graduates from a small subset of universities. Ten of the top 11 institutions were common to both men and women faculty (Table 3-16). Eleven

TABLE 3-14 Chemistry Faculty, by Sex and Rank, 2001

Rank	Total	Men	Women
Assistant professor	464	379	85 (18.3%)
Associate professor	408	335	73 (17.9%)
Full professor	1,605	1,502	103 (6.4%)

SOURCE: American Chemical Society (2001). *Directory of Graduate Research*. Washington, DC: American Chemical Society.

TABLE 3-15 Proportion of Chemistry Doctorates Who Obtain Chemistry Faculty Positions at Research I Institutions, by Sex and Year of PhD

Years	Chemistry PhDs Granted	Chemistry PhDs Who Obtain an R1 Faculty Position
Women		
1966-70	686	14 (2.0%)
1971-75	928	28 (3.0%)
1976-80	1,038	8 (0.8%)
1981-85	1,488	47 (3.2%)
1986-90	2,231	54 (2.4%)
1991-95	2,964	50 (1.7%)
1996-99	2,545	31 (1.2%)
Men		
1966-70	8,689	278 (3.2%)
1971-75	8,730	214 (2.5%)
1976-80	6,805	195 (2.9%)
1981-85	7,163	244 (3.4%)
1986-90	7,732	233 (3.0%)
1991-95	7,931	226 (2.8%)
1996-99	7,412	135 (1.8%)

SOURCES: *Chemistry PhDs:* National Science Foundation (1966-2001). *Survey of Earned Doctorates.* Arlington, VA: National Science Foundation; data accessed through WebCASPAR. *Chemistry Faculty:* American Chemical Society (2001). *Directory of Graduate Research.* Washington, DC: American Chemical Society.

departments graduated 54.6% of the US-trained men future RI faculty; Harvard University and the University of California, Berkeley, trained by far the most. For women, 11 departments graduated 51.7% of the US-trained women future RI faculty members, and Berkeley trained by far the most.

During the years 1988-1997, women received 26.4% of the doctorates in chemistry. A lower proportion of women doctorates obtained faculty positions at Research I institutions than did men doctorates (Table 3-17). Of those Research I universities that hired more than 5 faculty, 4 hired above the pool, 7 hired at about the pool, and 19 hired substantially below the available pool of women chemistry PhD graduates.

Programs designed to increase the representation of women chemistry faculty need to take into account cuts in the number of full-time faculty slots at doctorate-granting institutions, as demonstrated by the larger proportion but smaller number of women faculty (Table 3-18). This shrinkage of the tenure track is a general phenomenon. The academic employment of

TABLE 3-16 Institutions Training the Greatest Number of Chemistry Faculty at Research I Institutions, by Sex and Year of PhD

Men Faculty Members[a]		Women Faculty Members[b]	
Institution	Faculty Members[c]	Institution	Faculty Members[c]
Harvard	179	Berkeley	32
Berkeley	175	California Institute of Technology	15
MIT	123	Harvard	10
California Institute of Technology	96	MIT	10
Wisconsin	92	Yale	10
Stanford	82	Cornell	10
University of Illinois, Urbana-Champaign	75	University of Illinois, Urbana-Champaign	8
Columbia	68	UCLA	8
Chicago	62	Stanford	7
Yale	52	Columbia	7
Cornell	51	Chicago	7
Total:	1,055	Total:	124

[a]54.6% of US-trained male faculty members.

[b]51.7% of US-trained female faculty members.

[c]Number of PhDs trained at institution who subsequently hold faculty position at RI institution.

SOURCE: American Chemical Society (2001). *Directory of Graduate Research.* Washington, DC: American Chemical Society.

science and engineering PhDs increased from 118,000 in 1973 to 258,300 in 2003, full-time faculty positions grew more slowly than postdoctoral and other full- and part-time positions, and growth was slower than in the government and business sectors.[115]

CONCLUSION

Individual efforts can have dramatic effects but sustained change is unlikely unless there is a transformation of the process by which students and faculty are educated, trained, recruited, and retained. To increase the numbers of women in science and engineering education and academic careers, policy action should focus on specific lever points: the transition to

[115]National Science Board (2004). *Science and Engineering Indicators, 2004.* Arlington, VA: National Science Foundation, Table 5-6.

TABLE 3-17 Number of Faculty Hired at Selected Research I Institutions, by Sex, 1988-1997

| Hiring Institution[a] | Number of Faculty Hired | | | |
	Men	Women	Total	% Women
University of California, Berkeley	49	19	68	27.9
Harvard University	32	3	35	8.6
California Institute of Technology	27	6	33	18.2
MIT	25	0	25	0.0
Stanford University	23	5	28	17.9
University of Wisconsin, Madison	19	2	21	9.5
University of Illinois, Urbana-Champaign	18	2	20	10.0
Yale University	15	5	20	25.0
University of California, Los Angeles	13	4	17	23.5
University of Chicago	12	4	16	25.0
Columbia University	12	1	13	7.7
Cornell University	12	6	18	33.3
North Carolina State University	10	2	12	16.7
University of Texas, Austin	10	0	10	0.0
Northwestern University	8	1	9	11.1
University of Pennsylvania	8	0	8	0.0
University of Arizona	7	0	7	0.0
University of Michigan, Ann Arbor	7	1	8	12.5
University of Minnesota	7	2	9	22.2
Ohio State University	6	0	6	0.0
University of California, Irvine	5	1	6	16.7
University of California, San Diego	5	1	6	16.7
Princeton University	4	2	6	33.3
University of Colorado, Boulder	3	3	6	50.0
Pennsylvania State University	5	0	5	0.0
Purdue University	5	0	5	0.0
University of Southern California	5	0	5	0.0
Rochester University	4	1	5	20.0
Texas A&M University	4	1	5	20.0
Iowa State University	3	2	5	40.0

[a]Only Research I universities that produced more than 5 faculty members are included.

SOURCE: American Chemical Society (2001). *Directory of Graduate Research.* Washington, DC: American Chemical Society.

college, graduate school faculty interactions, application and recruitment to faculty positions, and retention of faculty.

Increasing the number of women and underrepresented minority-group faculty substantially will require assistance from faculty, individual departments, and schools; oversight and leadership from provosts and presidents; and sustained normative pressure, possibly from external sources. As dis-

TABLE 3-18 Women PhD Chemists Working Full-Time at PhD-Granting Institutions, by Rank and Sex, 1990-2005

	Percent Women					Total Number of Women				
	1985	1990	1995	2000	2005	1985	1990	1995	2000	2005
Full professor	3.1	4.3	5.3	7.9	10.6	1,655	1,623	1,892	1,696	1,274
Associate professor	9.2	12.2	14.5	18.0	23.0	564	517	615	534	414
Assistant professor	12.1	18.4	22.4	25.2	26.0	431	511	557	563	389
Instructor, adjunct	23.4	30.8	40.4	39.9	37.0	141	133	203	271	167
Research appointment	25.3	20.5	22.5	24.0	19.8	225	728	1,153	883	359
Other nonfaculty	N/A	27.6	26.9	30.6	30.0	N/A	225	405	310	172
No ranks	0.0	0.0	23.5	10.0	0.0	11	7	17	13	3
Total	8.3	12.8	15.9	18.5	18.7	3,058	3,744	4,842	4,270	2,844

NOTE: N/A indicates data not available.

SOURCE: American Chemical Society (2006). *Directory of Graduate Research.* Washington, DC: American Chemical Society.

cussed in the previous chapter, the first step is to understand that women are as capable as men of contributing to the science and engineering enterprise. As discussed in the next chapter, the science and engineering community needs to come to terms with the biases and structures that impede women from realizing their potential. The data show that policy changes are sustainable only if they create a "new normal," a new way of doing things. The community needs to work together, across departments, through professional societies, and with funders and federal agencies, to bring about gender equity so that our nation can perform at its full potential.

4

Success and Its Evaluation in Science and Engineering

CHAPTER HIGHLIGHTS

Progress in academic careers depends on evaluations of one's accomplishments by those more senior in a process widely believed to be objective. Research shows, however, that bias negatively affects the evaluations and judgments made about women scientists and engineers and their work. Women consequently are not only underrepresented in numerous science and engineering fields, but are also likely to work in less prestigious institutions than men, to hold lower rank, to take longer to be promoted and tenured, to win fewer awards and honors, and to be named less often to positions of leadership in their institutions and disciplines.

One of the key factors in career advancement is productivity, as measured by the number of published papers that carry the faculty member's name. Women scientists and engineers have long been considered less productive than men because they published fewer papers. Evidence shows, however, that productivity is not an independent characteristic of individuals but rather a reflection of their positions in the academic hierarchy and the access to resources that those positions make possible. When academic position, available resources, type of institution, and other personal and institutional factors are held constant, men and women scientists and engineers are equally productive. Other evidence indicates that women's publications have greater average impact than men's.

Many people believe that discrimination involves explicit, blatant hostility, but current bias against women scientists and engineers is often subtle, implicit, and unexamined. Under prevailing gender schemas, competent women are often viewed as "overaggressive" and "not nice" whereas traditionally subservient women are seen as "incompetent." In addition, organizational rules and policies that appear egalitarian often produce different results for men and women. The playing field is not level. Women and minority groups make up an increasing proportion of the labor force. They also are an increasing proportion of the pool of students from which universities can recruit faculty. To capture and capitalize on this talent, policies adopted when the workplace was more homogeneous need to be changed to create organizational structures that manage diversity effectively. Equity efforts need to address the systemic changes required to build and sustain educational, research, and workplace environments that promote effective participation in an increasingly pluralistic society.

FINDINGS

4.1   Throughout a scientific or engineering career, advancement depends on judgments of one's performance by more senior scientists and engineers. A substantial body of research shows these judgments contain arbitrary and subjective components that disadvantage women. The criteria underlying the judgments developed over many decades when women scientists and engineers were a tiny and often marginal presence and men were considered the norm.

4.2   Gender bias—often unexamined, and held and acted on by people of both sexes who believe themselves unbiased—has affected many women scientists' chances of career progress. Minority-group women face the double bind of racial and gender bias.

4.3   Incidents of bias against individuals not in the majority group tend to have accumulated effects. Small preferences for the majority group can accumulate and create large differences in prestige, power, and position. In academic science and engineering, the advantages have accrued to white men and have translated into larger salaries, faster promotions, and more publications and honors relative to women.

4.4   Women have the qualities needed to succeed in academic careers and do so more readily when given an equal opportunity to achieve. For example, publication productivity is one of the most important factors by which scientists are evaluated for hiring, promotion, and tenure. Women scientists' publication productivity has increased over the last 30 years and now matches men's. The critical factor affecting publication productivity is access to institutional resources; marriage, children, and elder-care responsibilities have minimal effects.

4.5 Career impediments based on gender or racial or ethnic bias deprive the nation of an important source of talented and accomplished researchers.

RECOMMENDATIONS

4.1 Trustees, university presidents, and provosts should provide clear leadership in changing the culture and structure of their institutions to recruit, retain, and promote women—including minority women— into faculty and leadership positions.

4.2 University leaders should work with their faculties and department chairs to examine evaluation practices to focus on quality of contributions and their impact.

4.3 Deans, department chairs, and their tenured faculty should take the responsibility for creating a productive environment and immediately implement programs and strategies shown to be successful in minimizing the effect of biases in recruiting, hiring, promotion, and tenure.

4.4 Faculties and their Senates should initiate a full faculty discussion of climate issues.

4.5 Universities should provide management and leadership training for deans, department heads, search committee chairs, and other faculty with personnel management responsibilities; they should also provide management training to new faculty as part of a professional development core.

4.6 University leaders should, as part of their mandatory management efforts, hold leadership workshops for deans, department heads, search committee chairs, and other faculty with personnel management responsibilities, that include an integrated component on diversity and strategies to overcome bias and gender schemas and strategies for encouraging fair treatment of all people. It is crucial that these workshops are integrated into the fabric of the management of universities and departments.

4.7 Deans, department chairs, and their tenured faculty should develop and implement programs that educate all faculty members and students in their departments on unexamined bias and effective evaluation; these programs should be *integrated into* departmental meetings and retreats, and professional development and teacher-training courses. For example, such programs can be incorporated into research ethics and laboratory management courses for graduate students, postdoctoral scholars, and research staff and can be part of management leadership workshops for faculty, deans, and department chairs.

4.8 Scientific and professional societies should provide professional development training for members that includes a component on bias in evaluation; develop and enforce guidelines to ensure significant representation of women on meeting speaker lists, on editorial boards, and in other significant leadership positions; and work to ensure that women are recognized for their contributions to the nation's scientific and engineering enterprise through nominations for awards and leadership positions.

4.9 Honorary societies should review their nomination and election processes to address the underrepresentation of women in their memberships.

4.10 Journals should examine their entire review process, including the mechanisms by which decisions are made to send a submission to review, and take steps to minimize gender bias, such as blinded reviews.

4.11 Federal funding agencies and foundations should work with scientific and professional societies to host mandatory national meetings that educate members of review panels, university department chairs, and agency program officers about methods that minimize the effects of gender bias in evaluation. The meetings should be held every 2 years for each major discipline and should include data and research presentations on subtle biases and discrimination, department climate surveys, and interactive discussions or role-modeling. Program effectiveness should be evaluated on an ongoing basis.

4.12 Federal funding agencies should collect, store, and publish composite information on demographics, field, award type and budget request, review score, and funding outcome for all funding applications.

4.13 Funding organizations should expand support for research on the efficacy of organizational programs designed to reduce gender bias, and for research on bias, prejudice, stereotype threat, and the role of leadership in achieving gender equity.

To build a successful academic career, a scientist or engineer must succeed—and be seen by colleagues and superiors to have succeeded—at each of a number of increasingly demanding stages of development. Judgments of performance are widely thought to be objective, but a substantial body of research shows that they are significantly affected by biases.

The effect of any specific instance of bias may not in itself be large—receiving a somewhat lower evaluation or a less enthusiastic recommendation than would be true in the absence of bias, not being invited to chair a session at a meeting, or being excluded from conversations in a friendship network.

Such instances of bias would not prevent a person from doing research or pursuing a career. A growing body of evidence shows, however, that such incidents of bias tend to accumulate. In a highly competitive field in which reputation and influence are crucial aspects of professional standing, small preferences can accumulate into large differences in prestige, power, and position (Box 1-4). In academic science and engineering, the advantages accrued to white men have translated into increased salaries, faster promotions, and more publications and honors relative to women.

BUILDING A CAREER

A career has four interlocking dimensions: education, position, productivity, and recognition.[1] Whether a given scientist or engineer succeeds in building such a career depends on a number of factors, some personal and some institutional—as well as luck or happenstance. Does he or she possess the qualities of intellect, character, and personality needed to succeed when there is high-stakes competition? Does he or she work on research questions that produce results worthy of publication and citation? Does he or she succeed in obtaining adequate funding to carry out research? Does he or she develop relationships that help to advance the research and the career? Do the institutions where he or she was educated and trained and where he or she attempts to establish and further a career provide advantages or impose disadvantages that make success more or less likely?

Productivity

College and university faculty members fulfill three main functions: teaching, research, and service in various capacities, such as committee members or department officials involved in running the institution. For purposes of hiring and advancement to higher rank, however, research productivity—defined as authorship of peer-reviewed publications—is

---

[1]MF Fox and JS Long (1995). Scientific careers: Universalism and particularism. *Annual Review of Sociology* 21:45-71. For a discussion of education and position, see Chapter 3.

weighed most heavily,[2] even though efforts have been made to expand the definition of scholarship to include teaching, the integration of knowledge, grants awarded, and applications of research in addition to original discoveries.[3]

Publications, particularly those in high-prestige journals or conference proceedings, carry the greatest weight.[4] That is true regardless of whether the responsibilities of the faculty member's position actually involve doing research or instead focus on administration, teaching, or service. Faculty productivity measured by quantity of publications has also been shown to correlate with stamina and opportunity but not with creativity or measured intelligence.[5] And studies show that teaching and research have opposite relationships to publication productivity: increased time commitments to teaching are associated with decreased publication productivity.[6]

Observers have argued that emphasis on number of publications overvalues the work of men scientists and engineers at the expense of women because of the unequal allocation of tasks that characterizes academic life. Women, on average, devote more time than men to teaching and service, while men, on average, devote more time than women to research.[7] Recent evidence from faculty surveys indicates that more women than men faculty feel that mentoring as a service activity is undervalued by their department (Figure 4-1). Some have suggested that discrepancy reflects value differences between the sexes, namely that women give greater emphasis to such nurturing activities as teaching and advising students and men give greater emphasis to competition. Others argue that the discrepancy reflects the fact that women generally have less power and less opportunity to obtain positions at research universities, where support systems and resources clearly increase faculty productivity.[8]

---

[2]M Skolnik (2000). Does counting publications provide any useful information about academic performance? *Teacher Education Quarterly* 27(2):15-25.

[3]E Boyer (1990). *Scholarship Reconsidered: Priorities of a Professoriate.* Princeton, NJ: Princeton University Press.

[4]Skolnik (2000), ibid; J Long, P Allison, and R McGinnis (1993). Rank advancement in academic careers: Sex differences and the effects of productivity. *American Sociological Review* 58(8):703-722.

[5]MF Fox (1985). Publication, performance and reward in science and scholarship. In *Higher Education: Handbook of Theory and Research*, Vol. 1, ed. JC Smart, New York: Agathon.

[6]MF Fox (1992). Research, teaching, and publication productivity: Mutuality versus competition in academia. *Sociology of Education* 65(4):293-305.

[7]SM Park (1996). Research, teaching and service: Why shouldn't women's work count? *The Journal of Higher Education* 67:46-84; EE Gottlieb and B Keith (1997). The academic research-teaching nexus in eight advanced-industrialized countries. *Higher Education* 34:397-420.

[8]Fox (1985), ibid; H Dundar and DR Lewis (1998). Determinants of research productivity in higher education. *Research in Higher Education* 39(6):607-631.

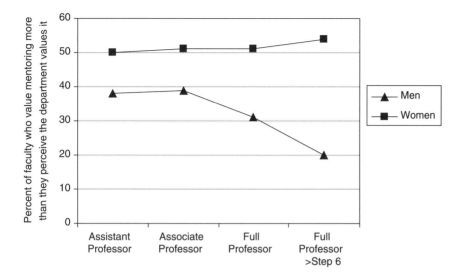

FIGURE 4-1 Individual and perceived institutional value of student mentoring, by rank and sex.

NOTE: The survey asked faculty to rate whether they valued mentoring more, the same, or less than they perceived their department valued mentoring.

SOURCE: University of California Faculty Climate Survey, 2003. Available at *http://www.ucop.edu/acadadv/berkeley-response/faculty-climate.pdf.*

Especially during the probationary years, graduate students, postdoctoral scholars, and assistant professors feel intense pressure to prove that they are not only productive, but serious about their science and engineering careers. They often spend very long hours at their work and try to show a total commitment to an academic career. "By its nature, academic work is potentially boundless: there is always one more question to answer; one more problem to solve; one more piece to read, to write, to see, or to create."[9] In addition, for scientists or engineers working on federal grants, the granting agencies impose time accounting requirements.[10]

---

[9]JW Curtis (2004). Balancing work and family for faculty: Why it's important. *Academe* 90(6), *http://www.aaup.org/publications/Academe/2004/04nd/04ndtoc.htm.*

[10]J Couzin (2006). US rules on accounting for grants amount to more than a hill of beans. *Science* 311:168-169.

Some have suggested that a postdoctoral fellow intent upon a research career should be spending 60-80 hours per week in the laboratory and clinical fellows 80-120 hours per week.[11] The National Science Foundation (NSF) has determined the average workweek for science and engineering faculty to be 50.6 hours per week.[12] At one research university, faculty with and without children reported engaging in professional work 51-60 hours per week, but women faculty with children spend substantially more time than men faculty with children on household and child-care responsibilities (Figure 4-2).[13] Those findings mirror what is seen in a national sample of science and engineering doctorates. Men engage in professional work an average of 0.7 hour per week more than women, but the difference was associated with having children living in the household. Men and women without children reported working 49 hours per week, and women with children—but not men with children—reported working 46 hours per week.[14]

Those statistics belie the nature of work for a scientist or engineer, whose productivity does not depend solely on total hours logged in the laboratory. Indeed, other sorts of work—including reading literature, going to meetings, and discussions with colleagues—may occur off site but are no less important. For persons with major caregiving responsibilities, particularly the care of children or other dependent family members, the limitless time demands of a competitive academic career present a major challenge. The great majority of those bearing caregiving responsibilities are women, and their effort in their family responsibilities does not count as "work" in the academic schema, but rather as a distraction from work.

---

[11]S Kern (2002). Fellowship Goals for PhDs and MDs: A primer on the molecular biology postdoctoral experience. Cancer Biology and Therapy 1:74-85. Kern notes the total hours include research and reading; he also notes that the routine 80-120 hours in clinical training "may be incompatible with a researcher's need for creativity and precision."

[12]TB Hoffer and K Grigorian (2005). *All in a Week's Work: Average Workweeks of Doctoral Scientists and Engineers* (NSF 06-302). Arlington, VA: National Science Foundation, *http://www.nsf.gov/statistics/infobrief/nsf06302/nsf06302.pdf.*

[13]WH Gmelch, PK Wilke, and NP Lovrich (1986). Dimensions of stress among university faculty: Factor-analytic results from a national survey. *Research in Higher Education* 24:266-286; MA Mason and M Goulden (2004). Marriage and baby blues: Redefining gender equity in the academy. *Annals of the American Academy of Political and Social Science* 596(1):86-103, *http://ann.sagepub.com/cgi/reprint/596/1/86.*

[14]Hoffer and Grigorian (2005), ibid.

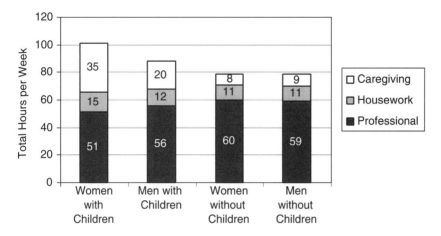

FIGURE 4-2 University of California faculty, 30-50 years old, self-reported hours per week engaged in professional work, housework, and caregiving.

SOURCE: Adapted from: MA Mason, A Stacy, and M Goulden (2003). *University of California Faculty Work and Family Survey, http://ucfamilyedge.berkeley.edu/ workfamily.htm.*

> The "ideal worker" is someone whose commitment to work is unlimited by child bearing or rearing—i.e., a man. Success in academia today continues to be aligned with traditional masculine stereotypes of autonomy, competitiveness and heroic individualism. The 'ideal worker' is someone for whom work is primary, the demands of family, community, and personal life secondary, and time to work unlimited.
>
> —Ellen Ostrow, clinical psychologist and founder of Lawyers Life Coach[15]

Sex Differences in Publication Productivity

Why is publication productivity important? It is through publications that research results are communicated and verified. Publication productivity is both the cause and the effect of status in science and engineering.

---

[15]E Ostrow (2002). The backlash against academic parents. *Chronicle of Higher Education* (February 22), *http://chronicle.com/jobs/2002/02/2002022202c.htm.*

Several researchers have shown that publication productivity reflects and partially accounts for the depressed rank in status of women in science and engineering.[16] However, this assumes that it is the number of papers that is important and does not account for differences in the impact of papers.

In decades past, data have shown an apparent gender gap in the numbers of papers published by men and women faculty. In a study of scientists who received PhDs in 1969-1970, Cole and Zuckerman estimated that, on average, women published slightly more than half (57%) as many papers as men.[17] Little information is available on publication rates for minority-group scientists.[18]

The root of the difference in publication productivity is an essential question. Several studies have examined the effect of family-related factors. Although more women than men leave academe because of family responsibilities, research on the effects of marriage, children, or elder-care responsibilities has yielded mixed results.[19] The critical variable appears to be *access to resources*. A recent longitudinal analysis by Xie and Shauman of faculty in postsecondary institutions in 1969, 1973, 1988, and 1993 shows that the sex difference in research productivity has declined—from a female:male ratio of 0.580:1 in 1969 to 0.817:1 in 1993. In that period, the primary factor affecting women scientists' research productivity was their overall structural position, such as institutional affiliation and rank. When type of institution, teaching load, funding level, and research assistance are factored in, the productivity gap disappears.[20]

---

[16]G Sonnert and G Holton (1996). Career patterns of women and men in the sciences. *American Scientist* 84:63-71; EG Creamer (1998). Assessing faculty publication productivity: Issues of equity (ASHE-ERIC Higher Education Report 26(2)). Washington, DC: George Washington University; LJ Sax, S Hagedorn, M Arredondo, and FA Dicrisi (2002). Faculty research productivity: Exploring the role of gender and family-related factors. *Research in Higher Education* 43(4):423-446; MF Fox (2005). Gender, family characteristics, and publication productivity among scientists. *Social Studies of Science* 35(1):131-150.

[17]JR Cole and H Zuckerman (1984). The productivity puzzle: Persistence and change in patterns of publication of men and women scientists. *Advances in Motivation and Achievement* 2:217-258; see also JS Long (1992). Measures of sex differences in scientific productivity. *Social Forces* 71:159-178; there appears to be a publication productivity gap between men and women and white and minority students in graduate school, see Chapter 3 and MT Nettles and CM Millett (2006). *Three Magic Letters: Getting to PhD*. Baltimore, MD: Johns Hopkins Press.

[18]MF Fox and JS Long (1995). Scientific careers: Universalism and particularism. *Annual Review of Sociology* 21:45-71; W Pearson (1985). *Black Scientists, White Society, and Colorless Science: A Study of Universalism in American Science*. Millwood, NY: Associated Faculty.

[19]Reviewed in LJ Sax, S Hagedorn, M Arredondo, and FA Dicrisi (2002), ibid.

[20]Y Xie and KA Shauman (1998). Sex differences in research productivity: New evidence about an old puzzle. *American Sociological Review* 63(6):847-870.

Another analysis provides a clear illustration of the correlation between productivity, institutional affiliation, and rank.[21] Overall, men academic scientists and engineers produced 30% more publications than women academic scientists and engineers, but when men at Research I universities were compared with women at the same type of institution, the productivity gap fell to 25%. Women were much more likely to be in non-tenure-track posts than men, and comparing only scientists and engineers who held faculty positions reduced the productivity gap to 13%. Focusing on tenured faculty members found tenured men with only 8% more publications than their women tenured colleagues. The difference in publication productivity between men and women who are full professors of science or engineering at the Research I institutions was under 5%.

The effect of a scientist's institutional affiliation on his or her productivity is so great that the prestige of the department or university has been found to affect scientists' productivity, rather than the other way around. Prestige serves as a symbolic stand-in for an array of characteristics that can foster or hamper productivity, including financial, physical, and staff resources and intellectual environment. Evidence shows that when scientists move to more prestigious institutions, their productivity increases.[22]

Another essential question is whether number of papers is the appropriate metric of productivity. In a study of biochemists, Long found that articles by women received, on average, more citations than articles with men primary authors.[23] Some have argued that both quantitative and qualitative measures of productivity should be taken into account in making important decisions about a scientist's career.[24] Indeed, recent metrics have been developed to measure citations of an article—its "impact factor"—as well as the prestige of the journal in which it is published.[25]

Recognition

Another indicator of scientific productivity, and one especially germane to career advancement, is recognition in the field. Being invited to

[21]National Research Council (2001). *From Scarcity to Visibility: Gender Differences in the Careers of Doctoral Scientists and Engineers*. Washington, DC: National Academy Press, *http://www.nap.edu/catalog/5363.html*.

[22]P Allison and S Long (1990). Departmental effects on scientific productivity. *American Sociological Review* 55:119-25.

[23]JS Long (1992). Measures of sex differences in scientific productivity. *Social Forces* 71:159-178.

[24]Sonnert and Holton (1996), ibid.

[25]P Ball (2006). Prestige is factored into journal ratings. *Nature* 439(16):770-771, *http://www.nature.com/nature/journal/v439/n7078/pdf/439770a.pdf*.

speak at major professional society meetings is one type of recognition, but women are not well represented among symposium speakers and keynotes (Box 4-1).

Recognition of lifetime achievement by election to a high-prestige honorific society is a cherished honor. However, the numbers of women elected to such societies as the National Academy of Sciences, the National Academy of Engineering, the Institute of Medicine, the American Academy of Arts and Sciences, and the American Philosophical Society, or awarded such prestigious honors as the Lasker Prize or the National Medal of Science have been small (Table 4-1).

Some organizations point to the low numbers of women who are "eligible" for honors and awards; to a first approximation, the nomination pool for lifetime achievement honors, such as election to an honorific society, is the cohort who received PhDs about 30 years ago. Indeed, the representation of women in that cohort is quite small. Recent classes of electees, however, have included younger people, and not all societies elect solely PhD recipients. A recent report from the InterAcademy Council (IAC) concludes that the disproportionately small number of women in the science and technology enterprise, particularly in leadership positions, is a major hindrance to strengthening science capacity worldwide.[26] The IAC called upon all academies to address the underrepresentation of women in their memberships, in particular by implementing internal management practices that encourage and support women, and by influencing policy makers and other leaders to bring about broader change.

As with the tenure-track applicant pool (see Chapter 3), the nominee pool for honors and awards likely underrepresents the available pool of excellent women researchers. A case in point is the recent experience with the Pioneer Awards offered by the National Institutes of Health (NIH) (Box 4-2). In its first year, not only did the new program designed for early-career researchers not select any women, but all the awardees were well established and in middle to late career. In response to community concern, NIH took the time and energy to diagnose the problem, and found that several small changes in the program announcement and attention to the selection process changed the outcome greatly in the program's second year.

One issue brought to the fore by the Pioneer Award was the difference in the number of women who self-nominated as opposed to those who were nominated by mentors or peers. It appears, as with hiring, that relying on

---

[26]InterAcademy Council (2006). *Women for Science*. Amsterdam: InterAcademy Council, *http://www.interacademycouncil.net/?id=11228*. The IAC is an organization created by 90 science academies across the globe.

established networks can lead to underrepresentation of women in the nominee pool.[27] One organization, the Committee on the Advancement of Women Chemists (COACh), is working with professional societies to ensure that qualified women are nominated for awards and leadership positions (Box 4-3).

LEADERSHIP POSITIONS

Women, especially minority-group women, are underrepresented in science and engineering faculties at all levels.[28] The dearth of women is even more pronounced in the upper tiers of the academy. In addition to being outnumbered, women have lower salaries,[29] are awarded less grant money,[30] and perceive the scientific workplace as unwelcoming and even hostile.[31] Few women are chief editors of top-rated journals and their representation varies substantially by field (Table 4-2). Even a cursory glance at most organization charts in research organizations shows that women are underrepresented, not only in senior faculty positions but also in leadership positions. According to a recent study of academic medical

---

[27]Networks have also been shown to affect decisions to publish; as gender balance improves within a field, network access changes, and the representation of women as authors also improves. See JM McDowell, LD Singell, and M Stater (2006). Two to tango? Gender differences in the decisions to publish and coauthor. *Economic Inquiry* 44(1):153-168.

[28]DJ Nelson (2005). *A National Analysis of Diversity in Science and Engineering Faculties at Research Universities, http://cheminfo.chem.ou.edu/faculty/djn/diversity/briefings/Diversity %20Report%20Final.pdf;* J Handelsman, N Cantor, M Carnes, D Denton, E Fine, B Grosz, V Hinshaw, C Marrett, S Rosser, D Shalala, and J Sheridan (2005). More women in science. *Science* 309(5738):1190-1191; CA Trower and RP Chait (2002). Faculty diversity: Too little for too long. *Harvard Magazine* 104(4), *http://www.harvard-magazine.com/on-line/ 030218.html.*

[29]Trower and Chait (2002), ibid; PD Umbach (2006). *Gender Equity in the Academic Labor Market: An Analysis of Academic Disciplines.* Paper presented at the 2006 annual meeting of the American Educational Research Association, San Francisco, CA, April 7-11, *http://myweb.uiowa.edu/pumbach/AERA2006_equitypaper.pdf.*

[30]SD Hosek, AG Cox, B Ghosh-Dastidar, A Kofner, N Ramphal, J Scott, and SH Berry (2005). *Gender Differences in Major Federal External Grant Programs.* Washington, DC: RAND.

[31]D Olsen, SA Maple, and FK Stage (1995). Women and minority faculty job satisfaction: Professional role interests, professional satisfactions, and institutional fit. *Journal of Higher Education* 66(3):267-293; Trower and Chait (2002), ibid; ALW Sears (2003). Image problems deplete the number of women in academic applicant pools. *Journal of Women and Minorities in Science and Engineering* 9:169-181; LA Krefting (2003). Intertwined discourses of merit and gender: Evidence from academic employment in the USA. *Gender, Work, and Organization* 10(2):260-278; RR Callister (2006). The impact of gender and department climate on job satisfaction and intentions to quit for faculty in sciene and engineering fields. *Journal of Technology Transfer* 31:367-375.

EXPERIMENTS AND STRATEGIES

BOX 4-1 Speaker Representation at Scientific and Professional Society Meetings

The invitation to speak at a professional or academic society conference is one of the key benchmarks of a successful academic career. To ensure the proper recognition and advancement of women scholars in science and engineering, it is essential that the process for inviting conference speakers be absent of gender bias. Invited and distinguished conference speakers are usually selected by program committees and the speaker nomination process often fails to ensure adequate gender representation. Program committees lacking gender diversity tend to result in a lack of diversity among invited speakers.[a] The common practice of program committee members nominating themselves as invited speakers augments this effect.[b]

Table B4-1 presents data on the percentage of invited speakers to speak at prestigious symposia[c] at professional and scientific society conferences who were women in a number of disciplines. It has proven challenging to ensure that speakers at society-sponsored events reflect the diverse membership of the society with respect to appropriate representation by gender.

TABLE B4-1 Speakers at 2004-2005 Scientific and Professional Society Meetings, by Sex

Conference (2004-2005)[d]	% of Invited Speakers Who Were Women	Total Number of Invited Speakers
American Association for Artificial Intelligence (AAAI)	17	12
American Chemical Society (ACS)	18	174
American Society for Cell Biology (ASCB)	36	22
American Society of Mechanical Engineers (ASME)[e]	6	17
International Conference on Computer Graphics and Interactive Techniques[f]	17	78
Oceanic Engineering Society Meeting[g]	4	72
Federation of Clinical Immunological Societies (FOCIS)[h]	22	480
Society for Neuroscience (SFN)	9	11

SOURCES: *www.aaai.org, www.acs.org, www.ascb.org, www.siggraph.org, www.ieee.org, www.focisnet.org, www.sfn.org.*

Some societies have implemented speaker selection criteria to mandate that those who propose symposia specifically consider diversity of suggested speakers. At the American Society for Cell Biology (ASCB) 45th Annual Meeting, 36% of the invited speakers were women, which is an appropriate reflection of the nearly

40% of women professors in biological sciences. ASCB employs the following speaker selection guidelines:[i]

- Invite co-organizers who look different than you do.
- Actively seek suggestions for speakers.
- Scan programs of past meetings in different, but related, fields.
- Avoid the usual suspects (avoid the cadre of major figures who speak multiple times and "[fly] in just for the talk").
- Adjust your tentative program to ensure diversity.

The Federation of Clinical Immunological Societies (FOCIS) has gone one step further and reformed the way in which invited speakers are selected. For mini-symposium speakers at their 12th annual International Congress of Immunology (participants were from 86 countries, and about half were women), FOCIS instituted an abstract review process that was blinded as to author and institution. This resulted in 48% of 976 oral presenters being women. For speakers and chairs, the program committee used research excellence and publication impact criteria for speaker selection. Twenty-two percent of the 480 invited speakers were women, a substantial increase from the previous year, when only 10% of the invited speakers were women.[j]

Other organizations that sponsor and organize scientific conferences instruct and encourage conference planners to include appropriate gender representation among invited speakers and planning committees. The NIH encourages a "concerted effort to achieve appropriate representation of women" as conference organizers, speakers, and attendees for all meetings it sponsors.[k] Gordon Research Conferences and Keystone Symposia sponsor topically focused interdisciplinary research symposia with a small number of participants to foster discussion and collaboration. Both organizations instruct conference organizers to represent the gender diversity of the discipline when inviting conference speakers.[l]

---

[a]S Forsburg (2004). Ensuring diversity at the podium. *The ASCB Newletter* 27(2):13-14.
[b]A Lagendijk (2005). Pushing for power. *Nature* 438:429.
[c]Prestigious symposia include plenary sessions, keynote addresses, panels, named lectures, and award symposia.
[d]All conferences except FOCIS were held in 2005.
[e]Data from 2005 International Mechanical Engineering Congress and Exhibition.
[f]Association for Computing Machinery (ACM) conference of 2005 with highest attendance (~29,000).
[g]Institute of Electrical and Electronics Engineers (IEEE) conference of 2005 with highest attendance (~50,000).
[h]Data from 12th International Congress of Immunology.
[i]Forsburg (2004), ibid.
[j]MM Newkirk, E Richie, and JK Lunney (2005). Advancing women scientists: The immunology experience. *Nature Immunology* 6(9):855.
[k]*http://grants.nih.gov/grants/guide/notice-files/NOT-OD-03-066.html.*
[l]*http://www.grc.org, www.keystonesymposia.org.*

TABLE 4-1 Percentage of Women Nominated to an Honorific Society or for a Prestigious Award and the Percentage of Women Nominees Elected or Awarded, 1996-2005

	% Nominated	% Nominees Elected
Society		
American Philosophical Society[a]	14.6	23.7
Mathematical and physical sciences	19.0	24.0
Biological sciences	11.5	23.3
American Academy of Arts and Sciences	N/A	15.8
Mathematical and physical sciences	N/A	11.6
Biological sciences	N/A	20.0
Institute of Medicine[b]	19.2	22.7
National Academy of Engineering	5.3	6.0
Aerospace engineering	3.1	7.1
Bioengineering	6.9	4.6
Chemical engineering	5.9	5.2
Civil engineering	4.1	2.4
Computer science and engineering	11.9	8.6
Electric power and energy systems engineering	3.1	2.3
Electronics engineering	2.8	3.7
Industrial manufacturing and operations systems engineering	4.9	4.3
Materials engineering	5.7	7.8
Mechanical engineering	2.5	5.6
Petroleum mining and geological engineering	9.5	8.7
Special fields and interdisciplinary engineering	5.7	6.3
National Academy of Sciences	12.5	15.6
Award		
Lasker Prize	6.1	4.0
National Medal of Science[c]	N/A	12.0
Behavioral and social science	N/A	0
Biological sciences	N/A	26.1
Chemistry	N/A	15.4
Engineering	N/A	0
Mathematical and computer sciences	N/A	15.4
Physical sciences	N/A	0
NIH Pioneer Award[d]		
First program year (2004)	22.0	0.0
Second program year (2005)	26.0	46.2

[a]Data from 2000 to 2005.
[b]Data from 1999 to 2005.
[c]Data from 1996 to 2003.
[d]Award first offered in 2004.

N/A: demographic information not solicited or maintained for nominations.

SOURCE: Data were provided by membership departments of listed organizations and awards.

centers, women made up 18% of section chiefs, 11% of department chairs, and 10% of deans.[32] At the Department of Energy national laboratories, women make up 11% of scientific directors and 3% of directors and deputy directors (Table 4-3). Similar proportions of women serve in leadership posts at the NSF engineering research centers and science and technology centers (Tables 4-4 and 4-5).

Grants and Contracts

Grants and contracts offer another measure of leadership. At NIH over the last 20 years the participation of women has grown in all extramural grant budget categories. For the traditional research project grants (RPGs), also known as R01s, the percentage going to women increased from 17% to 24% from 1990 to 2004. Over the period 1983-2004, the share of grants going to women has increased from 13% to 24% for all RPGs[33] and 17% to 39% for career development awards. Representation of women among principal investigators on center awards has increased from 4% to 17%, but this is still far below the level of participation of women in the individual investigator grant categories.

The average size of grants varies considerably across budget category, and the differences in sizes of grants to women and men vary as well. In FY 2004, the biggest differences in the average award are for centers, where women serve as principal investigators on grants that are on average only 60% as large as those for men. The average size of the NIH Small Business Innovation Research Program and Small Business Technology Transfer Program awards for women slightly exceeds that of men. And the average RPG and career development award for women is about 90% of the size for men (Figure 4-3).[34]

Evaluation of Leaders

Underlying this skewed representation of women in leadership positions are sex differences in the expectation and evaluation of leadership. For example, both men and women hold more negative attitudes toward women than toward men authorities, although women's explicit attitudes

---

[32]Association of American Medical Colleges (2005). *Analysis in Brief: The Changing Representation of Men and Women in Academic Medicine.* Washington, DC: AAMC.

[33]The RPG category constitutes 79% of NIH extramural awards and 75% of the extramural dollars.

[34]Office of Extramural Research (2005). *Sex/Gender in the Biomedical Science Workforce.* National Institutes of Health, *http://grants2.nih.gov/grants/policy/sex_gender/q_a.htm#q5.*

EXPERIMENTS AND STRATEGIES

BOX 4-2 Pioneer Award

The NIH director's Pioneer Award was created in 2004 as part of the NIH Roadmap for Medical Research. The award was designed to promote "exceptionally creative scientists taking innovative approaches to major challenges in biomedical research." In its first year, outside nominations and self-nominations were solicited. The application consisted of a five-page essay and three letters of recommendation. Of the 1,300 nominations, 20 applicants were asked to interview. All of the awardees were men. Although all were doing exceptional research, they were not representative of the intended target audience—early career researchers.

The award program was in its first year, and NIH did not anticipate the large number of nominations, most of which occurred in the last few days. To review the applications, NIH had to recruit a sizable number of additional reviewers in a short period. As a result, 60 of the 64 reviewers were men. In addition, because self-nominations and external nominations were accepted, reviewers found it difficult to compare self-nomination essays describing applicants' own accomplishments with external nomination essays written on behalf of the nominees. Carnes et al.[a] suggest several evidence-based reasons why women scientists might have been disadvantaged in the Pioneer Award's nomination and selection process, including:

- Time pressure placed on evaluators would make it more likely for them to rely on stereotypic assumptions that favor men as scientists.
- Absence of face-to-face discussion of candidates disadvantages women.
- Ambiguity of performance criteria in combination with the word leadership tends to favor men.
- Weight given to letters of recommendation negatively affects women because letters written for women tend to be shorter, have more references to personal life, include more gender terms, contain fewer standout adjectives, and have more gender-stereotypic adjectives.
- The need for finalists to make a formal presentation where the nominee, and not the nominee's work, was the focus of the evaluation favors men because men scientists are more likely to meet the implicit assumption of what a scientist, pioneer, and leader should look like.

are more egalitarian than men's.[35] Martell and DeSmet had 151 managers judge the leadership effectiveness of men and women middle managers on various categories of leadership behavior.[36] They found that both men and women managers rated men higher on delegating behavior, and rated

---

[35]LA Rudman and SE Kilianski SE (2000). Implicit and explicit attitudes toward female authority. *Personality and Social Psychology Bulletin* 26(11):1315-1328.

[36]RF Martell and AL DeSmet (2001). A diagnostic-ratio approach to measuring beliefs about the leadership abilities of male and female managers. *Journal of Applied Psychology* 86(6):1223-1231.

Jeremy Berg, director of National Institute of General Medical Sciences, and Judith Greenberg, director of the Division of Genetics and Developmental Biology, took on the challenge of revamping the award selection process in 2005. Together, they implemented some minor changes that had a dramatic impact on the result. These changes included:

- Removed leadership potential from criterion.
- Engaged in outreach to women, minorities, and early career scientists to make sure people felt included and welcome to apply. The proportion of women in the applicant pool increased from 20% in the initial response to the call for applications in 2004 to 26% in 2005; and from 10% in the request for a full proposal in 2004 to 35% in 2005.
- Recruited a balanced pool of reviewers. There were 4% women in 2004 and 44% in 2005. Carnes also suggests that a reduction in the number of applicants (from 1,300 in 204 to 840 in 2005) and greater familiarity with the application process may have reduced time pressure on reviewers, and thus decreased the effects of implicit biases.[b] The fact that the award process was also in the public spotlight may also have reduced the likelihood that reviewers used stereotypes to identify candidates.[c]
- Oriented reviewers to read the nomination announcement, which especially encouraged women and minority-group members to apply. Asked reviewers to consider "innovation density" to level the playing field for younger applicants.
- Changed nominations to only self-nomination.

In 2005, of the 13 recipients of the Pioneer Award, 6 were women, one was an African American man, and all the winners were significantly younger—evidence that the procedural changes created the opportunity and environment in which a diverse pool of candidates could be seriously considered.

---

[a]M Carnes, S Geller, E Fine, J Sheridan, and J Handelsman (2005). NIH Director's Pioneer Awards: Could the selection process be biased against women? *Journal of Women's Health* 14(8):684-691; ML Carnes (2006). Gender: Macho language and other deterrents. *Nature* 442:868.

[b]M Carnes (2006). Gender: Macho language and other deterrents. *Nature* 442:868.

[c]PE Tetlock (1985). Accountability: A social check on the fundamental attribution error. *Social Psychology Quarterly* 48:227-236.

women higher on consulting behavior. Women rated women middle managers more favorably on inspiring, mentoring, problem solving, rewarding, and supporting; men either rated men and women equally or rated men more favorably on these behaviors.

Sinclair and Kunda found that the rating of women evaluators depended more on the nature of the evaluation than that of men.[37] Specifi-

---

[37]L Sinclair and Z Kunda (2000). Motivated stereotyping of women: She's fine if she praised me but incompetent if she criticized me. *Personality and Social Psychology Bulletin* 26(11):1329-1342.

EXPERIMENTS AND STRATEGIES

BOX 4-3 Breaking through the "Polycarbonate Ceiling"— The Committee on the Advancement of Women Chemists

The Committee on the Advancement of Women Chemists (COACh) was formed in 1998 and is working to increase the numbers and success of women scientists in academe. Initially focused on women in chemistry, it has expanded to include men and women in geology, physics, mathematics, computer science, and biology. COACh has two important missions: first, it brings senior women chemists together for networking events, interactive workshops, and mentoring support; and second, it actively seeks to improve the professional lot of women scientists at academic institutions at all levels.

COACh offers a series of workshops at professional meetings and institutions that are designed to enhance leadership skills, to expand women's professional networks, to improve institutional climate, and to level the playing field for all faculty. COACh has implemented professional skills workshops that provide negotiation, management, and leadership skills to help women to achieve their professional goals as faculty in the sciences. Through a variety of instructional and interactive approaches, these sessions provide an opportunity to share experiences with others and engage in small group discussions. Over 1,100 women academic scientists from around the country have participated in these workshops in the last 4 years. Nine of 10 women who have taken COACh workshops report increased negotiation and communication skills and reduced workplace stress.[a] Over 90% of COACh workshop attendees report mentoring other women in the skills they learned.[b] COACh workshops specifically designed to address issues of minority-group women scientists have recently been launched.

COACh also conducts research on institutional climate and factors contributing to the low number and advancement of women chemistry faculty, including collecting data and personal stories of sexism that women scientists still suffer.[c] COACh is working to ensure that women are nominated for awards and leadership positions and is working with academic institutions to help them to eliminate biases and barriers that work against underrepresented groups in the sciences. COACh efforts are jointly sponsored by NSF, NIH, and the Department of Energy (DOE). More details about COACh and its programs can be found on its Web site at *http://coach.uoregon.edu.*

---

[a]MW Leslie (2005). *Women Learn How to Pierce the 'Polycarbonate Ceiling' in Chemistry Careers. http://www. Eurekalert.org/pub_release/2005-09/uoo-wlh092105.php.*
[b]G Richmond (2006). Presentation to the committee, February 13, 2006.
[c]A Schneider (2000). Support for a rare breed: Tenured women scientists. *Chronicle of Higher Education,* November 10.

TABLE 4-2 Percentage of Women Chief Editors at Top-Ranked Journals, by Field

Field	Top Journals[a]	% Women Editors[b]
Overall	CA: A Cancer Journal for Clinicians, Annual Review of Immunology, New England Journal of Medicine, Annual Review of Biochemistry, Nature Reviews Cancer, Science, Nature Reviews Immunology, Reviews of Modern Physics, Nature Reviews Molecular Cell Biology, Cell	40%
Biology	PLOS Biology, Quarterly Review of Biology, FASEB Journal, Bioessays, Biological Reviews, Philosophical Transactions of the Royal Society B, Bioscience, Journal of Biological Rhythms, Proceedings of the Royal Society, London: B-Biological Sciences, Radiation Research	10%
Medical	New England Journal of Medicine, Lancet, JAMA, Annals of Internal Medicine, Annual Review of Medicine, British Medical Journal, PLOS Medicine, Archives of Internal Medicine, Canadian Medical Association Journal	50%
Chemistry[c]	Chemical Reviews, Surface Science Reports, Nature Materials, Progress in Solid State Chemistry, Chemical Society Reviews, Annual Review of Physical Chemistry, Accounts of Chemical Research, Aldrichimica Acta, Nano Letters (2 chief editors), Coordination Chemistry Reviews	9%
Computer science[c]	ACM Computing Surveys, Bioinformatics, Human-Computer Interactions, Journal of the American Medical Informatics Association, VLDB Journal (3 chief editors), Journal of Machine Learning Resarch, Neuroinformatics (3 chief editors), IEEE Transactions on Pattern Analysis and Machine Intelligence, International Journal of Computer Vision (2 chief editors),	13%
Engineering[c]	Annual Review of Biomedical Engineering, Progress in Quantum Electronics, Journal of Catalysis, Biomaterials, Chemistry and Physics of Carbon, Environmental Science and Technology, International Journal of Plasticity, IEEE Transactions on Medical Imaging, Proceedings of IEEE, IEEE Transactions on Pattern Analysis	0%

continued

TABLE 4-2 Continued

Field	Top Journals[a]	% Women Editors[b]
Mathematics	Journal of the American Mathematics Society, Annals of Mathematics, Computational Complexity, Journal de Mathematiques Pures et Appliquees, Bulletin of the American Mathematics Society, ACTA Math-Djursholm, Inventiiones Mathematica, Journal of the European Mathematics Society, Memoirs of the American Mathematical Society, and Duke Mathematical Journal	20%
Physics	Reviews of Modern Phyics, Annual Review of Astronomy and Astrophysics, Surface Science Reports, Nature Materials, Astrophysics Journal Supplement Series, Materials Science and Engineering Reviews, Physical Reports, Advances in Physics, Astronomy and Astrophysics Review, Reports on Progress in Physics	0%
Psychology	Annual Review of Psychology. Psychological Bulletin, Psychology Review, Psychotherapy and Psychosomatics, Neurobiology of Learning and Memory, Cognitive Psychology, Psychosomatic Medicine, Health Psychology, Psychological Medicine, Biological Psychology, and Cognitive Psychology	9%
Social sciences[c]	Research in Organic Behavior, Evolution of Human Behavior, Econometrica, Social Science and Medicine, Psycho-Oncology, Sociology of Health and Illness, AIDS and Behavior, Future Child, Accident Analysis and Prevention, Hastings Center Report	40%

[a]Top 10 journals were determined by impact factor using the Thompson ISI rating system; in some fields there are more than 10 due to a tie.

[b]Included only chief editor position; some journals have more than one chief editor.

[c]The top 10 journals in these fields were determined by looking at all subdisciplines within the larger field using Thompson ISI Journal Citation Reports, for example, Chemistry includes the subdisciplines of Physical Chemistry, Analytical Chemistry, Biochemistry, etc.

SOURCE: *Journals:* Thompson ISI 2005 Journal Citation Reports. *Editors:* individual journal Web sites, August 2006.

cally, women evaluators were viewed as less competent than men evaluators after providing negative feedback to a rater but not after providing positive feedback. Other studies find mixed evidence of sex differences in the evaluation of leaders. A meta-analysis of perceptions of men's and women's leadership showed no sex differences when the data were analyzed in the aggregate. Yet, although men and women were found to be equally effective in leadership positions overall, both sexes were found to be more effective in gender-congruent roles.[38] That these findings from the world of business cross into science and engineering is evident in Tables 4-2 to 4-4 in the difference in representation of women in scientific director positions versus administrative director positions.

EVALUATION OF SUCCESS

People pursue their careers in organizations and workplaces populated by others and governed by rules, norms, and practices quite independent of any individual worker's control. Persistent wage and employment sex differentials exist in the labor market as a whole and for scientists in particular.[39] Research has amply documented discrimination against women and minority-group members in hiring and evaluation, especially in traditionally male fields.[40] Social psychologists argue that most discriminatory behavior takes the form of implicit bias and results from gender schemas, the largely unexamined sets of ideas people hold concerning gender roles.[41] For example, women's performance ratings exceed men's in jobs that are sex-typed female, one meta-analysis found, but suffer in comparison with men in jobs considered male.[42] One program is using theater to examine the heretofore unexamined biases that affect interactions and decision making (Box 4-4).

---

[38]AH Eagly and MC Johannesen-Schmidt (2001). The leadership styles of women and men. *Journal of Social Issues* 57(4):781-797.

[39]JG Altonji and RM Blank (1999). Race and gender in the labor market. In *Handbook of Labor Economics, Volume 3*, eds. O Ashenfelter and D Card. Amsterdam: Elsevier Science; D Ginther (2001). Does science discriminate against women? *Federal Reserve Bank of Atlanta Working Papers* No. 02(2001):66, *http://www.frbatlanta.org/publica/work_papers/wp01/wp0102.htm.*

[40]V Nieva and B Gutek (1980). Sex effects on evaluation. *Academy of Management Review* 5:267-276; ME Heilman, AS Wallen, D Fuchs, and MM Tamkins (2004). Penalties for success: Reactions to women who succeed at male gender-typed tasks. *Journal of Applied Psychology* 89(3):416-427; for example, see: M Bertrand and S Mullianathan (2004). Are Emily and Greg more employable that Lakisha and Jamal? *American Economic Review* 94(4):991-1013.

[41]V Valian (1998). *Why So Slow? The Advancement of Women.* Cambridge, MA: MIT Press; MR Banaji and AG Greenwald (1995). Implicit gender stereotyping in judgments of fame. *Journal of Personality and Social Psychology* 68:181-198; M Biernat and ER Thompson (2002). Shifting standards and contextual variation in stereotyping. *European Review of Social Psychology* 12:103-137; LA Rudman and P Glick (2001). Gender effects on social influence and hireability: Prescriptive gender stereotypes and backlash towards agentic women. *Journal of Social Issues* 57(4):743-762.

[42]HK Davison and MJ Burke (2000). Sex discrimination in simulated employment contexts: A meta-analytic investigation. *Journal of Vocational Behavior* 56:225-248.

TABLE 4-3 Department of Energy National Laboratory Leadership Positions

Laboratory	Director and Deputy Directors		Scientific Directors		Administrative Directors		Notes
	Male	Female	Male	Female	Male	Female	
Ames	2	0	11	0	7	7	Division directors and unit directors
Argonne	3	0	23	0	12	5	Division directors, associate directors, and unit directors
Brookhaven	3	0	17	1	22	8	Directors, associate directors, and unit directors
Fermi	4	0	19	2	10	5	Division directors, division deputies, unit heads and associate unit heads
Idaho	4	0	6	0	8	3	Directors, deputy directors, and associate laboratory directors
Lawrence Berkeley	3	0	15	0	11	0	Directors, deputies, and associates
Lawrence Livermore	3	1	8	2	7	3	Directors, associate laboratory directors, division directors, and department heads

Los Alamos	2	0	4	1	2	1	Director, deputy directors, and associate directors
Renewable Energy	1	0	15	7	7	2	Directors, associate laboratory directors, and division directors
Oak Ridge	3	0	5	1	10	3	Directors, deputy directors, associate laboratory directors, and division directors
Pacific Northwest	3	0	4	0	6	4	Directors, associate laboratory directors, and division directors
Sandia	1	0	1	2	N/A	N/A	Director and deputy directors
Total (%)	32 (3%)	1 (3%)	128	16 (11%)	102	41 (29%)	

NOTES: **Scientific directorates** include Biology, Science and Technology, Research, Materials Science, Engineering, Chemistry, and Physics. **Administrative directorates** include Human Resources; Diversity; Administration; Security and Facility Operations; Technical Services; Information Technology; Legal; Business Support Services; Communications; Public Affairs; Environment, Safety, Health and Quality; Partnerships; Technology Transfer and Economic Development; Education Programs; and Infrastructure. N/A = not available.

SOURCE: Personnel data obtained from organizational charts published on-line by each laboratory. Data retrieved February 16, 2006.

TABLE 4-4 National Science Foundation Engineering Research Center Leadership Positions

Engineering Research Center (ERC)	Director and Deputy Directors		Scientific Directors		Administrative Directors		Notes
	Male	Female	Male	Female	Male	Female	
Georgia Tech/Emory Center for the Engineering of Living Tissues	2	1	7	1	0	4	
Computer-Integrated Surgical Systems and Technology ERC	1	0	1	1	3	2	
Biomimetic MicroElectronic Systems	2	0	7	0	1	3	
VaNTH ERC in Bioengineering Educational Technologies	4	2	4	0	1	1	Directors includes director, codirector, and assistant director
Engineered Biomaterials ERC	1	1	3	0	2	0	
Center for Advanced Engineering Fibers and Films	2	0	2	1	2	2	
Center for Environmentally Beneficial Catalysis	5	0	10	1	5	1	Directors include director and associate director. Each person has one or two titles; some may appear in multiple columns
ERC for Reconfigurable Machining Systems	2	0	3	1	1	2	Science directors includes thrust leader and senior team member

Center							Notes
Pacific Earthquake ERC	2	0	7	1	2	2	Each person has one or two titles; they may appear both on director and science director columns
Mid-America Earthquake Center	2	0			1	2	Thrust leader information not available
Multidisciplinary Center for Earthquake Engineering Research	2	0	4	1	6	1	
ERC for Extreme Ultraviolet Science & Technology	1	1	5	2	2	1	One woman is both a director and co-thrust leader on two science thrusts, thus appearing three times in the table
ERC for Collaborative Adaptive Sensing of the Atmosphere	5	1	4	0	1	2	Director includes director, and deputy and associate directors
Center for Wireless Integrated MicroSystems	4	0	5	0	2	2	Director includes director, and deputy and associate directors.
Center for Subsurface Sensing and Imaging Systems	6	0					Director includes director and associate directors; detailed scientific and administrative directorate information not available.
Integrated Media Systems Center	2	0	5	1	3	1	Director includes director and deputy directors
Center for Power Electronics Systems	6	0	6	1	1	2	Director includes campus directors
Total (%)	49	6 (11%)	73	11 (13%)	33	28 (46%)	

SOURCE: Personnel data obtained from organizational charts published on-line by each center. Data retrieved May 1, 2006.

TABLE 4-5 National Science Foundation Science and Technology Center Leadership Positions

Science and Technology Center (STC)	Director and Deputy Directors		Scientific Directors		Administrative Directors		Notes
	Male	Female	Male	Female	Male	Female	
Adaptive Optics		1					Names of leadership unavailable beyond director
Advanced Materials for Water Purification	1	0	6	0	2	2	
Behavioral Neuroscience	1	0	5	0	3	3	Scientific directors includes core heads
Biophotonics	2	0	14	4	3	2	Includes senior management only. Scientific directors includes project leaders for projects under three main thrusts
Earth-Surface Dynamics	1	1	6	0	0	3	Science directors include integrated project leaders and managers
Embedded Networked Sensing	1	1	11	0	2	1	Scientific directors includes principal investigators listed on organization chart under research areas
Environmentally Responsible Solvents and Processes	3	0	4	0	2	1	

Research Area							Notes
Integrated Space Weather Modeling	2	0	2	2	3	0	
Materials and Devices for Information Technology Research	2	0	2	0	5	2	Administrative directors includes associate directors. Scientific directors includes only thrust leaders
Nanobiotechnology	2	1	5	0	0	1	
Remote Sensing of Ice Sheets	2	0	9	0	2	1	Scientific directors includes research team leaders
Sustainability of Semi-arid Hydrology and Riparian Areas	1	1	10	9	3	0	Scientific directors includes macro-theme leaders Administrative directors excludes program coordinator and business manager
Ubiquitous Secure Technology	2	0	2	1	4	1	Director includes director and executive director. Scientific director includes coordinators of the three research areas
Total (%)	**20 (20%)**	**5 (20%)**	**76 (17%)**	**16 (17%)**	**29**	**17 (37%)**	

SOURCE: Personnel data obtained from organizational charts published on-line by each center. Data retrieved May 1, 2006.

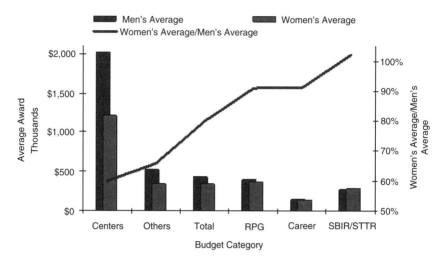

FIGURE 4-3 Average NIH research grant award to women and men by budget category, FY 2004.

SOURCE: Office of Extramural Research (2005). *Sex/Gender in the Biomedical Science Workforce*. National Institutes of Health, *http://grants2.nih.gov/grants/policy/sex_gender/q_a.htm#q5*.

Many academic scientists and engineers believe that they function within a meritocratic system that objectively rewards ability and productivity, and that careers should be open to talent.[43] The institutions making up that system, however, are differentiated by major distinctions of prestige, power, and available resources. As described above, those factors influence the ability to do research and influence the evaluation of efforts. The characteristics and policies of an institution therefore can exert a major influence on career outcomes.

Because the path to an academic career is long and consists of multiple steps, any advantages or disadvantages that befall a scientist or engineer, even apparently small ones, can accumulate and lead to further advantages or disadvantages.[44] The reputation of one's degree institutions, the connec-

---

[43]Reviewed in MF Fox and JS Long (1995). Scientific careers: Universalism and particularism. *Annual Review of Sociology* 21:45-71.
[44]RK Merton (1973). *The Sociology of Science: Theoretical and Empirical Investigations*. Chicago, IL: University of Chicago Press.

tions and eminence of one's mentors, the resources of the laboratories where one works, the significance of the problems one works on, the stature of the journals in which one publishes—these and many similar factors can foster or impair a researcher's rise in the academic world.

Gender Bias in Evaluation

Deeply ingrained in the culture of academic science is the assumption that merit, as revealed by the purportedly objective process of peer review, determines the distribution of status, rewards, and opportunities. From Marie Curie to Christiane Nüsslein-Volhardt, prominent women have had their work recognized because it was so important and original. Research, however, has shown that gender colors evaluation of scientific and engineering accomplishment and thus affects the opportunities and rewards that women receive. In the intense competition for academic standing, even small differences in advantage can accumulate over the span of a career and create large differences in status and prestige. That results in white men scientists and engineers often receiving greater rewards for their accomplishments than women or minority-group members.[45]

A study of the peer-review scores awarded on applications for postdoctoral fellowships in Sweden—the country named by the United Nations as the world leader in gender equality—revealed that men received systematically higher competence ratings than equally productive women. A woman, in fact, had to be more than twice as productive as a man to be judged equally competent. "It is not too far-fetched to assume that [similar] gender-based discrimination may occur elsewhere," the researchers suggested. They argued that the documented discrepancy in the perception of female work could "entirely account" for the shortage of women in senior faculty positions.[46] Other research suggests that there is a similar gendered evaluation of research grants in the United States.[47]

Gendered evaluation runs deep in science. Tregenza, studying journal peer review in ecology, a field in which senior academics are predominantly male and younger researchers are close to gender parity, found differences in acceptance rates across journals according to the sex of the first au-

[45]V Valian (1999). *Why So Slow: The Advancement of Women.* Cambridge: MIT Press.

[46]C Wennerås and A Wold (1997). Nepotism and sexism in peer review. *Nature* 387: 341-343.

[47]I Broder (1993). Review of NSF economics proposals: Gender and institutional patterns. *American Economic Review* 83:964-970. This researcher found female reviewers rated female-authored proposals lower than did male reviewers of the same proposals, while no gender differences in the review of male proposals was observed.

EXPERIMENTS AND STRATEGIES

BOX 4-4 Center for Research on Learning and Teaching (CRLT) Theater Program: NSF ADVANCE at the University of Michigan[a]

Interactive theater can be used to build community, raise awareness, and stimulate discussion.[b] It has been used to confront issues that are difficult to resolve due to conflicts between ideals and practice.[c] The Center for Research on Learning and Teaching (CRLT) Theater Program, sponsored by the NSF ADVANCE program at the University of Michigan, uses interactive performances to demonstrate how faculty interactions shape and reflect the climate. They have developed performances that explore search committee discussions of job candidates, mentoring of junior faculty, and committee meeting discussions of tenure candidates. The performances are based on extensive faculty interviews, focus groups, and faculty and administrative consultation and review conducted at the University of Michigan.

The main component of the CRLT Theater Program is the CRLT Players, a theater troupe composed of professional and student actors who use interactive sketches to draw attention to everyday issues in academe surrounding pedagogy, diversity, and inclusion. Using research from the experiences of faculty members and students, the players present different viewpoints to draw the audience in with a mix of comedy and drama. At the end of the show, the actors continue to play their roles during a question-and-answer session with the audience.

In one theater presentation, the CRLT Players enact a meeting of search committee for a faculty position in the computer science department. The actors discuss which of two candidates—one man, one woman—they should hire. The five men and one woman simulating the search committee debate their research backgrounds, credentials, potential family plans, and gender diversity in the department. The scene ends with the chair stating that he would give the name of the man candidate to the dean for hiring. After the presentation, faculty observing the skit question the actors, who, in turn, answer the questions while remaining in character. The audience is allowed to critique the discussions and results of the search committee.

---

thor.[48] Some researchers argue that journals should use blinded peer review to minimize gender bias (Box 4-5). Trix and Penska evaluated letters of recommendation written by senior professors in support of men and women candidates for US medical school faculty positions and found that gender stereotyping systematically resulted in women candidates receiving less favorable recommendations than men.[49]

---

[48]T Tregenza (2002). Gender bias in the refereeing process? *TRENDS in Ecology and Evolution* 17(8):349-350.

[49]F Trix and C Psenka (2003). Exploring the color of glass: Letters of recommendation for female and male medical faculty. *Discourse and Society* 14(2):191-220. All of the letters examined were for successful candidates.

The program seems to be effective at multiple levels. Immediate feedback is provided during the question-and-answer session to help the troupe improve their performance. Audience members are asked to fill out a survey at the end of each performance. And the ADVANCE program also monitors long-term effects on department and university policies and procedures.[d]

Audience members have given consistently high ratings to the relevance and effectiveness of the performances:

- Both men and women rate the issues and topics raised as useful (4 on scale of 5, n=519).
- More women than men found the issues raised reflected personal experiences (3.38-3.91 for women, 2.8-3.53 for men).
- Both men and women found the audience/actor interactive discussion enhanced their understanding of the issue (4 on scale of 5).

The CRLT performance centered on mentoring was used to augment the development and roll-out of the *Faculty Advising Faculty Handbook* and departmental mentoring plans. In general, based on follow-up correspondence with attendees on what worked and what did not, it has become clear that the performances have caused faculty members to reflect on their own behavior and on group dynamics during various committee meetings. They have found that the most critical issues are setting, audience composition, and framing—giving the target audience a reason to care about the information presented and way to make use of it.

---

[a]*http://www.crlt.umich.edu/theatre/theatre.html.*

[b]N Chesler and M Chesler (2005). Theater as a community-building strategy for women in engineering: Theory and practice. *Journal of Women and Minorities in Science and Engineering* 11(1):83-96.

[c]KH Brown and D Gillespie (1999). Responding to moral distress in the university: Augusto Boal's theater of the oppressed. *Change* (September-October):34-39.

[d]D LaVaque-Manty, J Steiger, and A Stewart (forthcoming). Interactive theater: Raising issues about the climate with science faculty. In *Transforming Science and Engineering: Advancing Academic Women*. Eds. AJ Stewart, J Malley, and D LaVaque-Manty. Ann Arbor, MI: University of Michigan.

Steinpreis and colleagues examined gender stereotyping in evaluation of curricula vitae (CVs). They sent academic psychologists CVs ostensibly submitted by men and women candidates for an assistant professorship and for tenure. In fact, the documents recounted the career of a real woman psychologist who had been hired as an assistant professor and attained early tenure. The CVs for each career level were identical, except that half of respondents received a version identified by a stereotypically male name and half by a stereotypically female name. Both men and women faculty members showed a significant preference for hiring the man, rating "his" research, teaching, and service above the identical record of the woman candidate. Although the "man" and "woman" tenure candidates proved

FOCUS ON RESEARCH

BOX 4-5 Blinded Peer Review

High publication demands and the low acceptance rate of peer-review journals place journal editors and their reviewers in a powerful position. Journal reviewers have a vital role not only in influencing the journal editor's publication decisions, but also in the very nature and direction of scientific research. Because of their influence in peer-review outcomes, journal editors and reviewers are aptly described as the "gatekeepers of science."[a] Almost all English-language scientific and medical journals use *anonymous review*, in which authors do not learn the names of reviewers, but fewer than 20% use *blinded review*, in which reviewers do not learn the names of authors.[b] Journal editors who use blinded review have argued that blinding serves to decrease bias in the review process. Indeed, several studies have examined the effect of blinding and found that it reduced reviewer bias with regard to personal characteristics of the authors, including nationality, institutional affiliation, sex, friendship with the reviewer, race or ethnicity, and intellectual conformity with the reviewer.[c]

This phenomenon was demonstrated with alarming clarity in an study examining the effects of blinding auditions for symphony orchestras, where, similar to universities, the training period is long, there are many more candidates than slots available, and in which number of positions is highly fixed and turnover is slow. The practice of "blind" auditions (placing a screen between the player and the judge) increased by 50% the probability that women would advance out of preliminary rounds, and explained between 30 to 55% of the increase in the proportion of women among new hires and between 25 to 46% of the increase in the percentage of women in the orchestras from 1970 to 1996.[d]

Additional research controlling for a variety of author, article, and journal attributes shows that articles published in journals using blinded peer review were

equally likely to be promoted on the basis of the superb CV, respondents were 4 times more likely to ask for supporting evidence about the woman, such as a chance to see her teach or proof that she had won her grants on her own, than they were for the man.[50] Earlier research has shown that department chairmen evaluating male and female applicants with identical records tended to hire the men as associate professors and the women as assistant professors.[51]

---

[50]R Steinpreis, K Sanders, and D Ritzke (1999). The impact of gender on the review of the curriculum vitae of job applicants and tenure candidates: A national empirical study. *Sex Roles: A Journal of Research* 41:509-28.

[51]L Fidell (1970). Empirical verification of sex discrimination in hiring practices in psychology. *American Psychologist* 25:1094-1098.

cited significantly more than articles published in journals using nonblinded peer review.[e] Some have suggested that in addition to blinded review, journal editors conduct periodic internal and external evaluations of their journals' peer-review process and outcomes to ensure that review bias is minimized.[f]

[a]M Hojat, JS Gonnella, and AS Caelleigh (2003). Impartial judgment by the "gatekeepers" of science: Fallibility and accountability in the peer review process. *Advances in Health Sciences Education* 8(1):75-96.

[b]M Fisher, SB Friedman, B Strauss (1994). The effects of blinding on acceptance of research papers by peer review. *JAMA* 272:143-146.

[c]JS Ross, CP Gross, MM Desai, Y Hong, AO Grant, SR Daniels, VC Hachinski, RJ Gibbons, TJ Gardner, and HM Krumholz (2006). Effect of blinded peer review on abstract acceptance. *JAMA* 295:1675-1680; M Fisher, SB Friedman, and B Strauss (1994). The effects of blinding on acceptance of research papers by peer review. *JAMA* 272:143-146; RM Blank (1991). The effects of double-blind versus single-blind reviewing: Experimental evidence from the *American Economic Review. American Economic Review* 81:1041-1067; RA McNutt, AT Evans, RH Fletcher, and SW Fletcher (1990). The effects of blinding on the quality of peer review. A randomized trial. *JAMA* 263(10):1371-1376; MA Ferber and M Teiman (1980). Are women economists at a disadvantage in publishing journal articles? *Eastern Economic Journal* 6(3-4):189-193; but also see S van Rooyen, F Godlee, S Evans, R Smith, and N Black (1998). Effect of blinding and unmasking on the quality of peer review: A randomized trial. *JAMA* 280(3):234-237.

[e]C Rouse and C Goldin (2000). Orchestrating impartiality: The impact of "blind" auditions on female musicians. *American Economics Review* 90:715-741. The study was based on a final analysis sample of 14,133 individuals and 592 audition segments.

[e]DN Laband and MJ Piette (1994). A citation analysis of the impact of blinded peer review. *JAMA* 272(2):147-149.

[f]Hojat et al. (2003), ibid; DJ Rennie (1998). Peer review in Prague. *JAMA* 280(3):214-215.

The University of Wisconsin-Madison's Women in Science and Engineering Leadership Institute (WISELI) provides workshops to train search committee chairs on good search methods and to sensitize them to hiring bias (Box 4-6).[52] WISELI recommends spending 15-20 minutes on each application, reading the entire application rather than relying on one measure of performance, developing criteria for evaluations that can be consistently applied, and periodically evaluating decisions to determine whether qualified women and minority-group members were included.[53] The Uni-

[52]Women in Science and Engineering Leadership Institute. *Training for hiring committees.* University of Wisconsin-Madison: WISELI, *http://wiseli.engr.wisc.edu/initiatives/hiring/training_hiring.html#Workshops.*

[53]Women in Science and Engineering Leadership Institute, University of Wisconsin-Madison, ibid.

EXPERIMENTS AND STRATEGIES

BOX 4-6 Searching for Excellence and Diversity: Workshops for Search Committee Chairs at the University of Wisconsin-Madison

The Women in Science and Engineering Leadership Institute (WISELI) at the University of Wisconsin-Madison offers workshops for faculty chairs of search committees that aim to increase the diversity of candidates recruited and hired for faculty and administrative positions. Relying on principles of active learning and peer education, the workshops encourage faculty to share search experiences and strategies across department and school/college boundaries.[a] The workshops emphasize the *5 Essential Elements of a Successful Search.*[b] An introduction to and discussion of the effects of unconscious biases and assumptions on evaluation of candidates is an important feature of the workshop experience. From 2003 through 2006, 152 faculty members representing 70 different departments (57% of all departments in the university) participated in the workshops.

WISELI has been evaluating the success of this approach to improving the hiring process at UW-Madison by tracking:

(1) **Workshop participants' ratings of the usefulness of the workshops.**[c] Overall, all workshop participants who responded to our request for feedback (N=65; 42% response rate) indicated that the workshop they attended was "Somewhat" or "Very" useful; none reported that the workshop was not at all useful. Similarly, all respondents reported that they would recommend the workshop to others, and no respondents indicated they would not recommend the workshop.

(2) **Self-reported gains in skill related to the search process on an all-faculty survey.**[d] Workshop participant responses on the 2006 *Study of Faculty Worklife at the UW-Madison* (N=1,230; 56% response rate) indicate that participants did significantly increase their skill in the following areas: establishing search procedures to ensure the equitable review and hiring of candidates and creating a welcoming environment for new hires.

(3) **Survey responses of new faculty satisfaction with various elements of the search process.**[e] New hires in departments that sent at least one faculty member to the WISELI training reported an increase in their satisfaction with the hiring process, while departments that did not participate saw a decrease in their new members' satisfaction with the hiring process, from 2003 (before the workshops were implemented) to 2006 (Figure B4-6A).

---

[a] *http://wiseli.engr.wisc.edu/initiatives/hiring/training_hiring.html.*
[b] *http://wiseli.engr.wisc.edu/initiatives/hiring/SearchBook.pdf.*
[c] C Pribbenow, C Maidl, and J Winchell (2005). *WISELI's Workshops for Search Chairs: Evaluation Report.* Madison, WI: University of Wisconsin.
[d] *http://wiseli.engr.wisc.edu/Products/facultyversion06.pdf.*
[e] E Fine and J Sheridan (2006). *Searching for Excellence & Diversity—Training Workshops for Search Committees.* Poster presentation, 5th Annual ADVANCE Institutional Transformation Principal Investigators Meeting. Washington, DC, May 17, *http://wiseli.engr.wisc. edu/initiatives/hiring/UWMadison_Poster2006_2.ppt.*

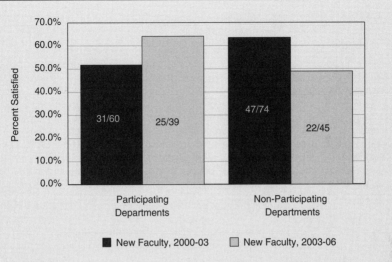

FIGURE B4-6A

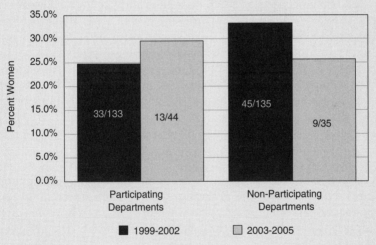

FIGURE B4-6B

(4) **Actual percentages of women and minority faculty hired.**[f] Departments who sent at least one faculty member to a workshop showed a 19% increase in the percentage of their new assistant professors who were women, compared to a 23% *decrease* for those departments that did not participate (Figure
B4-6B).

---

[f]Fine and Sheridan (2006), ibid.

continued

BOX 4-6 Continued

These measures indicate that WISELI's approach to educating search committee chairs appears to be working, although many other factors such as the motivation of the individual search committee chairs and departments are likely to also play an important role.

WISELI plans to continue implementing workshops across the UW-Madison campus, expanding them beyond faculty and administrative searches to searches for other staff as well. One large college made participation in these workshops mandatory for all search committee chairs beginning in 2005/2006. WISELI is also visiting other campuses to offer a day-long session, "Searching for Excellence & Diversity: Implementing Training for Search Committees," to help universities, university systems, and/or regional collectives develop and present search workshops on their own campuses.[g]

---

[g]http://wiseli.engr.wisc.edu/initiatives/hiring/ImplementingTraining.htm.

---

versity of Michigan has its STRIDE (Strategies and Tactics for Recruiting to Improve Diversity and Excellence) program,[54] which uses senior professors of science and engineering who have been trained by social scientists to work with recruitment committees to overcome biases. University administrators can make departments accountable by making participation in such programs a condition for undertaking a faculty search. Building in a measure of accountability reduces the use of stereotypes in choosing job candidates.[55]

Understanding Discrimination[56]

Although women today in the United States have many more opportunities than women of previous generations, many societal traditions inhibit their full participation in the technical workforce. Women have been struggling for access into universities and entrance into the labor force since the

---

[54]University of Michigan STRIDE Web site, *http://sitemaker.umich.edu/advance/stride*. See AJ Stewart, D LaVaque-Manty, and JE Malley (2004). Recruiting women faculty in science and engineering: Preliminary evaluation of one intervention model. *Journal of Women and Minorities in Science and Engineering* 10(4):361-375.

[55]PE Tetlock (1985). Accountability: A social check on the fundamental attribution error. *Social Psychology Quarterly* 48:227-236.

[56]See Appendix C for a discussion of the theories of discrimination. Excerpted from National Research Council (2004). *Measuring Racial Discrimination*. Washington, DC: The National Academies Press, pp. 55-70, *http://fermat.nap.edu/catalog/10887.html*.

middle of the 19th century.[57] But, admission was only half the battle. Women were often co-opted into the science and engineering professions to provide lower-cost labor necessary to combat temporary workforce shortages. In addition, as described in Chapter 5, when women are hired into faculty or upper management, institutions do not provide contexts conducive to their productive potential or retention.[58]

Subtle, Implicit, or Unexamined Bias

Even as gender equity gains ground and a national consensus has developed that explicit racial hostility is abhorrent,[59] people may still hold prejudiced attitudes, stemming in part from the US history of overt sex and racial prejudice. Although prejudicial attitudes do not necessarily result in discriminatory behavior with adverse effects, the persistence of such attitudes can result in unconscious and subtle forms of discrimination in place of more explicit, direct hostility. Such subtle prejudice is often abetted by differential mass-media portrayals[60] and by de facto segregation in education and occupations. All manifestations of subtle prejudice constitute barriers to full equality of treatment. Subtle prejudice is much more difficult to document than more overt forms, and its effects on discriminatory behavior are more difficult to capture. However, *subtle* does not mean trivial or inconsequential; subtle prejudice can result in major adverse effects. More recently, legal scholars have begun to use the term *unexamined* to describe such discriminatory behavior, arguing that it shifts the burden of proof and acknowledges that such behavior can be changed.[61]

---

[57]BM Solomon (1985). *In the Company of Educated Women: A History of Women and Higher Education in America.* New Haven, CT: Yale University Press; R Oldenziel (2000). Multiple entry visas: Gender and engineering in the US, 1870-1945. In *Crossing Boundaries, Building Bridges: Comparing the History of Women Engineers 1870s-1990s,* eds. A Canal, R Oldenziel, and K Zachmann, Amsterdam: Overseas Publishers Association.

[58]C Vogt (2006). Women's participation in ICT careers in industrialized nations. In *Explaining Gendered Occupational Outcomes,* eds. J Eccles and H Watt. Washington, DC: American Psychological Association.

[59]R Inglehart and P Norris (2003). *Rising Tide: Gender Equality and Cultural Change.* New York: Cambridge University Press; LD Bobo (2001). Racial attitudes and relations at the close of the twentieth century. In *America Becoming: Racial Trends and their Consequences,* Vol. 1, eds. NJ Smelser, WJ Wilson, and F Mitchell. Washington, DC: National Academy Press.

[60]PG Davies, SJ Spencer, DM Quinn, and R Gerhardstein (2002). Consuming images: How television commercials that elicit stereotype threat can restrain women academically and professionally. *Journal of Personality and Social Psychology* 33:561-578.

[61]JC Williams (2006). Moving beyond the "Chilly Climate" to a new model for spurring organizational change. In *Biological, Social, and Organizational Components of Success for Women in Science and Engineering.* Washington, DC: The National Academies Press.

Pervasive, unexamined gender bias has played a major role in limiting women's opportunities and careers because American culture generally stereotypes science, mathematics, and engineering as domains appropriate to white men and much less suitable for women or members of racial or ethnic minorities. If gender bias takes a so-called benevolent form, women are viewed as pure and morally superior, although not suited for male occupations. Under a hostile form of gender bias, women who aspire to traditionally masculine roles are seen as undermining or attacking the rightful prerogatives of men. The combination of those biases often causes competent women to be perceived as "not nice" or even "overly aggressive" and traditionally subservient women to be perceived as "incompetent" and "trivial."[62]

As described in Chapter 2, in-group and out-group stereotypes can lead to lower test performance and reduce confidence and can lead some women and members of underrepresented minorities to develop less interest in pursuing science- and mathematics-based careers, even when they major in those fields. It can also affect students' interest in taking on the leadership roles that are necessary for success in academic research.[63] The tendency to see women and minority-group members as less competent than white men and their accomplishments as less worthy and significant is a prominent component of the "glass ceiling," the well-known complex of attitudes and biases that keeps women and minorities in many organizations and professions out of the most powerful, influential, and prestigious positions because they are assumed to be unfit for leadership.[64] Stereotyping and cognitive bias thus create a "built-in headwind" for women and minorities in the sciences and engineering.

---

[62]P Glick and S Fiske (1996). The Ambivalent Sexism Inventory: Differentiating hostile and benevolent sexism. *Journal of Personality and Social Psychology* 70:491-512.

[63]CM Steele and J Aronson (1995). Stereotype threat and the intellectual test performance of African Americans. *Journal of Personality and Social Psychology* 69:797-811; M Inzlicht and Ben-Zeev (2000). A threatening intellectual environment: Why women are susceptible to experience problem-solving deficits in the presence of men. *Psychological Science* 11:365-371; J Keller (2002). Blatant stereotype threat and women's performance: Self-handicapping as a strategic means to cope with obtrusive negative performance expectations. *Sex Roles: A Journal of Research* 47:193-198; T Schmader, M Johns, and M Barquissau (2004). The costs of accepting gender differences: The role of stereotype endorsement in women's experience in the math domain. *Sex Roles: A Journal of Research* 50:835-850; PG Davies, SJ Spencer, and CM Steele (2005). Clearing the air: Identity safety moderates the effects of stereotype threat on women's leadership aspirations. *Journal of Personality and Social Psychology* 88:276-287.

[64]JC Williams (2004). Hitting the maternal wall. *Academe* 12(6), http://www.aaup.org/publications/Academe/2004/04nd/04ndwill.htm; JC Alessio and J Andrzejski (2000). Unveiling the hidden glass ceiling. *American Sociological Review* 26 (2):311-315.

The main effect of subtle prejudice seems to be to favor the in group rather than to directly disadvantage the out group.[65] One might, for example, fail to promote someone on the basis of race, perceiving the person to be deferential, cooperative, and "nice" but essentially incompetent, whereas a comparable in-group member might receive additional training or support to develop greater competence. Conversely, one might acknowledge an out-group member's exceptional competence but fail to see the person as sociable and comfortable—and therefore not fitting in, not "one of us," and less collegial—and on that account fail to promote the person as rapidly.

The Case for Diversity: "There Goes the Neighborhood?"

There have been dramatic changes in workforce demographics over the last 40 years. As discussed in Chapter 1, women and minority groups make up an increasing proportion of science and engineering students and the technical labor force.[66] The benefits of workforce diversity seem clear in knowledge-based innovative work requiring creativity and flexibility.[67] In the past decade, a number of reports and popular books have touted the benefits of workplace diversity,[68] connecting it to enhanced group problem solving, increased creativity, and increased profits.[69] A vast and growing body of research provides evidence that a diverse student body, faculty, and

---

[65]MB Brewer and R Brown (1998). Intergroup relations. In eds. D Gilbert, ST Fiske, and G Lindzy, *The Handbook of Social Psychology*, 4th edition. New York: McGraw-Hill.

[66]See, for example, A Antonio (2003). Diverse student bodies, diverse faculties. *Academe* 89(6):14-18.

[67]M Polyani (1962). The Republic of Science: Its political and economic theory. *Minerva* 1:54-74; NL Johnson (2000). *Developmental Insights into Evolving Systems: Roles of Diversity, Non-selection, Self-organization, Symbiosis.* Paper presented at Seventh International Conference on Artificial Life. Portland OR, August 1-6; see also review in SE Jackson, KE May, and K Whitney (1995). Understanding the dynamics of diversity in decision-making teams. In *Team Effectiveness and Decision-Making in Organizations*, eds. RA Guzzo and E Salas. San Francisco: Jossey-Bass.

[68]See, for example, WB Johnstone and AE Packer (1987). *Workforce 2000: Work and Workers for the Twenty-First Century.* Indianapolis, IN: Hudson Institute; A Morrison (1996). *The New Leaders: Leadership Diversity in America.* San Francisco: Jossey-Bass.

[69]CJ Nemeth (1985). Dissent, group process, and creativity: The contribution of minority influence. *Advances in Group Processes* 2:57-75; CJ Nemeth (1995). Dissent as driving cognition, attitudes, and judgments. *Social Cognition* 13:273-291;TH Cox (1993). *Cultural Diversity in Organizations: Theory, Research, and Practice.* San Francisco: Berrett-Koehler; PL McLeod, SA Lobel, and TH Cox (1996). Ethnic diversity and creativity in small groups. *Small Group Research* 27:248-265; S Nelson and G Pellet (1997). *Shattering the Silences*

staff benefits the joint missions of teaching and research.[70] However, if the structural conditions and individual perspectives do not exist to harness their benefit, diverse workgroups can lead to increased workplace tension, team fragmentation, and increased staff turnover.[71] Ineffective processes and policies are manifested as workplace bias: differences in career outcomes by gender or race/ethnicity that are not attributable to the differences in skills, qualifications, interests, or preferences that individuals bring to the employment setting.[72]

> Diversity and discussions of it can be turbulent and uncomfortable, but it also is clarifying, illuminating, leading to a deeper understanding of one's self and one's world. Diversity advances innovation. Diversity powers excellence.
>
> —Shirley Jackson, President,
> Rensselaer Polytechnic Institute (2005)[73]

Businesses and universities realize that to capture and capitalize on this talent, they need to change policies adopted when the workplace was more homogeneous and create new organizational structures.[74] Most organizational efforts have focused on race and gender, but many also incorporate other aspects of diversity, including socioeconomic status, ethnic heritage, sexual orientation, and disability status.[75] At the same time, organizations must consider increasing challenges to the concept of affirmative action and the discontinuation of programs seen to be providing advantage to any

---

[videorecording]. San Francisco: Gail Pellet Productions; A Antonio (2002). Faculty of color reconsidered: Reassessing contributions to scholarship. *Journal of Higher Education* 73:582-602; CSV Turner (2000). New faces, new knowledge. *Academe* 86:34-37; JF Milem (2003). The educational benefits of diversity: Evidence from multiple sectors. In *Compelling Interest: Examining the Evidence on Racial Dynamics in Higher Education,* eds. M Chang, et al. Stanford, CA: Stanford Education; DA Thomas (2004). Diversity as strategy. *Harvard Business Review* 82(9):98-108.

[70]See WISELI's *Benefits and Challenges of Diversity, http://wiseli.engr.wisc.edu/initiatives/climate/Benefits_Challenges.pdf.*

[71]See review by Jackson, May, Whitney (1995), ibid.

[72]WT Bielby (2000). Miminizing workplace gender and racial bias. *Contemporary Sociology* 29(1):120-129.

[73]UCSC Chancellor's Inaugural Symposium, November 3, 2006, *http://celebration2005. ucsc.edu/symposium.asp.*

[74]WB Johnstone and AE Packer (1987), ibid.

[75]See, for example, M Loden (1995). *Implementing Diversity.* Burr Ridge, IL: McGraw-Hill.

specific group.[76] Equity efforts need to address not just *individual* needs but also the *systemic changes* needed to build and sustain educational, research, and workplace environments that promote effective participation in an increasingly pluralistic society. As described below (Box 4-7), such structures would include proactive recruiting, programs to enhance team-building and interpersonal skills, compensation equity, family friendly policies, mentoring and career development programs for junior and senior employees, and accountability through annual appraisals and evaluations.

Accountability and Evaluation

Program evaluation must be an integral part of any diversity initiative. Models for some best practices have begun to emerge from some AD-VANCE institutions (Box 5-5).[77] However, none of the ADVANCE institutions have to date completed their 5-year institutional transformation grant, so evaluation of the success of these programs is not possible. Progress can be gleaned from annual reports to NSF[78] and on many of the individual program Web sites.

Effective assessment is an iterative self-diagnostic process. It ideally involves continuous cycles of program improvement and refinement. A program should incorporate a hypothesis, a set of measurable goals, and should collect baseline (formative) and outcomes (summative) data to test that hypothesis. Reasoned analyses and plans are followed by "experimental" trials with continuous testing, learning, and program refinement from those planned trials. A percentage of total program funding should be allotted to evaluation activities and an individual should be designated to be responsible for data collection and analysis; 5% of total project funding is a common allocation for evaluation in federal programs.[79]

---

[76]G Custred and T Wood (1996). California's Proposition 209, *http://www.acri.org/209/ 209text.html*; *Gratz v. Bollinger*, No. 02-516, 123 S. Ct. 2411 (2003); *Grutter v. Bollinger*, No. 02-241, 123 S. Ct. 2325 (2003); A Klein (2004). Affirmative-action opponents suffer setbacks in Colorado and Michigan. *Chronicle of Higher Education* 50(31):A23; R Roach (2005). Ford diversity fellows urged to defend affirmative action. *Diverse Issues in Higher Education, http://www.diverseeducation.com/artman/publish/article_4898.shtml*; P Schmidt (2006). From "Minority" to "Diversity". The transformation of formerly race-exclusive programs may be leaving some students out in the cold. *Chronicle of Higher Education* 52(22): A24; P Schmidt (2006). Southern Illinois U. and Justice Dept. near accord on minority fellowships. *Chronicle of Higher Education* 52(22):A26; R Clegg (2006). Faculty hiring preferences and the law. *Chronicle of Higher Education* 52(37):B13.

[77]See SV Rosser (2006). Creating an inclusive work environment. In: *Biological, Social, and Organizational Components of Success for Women in Science and Engineering*. Washington, DC: The National Academies Press.

[78]Available at *http://www.nsf.gov/advance*.

[79]National Research Council (1996). *The National Scholars Program: Excellence with Diversity for the Future*. Washington, DC: National Academy Press.

FOCUS ON RESEARCH
BOX 4-7 Making Diversity Work

"If you think managing diversity is a *program*, you don't get it."[a]

Considerable research has shown the barriers limiting the appointment, retention, and advancement of women faculty. The question is how to move beyond these barriers and make diversity work. An evaluation of a wide-ranging campus diversity initiative in the University of California system provides specific lessons for academe. Programs that were effective had three key components: the campus had a framework for monitoring progress, a commitment to analyze and use data for organizational change, and a commitment to take corrective action.[b]
These results mirror what is found in other organizations that have implemented successful diversity management programs. Several researchers have examined program efficacy using a variety of techniques, including tracking of workforce composition and employment practices,[c] and case studies in industry[d] and federal agencies.[e] While there are some important differences, there are some common factors that successful programs—those shown to improve workforce diversity—exhibit. These benchmarks of success are:

1. Management involvement (CEO, President)—resource commitments, internal communication of goals, alignment of strategic goals and organizational mission.
2. Close tailoring of diversity initiative to organizational needs, starting with performance of an organizational survey to identify demographics, issues, and needs.
3. Program not specific to a demographic group.[f]
4. Changes individual behavior.
5. Changes personnel systems and existing organizational procedures and practices.
6. Involves organizational development—participation of top managers, sequencing of educational programs so that managers back up training of nonsupervisory staff, long-term effort to reach a large proportion of employees, and considerations of the length and depth of programs.
7. Incorporates measurables and accountability—regular monitoring of patterns of job segregation, pay, and career advancement by gender and race/ethnicity; and explicit evaluation of managers and supervisors in contributing to initiative goals.

Industries that have large research and development (R&D) components may be most likely to hold lessons for academia. In this context, several actions are correlated with increased workforce diversity:[g]

• Mentoring programs have been highly effective in moving white and African American women and African American men into management.
• Culture audits and surveys of workers have resulted in increases in white and African American women in management, whereas they show mixed effects in non-R&D industries.
• Targeted recruitment is particularly effective in R&D industries.

Overall, these findings support the creation of systems of authority and accountability (diversity committees, affirmative action plans) (Box 6-2), the use of targeted searches and incentives (Box 3-6), the use of surveys to assess university culture (Box 6-7), and the implementation of mentoring programs (Box 6-3). While diversity training is helpful in R&D intensive industries, it is important to note that corporate diversity training is very different from the sort of diversity initiatives found in the ADVANCE programs (Box 5-5), in which academic scientists rather than hired consultants lead training and create ongoing feedback and learning systems (Boxes 4-3, 4-4, and 4-6). Such training systems are akin to diversity committees, which are quite effective in both R&D industries and elsewhere. To derive maximal benefits from diversity, members of academic communities must show respect for each other's cultural and stylistic preferences and awareness of unconscious assumptions and behaviors that may influence interactions. Only when differences are openly discussed and learned from do the positive effects of diversity accrue; open discussion makes it possible for the groups to create psychological safety.[h] The goal is to create a climate in which everyone feels personally safe, listened to, valued, and treated fairly and with respect.

---

[a]F Miller (1992). *Discussant commentary. Leadership Diversity Conference: Beyond Awareness into Action.* Center for Creative Leadership, Greensboro, NC.

[b]DG Smith, S Parker, AR Clayton-Pedersen, JF Moreno, and DH Teraguchi (2006). *Building Capacity: The Study of Impact of The James Irvine Foundation Campus Diversity Initiative.* Irvine, CA: The James Irvine Foundation.

[c]A Kalev, F Dobbin, and E Kelly (2006). *Best Practices or Best Guesses? Diversity Management and the Remediation of Inequality* (Working Paper). Cambridge, MA: Harvard University, *http://www.wjh.harvard.edu/~dobbin/cv/working_papers/eeopractice1.pdf.*

[d]M Bendick, ML Egan, and SM Lofhjelm (1998). *The Documentation and Evaluation of Anti-Discrimination Training in the United States.* Geneva: International Labor Organization; JA Gilbert, BA Stead, and JM Ivancevich (1999). Diversity management: A new organizational paradigm. *Journal of Business Ethics* 21:61-76; R Ely (2004). A field study of group diversity, participation in diversity education programs and performance. *Journal of Organizational Behavior* 25(6):755-780.

[e]KC Naff and JE Kellough (2003). Ensuring employment equity: Are federal diversity programs making a difference? *International Journal of Public Administration* 26(12):1307-1336.

[f]Some research indicates that broad diversity initiatives may not help, and in some cases may hinder, the promotion of minorities; reviewed in Naff and Kellough (2003). Other research indicates that reducing the saliency of group identity helps to reduce backlash by majority groups; reviewed in Gilbert et al. (1999), ibid; Bendick et al. (1998), ibid. It should be noted in this context that those programs shown to be effective at increasing the retention of women faculty are almost immediately broadened to include all faculty (Box 6-3).

[g]F Dobbin and A Kalev (2006). *Diversity management and managerial diversity: Addendum to "Best Practices or Best Guesses."* Special Report to the National Academies Committee on Women in Academic Science and Engineering.

[h]RJ Ely and DA Thomas (2001). Cultural diversity at work: The effects of diversity perspectives on work group processes and outcomes. *Administrative Science Quarterly* 46:202-228.

EXPERIMENTS AND STRATEGIES

BOX 4-8 Specific Steps for Overcoming Bias

1. Avoid language that activates unexamined and implicit biases (Box 2-4).
2. Make positive role models visible (see Boxes 2-4 and 4-2).
3. Include women and minority-group members on evaluation committees (Box 4-2).
4. Create an enhanced sense of community and partnership (Box 5-2).
5. Discuss possible bias and challenge decisions openly (Box 4-4).
6. Make the community aware of the research on bias and emphasize the neutral effect of the gender of the evaluator, thereby defusing the issue and avoiding accusations and defensiveness (Box 4-9).
7. Define criteria at the outset of the selection process to ensure that they select the best academic traits rather than simply replicating past patterns (Boxes 4-1, 4-6, and 4-7).
8. Hold accountable people and committees that conduct evaluations of people for hiring, tenure, promotion, and awards (Boxes 4-2, 4-6, and 4-7).

FOCUS ON RESEARCH

BOX 4-9 Top Research Articles on the Effects of Bias on Evaluation[a]

Each of the 19 institutions that have received NSF ADVANCE grants were asked which research publications have proven most effective in their institutional transformation projects. The most-cited publications were these:

RE Steinpreis, KS Anders, and D Ritzke (1999). The impact of gender on the review of the curricula vitae of job applicants and tenure candidates: A national empirical study. *Sex Roles: A Journal of Research* 41:509-528.
F Trix and C Psenka (2003). Exploring the color of glass: Letters of recommendation for female and male medical faculty. *Discourse and Society* 14(2):191-220.
V Valian (1999). *Why So Slow: The Advancement of Women.* Cambridge: MIT Press.
C Wennerås and A Wold (1997). Nepotism and sexism in peer-review. *Nature* 387: 341-343.

---

[a]All 19 ADVANCE institutions were polled on the top 3-5 articles that have proven the most effective in their institutional transformation projects. Poll conducted between January 20 and March 20, 2006.

The committee has prepared a detailed scorecard for the purposes of measuring progress toward improving the representation of women in university programs and faculties (Box 6-7). Measurables include

• Changes in the representation of women and minorities in the student body, new faculty interviews, hire offers, faculty rank positions, and in administrative positions.
• Changes in hiring, promotion, tenure, retention, and turnover. Exit interviews can be an important means of evaluating reasons for turnover and designing retention programs (Box 3-5).
• Differences in salary or resource allocation.

BEYOND BIAS

The underrepresentation of women and minorities in science and engineering faculties stems from a number of issues that are firmly rooted in our society's traditions and culture. To accelerate the rate at which women and minority-group members take their places as leaders in science and engineering, it is essential that all members of the scientific and engineering community—men and women alike—reflect on their own values, beliefs, and behavior to ensure that they do not further stereotypes, prejudices, policies, practices, or climates that discourage or exclude women and minorities from academe (Box 4-8).

A powerful way to reduce evaluation bias has been to bring to the attention of those performing evaluations—including provosts, department chairs, and search committees—the research in the field (Box 4-9).

CONCLUSION

Our analysis shows that women possess the qualities needed to succeed in academic careers and can do so when given an equal opportunity to achieve. Furthermore, reducing the homogeneity of faculty enhances problem solving, teaching, and research. The need to eliminate bias against women scientists and engineers—whether explicit, covert, or unexamined—is therefore more than a moral or legal obligation of universities. It is a requirement for assuring a scientific workforce of the highest quality. Only the best possible scientific workforce will permit the nation to compete in an increasingly global world of science and engineering.

5

Institutional Constraints

CHAPTER HIGHLIGHTS

In addition to bias, systematic constraints and expectations built into academic institutions have impeded the careers of women scientists and engineers. The traditional scientific or engineering career presumes the model of an out-of-date male life course. It is predicated on the assumption that the faculty member will have an unlimited commitment to his or her academic career throughout his or her working life. Attention to other serious obligations, such as family, is taken to imply lack of dedication to one's career. Historically, that career model depended on a faculty member having a wife to take care of all other aspects of life, including the household, family, and community. The model still fits some men but is increasingly unsuitable for both men and women who need or want to participate in other activities important to them and their communities.

The traditional career model is clearly difficult for women scientists and engineers to fulfill, especially if they have children. Because the burden of family, household, and community care generally falls more heavily on women than on men—and because women seldom have substantial spousal support—women scientists and engineers often experience intense conflict between their family and professional roles. A well-documented complex of biases known as the maternal wall or family responsibilities discrimi-

nation hampers the career advancement of women scientists and engineers with children and the minority of male scientists and engineers who bear major caregiving responsibilities. Those on highly competitive academic career tracks are aware of these issues and often make compromises to lessen the conflict or choose not to avail themselves of accommodations for which they are eligible, such as stopping the tenure clock or reducing work responsibilities, out of fear of damaging their career prospects. Women scientists and engineers in fast-track positions, for example, are less likely than those on less competitive career tracks to be married or to have children. Those who are mothers tend to have fewer children than comparable men. Furthermore, the perseverance of women scientists and engineers is seldom perceived as evidence of the very high level of devotion to their profession that it represents.

Anti-discrimination law requires universities to remedy conditions that differentially affect women's entry into and promotion in academic scientific and engineering careers. Under recent legal decisions, the existence of stereotyping can serve as proof of discrimination. Legal trends thus encourage institutions to reduce stereotyping and also to change the institutional practices and norms that limit women's advancement. Other steps needed to remove barriers include documenting the status and progress of underrepresented groups, establishing a work environment that is explicitly inclusive, and providing services that allow scientists and engineers to be productive while meeting their responsibilities outside of work. All those steps require leadership—and resource commitments—at the highest department and institutional levels. The most necessary and most difficult change is a thorough reconsideration of the long-accepted recruitment and evaluation practices implicit in the outdated academic career model.

FINDINGS

5-1. Systematic structural constraints built into academic institutions have impeded the careers of women scientists and engineers. A successful academic career has traditionally involved the presumption that unlimited attention can be given to that throughout one's life.

5-2. Deviation or delay, any substantial hiatus, or serious attention to responsibilities outside of the academic realm have harmed faculty members' ability to compete successfully because it has been taken to indicate a lack of seriousness about their careers.

5-3. Scientists and engineers without substantial spousal support, particularly those who shoulder major caregiving responsibilities, are disadvantaged in meeting the norms and expectations of academe.

5-4. The mere existence of apparently family-friendly policies at universities will not reduce the pressure on women faculty or their fear that family life will damage or even destroy their careers.

5-5. Well-planned, data-driven efforts to remove institutional constraints on women academics' careers can produce significant results.

5-6. Whether those efforts involve "small wins" or institution-wide transformations, to be successful they must be based on accurate information about the existing situation, attention to problematic elements in the institution's culture and practices, input from affected persons to help to identify those elements, evaluation of results, and buy-in from leadership at all institutional levels. Recalcitrance at lower levels can torpedo top-down initiatives, and bottom-up efforts can sink without support from those with power at top levels.

5-7. Adequate data gathering, planning, implementation, and evaluation of changes require the dedication of sufficient resources to the objective of increasing diversity.

RECOMMENDATIONS

5-1. For lasting change to occur, academic institutions, professional societies, and federal agencies should work together to provide leadership on issues of equity, hold their constituents accountable for change, and provide clear methods and measures for compliance.

5-2. University leaders should incorporate into campus strategic plans goals of counteracting bias against women in hiring, promotion, and treatment. This includes working with the inter-institution monitoring organization (see recommendation 5-7 below) to perform annual reviews of the composition of their student body and faculty ranks, publicizing progress toward the goals annually, and providing a detailed annual briefing to the entire board of trustees.

5-3. University leaders should take action immediately to remedy inequities in hiring, promotion, and treatment.

5-4. University leaders should require evidence of a fair, broad, aggressive search, before approving appointments and hold departments accountable for the equity of their search process and outcomes even if it means canceling a search or withholding a faculty position.

5-5. University leaders should develop and implement hiring, tenure, and promotion policies that take into account the flexibility that faculty need across the life course, allowing integration of family, work, and community responsibilities. They should provide central policies and funding for faculty and staff on leave and should visibly and vigorously support campus programs that help faculty with children or other caregiving responsibilities to maintain productive careers. These programs should, at a minimum, include provisions for paid parental leave for faculty, staff, postdoctoral scholars, and graduate students; facilities and subsidies for on-site and community-based child care; dissertation defense and tenure clock extensions; and family-friendly scheduling of critical meetings.

5-6. Faculties and their senates should immediately review their tenure processes and timelines to ensure that hiring, tenure, and promotion policies take into account the flexibility that faculty need across the life course and do not sacrifice quality in the process of meeting rigid timelines.

5-7. The committee recommends that the American Council on Education convene national higher education organizations, including the Association of American Universities, the National Association of State Universities and Land Grant Colleges, and others to discuss implementation of an oversight/intermediary body. Analogous to the National Collegiate Athletics Association, this body would act as an intermediary between academic institutions and federal agencies in establishing norms and measures, in collecting data, and in cross-institution monitoring of compliance and accountability. A primary focus of the discussion should be on defining the scope and structure of data collection.

5-8. Scientific and professional societies should serve in an analogous role to individual national governing bodies for sports and set professional and equity standards and collect and disseminate field-wide education and workforce data.

5-9. Universities and scientific and professional societies should provide child-care and elder-care grants or subsidies to enable their members to attend work-related conferences and meetings.

5-10. Federal funding agencies and foundations should ensure that their practices—including rules and regulations—support the full participation of women and do not reinforce a culture that fundamentally discriminates against women. All research funding agencies and foundations should make it possible to use grant monies for dependent-care expenses necessary to engage in off-site or after-hours research-related activities or to attend work-related conferences and meetings. They should establish policies for extending grant support for researchers who take a leave of absence due to caregiving responsibilities, and create additional funding mechanisms to provide for interim technical or administrative support during a leave of absence related to caregiving.

5-11. Federal agencies and foundations should lay out clear guidelines and leverage their resources and existing laws to increase the science and engineering talent developed in this country, including enforcing federal anti-discrimination laws at universities and other higher education institutions through regular compliance reviews and prompt and thorough investigation of discrimination complaints.

5-12. Federal enforcement agencies should ensure that the range of their enforcement efforts covers the full scope of activities involving science and engineering that are governed by the anti-discrimination laws. If violations are found, the full range of remedies for violation of the anti-discrimination laws should be sought.

5-13. Federal enforcement efforts should evaluate whether universities have engaged in any of the types of discrimination banned under the anti-discrimination laws, including: intentional discrimination, sexual harassment, retaliation, disparate impact discrimination, and failure to maintain required policies and procedures.

5-14. Federal compliance review efforts should encompass a sufficiently broad number and range of institutions of higher education to secure a substantial change in policies and practices nationwide. Types of institutions that should be included in compliance reviews include 2-year and 4-year institutions; institutions of undergraduate education; institutions that grant graduate degrees; state universities; private colleges; and educational enterprises, including national laboratories and independent research institutes, which may not be affiliated with universities.

5-15. Federal enforcement agencies, including the Equal Employment Opportunity Commission (EEOC); the Department of Justice, the Department of Labor, and the Department of Education; and individual federal granting agencies' Offices of Civil Rights should encourage and provide technical assistance on how to achieve diversity in university programs and employment. Possible activities include providing technical assistance to educational institutions to help them to comply with anti-discrimination laws, creating a clearinghouse for dissemination of strategies that have been proved effective, and providing awards and recognition for model university programs.

5-16. Congress should take steps necessary to encourage adequate enforcement of anti-discrimination laws, including regular oversight hearings to investigate the enforcement activities of the Department of Education, the EEOC, the Department of Labor, and the science granting agencies, including the National Institutes of Health and the National Science Foundation, the Department of Defense, the Department of Agriculture, the Department of Energy, the National Institute of Standards and Technology, and the National Aeronautics and Space Administration.

A number of factors disadvantage women scientists and engineers compared with their men colleagues. Bias plays an important role, but it is only one of the features of academic life that creates obstacles for women. Various institutional practices—especially those related to recruitment, tenure, and promotion—have differential effects on women and men. Such practices can have unintended detrimental effects on people whose circumstances do not fit the traditional assumptions on which these practices were based.

The traditional image of the "ideal" scientist or engineer (see below) tends to disadvantage women and advantage men. Even when an institution applies its rules and practices without explicit regard to sex, members of a group that constitutes a small minority in the organization—one less valued and less influential in setting norms—experience the effects of rules and practices differently from members of the more prestigious majority group. That often works to the detriment of the minority. Seemingly neutral practices, based as they are on the life experiences and characteristics of men, can create barriers to the careers of women in science and engineering.

Social connections between academic institutions and other institutions—such as church, day care, schools, health care, or banks—can constrain the options of some people but not others, particularly with regard to expected work schedules. Women still bear the brunt of caregiving and experience the major conflict with such expectations. Institutions will need to recognize the features of their institutional life that disproportionately and systematically burden women and accordingly change policies and practices. Simple one-shot efforts will not remedy the effects of long-standing and pervasively male-biased expectations and norms. Careful analysis of particular situations and thoughtfully designed, multipronged approaches are needed to bring real change and foster the advancement of women scientists and engineers.

THE "IDEAL" SCIENTIST OR ENGINEER

As discussed in the previous chapters, an important constraint on women's careers is the traditional image of who merits an academic position. Not only are men presumed competent while women have to prove their worth, the traditional career model assumes that aspiring researchers can devote the decades of their twenties and thirties single-mindedly to their careers. Deviation or delay in following that course, any substantial hiatus or serious attention to responsibilities outside the academic realm, have traditionally harmed the scientist's or engineer's ability to compete successfully because it has been taken to indicate a lack of seriousness about one's career.

In that model, scientists and engineers may marry, become parents, and participate in family life while pursuing their demanding careers because they have full-time spousal support to assume the major household responsibilities, including rearing children and running the home. It thus presumes a life course and social role that no longer fits many men and does not fit most women.[1] The model clearly does not take into account the life course of women who wish to become parents inasmuch as it requires unbroken concentration on work during the peak female reproductive years. Nor does it take into account the needs of unmarried, divorced, or widowed scientists and engineers who shoulder household, family, and community obligations without spousal support. It is a model that fits the lifestyle of an ever smaller group of people. Furthermore, this outdated model may not fit current trends in science and engineering, which call for more collaborative and less single-minded and individualistic approaches. The need is urgent to transform academic norms and expectations so that the academy can continue to attract the best people.

Beyond the assumptions about timing, the traditional career model assumes that successful faculty members will become part of a community of colleagues in their laboratories, departments, and disciplines, and will receive the guidance and support of senior faculty members. For that to occur, aspiring scientists and engineers must gain acceptance and a feeling of belonging among their colleagues. As discussed in Chapter 3, women constitute a minority—and often a very small minority—in many scientific and engineering fields, and commonly feel isolated, left out, or not accepted. Bringing women and other minority groups into the mainstream is a necessary prerequisite to capturing the talent of the diverse workforce (Box 4-7).

---

[1]E Ostrow (2002). The backlash against academic parents. *Chronicle of Higher Education* (February 22), *http://chronicle.com/jobs/2002/02/2002022202c.htm.*

> Assertiveness and single-mindedness are easier to measure quantitatively than the qualities that we are really interested in, intellectual curiosity, dedication, and so on, which have more human dimensions. Assertiveness and single-mindedness are stand-ins that worked pretty well for a large group of men in previous generations. Even though they are no longer very appropriate, our system still selects for them. And because it "works" (at least if you ignore gender discrimination and such things), we haven't tried very hard to do better.
>
> —Howard Georgi, Mallinkrodt Professor of Physics, Harvard University[2]

RECRUITMENT

Are the recruitment practices used by academic institutions inviting and accessible to women? To understand how to increase the proportion of women and minority-group applicants, universities are studying their own recruitment and hiring practices. In one example, the University of California, Berkeley (UCB) examined department-level data on hiring and recruitment practices and noted which practices correlated with hiring women above, at, or below their percentage in the applicant pool.[3] Departments that were successful in recruiting women did not assume that women feel sufficiently confident or included to send in an application. Merely taking such steps as designating an affirmative action officer to serve on the search committee or stating in the job announcement that women and minority-group members are encouraged to apply correlated with hiring below the level of the applicant pool. However, departments that hired at or above the level of women in the applicant pool used specific strategies that included getting input from graduate students, selecting diverse search committees, and establishing relationships with women at professional meetings and inviting them to apply.

Conflict between work and family also affects the applicant pool. Mason and Goulden have found that married women who have children are

[2]H Georgi (2000). The back page: Is there an unconscious discrimination against women in science? *American Physical Society Newsletter, http://schwinger.harvard.edu/~georgi/women/backpage.htm.*

[3]A Stacy (2006). Recruitment practices. In *Biological, Social, and Organizational Components of Success for Women in Science and Engineering.* Washington, DC: The National Academies Press.

50% less likely to gain faculty positions, compared with single women or married men who have children.[4] Ginther, examining career progression by field, found single women scientists and engineers 16% more likely than single men to be in tenure track jobs 5 years after the PhD while married women with children were 45% less likely than married men with children to be in tenure-track positions. Having children, especially young children, decreases the likelihood of women's obtaining a tenure-track job by 8% to 10% in all science and engineering fields but has no significant impact on men. Ginther attributes those differences to the coincident timing of the tenure and biological clocks and to women's role as primary caregivers for children.[5]

Narrow position specifications also affect the applicant pool and the numbers of women hired. There is mounting evidence that women are choosing to work at the boundaries of disciplines. Among the science, technology, engineering, and mathematics (STEM)[6] faculty at UCB, 26% of the women and 15% of the men have joint appointments. Women tend to hold joint appointments in business, biology, law, city and regional planning, economics, and environmental science. In one of the newer departments, bioengineering, half of the faculty are women. When the biological sciences were restructured to include broad, multidisciplinary approaches, the proportion of women faculty increased to 50%.

> I can't tell you how many times I have reviewed searches in which the people—predominantly women and minority-group members—were not hired, because they didn't "fit".
>
> —Angelica Stacy, Professor of Chemistry and Associate Vice Provost for Faculty Equity, University of California, Berkeley (2006) [7]

As part of its diversity initiative, UCB has started to hold some full-time equivalent faculty positions centrally to encourage groups of faculty and

---

[4]M Mason and M Goulden (2004). Marriage and baby blues: Redefining gender equity in the academy. *Annals of the American Academy of Political Social Science* 596:86-103.

[5]D Ginther (2006). Economics of gendered distribution of resources in academe. In *Biological, Social, and Organizational Components of Success for Women in Academic Science and Engineering*. Washington, DC: The National Academies Press.

[6]At UCB, STEM denotes science, technology, engineering, and mathematics but does not include biology or health sciences.

[7]A Stacy (2006). Recruitment practices. In *Biological, Social, and Organizational Components of Success for Women in Academic Science and Engineering*. Washington, DC: The National Academies Press.

departments to pool resources and propose hires in new multidisciplinary research areas. The University of Wisconsin, Madison, and a number of other institutions have similar central-hire or cohire programs based on a commitment to enhance interdisciplinary research.[8] Those policies counteract the tendency of departments to hire people to fill the mainstream slots, rather than moving the institutions forward into new fields. To accomplish the latter, institutional leadership is important.

INSTITUTIONAL INTERACTIONS

As shown in Chapter 4, distinctions based on sex and race or ethnicity emerge from the identification of people as members of a group, rather than their identification as individuals. Our findings on the education and career trajectories of men and women scientists and engineers do not reveal differences in ability, training, or even productivity that explain the sex differences in career progression. Rather, a web of factors—including psychosocial features, family patterns, institutional requirements, and aspirations and expectations—combine to produce unequal career outcomes for men and women. Various institutions of society—including family, schools, and employers—interact to create obstacles to women's careers.

Those interactions strongly influence the differential choices that men and women make at crucial points along their educational and career progressions. Such choices are not necessarily voluntary. Rather, career choices reflect the broad social structure and therefore tend to reinforce the current sex segregation of occupations.[9] Examples include the greater propensity of women scientists to enter biological science rather than physical science fields and the lower propensity of men than women in general to respond to career setbacks by withdrawing from the workforce and devoting themselves to family responsibilities. Indeed, the latter may be a rational response for women who perceive their career success as adversely affected by factors they cannot (or choose not to) change, such as being female or having children.

The set of societal and institutional connections around family formation are particularly complex and have starkly different effects on men and women scientists and engineers. The institutions on which parents depend for support in caring for their families typically have rules, traditions, as-

---

[8]NAS/NAE/IOM (2004). *Facilitating Interdisciplinary Research*. Washington, DC: The National Academies Press, Chapter 5.

[9]Y Xie and KA Shauman (1998). Sex differences in research productivity: New evidence about an old puzzle. *American Sociological Review* 63(6):847-870.

sumptions, and policies of their own that may conflict with those of laboratories and universities. Familial roles embody implications about available time, energy, and income. Day care providers, schools, and other child-centered organizations run on calendars that assume that parents can be available at particular hours, on particular days, or for entire seasons of the year and can afford particular costs. Laboratories assume that scientists or engineers are available when needed for research, and departments assume that researchers are free to travel to present results and deal with collaborators. Fellowship and hiring committees assume that people are free to relocate to maximize career opportunities.

The importance of institutional connections shows up in the differential career effects of marriage and the presence of young children. They spur the career advancement of men but slow the advancement of women.[10] On average, 64.4% of women doctoral scientists and engineers in tenure or tenure-track careers are married; 83.4% of men are married, 42.2% of women have children, and 50% of men have children. These proportions differ by field, but have not changed substantially between 1993 and 2003 (Figure 5-1). Of those women who are married, more women scientists and engineers are married to men who work full time (Figure 5-2), and depending on field, 64% to 81% of women scientists and engineers marry fellow scientists and engineers (Figure 5-3).

The academic job market is national. Geographic mobility is important for career advancement. At a minimum, most successful academics relocate from where they did their graduate work. A number of lines of evidence indicate that mobility of women academics differs from that of men, and that this is tied to the increased likelihood that more women than men are in dual-career marriages, particularly in marriages to other academics. Research since the 1970s shows that women academics are more likely to be living in large urban areas, a strategy that increases the likelihood that both partners in a dual-career marriage will find satisfactory employment.[11]

---

[10]Y Xie and KA Shauman (2003). *Women in Science: Career Processes and Outcomes.* Cambridge, MA: Harvard University Press; D Ginther (2006). The economics of gender differences in employment outcomes in academia. In *Biological, Social, and Organizational Components of Success for Women in Academic Science and Engineering.* Washington, DC: The National Academies Press; MA Mason and M Goulden (2004). Marriage and baby blues: Redefining gender equity in the academy. *Annals AAPSS* 596:86-103.

[11]J Mincer (1978). Family migration decisions. *Journal of Political Economy* 86:749-773; RH Frank (1978). Family location constraints and the geographic distribution of female professionals. *Journal of Political Economy* 86:117-130; G Marwell, RA Rosenfeld, and S Spilerman (1979). Geographic constraints on women's careers in academia. *Science* 205:1225-1231; RA Rosenfeld and JA Jones (1987). Patterns and effects of geographic mobility for academic women and men. *Journal of Higher Education* 58(5):493-515; KA Shauman and Y Xie (1996). Geographic mobility of scientists: Sex differences and family constraints. *Demography* 33(4):455-468.

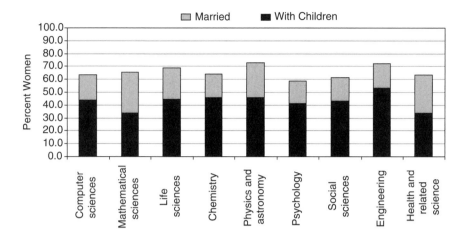

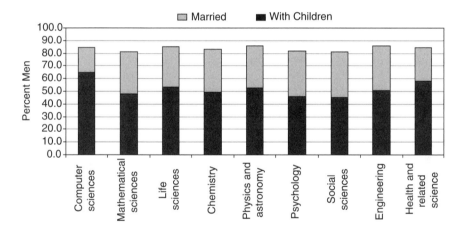

FIGURE 5-1 Percent of women and men doctoral scientists and engineers in tenured or tenure-track positions, by sex, marital status, and presence of children, 2003.
SOURCE: National Science Foundation (2003). *Survey of Doctorate Recipients, 2003.* Arlington, VA: National Science Foundation.

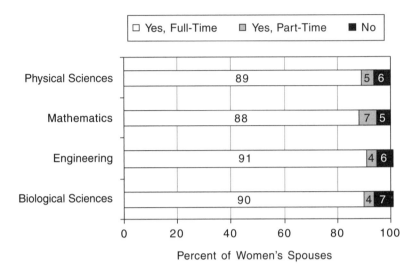

Percent of Women's Spouses

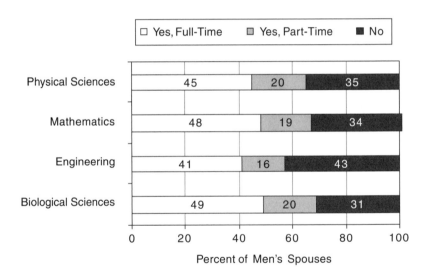

Percent of Men's Spouses

FIGURE 5-2 Spousal employment of science and engineering PhDs, 30-44 years old in 1999: Married PhDs.
SOURCE: National Science Foundation (1999). *Survey of Doctoral Recipients*. Arlington, VA: National Science Foundation.

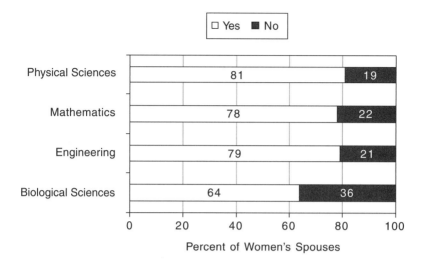

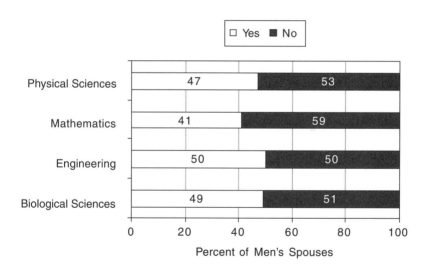

FIGURE 5-3 Employment expertise of spouses of science and engineering PhDs, 30-44 years old in 1999: Married PhDs with employed spouses.
NOTES: Yes = married to another scientist or engineer; No = not married to another scientist or engineer.
SOURCE: National Science Foundation (1999). *Survey of Doctoral Recipients.* Arlington, VA: National Science Foundation.

Irrespective of sex, unmarried scientists have the highest mobility rates, and scientists married to nondoctorate professionals have the lowest mobility rates. Life scientists and physical scientists have higher mobility rates than social scientists. The main difference in mobility by sex centers on the presence of young children. Women's mobility appears much more constrained than men's by preschool (women 11% less likely to move) and elementary-age children (women 39% less likely to move).[12] Whatever the reasons, early parenthood often corresponds with the early years of the mother's scientific or engineering career, so lower mobility limits many women's ability to respond to career opportunities that may make a crucial difference in their ultimate career outcomes. Compromises made in initial faculty appointments can have long-term detrimental effects because the quality of colleagues and the resources available at the crucial early stages of a career affect productivity and visibility in a field. Men's geographic mobility does not appear constrained until their children reach their teens.[13] By that time, an academic career is generally well established and lessened mobility may have a smaller effect on ultimate outcomes.

All those considerations indicate that differences in career trajectories for men and women are generated and reinforced by the social structures in which people are situated and by the networks of interactions in which they participate. Increasing women's representation in science and engineering requires many social, cultural, and economic changes that are large in scale and interdependent.[14]

Family Responsibilities and the Bias Against Caregivers

Underlying the disproportionate disadvantage for the careers of women academic scientists and engineers of parenthood or other significant care responsibilities is a strong cultural devaluation of femininity and a consequent bias against caregivers that is deeply embedded in a number of practices and attitudes in academe.[15] American culture generally stereotypes caregiving as feminine work; many more women than men carry the main or exclusive responsibility for caregiving—whether of children or of elderly

---

[12]Shauman and Xie (1996), ibid.

[13]Shauman and Xie (1996), ibid.

[14]Y Xie and KA Shauman (2003). *Women in Science: Career Processes and Outcomes.* Cambridge, MA: Harvard University Press; JC Williams (2000). *Unbending Gender: Why Work and Family Conflict and What to Do About It.* New York: Oxford University Press.

[15]Williams (2000), ibid; R Drago, C Colbeck, KD Stauffer, A Pirretti, K Burkum, J Fazioli, G Lazarro, and T Habasevich (2005). Bias against caregiving. *Academe* 91(6), *http://www.aaup.org/publications/Academe/2005/05so/05sodrag.htm.*

or disabled relatives—within their families.[16] This is reflected in the fact that overall, women between the ages of 20 and 40 take off more time from work than men to care for children, including disability leave and more time in the hospital.[17] In the United States, 9 in 10 women return to work within a year after the birth of a child;[18] family leave coverage increases the likelihood that a woman will return to work after childbirth.[19] After age 45, the differences in disability leave reverse. Men experience more episodes of chronic illness, longer hospital stays, and are more likely to go on long-term disability.[20]

In academe, caregiving is often seen as competing for the time and attention needed to succeed in highly competitive fields and, therefore, as indicating a lack of dedication to a scientific career. The determination to overcome the difficulties inherent in doing science while bearing caring responsibilities is somehow not generally seen as indicating the even greater dedication to science or engineering that it represents.[21]

> I really felt by having a child I gave up a lot of respect I had worked very hard to earn.
>
> —Anonymous woman professor, 2001[22]

---

[16]E Lehrer and M Nerlove (1986). Female labor force behavior and fertility in the United States. *Annual Review of Sociology* 12:181-204.

[17]I Akerlind, K Alexanderson, G Hensing, M Liejon, and P Bjurulf (1996). Sex differences in absence in relation to parental status. *Scandinavian Journal of Social Medicine* 24(1):27-35; JP Vistnes (1997). Gender differences in days lost from work due to illness. *Industrial and Labor Relations Review* 50(2):304-323.

[18]S Desai and LJ Waite (1991). Women's employment during pregnancy and after the first birth: Occupational characteristics and work commitment. *American Sociological Review* 56(4):551-566.

[19]KL Brewster and RR Rindfuss (2000). Fertility and women's employment in industrialized nations. *Annual Review of Sociology* 26:271-296; J Waldfogel, Y Higuchi, and M Abe (1999). Family leave policies and women's retention after childbirth: Evidence from the United States, Britain, and Japan. *Journal of Population Economics* 12:523-545.

[20]S Gjesdal and E Bratburg (2002). The role of gender in long-term sickness absence and transition to permanent disability benefits. *The European Journal of Public Health* 12(3):180-186; A Case and C Paxson (2005). Sex differences in morbidity and mortality. *Demography* 42(2):189-214.

[21]For example, see J Fletcher (2001). *Disappearing Acts. Gender, Power, and Relational Practice at Work.* Cambridge, MA: MIT Press.

[22]Participant in leadership workshop hosted by the Committee on the Advancement of Women Chemists (COACh).

The Maternal Wall

Women attempting to pursue scientific or engineering careers while also carrying major child-care responsibilities encounter a well-documented complex of constraints and biases called the *maternal wall*, which contributes to the scarcity of women in the upper faculty ranks.[23] Research has shown that the maternal wall, also known as *family responsibilities discrimination*, penalizes mothers, potential mothers, and fathers who seek an active role in family care.[24] The researchers document that mothers experience gender stereotyping in how jobs are defined, in the standards to which they are held, and in assumptions that are made about them and their work; for example, a man who is absent is assumed to be presenting a paper, whereas a woman who is absent is assumed to be taking care of her children. Mothers also face negative assumptions about their competence, specifically, that they are less competent or committed than other workers. Similarly, fathers who take parental leave or even a short leave to deal with family matters often receive fewer rewards and lower performance ratings and are viewed as less committed.

> I have been under a lot of stress dealing with expectations after having a child. In the eyes of the departmental administration I was no longer a faculty member but had become a "pregnant female." There was no prior experience with this overlap so the expectations of me were way out of line with how we normally treat faculty.
>
> —Anonymous woman professor, 2001[25]

Because of those effects, parenthood, especially when it begins early in an academic career, affects women's prospects for advancement far more adversely than men's. Motherhood has been identified as the factor most

---

[23]JC Williams (2004). Hitting the maternal wall. *Academe* 90(6), *http://www.aaup.org/publications/Academe/2004/04nd/04ndwill.htm.*

[24]JC Williams and HC Cooper (2004). The public policy of motherhood. *Journal of Social Issues* 60(4):849-865; C Etaugh and G Gilomen (1989). Perceptions of mothers: Effects of employment status, marital status, and age of child. *Sex Roles: A Journal of Research* 20:59-70; C Etaugh and C Moss (2001). Attitudes of employed women toward parents who choose full-time or part-time employment following their child's birth. *Sex Roles: A Journal of Research* 44:611-619; SJ Correll and S Benard (2005). Getting a job: Is there a motherhood penalty? *Presentation at American Sociological Association Annual Meeting, August 15, 2005, Philadelphia, PA, http://sociology.princeton. edu/programs/workshops/Correll_Benard_manuscript.pdf.*

[25]Participant in leadership workshop hosted by COACh.

likely to preclude a woman with science or engineering training from pursuing or advancing in an academic career.[26] As discussed above, women scientists and engineers disproportionately marry fellow scientists and engineers.[27] For example, 44% of women members of the American Physical Society are married to physicists, and another 25% are married to other scientists. 80% of women mathematicians and 33% of women chemists are married to men in their fields.[28] Marrying within an academic discipline, termed *disciplinary endogamy*, is more widespread in the sciences and engineering than in other academic fields. It can create problems for hiring (especially for women), because most universities do not have dual-career hiring policies.[29] Even in the 1980s, 20% of faculty resignations were related to spousal employment.[30] Wolf-Wendel and colleagues have surveyed dual-career policies at 360 institutions of higher education, performed case studies of five colleges and universities, and compiled a detailed compendium of institutional policies and practices.[31]

That said, women on highly competitive academic career tracks are less likely to marry or reproduce and more likely to divorce than comparable men or than women in lower-level academic posts.[32] A longitudinal study of more than 160,000 academics shows that two-thirds of women who took academic jobs on the fast track before they had become mothers never had children.[33] While there was no change in marriage rates of PhD recipients from 1978 to 1994, both men and women PhDs are increasingly

---

[26]Y Xie and KA Shauman (2003). *Women in Science: Career Processes and Outcomes.* Cambridge, MA: Harvard University Press; D Ginther (2006). The economics of gender differences in employment outcomes in academia. In *Biological, Social, and Organizational Components of Success for Women in Academic Science and Engineering.* Washington, DC: The National Academies Press; MA Mason and M Goulden (2004). Marriage and baby blues: Redefining gender equity in the academy. *Annals AAPSS* 596:86-103.

[27]MA Mason and M Goulden (2002). Do babies matter? The effect of family formation on the lifelong careers of academic men and women. *Academe* 88(6):21-27, *http://www.aaup.org/ publications/Academe/2002/02nd/02ndmas.htm.*

[28]Stanford Study on Dual-Career Couples, see *http://news-service.stanford.edu/news/2005/ november9/dual-110905.html;* LE Wolf-Wendel, SB Twombly, and S Rice (2000). Dual-career-couples: Keeping them together. *Journal of Higher Education* 71(3):291-321.

[29]LE Wolf-Wendel, S Twombly, and S Rice (2000). The two-body problem: Dual-career-couples hiring practices in higher education. *The Journal of Higher Education* 71(3):291-321.

[30]D Burke (1988). *A New Academic Marketplace.* New York: Greenwood Press.

[31]L Wolf-Wendel, SB Twombly, and S Rice (2003). *The Two-Body Problem: Dual-Career-Couple Hiring Practices in Higher Education.* Baltimore: Johns Hopkins University Press.

[32]Drago et al. (2005), ibid; B Sullivan, C Hollenshead, and G Smith (2004). Developing and implementing work-family policies for faculty. *Academe* 90(6), *http://www.aaup.org/ publications/ Academe/2004/04nd/04ndsull.htm.*

[33]Mason and Goulden (2002), ibid.

delaying having children until later in their career.[34] About 45% of women who have tenure do not have children. That rate of childlessness—much higher than among tenured men—reflects the belief of many young female academics that they must choose between tenure and children and can have one only at the cost of the other.[35]

Given the tie between gender and caregiving, ostensibly gender-neutral institutional policies often seriously disadvantage women scientists and engineers. They may be as apparently innocuous as providing funding to cover travel expenses but not additional child care expenses for scientists attending out-of-town conferences to present papers. The widely used 7-year tenure clock and the pressure on tenure candidates to show early promise, although apparently gender-neutral, often force women to choose between taking time out for pregnancy, childbirth, and child care, or pursuing a fast-track career.

Scientists and engineers are generally well aware of the bias against caregivers, and those seeking fast-track academic careers use a number of strategies to keep family responsibilities from damaging their careers. One is to minimize family commitments that interfere with career progress. The most obvious method is avoiding marriage and parenthood. Overall, 17% of women at research universities stay single, as opposed to 10% of men; 30% of women but only 13% of men have limited their number of children to avoid anticipated career damage; 18% of women but only 8% of men have delayed their second child for the same reason.[36]

A number of universities permit faculty members to request that the tenure clock stop for a period or that their workload be temporarily lightened to mitigate the career effects of childbearing and childrearing. Many academics, however, fearful of seeming to lack dedication and seriousness, decline to avail themselves of those opportunities. Over a 7-year period at one large research university, for example, only four parents of either sex, of the 257 on the tenure track, took advantage of official family leave.[37] That tactic typifies the effort to deflect attention from one's family responsibilities. Other tactics include missing children's events and returning to

---

[34]M Mason and M Goulden (2004). Marriage and baby blues: Redefining gender equity in the academy. *Annals of the American Academy of Political Social Science* 596:86-103.

[35]R Drago (2006). The value of work-family policies. In *Biological, Social, and Organizational Components of Success for Women in Academic Science and Engineering*. Washington, DC: The National Academies Press.

[36]A Stacy (2006), ibid.

[37]Drago et al. (2005), ibid.

work earlier than desired after a birth. Studies show that more women than men engage in these tactics, which adds to their stress. For faculty—men and women—who engage in bias avoidance behaviors, time to tenure was reduced and age at tenure was reduced by over a year.[38]

Thus, the mere existence of apparently family-friendly policies at universities will not reduce the pressure on women faculty or their fear that family life will damage or even destroy their careers. Rather, to reduce the conflict between work and family that faculty members experience, university leaders, including top administrators and department chairs, must adopt policies that recognize and mitigate the disadvantages imposed by caregiving and, through word and deed, demonstrate their belief that faculty members can combine a high level of professional achievement with family life (Box 5-1).[39]

Glass Ceilings

In addition to the maternal wall, women scientists must contend with the "glass ceiling," another complex of attitudes and practices that keeps women in many organizations and professions out of the most powerful, influential, and prestigious positions because they are assumed to be unfit for leadership.[40] The tendency to see women as less competent than men and their accomplishments as less worthy and significant is a prominent component of the glass ceiling. Scientific and professional societies and universities need to recognize talented women and provide opportunities to serve in leadership roles; these can be as various as keynote speaker, center director, elected position, prestigious award, or an administrative position.[41] That said, the eagerness to find talented women sometimes causes them to be promoted before they have had enough experience. As with any

---

[38]Drago, et al. (2005), ibid.

[39]K Ward and L Wolf-Wendel (2004). Fear factor: How safe is it to make time for family? *Academe* 90(6), *http://www.aaup.org/publications/Academe/2004/04nd/04ndward.htm.*

[40]JC Williams (2006). Long time no see: Why are there still so few women in academic science and engineering. In *Biological, Social, and Organizational Components of Success for Women in Academic Science and Engineering.* Washington, DC: The National Academies Press; JC Alessio and J Andrzejski (2000). Unveiling the hidden glass ceiling. *American Sociological Review* 26(2):311-315.

[41]If University leaders do appoint women to positions of prominence, where they can gain leadership experience, these women have a high probability of going on to even greater things. For example, every woman ever appointed to the position of Provost at Yale has as her next job become President of a prestigious university (Hanna Gray, President of University of Chicago; Judith Rodin, President of the University of Pennsylvania; Alison Richard, Vice Chancellor of Cambridge University; and Susan Hockfield, President of the Massachusetts Institute of Technology).

DEFINING THE ISSUES

Box 5-1 Universities Reaffirm Pledge for Gender Equity[a]

In 2001, nine universities came together as a group to state publicly that "institutions of higher education have an obligation, both for themselves and for the nation, to develop and utilize fully all the creative talent available." They reaffirmed that statement in 2005, recognizing that barriers to the full participation of women still exist, not only in science and engineering, but also in academic fields throughout higher education.

"In the summer of 2005, representatives from our nine universities convened to share best practices and specific initiatives addressing faculty with family responsibilities. While considerable progress has been made since 2001, we acknowledge that there are still significant steps to be taken toward making academic careers compatible with family caregiving responsibilities. Our goal as research universities is to create conditions in which all faculty are capable of the highest level of academic achievement. Continuing to develop *academic personnel policies, institutional resources, and a culture that supports family commitments* is therefore essential for maximizing the productivity of our faculty. The future excellence of our institutions depends on our ability to provide equitable and productive career paths for all faculty."

—David Baltimore, California Institute of Technology; Lawrence H. Summers, Harvard University; Susan Hockfield, Massachusetts Institute of Technology; Shirley M. Tilghman, Princeton University; John Hennessy, Stanford University; Robert Birgeneau, University of California, Berkeley; Mary Sue Coleman, University of Michigan; Amy Gutmann, University of Pennsylvania; Richard C. Levin, Yale University

---

[a]*http://www.berkeley.edu/news/media/releases/2005/12/06_geneq.shtml.*

---

promotion, this works only if there is enough advice and support from above. The Committee on the Advancement of Women Chemists (COACh) program is an example of what can be done to "break" the glass ceiling (Box 4-3).[42]

PIONEERS AND TIPPING POINTS

The obstacles and impediments that women scientists and engineers experience as they pursue careers in academic institutions do not arise

---

[42]See also J Sheridan, PF Brennan, M Carnes, and J Handelsman (2006). Discovering directions for change in higher education through the experiences of senior women faculty. *Journal of Technology Transfer* 31:387-396.

solely from institutional constraints, stereotyping, or bias. Organizational studies show that introducing members of previously excluded groups into social units creates predictable attitudes and reactions among both the new arrivals and the established group members. The exact nature of these behaviors depends in part on the personalities and attitudes of the established members and on the number of newcomers relative to the group at large.[43] Sometimes the members engage in bullying or threatening behavior, at other times, welcoming and supportive behavior. The reactions evolve as the proportion changes.[44]

Bullying behavior is often systematically applied to women and can persist even in the highest levels of the academic hierarchy. Bullying is an abuse or misuse of power characterized by work-oriented aggression and is distinct from sexual harassment in nature and target of the aggression.[45] Work-related bullying may involve excessive assignment of work, reassignment of responsibilities, unfair criticism, and excessive monitoring. Bullies tend to target newcomers, particularly those from groups not well-represented in the workplace. In science and engineering academic environments, this means women are often targeted. Furthermore, gender plays a role in the form and perception of bullying. So, although both men and women are bullied, women tend to be affected differently. The combined effects of being more likely to be targeted, less likely to report bullying behavior, and lacking support structures can translate to a hostile environment for women in high academic and administrative positions. Mentoring programs have been effective at strengthening the support infrastructure and helping women faculty survive and overcome bullying. Ombuds offices are another avenue providing advocacy and support for those targeted.

For the small numbers of women in faculty and leadership positions in science and engineering a major issue is singularity or tokenism (Box 5-2). Numerical representation is an influential structural characteristic of most work organizations. Minority-group size affects attitudes, achievement, and the frequency and quantity of interpersonal contact between

---

[43]B Reskin and P Roos (1990). *Job Queues, Gender Queues: Explaining Women's Inroads into Male Occupations*. Philadelphia: Temple University Press.

[44]J Martin (2006). Gendered organizations. In *Biological, Social, and Organizational Components of Success for Women in Academic Science and Engineering*. Washington, DC: The National Academies Press.

[45]R Simpson and C Cohen (2004). Dangerous work: The gendered nature of bullying in the context of higher education. *Gender, Work and Organization* 11(2):163-186; R Young and H Sweeting (2004). Adolescent bullying, relationships, psychological well-being, and gender-atypical behavior: A gender diagnosticity approach. *Sex Roles: A Journal of Research* 50(7/8):525-537.

majority and minority group members[46] and may also affect salaries.[47] However, as dicussed in Chapter 4 (Box 4-7) the reliance on quotas to eliminate the occupational inequalities faced by tokens, the "add women and minority-group members and stir" model, may hinder the integration of the workplace if the underlying institutional structures are not addressed.[48]

Pioneering women scientists and engineers who are among the first of their sex to enter a field or laboratory or to be hired in a department face the predictable problems of tokenism and scarcity, including social isolation and extreme visibility.[49] The problems are more pronounced for pioneering women who belong to underrepresented racial or ethnic minorities.[50] Thus, even when women scientists and engineers achieve high academic rank in research I universities, full equality with their male colleagues often eludes them.

A survey of women science faculty members at MIT, for example, found that those in junior positions felt that their departments supported them and that gender bias would not threaten their future careers. Many of the women in tenured senior positions found themselves effectively "invisible" and "marginalized" within their departments and excluded from par-

---

[46]RM Kanter (1977). *Men and Women of the Corporation.* New York: Basic Books; N Toren and V Kraus (1987). The effects of minority size on women's position in academia. *Social Forces* 65:1090-1100; PB Jackson, PA Thoits, and HF Taylor (1995). Composition of the workplace and psychological well-being: The effects of tokenism on America's black elite. *Social Forces* 74(2):543-557; M Gladwell (2000). *The Tipping Point: How Little Things Can Make a Big Difference.* Boston: Little, Brown.

[47]M Bellas (1997). Disciplinary differences in faculty salaries: Does gender play a role? *Journal of Higher Education* 68(3):299-321.

[48]J Yoder (1991). Rethinking tokenism: Looking beyond numbers. *Gender and Society* 5(2):178-192; L Zimmer (1998). Tokenism and women in the workplace: The limits of gender-neutral theory. *Social Problems* 35(1):64-77; J Crocker and KM McGraw (1984). What's good for the goose is not good for the gander: Solo status as an obstacle to occupational achievement for males and females. *American Behavioral Scientist* 27(3):357-369; TF Pettigrew and J Martin (1987). Shaping the organizational context for Black American inclusion. *Journal of Social Issues* 43(1):41-78; J Martin (2006). Gendered organizations: Scientists and engineers in universities and corporations. In *Biological, Social, and Organizational Components of Success for Women in Academic Science and Engineering.* Washington, DC: The National Academies Press.

[49]RM Kanter (1997). *Men and Women of the Corporation.* New York: Basic Books; J Crocker and KM McGraw (1984), ibid.

[50]SM Malcom, PQ Hall, and JW Brown (1975). *The Double Bind: The Price of Being a Minority Woman in Science* (Pub. # 76-R-3). Washington, DC: American Association for the Advancement of Science; J Lach (1999). Minority women hit a "concrete ceiling". *American Demographics* 21(9):8-19.

FOCUS ON RESEARCH

BOX 5-2 Workplace Pioneers: "Men in Skirts"

When these women enter the workforce, they all begin with a common assumption: I have a chance. They believe their degrees, their raw talent, their ingenuity, and their industry will be the keys to their success. Then somewhere along the way, the women—especially the black women—begin to see that people still question their intelligence, and discount what they think. They are told to wait for opportunities, to prove themselves. So they wait. They continue to prove themselves. They contribute to the company's bottom line, they take on leadership positions, and they put in excessive time, often to the detriment of their personal lives. Yet, even the most successful women reach the point where they realize their own expectations haven't been met. That the rewards are not always commensurate with the costs. Many keep searching—and aching—for an answer. Others find this too toxic, and regrettably, bow out.[a]

Commitment to an organization is directly related to a person's comfort with their relationship to the organization: are opinions, experiences, and perspectives heard and respected?[b] Are contributions valued? Most newcomers enter the workplace expecting no difficulty fitting in. However, when a newcomer is identified by the current workers as an outsider—whether that determination be based on demographic factors such as race or gender, or cultural, physical, or role-related factors[c]—that optimism can turn to a sense of being tolerated rather than accepted.[d] The resulting emotional conflict is likely to lead to increased absence and turnover.[e]

---

[a]ELJ Edmonson Bell and SM Nkomo (2001). *Our Separate Ways: Black and White Women and the Struggle for Personal Identity.* Boston, MA: Harvard Business School Press.
[b]B Schneider (1987). The people make the place. *Personnel Psychology* 40: 437-453.
[c]JE McGrath, JL Berdahl, and H Arrow (1995). Traits, expectations, culture and clout: The dynamics of diversity in workgroups. In *Diversity in Work Teams*, eds. SE Jackson and MD Ruderman. Washington, DC: American Psychological Association; LH Pelled (1996). Demographic diversity, conflict, and work group outcomes: An intervening process theory. *Organization Science* 7:615-631; TH Cox (1993). *Cultural Diversity in Organizations: Theory, Research, and Practice.* San Francisco: Berrett-Keohler; LK Larkey (1996). Toward a theory of communicative interactions in culturally diverse workgroups. *Academy of Management Review* 21:463-491; C Strangor, L Lynch, C Duan, and B Glass (1992). Categorization of individuals on the basis of multiple social features. *Journal of Personality and Social Psychology* 62:207-218; ML Maznevski (1994). Understanding our differences: Performance in decision-making groups with diverse members. *Human Relations* 47:531-552.
[d]SE Taylor and ST Fiske (1976). The token in the small group: Research findings and research implications. In ed. J. Sweeney, *Psychology and Politics: Collected Papers.* New Haven, CT: Yale University Press.
[e]BE McCain, C O'Reilly, and J Pfeffer (1983). The effects of departmental demography on turnover: The case of a university. *Academy of Management Journal* 26:626-641; C O'Reilly, DF Caldwell, and WP Barnett (1989). Work group demography, social integration, and turnover. *Administrative Science Quarterly* 34:21-37; SE Jackson, JF Brett, VI Sessa, DM Cooper, JA Julin, and K Peyronnin (1991). Some differences make a difference: Individual dissimilarity and group heterogeneity as correlates of recruitment, promotions, and turnover. *Journal of Applied Psychology* 76:675-689.

continued

BOX 5-2 Continued

There is an implicit assumption that the differences between groups are larger than the variance within groups. This leads to the phenomenon called "outgroup homogeneity." In effect, when it comes to values, personality traits, and other characteristics, people tend to see outsiders (members of a group to which one does not belong) as more alike each other than insiders (members of the group to which one belongs). As a result, outsiders are at risk of being seen as interchangeable or expendable, and they are more likely to be stereotyped.[f] Why is this? In-group members usually have less contact with outsiders,[g] but this is not the sole factor. People tend to organize and recall information about insiders in terms of persons rather than abstract characteristics.[h] In some cases, people are also more motivated to make distinctions among others with whom they will have future contact.[i] Together, these factors produce a group of differentiated insiders and a relatively homogeneous, undifferentiated outsider group. This tendency of people to favor their own group, known as insider bias, has been found in cultures around the world.[j]

Some researchers argue that increasing the number of outsiders in a group or organization will lead to a reduced perception of difference and hence reduced discrimination.[k] Others argue that increased numbers threaten the current majority group and lead to increased discriminatory behavior, termed *backlash,*[l] and suggest that any numerical increase must be combined with attention to status and power relationships.[m] Certainly, the historical representation of women in a job

---

[f]See review by S Plous (2003). The psychology of prejudice, stereotyping and discrimination: An overview. In *Understanding Prejudice and Discrimination*, ed. S Plous. New York: McGraw-Hill.

[g]MR Islam and M Hewstone (1993). Dimensions of contact as predictors of intergroup anxiety, perceived out-group variability, and out-group attitude: An integrative model. *Personality and Social Psychology Bulletin* 38:203-210; PW Linville and GW Fischer (1993). Exemplar and abstraction models of perceived group variability and stereotypicality. *Social Cognition* 11:92-125.

[h]TM Ostrom, SL Carpenter, C Sedikeides, and F Li (1993). Differential processing of ingroup and out-group information. *Journal of Personality and Social Psychology* 64:21-34; B Park and CM Judd (1990). Measures and models of perceived group variability. *Journal of Personality and Social Psychology* 59:173-191.

[i]PW Linville (1988). The heterogeneity of homogeneity. In *Attribution and Social Interaction: The Legacy of Edward E. Jones*, eds. JM Darley and J Cooper. Washington, DC: American Psychological Association.

[j]CL Aberson, M Healy, and V Romero (2000). Ingroup bias and self-esteem: A meta-analysis. *Personality and Social Psychology Review* 4:157-173; MB Brewer (1999). The psychology of prejudice: Ingroup love or outgroup hate? *Journal of Social Issues* 55:429-444.

[k]PM Blau (1977). *Inequality and Heterogeneity.* New York: Free Press; RM Kanter (1977). *Men and Women of the Corporation.* New York: Basic Books; BA Gutek (1985). *Sex and the Workplace.* San Francisco: Jossey-Bass; TH Cox (1993). *Cultural Diversity in Organizations: Theory, Research, and Practice.* San Francisco: Berret-Koehler; LK Larkey (1996). Toward a theory of communicative interactions in culturally diverse workgroups. *Academy of Management Review* 21:453-491.

[l]HM Blalock (1957). Percent non-white and discrimination in the South. *American Sociological Review* 22:677-682; JD Yoder (1991). Rethinking tokenism: Looking beyond the numbers. *Gender and Society* 5:178-192.

has tremendous impact on compensation, reward, mobility prospects, and workplace culture.[n] Women who are relatively new to traditionally male-dominated work settings often attract more attention, are evaluated more extremely, are perceived as outsiders, receive less support, and are more likely to be viewed as a disruptive force in the workplace than male co-workers.[o] Similar consequences are seen in workplaces with skewed racial distributions.[p]

Strategies used to bring newcomers into a group influence how people express and manage tensions related to diversity, whether members of traditionally underrepresented groups feel respected and valued by their colleagues, and how people interpret the meaning of their sex or racial identity at work. These, in turn, have implications for how well the workgroup and its members function. There are three basic strategies employed by groups and organizations to incorporate people with different backgrounds and perspectives: acceptance, assimilation, or convergence.

Acceptance. That "essential differences"[q] exist between groups is hotly debated;[r] empirical research shows that acceptance of the differences hypothesis does not alter power imbalances and can often exacerbate outsider status.[s]

---

[m]L Zimmer (1988). Tokenism and women in the workplace: The limits of gender-neutral theory. *Social Problems* 35:64-77; Alderfer (1992). Changing race relations embedded in organizations: Report on a long-term project with the XYZ corporation. In ed. SE Jackson, *Diversity in the Workplace: Human Resources Initiatives*. New York: Guilford Press; SJ South, CM Bonjean, WT Markham, and J Corder (1982). Social structure and intergroup interaction: Men and women of the federal bureaucracy. *American Sociological Review* 47:587-599; AM Konrad, S Winter, and BA Gutek (1992). Diversity in work group sex composition: Implications for minority or minority members. In *Research in the Sociology of Organizations*, eds. PS Tolbert and SB Bacharach. Greenwich, CT: JAI Press; J Martin (2006). Gendered organizations: Scientists and engineers in universities and corporations. In *Biological, Social, and Organizational Components of Success for Women in Academic Science and Engineering*. Washington, DC: The National Academies Press.

[n]B Gutek and B Morasch (1982). Sex ratios, sex-role spillover, and sexual harassment of women at work. *Journal of Social Issues* 38:55-74; P England (1992). *Comparable Worth: Theories and Evidence*. New York: Aldine de Gruyter.

[o]RM Kanter (1977). *Men and Women of the Corporation*. New York: Basic Books; DF Izraeli (1983). Sex effects or structural effects: An empirical test of Kanter's theory of proportions. *Social Forces* 62:153-165.

[p]TF Pettigrew and J Martin (1987). Shaping the organizational context for black American inclusion. *Journal of Social Issues* 43:41-78; PG Devine and AJ Elliott (1995). Are racial stereotypes really fading? The Princeton Trilogy revisited. *Personality and Social Psychology Bulletin* 21:1139-1150; G Wilson, I Sakura-Lemessy, and JP West (1999). Reaching for the top: Racial differences in mobility paths to upper-tier occupations. *Work and Occupations* 26:165-186.

[q]C Gilligan (1982). *In a Different Voice*. Cambridge, MA: Harvard University Press; MF Belenkey, BM Clincy; NR Goldberger, and JM Tarule (1986). *Women's Ways of Knowing: The Development of Self, Voice, and Mind*. New York: Basic Books; S Baron-Cohen (2002). *The Essential Difference: The Truth about the Male and Female Brain*. New York: Basic Books.

[r]S Harding (1986). *The Science Question in Feminism*. Ithaca: Cornell University Press; C Di Stefano (1990). Dilemmas of difference: Feminism, modernity, and postmodernism. In *Feminism/Postmodernism*, ed. LJ Nicholson, New York: Routledge.

continued

BOX 5-2 Continued

Assimilation of outsiders leads to feelings of inauthenticity—for women, the "men in skirts" phenomenon.[t] At the same time, some argue that there is little reason to assume that outsiders placed in an organization will be able to withstand pressure to conform.

Convergence. In workplace situations where repeated personal interaction is required, game theory indicates that cooperation is the preferred strategy, particularly where players are able to monitor each other[u] or mobility is low,[v] two conditions that often exist in the workplace. To achieve cooperation among diverse group members, research shows that creating a convergent environment in which group members are seen as individuals rather than group members reduces between-group differences and creates a common in-group identity—everyone rooting for the same team.[w] Empirical research shows that only the convergence per-

---

[s]CF Epstein (1988). *Deceptive Distinctions.* New Haven, CT: Yale University Press; MT Mednick (1989). On the politics of psychological constructs: Stop the bandwagon, I want to get off. *American Psychologist* 44:1118-1123; M Calas and L Smirich (1993). Dangerous liaisons: The feminine-in-management meets globalization. *Business Horizons* 36(2):71-81; J Flax (1990). Postmodernism and gender relations in feminist theory. In *Feminism/Postmodernism,* ed. LJ Nicholson, New York: Routledge; J Fletcher (2001). *Disappearing Acts: Gender, Power, and Relational Practice at Work.* Cambridge, MA: MIT Press; RJ Ely and DE Meyerson (2000). Theories of gender in organizations: A new approach to organizational analysis and change. *Research in Organizational Behavior* 22:105-153; R Barnett and C Rivers (2004). *Same Difference: How Gender Myths Are Hurting Our Relationships, Our Children, and Our Jobs.* New York: Basic Books.

[t]J Martin and D Myerson (1998). Women and power: Conformity, resistance, and disorganized coaction. In *Power and Influence in Organizations,* eds. RM Kramer and MA Neale. San Francisco: Sage Publications; AM Morrison (1992). New solutions to the same old glass ceiling. *Women in Management Review* 7(4):15-19; ELJ Edmonson Bell and SM Nkomo (2001). *Our Separate Ways: Black and White Women and the Struggle for Personal Identity.* Boston, MA: Harvard Business School Press.

[u]TR Palfrey and H Rosenthal (1994). Repeated play, cooperation and coordination: An experimental study. *Review of Economic Studies* 61:545-565.

---

ticipating in significant decisions. Even more striking, those extremely accomplished scientists reported that their sense of marginalization had grown as their careers advanced. Early in their careers, they, like their junior colleagues of today, had believed "that gender discrimination was 'solved' in the previous generation and would not touch them. Gradually, however, their eyes were opened to the realization that the playing field was not level after all."[51]

---

[51]Massachusetts Institute of Technology (1999). A study on the status of women faculty in science at MIT. *MIT Faculty Newsletter* 11(4), *http://web.mit.edu/fnl/women/women.htm.*

spective provides the rationale and guidance needed to achieve sustained bene-fits from diversity.[x] Convergence aims to ensure that practices are "identity-blind," or the *same for each individual.*[y] Unless done carefully, efforts to get decision-makers to attend to the actual traits of individuals can backfire, and increase the degree to which stereotypes shape decisions.[z] Done well, convergence promotes both the attitudinal and structural integration of individuals with diverse back-grounds and perspectives.[aa]

[v]JM Guttman (1996). Rational actors, tit-for-tat types, and the evolution of cooperation. *Journal of Economic Behavior and Organization* 29:27-56.

[w]SL Gaertner, JF Dovidio, BS Banker, MC Rust, JA Nier, GR Mottola, and CM Ward (2003). The challenge of aversive racism: Combating pro-white bias. In *Understanding Prejudice and Discrimination*, ed. S Plous, New York: McGraw-Hill; S Jaffee and JS Hyde (2000). Gender differences in moral orientation: A meta-analysis. *Psychological Bulletin* 126:703-726; GR Franke, DF Crown, and DF Spake (1997). Gender differences in ethical perceptions of business practice: A social role theory perspective. *Journal of Applied Psychology* 82:920-934; G Hofstede (2001). *Culture's Consequences: Comparing Values, Behaviors, Institutions and Organizations across Nations.* Thousand Oaks, CA: Sage.

[x]JA Gilbert, BA Stead, and JM Ivancevich (1999). Diversity management: A new organizational paradigm. *Journal of Business Ethics* 21:61-76; RJ Ely and DA Thomas (2001). Cultural diversity at work: The effects of diversity perspectives on work group processes and outcomes. *Administrative Science Quarterly* 46(2):229-273.

[y]WT Bielby (2000). Minimizing workplace gender and racial bias. *Contemporary Sociology* 29(1):120-129; AM Konrad and F Linnehan (1995). Formalized HRM structures: Coordinating Equal Employment Opportunity or concealing organizational practices? *Academy of Management Journal* 38:787-829.

[z]F Pratto and JA Bargh (1991). Stereotyping based on apparently individuating information: Trait and global components of sex stereotypes under attention overload. *Journal of Experimental Social Psychology* 27:26-47; ST Fiske, M Linn, and SL Neuberg (1999). The continuum model: Ten years later. In *Dual Process Theories in Social Psycholog,.* eds. S Chaiken and Y Trope. New York: Guilford Press.

[aa]LK Larkey (1996). Toward a theory of communicative interactions in a culturally diverse workgroups. *Academy of Management* Review 21:463-491.

If the number of women in a field or department grows to about 20% of total membership, a "critical mass" develops, and a social tipping point occurs.[52] Women now form a noticeable contingent in the organization and start to perceive their common interests, joining together to press for improvements in policies relevant to their needs, such as those concerning

[52]TF Pettigrew and J Martin (1987). Shaping the organizational context for Black American inclusion. *Journal of Social Issues* 43(1):41-78; M Gladwell (2000). *The Tipping Point: How Little Things Can Make a Big Difference.* Boston: Little Brown.

family issues. They also begin to appear in leadership positions. With these signs of solidarity, however, the first signs of backlash begin to appear among the men, who start to perceive women as a threat to the established order and to their traditional position and privileges. Men may begin to resist further hiring or promotion of women, sometimes overtly but often covertly.[53]

It seems that when I stand up for myself and speak my mind, I am told that I am crazy, that I am a trouble-maker. What makes this particularly difficult to deal with is that this is exactly opposite to the way I was treated when I first arrived here. For the first 3 or 4 years I had a voice and was seemingly a highly respected and contributing member of the department. Getting cut off and invalidated in this way seemed to correlate almost exactly with the many outward signs of my success as a scientist in my field. It was then that I did not receive the greater respect that I had seemingly earned. Instead, I was cut off and treated in a patronizing manner.

—Anonymous female associate professor, 2004[54]

If female representation continues to increase and reaches 40%-60% of the group, a second tipping point occurs. Now gender issues seem to matter less and attract less attention. Such issues as bias and inequality in hiring, pay and promotion seem to disappear. If the proportion of women continues to grow, however, a third tipping point occurs; at 90% gender segregation returns; the department or field is now perceived as female and therefore less appropriate to men. The changeover from male to female can bring substantial consequences, in that fields viewed as female are less prestigious and poorer paying than those viewed as male.[55]

---

[53]See discussion of tipping points in science and engineering fields in P England, P Allison, S Li, N Mark, J Thompson, M Budig, and H Sun (2004). *Why Are Some Academic Fields Tipping Toward Female? The Sex Composition of US Fields of Doctoral Degree Receipt, 1971-1998, http://www.stanford.edu/dept/soc/people/faculty/england/Tipping.pdf*; L Zhang (2004). *Crowd Out or Opt Out: The Changing Landscape of Doctorate Production in American Universities* (Working Paper 63). Ithaca, NY: Cornell Higher Education Research Institute. *http://www.ilr.cornell.edu/cheri/wp/cheri_wp63.pdf.*
[54]Participant in leadership workshop hosted by COACh.
[55]B Reskin and P Roos (1990). *Job Queues, Gender Queues: Explaining Women's Inroads into Male Occupations*. Philadelphia: Temple University Press; M Bellas (1997). Disciplinary differences in faculty salaries: Does gender play a role? *Journal of Higher Education* 68(3):299-321.

THE LEGAL LANDSCAPE

The need for universities to develop practices that provide women scientists and engineers an equal chance of career success is far more than a moral imperative. Under modern anti-discrimination law, it is also a legal requirement. The low representation of women in the upper reaches of academe was long attributed to the "chilly climate" of those high realms. Today, however, legal thinkers argue that remedial action must go beyond vague formulations of creating a culture of faculty support. Universities must meet their obligation as employers to provide a workplace free of unlawful discrimination.[56]

As discussed in Chapter 3, the numbers of women earning bachelor's and graduate degrees have increased, but in many fields of science and engineering, an increasing PhD pool has not necessarily led to increased representation of women on faculties.[57] What legal options exist to redress this situation? Some have argued for using the federal Title IX statute[58] to compel science and engineering departments to hire women by threatening to withhold federal funding from institutions that fail to do so.[59] That strategy has worked well to increase the number and accessibility of athletic programs for women.

Legal theory and practice have evolved to combine a numerical analysis of workplace representation with an analysis of the underlying policies and climate that affect occupational entry or promotion. The legal avenues for redressing workplace discrimination are detailed in Box 5-3. Effective use of both Title IX and Title VI is critical for women—and especially women of color—in science and engineering fields. In addition, Title VII of the Civil Rights Act of 1964[60] prohibits employment discrimination based on race, color, religion, sex, or national origin in any organization with more than 15 employees. It bars discrimination from recruitment through termination, and it has been used in most tenure denial cases. Even though

---

[56]JC Williams (2006). Long time no see: Why are there still so few women in academic science and engineering. In *Biological, Social, and Organizational Components of Success for Women in Academic Science and Engineering.* Washington, DC: The National Academies Press.

[57]A Stacy (2006). Recruitment practices. In *Biological, Social, and Organizational Components of Success for Women in Science and Engineering.* Washington, DC: The National Academies Press.

[58]Title 20 U.S.C. Sections 1681-1688. See *http://www.dol.gov/oasam/regs/statutes/titleix.htm.*

[59]DR Rolison (2003). Can Title IX do for women in science and engineering what it has done for women in sports? *American Physical Society News Online* 12(5):8.

[60]Pub. L. 88-352. For a full description, see *http://www.eeoc.gov/policy/vii.html.*

Title VII was originally intended to protect racial minorities from employment discrimination, it appears to have been more effective in remedying sex segregation.[61] The Equal Pay Act of 1963 bars sex-based wage differentials between people who do the same or substantially similar jobs. Executive Order 11246 requires all federal contractors to file a discrimination statement and affirmative action plans. The Family and Medical Leave Act applies to all workplaces with 50 or more employees and guarantees an employee 12 weeks per year of unpaid leave to care for a family member. Title IX, passed in 1972,[62] prohibits sex-based discrimination in or exclusion from any educational program or activity receiving federal financial assistance. Finally, constitutional standards of equal protection apply, but only for public organizations.

Traditionally, proving discrimination involved comparing a plaintiff—for example, a woman denied tenure who claimed to be the subject of discrimination—with a similarly situated person in the other group. Recent cases, however, have opened a promising new approach by finding that the existence of stereotyping can serve as proof of discrimination.[63] Thus, a woman caught under the glass ceiling for purportedly being "too aggressive" to be a collegial colleague, or one up against the maternal wall for "lacking dedication" to her career because she sought to reduce her hours during her child's infancy may have grounds for a suit.

Those legal trends can encourage institutions not only to take steps to reduce stereotyping but also to provide services and establish programs that meet federal requirements and remove constraints that limit faculty (usually women) who have caretaking responsibilities. One-third of academic institutions, for example, have family policies that appear to violate the Pregnancy Discrimination Act, which forbids treating pregnancy differently from other temporary disabilities.[64] Women—and, in some cases, men—academics who try to assert their rights under such laws as the Family and

---

[61]E Hirsh (2006). *Enforcing Equal Opportunity: The Impact of Discrimination Charges on Sex and Race Segregation in the Workplace* (Working Paper). Department of Sociology, University of Washington.

[62]Title 20 U.S.C. Sections 1681-1688. See *http://www.dol.gov/oasam/regs/statutes/titleix.htm.*

[63]*Price Waterhouse v. Hopkins,* 490 U.S. 228 (1989); *Back v. Hastings-on-Hudson,* 365 F.3d. 107 (2d Cir. 2004); *Lust v. Sealy Inc.,* 383 F.3d 580 (7th Cir. 2004). See discussion of glass ceiling and families responsibilities discrimination in JC Williams (2006). Long time no see: Why are there still so few women in academic science and engineering? In *Biological, Social, and Oganizational Components of Success in Academic Science and Engineering.* Washington, DC: The National Academies Press.

[64]S Thornton (2003). Maternity and childrearing leave policies for faculty: The legal and practical challenges of complying with Title VII. *University of Southern California Review of Law and Women's Studies* 12(2):161-190.

Medical Leave Act, which mandates 12 weeks of unpaid leave and the right to return to work, however, often find themselves pressured to return sooner than they wish and face increased scrutiny, adverse career consequences, and other forms of retribution.[65]

The odds in sex discrimination cases do not favor plaintiffs. In most sex discrimination cases that reach trial, universities win. Most cases never reach trial, however, because they are dropped or resolved during the litigation process (Box 5-4 for a description of types of discrimination warranting legal action). A report by the American Association of University Women revealed that women academics won only a minority of lawsuits alleging improper denial of tenure.[66] Bringing such a case usually entails substantial effort and financial risk and the possibility of being considered a troublemaker. "It taints all levels of your professional life at the university," according to a woman who sued and ultimately settled with the university. Although the legal process can be financially and emotionally draining, however, it can empower plaintiffs.

> Beyond the economic risks of charges, institutional theory calls attention to the role legal sanctions may play in cultivating a normative environment that discourages discrimination. One factor that constitutes firms' institutional environment is industrial sector. EEO charges and settlements against a single firm in an industry may reverberate throughout the entire industry, providing legal and normative pressure for change and raising legitimacy concerns for recalcitrant firms. For example, a sex discrimination settlement against Home Depot may serve as a wake up call to Lowe's or other home improvement stores to get more women out on the sales floor.
>
> —Elizabeth Hirsh, University of Washington (2006)[67]

In some cases, publicity generated by discrimination cases can benefit the plaintiff and women faculty because it attracts the attention of legislators, advocates, and other organizations that can work toward long-term safeguards against discrimination and improvements in hiring and promotion. In *Penk v. Oregon State Board of Higher Education* (816 F.2d 458

---

[65]Williams (2006), ibid.

[66]AAUW (2004). *Tenure Denied. Cases of Sex Discrimination in Academia.* Washington, DC: American Association of University Women Educational Foundation and Legal Advocacy Fund.

[67]Hirsh (2006), ibid.

DEFINING THE ISSUES

BOX 5-3 A Primer on Anti-discrimination Laws[a]

Title VII of the Civil Rights Act of 1964[b]

Title VII covers employees and applicants and bans employment discrimination based on sex, race, national origin, and religion by all employers with 15 or more employees, whether or not those employers receive federal funds. Title VII applies to employment in institutions of higher education. Thus, depending on the facts of their working arrangements, graduate fellows and teaching assistants can be covered under Title VII as employees, as well as under Title IX as students or employees. Title VII is enforced by the Equal Employment Opportunity Commission, which investigates and resolves discrimination complaints and can bring lawsuits on behalf of claimants. Individual commissioners may also file commissioner's charges to initiate investigations of discrimination even absent a specific complaint.

Title IX (20 USC § 1681)[c]

Title IX bans sex discrimination in education and covers (a) students, faculty and employees at institutions of higher education that receive federal funds and (b) students and employees of educational programs that are offered by other institutions that receive federal funds. Statutes parallel to Title IX bar discrimination by recipients of federal aid on the basis of race (Title VI of the Civil Rights Act of 1964), disability (Section 504 of the Rehabilitation Act of 1973), and age (the Age Discrimination Act of 1975). Every federal agency that gives funds to institutions of higher education or to other institutions that run educational programs—including all cabinet agencies (such as the Department of Education and the Department of Defense) and such agencies as the National Science Foundation, the National Institutes of Health, and the National Aeronautics and Space Administration—is obliged to enforce Title IX. Each federal agency has issued regulations delineating its enforcement responsibilities under the law, and each has the authority to investigate and resolve discrimination complaints and to initiate compliance reviews of recipients of federal aid. For educational programs, Title IX is enforced by the Department of Education and by each federal agency that provides federal funds to the program. The Department of Justice is charged with coordination of agency efforts under Title IX and is obliged to ensure overall enforcement of the statute.

---

[a]Adapted from JC Williams (2006). Long time no see: Why are there still so few women in academic science and engineering. In *Biological, Social, and Organizational Components of Success for Women in Science and Engineering*. Washington, DC: The National Academies Press.

[b]Title VII of the Civil Rights Act of 1964 (*Pub. L. 88-352*) amendments: The Civil Rights Act of 1991 (*Pub. L. 102-166*) (CRA) amends several sections of Title VII. In addition, section 102 of the CRA amends the Revised Statutes by adding a new section following section 1977 (42 U.S.C. 1981), to provide for the recovery of compensatory and punitive damages in cases of intentional violations of Title VII, the Americans with Disabilities Act of 1990, and section 501 of the Rehabilitation Act of 1973, *http://www.eeoc.gov/policy/vii.html*.

[c]Title IX (20 USC Section 1681) Education Amendments of 1972, *http://www.dol.gov/oasam/regs/statutes/titleix.htm*.

Executive Order 11246[d]

Executive Order 11246 bans discrimination and requires federal contractors (including universities) to maintain affirmative action plans that set goals and timetables for increasing the representation of women and underrepresented minorities in their workforces. The executive order is enforced by the Office of Federal Contract Compliance Programs of the Department of Labor, which has the authority to resolve complaints and undertake compliance reviews of federal contractors.

Equal Protection (a constitutional claim) (42 USC §1983)

Academics who teach in public universities can recover damages if they can prove that men were disadvantaged compared with women, as when parental leave is routinely offered to women but men are forbidden to or severely discouraged from taking it. Women in public universities also can sue if they are not given equal protection of the law.

Equal Pay Act (29 USC § 206)[e]

It is illegal to pay higher salaries to men than to women doing "equal work" in jobs that require substantially "equal skill, effort, and responsibilities. . . under equal working conditions" (29 USC § 206(d)(1)). One federal case, *Lovell* v. *BBNT Solutions, LLC,* 295 F. Supp. 2d 611 (E.D. Va. 2003), refused to apply a categorical rule excluding a part-time chemist from being compared with full-time chemists, in a ruling that suggests that professors on part-time tenure track should be paid the proportion of their salary equal to the proportion of a full-time schedule that they work (for example, 75% pay for a 75% workload).

Pregnancy Discrimination Act (PDA) (42 USC § 2000e-(k))[f]

Employers are required to treat pregnant professors "the same" as other workers whose ability to work is similar. Evidence of a violation of the PDA includes stereotyping a pregnant woman as incompetent or not committed to her career, stripping a pregnant woman of duties and opportunities, and imposing conditions on her that are not applied to nonpregnant employees.

---

[d]Executive Order 11246 of Sept 24, 1965. (Modified: October 13, 1967, August 8, 1968, October 5, 1978, December 28, 1978, December 16, 2002). *http://www.dol.gov/esa/regs/statutes/ofccp/eo11246.htm.*

[e]Equal Pay Act of 1963 *The EPA, which is part of the Fair Labor Standards Act of 1938, as amended (FLSA), and which is administered and enforced by the EEOC, prohibits sex-based wage discrimination between men and women in the same establishment who are performing under similar working conditions, http://www.eeoc.gov/policy/epa.html.*

[f]The Pregnancy Discrimination Act *amended Title VII of the Civil Rights Act of 1964 to prohibit sex discrimination on the basis of pregnancy. It was approved October 31, 1978, http://www.eeoc.gov/abouteeoc/35th/thelaw/pregnancy_discrimination-1978.html.*

continued

BOX 5-3 Continued

Family and Medical Leave Act of 1993 (FMLA) (29 U.S.C. § 2601)

The FMLA applies to all organizations with 50 or more employees; it gives professors and other university employees (including most postdoctoral scholars and some graduate students) the legal right to up to 12 weeks of unpaid leave per year if the employee or his or her child, partner, or parent has a serious health condition, or if he or she has or adopts a child. Giving leave is *mandatory*. Covered employers are prohibited from denying or interfering with leave, including implying that leave will be seen as a lack of commitment to career.

Americans with Disabilities Act (ADA) (42 USC § 12101)[g]

Employees may not be discriminated against because they are caring for a family member whose illness or disability is covered by the ADA.

---

[g]Americans with Disabilities Act (ADA) of 1990: Title I of the ADA, which became effective for employers with 25 or more employees on July 26, 1992, prohibits employment discrimination against qualified individuals with disabilities. Title I applied to employers with 15 or more employees beginning on July 26, 1994. Title V contains miscellaneous provisions which apply to EEOC's enforcement of Title I. The Civil Rights Act of 1991 (*Pub. L. 102-166*) (CRA) amends sections 101(4), 102 and 509 of the ADA. In addition, section 102 of the CRA amends the Revised Statutes by adding a new section following section 1977 (42 U.S.C. 1981) to provide for the recovery of compensatory and punitive damages in cases of intentional violations of Title VII, the Americans with Disabilities Act of 1990, and section 501 of the Rehabilitation Act of 1973, *http://www.eeoc.gov/policy/ada.html.*

(9th Cir. 1987)), the plaintiffs—women faculty—lost but the Oregon State legislature subsequently passed a law against discrimination in the state's institutions of higher education.

Are the outcomes of individual cases leading to lasting change in organizations? Affirmative action laws have made inroads for women, but they have not always resulted in better working conditions in industry or academe. Even in companies, many of which have private dispute processes, workers file 25,000 cases of sex discrimination a year with the EEOC. About one-fifth result in favorable outcomes for complainants. In a retrospective 10-year analysis of 2,000 firms that filed EEOC reports in 2000,[68] Hirsh has shown that sex discrimination lawsuits often cause other firms in the same industry sector to make pre-emptive changes, apparently to

---

[68]All firms with 50 or more employees are required to file EEOC reports annually.

DEFINING THE ISSUES

BOX 5-4 Types of Discrimination Banned under the Anti-discrimination Laws

- *Intentional discrimination*, including decision making based on stereotypes or paternalistic assumptions (for example, about the level of commitment mothers will make to the workplace).

- *Sexual harassment*, a form of intentional discrimination that occurs either where access to benefits (or avoidance of penalties) is conditioned on submission to sexual advances **or** where sexual or gender-based harassment (such as disparagement of women based on their sex) is sufficiently severe and pervasive that it (a) effectively denies a student access to educational benefits or results in a hostile educational environment or (b) effectively denies an employee access to employment benefits or results in a hostile work environment.

- *Retaliation*, a form of intentional discrimination, in which covered institutions penalize persons (whether students or employees) who complain about what they perceive to be discriminatory practices against themselves or others, whether or not those practices would ultimately be found to violate the law.

- *Disparate impact discrimination*, which occurs when apparently neutral practices (such as asking current faculty to recommend those who should be included in the applicant pool for new positions or requiring publication in particular journals as a condition of tenure) disproportionately disadvantage one sex and cannot be justified as an education or business necessity.

- *Failure to maintain required policies and procedures.* Under Title IX regulations, educational institutions are required, among other things, to establish and implement anti-discrimination policies and complaint procedures, appoint and publicize the identity of Title IX coordinators who will monitor the institution's Title IX compliance, and prohibit retaliation for complaints of or protests about discrimination. Under Executive Order 11246, federal contractors must maintain affirmative action plans to increase opportunities for female and minority-group employees.

---

avoid problems of their own.[69] That suggests that the pressure of EEOC enforcement is indirect—that firms are more sensitive to the enforcement mechanisms they experience in their institutional environments than to the direct coercive pressure that discrimination charges bring. Institutional theorists argue that the law plays a role in shaping organizational behav-

---

[69]E Hirsh (2006). *Enforcing Equal Opportunity: The Impact of Discrimination Charges on Sex and Race Segregation in the Workplace* (Working Paper). Department of Sociology, University of Washington. Research and development firms are about half as likely to be issued sex discrimination charges as firms in other industry sectors.

EXPERIMENTS AND STRATEGIES

BOX 5-5 National Science Foundation ADVANCE Program

One funding source that has been essential in providing awards to universities has been the National Science Foundation (NSF) ADVANCE program. This program offers awards for institutional solutions that empower women to participate more fully in science and technology.[a]

The precursor to ADVANCE at NSF was Professional Opportunities for Women in Research and Education (POWRE), an individual fellowship program designed to foster professional growth during the tenure-track years and to increase the pool of women role models in science and engineering. The POWRE fellowships, which were awarded to women on an individual level, did little to effect institutional change in universities and organizations or to help women integrate work and family life.[b]

Recognizing that POWRE could not facilitate institutional change on a permanent basis, NSF replaced it with ADVANCE in 2001. During the 2005-2006 year, ADVANCE supported the following types of projects:[c]

• **Institutional Transformation Awards** support academic institutional transformation to promote the increased participation and advancement of women scientists and engineers in academe. The awards support innovative and comprehensive programs for institution-wide change.

• **Leadership Awards** support the efforts of individuals, small groups, or organizations in developing national or discipline-specific leadership in enabling the full participation and advancement of women in academic science and engineering careers.

---

ior, not because sanctions deter noncompliance, but rather because the law cultivates a normative environment, a "new normal," that legitimates and motivates compliance.[70]

BRINGING INSTITUTIONAL CHANGE

Transforming academic institutions so that they will foster the career advancement of women scientists and engineers is a complex task. The NSF's ADVANCE program is geared specifically to promote such institutional transformation (Box 5-5). It reflects the increasing understanding that individual accommodations and help are not sufficient to bring gender

---

[70]WT Bielby (2000). Minimizing workplace gender and racial bias. *Contemporary Sociology* 29:120-129; B Reskin (2000). The proximate causes of employment discrimination. *Contemporary Sociology* 29(2):319-328; S Strum (2001). Second generation employment discrimination: A structural approach. *Columbia Law Review* 101(3):458-568.

• **Partnerships for Adaptation, Implementation, and Dissemination Awards** support the analysis, adaptation, dissemination, and use of existing innovative materials and practices that have been demonstrated to be effective in increasing representation and participation of women in academic science and engineering careers.

During the first funding cycle of the ADVANCE program, nine colleges and universities each received about $4 million from NSF over 5 years.[d] Some of the successful programs that have been funded through the ADVANCE program are the University of Michigan NSF ADVANCE Project (Box 4-4), the WISELI program at the University of Wisconsin-Madison (Box 4-6 and Box 6-4), the NSF Program for Institutional Transformation at the Georgia Institute of Technology,[e] and the Committee on the Advancement of Women Chemists (COACh) program (Box 4-3).

---

[a]S Rosser and JL Chameau (2006). Institutionalization, sustainability, and repeatability of ADVANCE for institutional transformation. *Journal of Technology Transfer* 31:335-344.

[b]M Kempf (2002). EmPOWREment and ADVANCEment for women: NSF programs for women in science, *www.sciencecareers.org.* September 27.

[c]*http://www.nsf.gov/funding/pgm_summ.jsp?pims_id=5383.*

[d]Kempf (2002), ibid.

[e]SV Rosser (2006). Creating an inclusive work environment. In *Biological, Social, and Organizational Components of Success for Women in Academic Science and Engineering.* Washington, DC: The National Academies Press.

---

equity to the academy; as discussed above and illustrated in Figure 3-5, long-standing sectorwide measures appear to be necessary to accomplish the integration of women into the academy.[71] The Sloan Foundation takes the approach one step further in offering rewards for academic institutions that demonstrate the implementation and effectiveness of flexible faculty career policies (Box 5-6).

Small-Win Experiments

A number of organizations have successfully fostered female employees' career advancement by undertaking experiments that produce small but important changes in work procedures, practices, or norms. In most

---

[71]N Hopkins (2006). Diversification of a university faculty: Observations on hiring women faculty in the schools of science and engineering at MIT. *MIT Faculty Newsletter* 18(4):1, 16-23, *http://web.mit.edu/fnl/volume/184/hopkins.html.*

TRACKING AND EVALUATION

BOX 5-6 The Alfred P. Sloan Awards for Faculty Career Flexibility[a]

The Alfred P. Sloan Foundation, in partnership with the American Council on Education and the Families and Work Institute, has created the Alfred P. Sloan Awards for Faculty Career Flexibility to promote institutional efforts in research universities toward broader implementation of flexible career policies, critical for recruiting and retaining talented women scientists and engineers. The awards, initiated in 2006, will provide five research institutions each a $250,000 grant to recognize leadership and accomplishments in implementing ground-breaking policies for tenured and tenure-track faculty. In addition, two $25,000 awards will be given to universities that have shown innovative practices in career flexibility. The Sloan awards reward those institutions that have career-flexible policies and incentives to programs seeking to develop policies and programs.

Institutions will be judged according to their use of the following models:

- Career on-ramps and off-ramps
- Extended time to tenure (tenure clock adjustment).
- Shortened time to tenure, with prorated standard of productivity.
- Active service and modified duties (full-time service, with selected reduced duties).
- Part-time appointments (allowing mobility between full-time and part-time work).
- Phased retirement (partial appointments for finite periods).
- Delayed entry or re-entry opportunities (including practices that foster later-than-usual career starts).

An expert review panel will use a two-part process to select awardees. In the first round, applicants fill out a survey about the career flexibility offered to tenured and tenure-track faculty. The score that the university receives on the questionnaire determines whether it can advance to the next stage. In the second round, the selected institutions will complete a survey of tenured and tenure-track faculty regarding perceptions of, access to, and use of flexible career policies and practices. Universities will also be asked to devise a university-wide plan for accelerating the development and use of career flexibility among faculty to achieve institutional goals. Applicants will be asked to develop this plan while administering the survey to the faculty. Each university that participates in the second round will receive information about their ratings on the institutional survey and an anonymous comparison to the average ratings of other award applicants.

---

[a]More information about the Sloan awards program can be found at *http://www.acenet. edu/Content/NavigationMenu/ProgramsServices/Leadership/SloanAwards/index.htm.*

organizations in which women's advancement and leadership opportunities have been limited, the problem is not old-style, overt sex discrimination, but rather unrecognized features of the organizational culture that affect men and women differently. Those features tend to be so embedded in organizational life as to be invisible. They generally also bear no obvious relationship to gender. The only indication that such issues exist may be an unexplained inability of the organization to attract, retain, or promote women in sufficient numbers despite an apparent willingness to do so.

In an approach to overcoming such problems called small-win experiments, members of the organization, preferably with the backing of leadership, systematically seek out the features and set about finding ways to change them. An example of such a constraining cultural feature in one organization was a looseness about punctuality and the length of meetings that made it difficult for many women—who often live with tighter time restrictions than men because of their family responsibilities—to attend all the meetings they needed to attend to keep abreast of developments in the organization. Overtly establishing a new norm that meetings start and end at the announced times is a small-win experiment that made the organization much more congenial to women.[72] In another example, the custom of giving major credit for a successful project to the lead scientist devalued the "invisible work" of other professionals and support staff, many of whom were women.[73] The solution was to establish a way to give public recognition to the importance of "invisible work" and the people who do it.

Successful small-win experiments must be carefully tailored to the specific circumstances of a particular organization (Box 5-7). That requires a close examination of the organization's culture to uncover unstated assumptions about what constitutes success and who attains it, as well as implicit norms about how work is done and recognition granted. The consequences of the assumptions and practices must also be examined, and then discrete, concrete ways of changing the ones that adversely affect women must be devised. Once the project is under way, however, "it's surprising how quickly people can come up with ideas for small wins—and how quickly they can be put into action."[74]

One career customization work analogue in the academy is the suggestion of "5 in 10," that is, any time within 10 years of hiring, a faculty member can choose 5 years on which to base his or her tenure application. Other customized tenure options are explored by the American Council on Education (Box 5-8).

---

[72]DE Meyerson and JK Fletcher (2005). A modest manifesto for shattering the glass ceiling. In *Harvard Business Review on Women in Business*. Boston, MA: Harvard Business School.

[73]R Rapoport, L Bailyn, JK Fletcher, and Bill Pruitt (2002). *Beyond Work-Family Balance: Advancing Gender Equity and Workplace Performance*. San Francisco: Jossey-Bass.

[74]Meyerson and Fletcher (2005), ibid, p. 85.

EXPERIMENTS AND STRATEGIES

BOX 5-7 Deloitte and Touche:
Leadership in Industry Case Study[a]

A corporate example shows how it is possible to bring together a number of such change processes with fairly dramatic effects on the number of women in leadership positions. Deloitte and Touche USA, LLP, has recognized that formal flexible work arrangements are not sufficient to bring about that result. They have instituted a process of "mass career customization" whereby employees have a series of choices about position and responsibilities, rate of career progress, location and schedule, and workload, which may shift during the career. It increased the number of women partners from 3 in 1982 to 116 in 2005—the highest percentage of women partners in the four biggest professional services firms. It also keeps in touch with people who have stopped out temporarily to raise children, paying their professional fees to make it easier for them to come back.

Lessons from the Deloitte and Touche Women's Initiative:

• Make sure that senior management is "front and center."
• Make an airtight case for cultural change.
• Let the world watch you.
• Begin with discussion as the platform for change.
• Implement a system of accountability.
• Promote work-life balance for men and women.

---

[a]DM McCracken (2000). Winning the talent war for women. *Harvard Business Review* Nov/Dec (Reprint R00611); Deloitte and Touche (2005). Why Flexible Work Arrangements Are not the Answer: The Case for Career Customization (internal document).

Identifying Barriers to Success in Science and Engineering

Universities across the country have begun to conduct studies of the institutional "climate" for women and minority-group scientists and engineers.[75] Among the issues addressed by the climate studies are whether there is fair representation of women and minorities at various levels of academe; whether space, research support, and salaries are fairly allocated; and whether university policies reflect an understanding of the challenges faced by scientists and engineers in underrepresented groups.[76] A data-

---

[75]The National Academies Committee on Women in Science and Engineering. *Gender Faculty Studies at Research I Institutions, http://www7.nationalacademies.org/cwse/gender_faculty_links.html.*

[76]American Psychological Association (2000). *Women in Academe: Two Steps Forward, One Step Back, http://www.apa.org/pi/wpo/academe/report.html;* Women in Science and Engineering Leadership Institute, University of Wisconsin-Madison. *Advice to the Top: Top 10*

DEFINING THE ISSUES

BOX 5-8 Creating Flexibility in Tenure-Track Faculty Careers[a]

On March 22, 2005, the American Council on Education (ACE) released the report, *An Agenda for Excellence: Creating Flexibility in Tenure-Track Faculty Careers,* which concluded that "higher education leaders urgently need to examine and proactively address the institutional climate that governs the entire career cycle of faculty, from entry-level to tenure-track positions to retirement."

The panel reports that, for a variety of reasons, an increasing number of new PhDs are leaving academe or opting for careers outside the traditional tenure-track path. To achieve a better balance between personal and professional life, some faculty, especially women, choose adjunct and non-tenure-track positions, despite low pay, minimal or no benefits, and potential lack of job security. The ACE report argues that in many fields, especially science and engineering, the United States cannot afford to lose its potential academic workforce, and US institutions of higher learning should "act immediately to attract the best faculty to the tenure-track professoriate."

The report makes the following general recommendations:[b]

• Allow colleges, schools, and departments in a university to establish their own agreed-on guidelines for interpreting criteria for promotion and tenure, taking into account heavy teaching loads, professional service activities, and student advising.

• Create flexibility in the probationary period for tenure review without altering the standards or criteria. Longer probationary periods should not be required for all faculty, but flexible timeframes of up to 10 years, with reviews at set intervals, should be offered. This option could benefit faculty who may need to be compensated for lost time or given additional time to prepare because of unanticipated professional or personal circumstances.

• Examine and actively address the work-life issues and professional climate of faculty members throughout the entire career cycle.

---

[a]American Council on Education (2005). *An Agenda for Excellence: Creating Flexibility in Tenure-Track Faculty Careers.* Executive Summary, *http://www.acenet.edu/bookstore/pdf/ 2005_tenure_flex_summary.pdf.*
[b]ACE Web site. *An Agenda for Excellence: Creating Flexibility in Tenure-Track Faculty Careers, http://www.acenet.edu/AM/Template.cfm?Section=Home&Template=/CM/HTML Display.cfm&ContentID=10401.*

---

driven approach to examining those concerns lends credibility to and enables a less confrontational discussion of the issues.[77]

Tips for Academic Leaders to Accelerate the Advancement of Women in Science and Engineering, http://wiseli.engr.wisc.edu/Products/Sex_and_Science.pdf; Harvard University (2005). *Report of the Task Force on Women Faculty, http://www.news.harvard.edu/gazette/daily/ 2005/05/women-faculty.pdf.*

[77]Harvard University (2005), ibid.

One approach to documenting the status of women in academic science and engineering is to combine quantitative data collection (see Chapter 3) with qualitative information obtained from faculty, students, and university leaders. For example, the Association for Women in Science (AWIS) created a Web-based interactive toolkit of surveys, literature, Web links, and guidelines to help universities to evaluate the climate for women on their campuses.[78] At the request of department chairs, confidential surveys are used to query faculty and students on department demographics, gendered practices and policies, and the climate for women. Departments are also asked to provide enrollment data. After collecting that background information, a panel of respected scientists who are familiar with climate issues meets with faculty, students, and administrators to discuss their views about the status of women in a department. The panel then makes recommendations based on the information collected and helps the department to implement them.

> We must grow our women leadership ranks. We must help our women and our men fit their lives into their work and their work into their lives, so that we can keep our pipeline robust. With women comprising nearly 50% of the labor force, we can't succeed in the marketplace unless we attract and retain a representative share of women at all levels of our organization, including partner, principal, and director.
>
> —Jim Quigley, Chief Executive Officer,
> Deloitte and Touche, USA, LLP (2005)[79]

The AWIS program was based on a site visit program established by the American Physical Society (APS) to evaluate physics departments. The goal of APS was to identify and intervene in both the generic and specific problems commonly experienced by women and minority groups in physics departments.[80] After a visit, a team submitted a written report of its findings, including suggestions for improvement, to the department chair. In turn, the department chair was asked to describe in writing actions taken to remedy the problems. Women's committees in professional societies have been a powerful force for change (Box 5-9).

A number of universities have used a similar approach internally. For

---

[78]CJ Didion, MA Fox, and ME Jones (1998). Cultivating academic careers: AWIS project on academic climate. *AWIS Magazine* 27(1):23-27, *http://www.awis.org/pubs/mentoring/98winter.pdf.*

[79]Deloitte and Touche (2005). *Why Flexible Work Arrangements Are not the Answer: The Case for Career Customization* (internal document).

[80]American Physical Society. *Improving the Climate for Women Site Visits. http://www.aps.org/educ/cswp/visits/index.cfm.*

EXPERIMENTS AND STRATEGIES

BOX 5-9 Women in Cell Biology

Women in Cell Biology (WICB) is widely credited with providing leadership in the inclusion of women in the society's annual meeting and in its officer ranks (see Box 4-1). WICB began in the early 1970s as an ad hoc group of women cell biologists who met during the American Society for Cell Biology (ASCB) annual meeting and distributed a photocopied newsletter. In 1992, ASCB invited WICB to become a standing committee of ASCB. Some of the activities that WICB offers at the annual ASCB meeting are

1. An annual Junior and Senior Award followed by an evening professional development program.
2. A Career Lunch Table program where persons self-select to talk to those with experience in a wide array of topics (such as teaching at liberal arts colleges, the shift from academe to biotechnology, and dual-career partnerships).
3. A professionally led workshop on such topics as conflict management.

In addition, WICB members write a column in the quarterly ASCB newsletter, and their Web site offers many links to various women in science resources, ranging from obtaining speakers in all fields of cell biology to balancing work and family life.[a]

---

[a]American Society for Cell Biology Web page, *http://www.ascb.org/.*

---

example, Duke University (Box 5-10) has used a combination of surveys, interviews, and focus groups. Other universities have also used quality of life surveys for internal information to help them to pinpoint critical areas on which to focus change efforts.

In addition to examining the campus climate, it is important that the university leadership make it known that it is committed to the advancement of women and minority groups. This may include drawing attention to the status of women, demonstrating that the inferior status of women is a problem for the entire university, noting that the campus has zero tolerance for sexual harassment and discrimination, and making deans and department heads accountable for what happens to women in their constituencies.[81]

---

[81]F Dobbin and A Kalev (2006). *Diversity Management and Managerial Diversity*, Addendum to "Best Practices or Best Guesses." Special Report to the National Academies Committee on Women in Academic Science and Engineering. This report supplements their analyses in "Best Practices or Best Guesses" by separating out industries that have large research and development components and that, thus, may be most likely to hold lessons for academe.

DEFINING THE ISSUES

BOX 5-10 Women's Initiative, Duke University

The Steering Committee for the Women's Initiative at Duke University released a study in September 2003 in which it surveyed faculty, staff, graduate students, undergraduates, and alumnae to understand the full range of experiences in the university.[a] The study found that the most salient issues for women at Duke are related to the positions that they hold at the university. Those issues can range from the effects of the tenure clock on faculty members; child-care responsibilities for young faculty, postdoctoral scholars, and graduate students; and the effects of social pressure on undergraduates.

The steering committee came to several important findings:

• Many graduate and professional students, men and women, said that communicating with faculty is often difficult.
• Graduate programs generally had not created comfortable environments for students who are diverse in terms of race, ethnicity, sexual orientation, culture, or family situation.
• Graduate and professional students, faculty, and staff consistently reported that juggling their professional and family lives is a major challenge.
• Women are not well represented in the regular rank faculty. The percentage of associate and full professors who are women has improved, but as is the case nationally, the percentage of women shrinks with increasing academic rank. Women at the full professor rank still make up a small percentage of the regular rank faculty.

Duke University is working to improve the campus climate for both women and men. A Commission on the Status of Women was appointed to monitor the conditions for women on campus and develop "smaller working groups around specific topics of concern." At the same time, the university announced that it would spend $1 million per year to "enhance the strategic hiring of women and minorities."[b] The university also decided to spend an additional $2 million to expand its day-care center, doubling the number of children it can handle from 76 to 153 and opening it up to graduate students for the first time.

Duke has made innovative investments in the community. The university has invested in day-care centers off-campus. This has benefited the entire community and allowed the facilities to leverage funds from the state. In exchange, the centers reserved a number of places for Duke faculty, staff, and graduate students.[c] In 2006, Duke will have 29 day-care centers participating in the program.[d]

---

[a]S Roth (2003). *The Steering Committee's Report on the Women's Initiative.* Durham, NC: Duke University, *http://www.duke.edu/womens_initiative/exec.htm.*

[b]R Wilson (2003). Duke and Princeton will spend more to make female professors happy. *Chronicle of Higher Education,* October 10.

[c]J Mathot (2005). Duke expands child care options. *Duke News,* September 9, *http://www.dukenews.duke.edu/2005/09/childcare.html.*

[d]*http://www.hr.duke.edu/dccp/.*

The American Psychological Association (APA) recommends that the individuals who "fail to make the corrections necessary for gender equity should be given feedback, and their effectiveness in correcting these problems should be reflected in their compensation."[82] Additional recommendations include establishing oversight committees within schools. For example, Harvard and Yale have created a position of senior vice provost for diversity and faculty development; Princeton for some time has had a person in charge of these issues. In each case, the person is a member of the university's central administration, is a highly respected member of the faculty, and has the ability to bring together people and practices from across the university and to initiate and implement new programs.[83] Other universities, such as Duke and MIT, have advisory committees or councils on faculty diversity.

ESTABLISHING AN INCLUSIVE WORK ENVIRONMENT

Reports suggest that both women and minority-group members perceive the climate of university science and engineering departments as "uninviting, unappealing, and unaccommodating,"[84] and they cite isolation as a reason for leaving.[85] Women tend to be less satisfied than men with their fit in their departments, the racial and ethnic diversity of their department faculty, and the quality of mentoring that they receive from senior faculty.[86] Good mentoring is important for postdoctoral scholars as they develop greater independence and for junior faculty as they navigate the professional and personal changes at the start of their faculty careers.[87] Mentoring is also a critical component in creating and maintaining a diverse workforce (Box 4-7). To foster mentoring, some universities pair junior faculty with a senior mentor who is encouraged to provide guidance, career advice, and even intervention on behalf of the junior faculty member.[88] In addition to providing mentoring to graduate students, postdoctoral fellows, and junior faculty, it is important to train and encourage all faculty to become good mentors.[89]

---

[82]APA (2000), ibid.

[83]Harvard University (2005), ibid.

[84]Trower and Chait (2002), ibid.

[85]Nelson (2005), ibid.

[86]CA Trower and JL Bleak (2004). *The Study of New Scholars. Gender: Statistical Report [Universities]*. Harvard Graduate School of Education.

[87]NAS/NAE/IOM (1997). *Adviser, Teacher, Role Model, Friend: On Being a Mentor to Students in Science and Engineering*. Washington, DC: National Academy Press.

[88]NAS/NAE/IOM (1997), ibid.

[89]Harvard University (2005). *Report from the Task Force on Women in Science and Engineering*.

Mentoring not only helps those being mentored, but helps mentors to attract new students, develop their professional networks, and stay abreast of the work in their fields.[90] Studies show that students and mentors feel more comfortable when paired with people of the same sex and ethnicity,[91] so the dearth of senior women and minority-group faculty may make it difficult for junior faculty and for students in these groups to find appropriate mentors.[92] Moreover, appropriate mentors may already be overburdened by service obligations.[93] Team mentoring may alleviate time pressures on individual mentors. Students and faculty can seek out different mentors for different issues; they may have one person with whom they talk with about how to manage the conflicts between work and other obligations, another about research, and a third about teaching.

Besides mentoring, it is important that faculty have role models. Although some argue that mentoring is by far more important for career progression,[94] "modeling oneself on an older person has been found to be a good way of creating a pathway into a career, making for likely early success."[95] Here, too, similarity is important. The percentage of women faculty is therefore also an indicator of academic success for women undergraduates.[96] The lifestyle of role models may be as important as their sex, however. If students or junior faculty see only single women or highly aggressive and "man-like" women, they may not see anyone who is an appropriate role model. Young women—and many young men—desire a different kind of lifestyle, and if the academy cannot make room for this variety, it will lose some of its potential contributors.

Women and minority-group members also report having limited opportunities to participate in department decision making and complain about being given "token" committee assignments.[97] MIT's report recommends actively seeking out women for influential positions in departments and on key committees.[98] APA recommends providing lines of communica-

---

[90]NAS/NAE/IOM (1997), ibid; Howard Hughes Medical Institute and Burroughs Wellcome Fund (2004). *A Practical Guide to Scientific Management for Postdocs and New Faculty.* Bethesda, MD: HHMI.

[91]M Nettles and C Millett (2006). *Three Magic Letters: Getting to PhD.* Baltimore, MD: Johns Hopkins University Press.

[92]Nelson (2005), ibid; J Bickel (2000). Encouraging the advancement of women. *JAMA* 283(5):671.

[93]APA (2000), ibid.

[94]C DeAngelis (2000). Women in academic medicine: New insights, same sad news. *The New England Journal of Medicine* 342(6):426-427.

[95]H Etzkowitz, C Kemelgor, M Neuschatz, and N Uzzi (1994). Barriers to women in Academic Science and Engineering. In eds. W Pearson Jr. and I Fechter, *Who Will Do Science? Educating the Next Generation,* Baltimore: John Hopkins University Press.

[96]Trower and Chait (2002), ibid.

[97]Trower and Chait (2002), ibid.

[98]MIT (1999), ibid.

tion between senior women faculty and administration and developing strategies for mutual rather than hierarchical use of power.[99]

Integrating Work into One's Whole Life

It is important that university leadership recognize that both men and women have interests and obligations outside work. Those may include spending time with family, performing community service, seeking educational opportunities, and engaging in leisure and hobby activities. Employers for Work-Life Balance, a UK-based public interest organization that works to implement and improve sustainable work-personal life strategies, defines the goal as "having a measure of control over when, where and how you work, leading to being able to enjoy an optimal quality of life."[100] A 2003 survey found that, when considering employers, graduates preferred flexibility to pay.[101] Although flexibility is an important component of such control, it is not sufficient, as the Deloitte and Touche example shows. Without more fundamental institutional transformation, such practices as flexible work arrangements, family leave policies, and education and training opportunities, however important, will not be sufficient for gender equity.

Maintaining the ability to combine productive work with outside interests and responsibilities is an issue for everyone, not just for parents. Nonetheless, because family care is so basic a responsibility and women are still the primary caretakers, it remains a key issue for women in academe.[102] The American Association of University Professors (AAUP) recommends that all institutions go beyond federal entitlements by offering paid disability leave for pregnancy regardless of what other leave policies universities have.[103] AAUP further recommends going beyond the provision of the Family and Medical Leave Act by extending provisions of leave for care of same-sex and domestic partners and for family members other than children and spouses and by providing some form of paid family care leave.

---

[99]APA (2000), ibid.

[100]Employers and Work-Life Balance. *http://www.employersforwork-lifebalance.org.uk/*.

[101]UK Graduate Careers survey (2003). Cited in *Employers for Work-Life Balance, http://www.employersforwork-lifebalance.org.uk/media/faqs_a1.htm#Q3*.

[102]R Drago and C Colbeck (2003). *Final Report from the Mapping Project: Exploring the Terrain of U.S. Colleges and Universities for Faculty and Families, http://lsir.la.psu.edu/workfam/mappingproject.htm*; M Mason and M Goulden (2002). Do babies matter? The effect of family formation on the lifelong careers of academic men and women. *Academe* 88(6).

[103]American Association of University Professors (2001). *Statement on Principles of Family Responsibilities and Work, http://www.aaup.org/statements/REPORTS/re01fam.htm*.

AAUP also suggests allowing the use of short-term emergency leave for contingencies, such as a lack of family care services.

Along these lines, the University of Washington ADVANCE program[104] offers awards of between $5,000 and $12,000 to faculty who are dealing with the birth of a child, caring for an ailing parent, or confronting other personal issues. The grants provide assistance in the form of released time, conference travel, research support, and so forth. Similarly, the Earth Institute at Columbia University offers "transition support grants" that provide partial salary support for women researchers during times at which they must limit their research productivity to tend to family affairs. The grants provide support for research assistants, postdoctoral scholars, or adjunct professors to assist women faculty with their research.[105]

Both Stanford University and Dartmouth University have announced graduate student childbirth and pregnancy leave policies (Box 6-6) that allow students to postpone or reduce academic requirements for up to 3 months while remaining eligible for full-time enrollment status and retaining access to university facilities, housing, and benefits. Harvard Law School's parental leave policy allows either parent who is the sole provider of care for 20 or more hours per week to take paid leave; this policy allows benefits to be extended to men and women without requiring that they be the *primary* caregivers, thereby "protecting mothers while encouraging fathers to engage in equal parenting."[106]

Enabling faculty to take time off for the birth or adoption of a child does not, however, solve a problem facing many faculty committed to both careers and children, namely, that the timeline for achieving tenure corresponds with many women's timelines for having children. One approach to easing that dilemma is to "stop the tenure clock" or delay tenure decisions for some period for women having children.[107] That would allow women to stop or reduce work while engaged in child care without suffering a

---

[104]University of Washington ADVANCE, *http://www.engr.washington.edu/advance/work-shops/index.html*.

[105]ADVANCE at The Earth Institute of Columbia University. *Transition Support Grants: Information for Application 2004*, *http://www.earthinstitute.columbia.edu/advance/pdf/ADV_Transition_Support.pdf*.

[106]J Williams (2005). Are your parental leave policies legal? *The Chronicle of Higher Education*, *http://chronicle.com/jobs/2005/02/2005020701c.htm*.

[107]R Colwell (2002). *Rethinking the Rules to Promote Diversity.* NSF Director Rita R. Colwell's Remarks to the American Chemical Society, *http://www.nsf.gov/od/lpa/forum/colwell/rc02081acsdiversity.htm*; Etzkowitz et al. (1994), ibid; Harvard University (2005). *Report of the Task Force on Women Faculty*; MA Mason, A Stacy, M Goulden, C Hoffman, and K Frasch (2005). *University of California Faculty Family Friendly Edge. An Initiative for Tenure-Track Faculty at the University of California, http://ucfamilyedge.berkeley.edu/*.

penalty during tenure review. Recognizing that child rearing is an issue for both men and women, some universities provide tenure clock extension to all assistant professors who have substantial responsibility for the care of young children.[108]

As shown in the Duke University example above, providing access to day care and other assistance with child rearing may also help to ease the burdens of parents seeking tenure or otherwise coping with juggling the competing demands of work and family. Recommendations include providing affordable child care, facilities for sick children, safe environments for children within the workplace, after-school care, child-care cooperatives, and lactation rooms.[109] Universities could also establish part-time tracks for parents during early child-rearing years that would allow parents to re-enter full-time work.[110] In addition, many institutions have adopted "active service-modified duties" policies so that workers can reduce their workload during busy times but still receive full pay.[111] These and other suggestions are summarized in the ACE report *An Agenda for Excellence: Creating Flexibility in Tenure-Track Faculty Careers* (see Box 5-8 above).

Even with parental leave and tenure clock extension policies in place, women have been reluctant to take advantage of the programs for fear of experiencing a backlash. Suggested remedies include making it clear that tenure clock extension and active service-modified duties policies are entitlements.[112] Instituting a minimal maternity leave policy and making tenure clock extension automatic upon granting maternity leave may ease this issue.[113] For example, since 2001 MIT has automatically extended the tenure clock for women tenure-track faculty who bear a child. Princeton University recently established an automatic extension for men and women for both birth and adoption. And UC-Berkeley includes in its letters asking for review of a candidate that reviewers must ignore any time extension due to family responsibilities.

Still, some fear that if leave policies and tenure clock stoppages are offered to both men and women, women will use them for their intended purpose, whereas men will use them to engage in scholarship, resulting in "upping the ante for tenure instead of leveling the playing field."[114] Drago

---

[108]Mason et al. (2005), ibid.

[109]Association for Women in Science. *Academic Climate: Addressing the Climate for Women in Academia. Recommended Strategies,* ibid.

[110]Mason and Goulden (2002), ibid.

[111]American Association of University Professors (2001), ibid; Mason et al. (2005), ibid.

[112]Mason et al. (2005), ibid.

[113]Harvard University (2005). *Report of the Task Force on Women Faculty.*

[114]LK Kerber (2005). We must make the academic workplace more human and equitable. *Chronicle of Higher Education* 51(28):B6.

and Colbeck[115] recommend neither expecting nor rewarding exceptional productivity during family leave periods or tenure clock stoppages to avoid "ramping up of performance bars."

Service Obligations

Scientists and engineers also have to deal with competing commitments in their work lives, and this particularly hits women and minority-group faculty. Because they are relatively few, the same people are repeatedly called upon to serve on university and community committees, boards, and service groups and to mentor women and minority-group students.[116] Even though women and minority-group faculty may feel overburdened by service obligations, they may be reluctant to decline these opportunities.[117] As a result, the mounting obligations may result in overload and stress.[118] Northwestern University's faculty diversity committee recommends mentoring women on when and how to decline service invitations.[119] Other recommendations include recognizing service contributions in annual merit, promotion, and tenure decisions[120] and calling on tenure committees to prize teaching and service as much as research.[121]

BREAKING THE CONSPIRACY OF SILENCE: MINORITY-GROUP WOMEN FACULTY

Women of color are peculiarly invisible in all the discussion of academic careers because they are either part of "women," a group that is mainly white, or "minorities," a group that is mainly male, particularly in the senior ranks.[122] Furthermore, they themselves are not a homogeneous group and this further hides their particular experiences and issues. So, for example, Turner and Myers[123] use 1990 census data and show that,

---

[115]Drago and Colbeck (2003), ibid.

[116]Association of American Law Schools (1996). Retaining faculty of color. *AALS Newsletter. http://www.aals.org/mlt3.html.*

[117]American Psychological Association (2000), ibid; AALS (1996), ibid.

[118]AALS (1996), ibid.

[119]Faculty Diversity Committee, Northwestern University (2004), *http://www. northwestern.edu/provost/committees/diversity/reports.html.*

[120]American Psychological Association (2000), ibid.

[121]Trower and Chait (2002), ibid.

[122]This is a long-standing issue; see for example GT Hull, B Smith, and PB Scott (eds) (1982). *All the Women are White, All the Blacks are Men, But Some of Us Are Brave.* Toronto: Hushion House.

[123]CSV Turner and SL Myers (2000). *Faculty of Color in Academe: Bittersweet Success.* New York: Allyn and Bacon.

whereas among Native Americans and Latinos women are better represented in faculties than are men, the opposite is the case for African Americans and Asian Americans. And even though African American women earn doctorates at higher rates than African American men, they have a smaller representation on faculties.[124] Among Asian Americans, 70% of faculty are male.[125]

Interviews with women faculty of color[126] have revealed how closely race and gender bias are linked in their experiences. Nonetheless, the salience of race appears to be higher, and these faculty members feel that white women, who are doing better than faculty of color of either sex, have a cultural bias that causes difficulties for women of color. As one noted; "the discipline is really dominated by Western European notions." In addition to having greater service obligations than whites in their universities because of their small numbers, women of color also are likely to have more extended responsibilities in their families and communities.[127] Finally, they are even more likely than white women to have their legitimacy in the class room challenged. For all those reasons, it is critical that this group not be made invisible by inclusion in larger groups that do not share their issues. They need special and specific attention. As Turner says, it is important to break the conspiracy of silence about this group.

FUNDING-AGENCY-DRIVEN INSTITUTIONAL TRANSFORMATION

In addition to the university-specific practices detailed above, both public and private organizations have created awards aimed at advancing women in science and engineering by providing financial support for both individual women investigators and the institutions that support them. The goal of the NSF ADVANCE program (Box 5-5) is to create institutional changes that will help all faculty and diminish distinctions by gender and race or ethnicity.

The Clare Boothe Luce (CBL) program, the largest source of private

---

[124]CB Leggon (2006). Women in science: Racial and ethnic differences and the differences they make. *Journal of Technology Transfer* 31:325-33.

[125]Leggon (2006), ibid; Harvey (2003). *20th Anniversary of the Minorities in Higher Education Annual Status Report 2002-2003.* Washington, DC: American Council on Education.

[126]CSV Turner (2002). Women of color in academe: Living with multiple marginality. *Journal of Higher Education* 73:74-93; D Jordan (2005). *Sisters in Science.* Ashland, OH: Purdue University Press.

[127]ELJ Edmondson Bell and SM Nkomo (2001). *Our Separate Ways.* Cambridge, MA: Harvard Business School Press.

funding for women in science and engineering, "strives to increase the participation of women in the sciences and engineering at every level of higher education and to serve as a catalyst for colleges and universities to be proactive in their own efforts toward this goal."[128] Among its programs, CBL provides "professorship" grants that support women at the beginning of the tenure track. In addition to allowing for a stipend and benefits, the CBL professorship allocates 20% of the total award for covering professional expenses, including child care. Professorship awards are proposed by an institution, and may only be used to hire new tenure-track faculty. CBL funding also provides universities with an incentive to advance their women faculty. Proposals must describe an institution's plan for increasing the external visibility of the candidate, nurturing her professional development, and incorporating her into a regular position at the end of the grant period. They must also demonstrate that the institution understands the factors that may hinder women's career advancement and must describe the university's policies for advancing women.

With a substantial proportion of women leaving the academic career path because of caregiving responsibilities, re-entry postdoctoral positions may be an effective "on-ramp" to bring these women back into academic science and engineering careers. The Harvard Women in Science and Engineering Task Force (Box 6-3) recommended "senior postdoctoral fellowships" and similar kinds of funding at key transition points to enable women to reach leadership levels; such grants have also been available to facilitate career re-entry through the NIH Mentored Research Scientist Development Award K01 grant mechanism.[129] The American Physical Society recently implemented the Hildred Blewitt Scholarship to support the career re-entry of a researcher who has had a career interruption due to family responsibilities.[130]

CONCLUSION

Considerable attention has been directed at understanding how to create work environments that provide women and minority-group members fair compensation and resources, networking opportunities, and appropriate integration of work and home responsibilities. Resistance to change is

---

[128]The Clare Boothe Luce Program. *Proposal Guidelines for Invited Colleges/Universities, http://www.hluce.org/4cbldefm.html.*

[129]Mentored Research Scientist Development Award (K01) Web page, *http://www.grants. gov/search/search.do?mode=VIEW&oppId=8425.*

[130]See American Physical Society Hildred Blewitt Scholarship Web page, *http://www.aps. org/educ/cswp/blewett/index.cfm.*

rooted in the worry that standards will be lowered if, for example, allowances are made for a young woman who has children while working toward tenure. Because academic institutions need the best *minds,* dedication and effort needs to be considered in context. It's like watching two racers complete an obstacle course in nearly the same time, while one carries a 100-pound pack on their back and the other is unencumbered. Currently, we favor the lightweight because they probably finished first. But we should think about the heavyweight, and realize their intrinsic ability is much greater—something we would miss if we didn't consider the context. Next year, or 5 years from now, that heavyweight's burden will likely be lower, and the lightweight's burden could have increased, due to aging parents or disease or a divorce. Judging intrinsic merit is important.

Programs already under way in universities and funding agencies across the nation illustrate that well-planned knowledge-based efforts to remove constraints on women academics' careers can produce substantial results. Whether those efforts involve "small wins" or institution-wide transformations, to be successful they must include use of accurate information about the existing situation, attention to problematic elements of institutional culture and practices, input from affected persons to help identify those elements, evaluation of results, and buy-in from leadership at all institutional levels.

Carrying out adequate data gathering, planning, implementation of changes, and evaluation requires that sufficient resources be dedicated to the objective of increasing diversity. Academic institutions must be joined by scientific and professional societies and federal agencies for lasting change to occur. All three sectors must provide leadership on issues of diversity, hold their constituents accountable for change, and provide clear measures and methods for compliance. Together, they can work to promote and ensure equity, increase the pool of talented scientists and engineers, and ensure their integration into the nation's economy.

6

Fulfilling the Potential of Women in Academic Science and Engineering

While the number and proportion of women earning science and engineering degrees has increased dramatically, the need for additional focused steps to increase the representation of women in science and engineering faculties is obvious and persistent. Universities and colleges play central roles both in the education of scientists and engineers and in the conduct of research and development. Progress toward equality on their campuses is crucial if we are to optimize the productivity of the nation's science and engineering enterprise.

ROOT CAUSES OF DISPARITIES

Making full use of the nation's scientific and technical talent, regardless of the sex, social, and ethnic characteristics of the persons who possess it, will require both understanding of the causes of inequality and effective remedies.

Biological explanations for the dearth of women professors in science and engineering have not been confirmed by the preponderance of research (**Chapter 2**). Studies of brain structure and function, of hormonal modulation of performance, of human cognitive development, and of human evolution provide no significant evidence for biological differences between men and women in performing science and mathematics that can account for the lower representation of women in these fields. The dramatic increase in the number of women science and engineering PhDs over the last 30 years clearly refutes long-standing myths that women innately or inherently lack the qualities needed for success; obviously, no changes in innate abilities could occur in so short a time.[1]

Surveys of the definite postgraduate plans of science and engineering doctoral recipients show that similar proportions of women and men plan for a career in academe. As shown in **Chapter 3**, despite similar career aspirations, women have not been able to translate their success at earning science and engineering PhDs into academic careers equal to those attained by men.

Academe is purportedly a meritocracy that rewards objectively determined accomplishment. However, many studies document that both bias and structural barriers built into academic institutions and the occupation of professor limit many women's ability to be hired and promoted in university faculties. In fact, the academy has perpetuated patterns of bias that devalue women and minorities and their abilities, aspirations, accomplishments, and roles. As described in **Chapter 4**, small but consistent differences in evaluation, often caused by gender bias, can have a sustained and substantial impact on career outcomes.

> I have always believed that contemporary gender discrimination within universities is part reality and part perception, but I now understand that reality is by far the greater part of the balance.
>
> —Chuck Vest, President, MIT[2]

A substantial body of research demonstrates that women are underrepresented at higher levels of business and academe because of the influence of gender schemas and the accumulation of disadvantage that such schemas generate.[3] Gender schemas systematically influence both women and men's perceptions and evaluations of competence and performance, and they cause women to be consistently underrated and men consistently overrated. Academic scientists and engineers show bias against women applying for grants, employment, and tenure. To achieve the same competence rating as a man, a woman must have a significantly superior

---

[1]J Handelsman, N Cantor, M Carnes, D Denton, E Fine, B Grosz, V Hinshaw, C Marrett, S Rosser, D Shalala, and J Sheridan (2005). More women in science. *Science* 309:1190-1199, *http://www.sciencemag.org/cgi/content/full/309/5738/1190*.

[2]Massachusetts Institute of Technology (1999). A study on the status of women faculty in science at MIT. *MIT Faculty Newsletter* 11(4), *http://web.mit.edu/fnl/women/women.html*.

[3]V Valian (1998). *Why So Slow? The Advancement of Women*. Cambridge, MA: MIT Press.

FOCUS ON RESEARCH

BOX 6-1 Benefits of Presumed Competence

Acquisition of human capital parallels the accumulation of advantage or disadvantage. Exposure to discrimination influences earnings and leads to inequalities in income across the career, particularly among the highly educated.[a] Those familiar with compound interest know that even a difference in return of 1% per year leads to a 25% lower total return over a 30-year period. A computer simulation of promotion practices shows a similar effect.[b] The model assumes a pyramidal organizational hierarchy and a tournament model of success, in which evaluation of early career success is necessary for promotion. A hypothetical corporation with eight levels is staffed at the bottom level by equal numbers of men and women, and 15% of the staff is promoted from one level to the next, but there is an evaluation bias in favor of men. With a 5% bias, only 29% of those promoted to the very top level of the organization were women, whereas 58% of the bottom-level positions were filled by women. Even more dramatic is the finding that when sex differences explained only 1% of the variance, an estimate that might be dismissed as trivial, only 35% of the highest-level positions were filled by women. Clearly, even small disadvantages can create significant disparities over time.

---

[a]D Tomaskoviv-Devey, M Thomas, and K Johnson (2005). Race and the accumulation of human capital across the career: A theoretical model of fixed-effects application. *American Journal of Sociology* 111:58-89.

[b]RF Martell, DM Lane, and C Emrich (1996). Male-female differences: A computer simulation. *American* Psychologist 51:157-158.

---

record.[4] Although most individual differences in treatment are typically quite subtle and seemingly small, these small but consistent advantages or disadvantages accumulate into significant discrepancies in salary, promotion, and prestige (Box 6-1).

In addition to bias, systematic structural constraints built into academic institutions have impeded the careers of women scientists.[5] As docu-

---

[4]C Wennerås and A Wold (1997). Nepotism and sexism in peer-review. *Nature* 387:341-343; R Steinpreis, KS Anders, and D Ritzke (1999). The impact of gender on the review of the curriculum vitae of job applicants and tenure candidates: A national empirical study. *Sex Roles* 41(7-8):509-528; Massachusetts Institute of Technology (1999). A study on the status of women faculty in science at MIT. *MIT Faculty Newsletter* 11(4), *http://web.mit.edu/fnl/women/women.html*.

[5]For example, see J Jacobs and S Winslow (2004). The academic life course: Time pressures and gender inequality. *Community, Work and Family* 7(2):143-161; B Baginole (1993). How to keep a good woman down: An investigation of the role of institutional factors in the process of discrimination against women academics. *British Journal of Sociology of Education* 14(3):261-274.

mented in **Chapter 5**, organizational rules and structures may appear neutral on the surface but can function in a way that leads to differential treatment of or differential outcomes for men and women. One example is the effect on productivity of unequal access to institutional resources.[6] Another is the assumption that faculty members have substantial spousal support. The evidence demonstrates that anyone lacking the work and family support provided by someone fulfilling the traditional role of wife is at a serious disadvantage in academe. Most faculty members no longer belong to households that fit that mold. In 2003, 64.4% of women and 83.5% of men tenured or tenure-track faculty were married; 42.2% of women and 50% of men faculty had at least one child in the household.[7] About 90% of the spouses of science and engineering women faculty are employed full-time; almost half the spouses of male faculty also work full-time (see Figures 5-2 and 5-3).[8] Furthermore, even within today's two-career households, women still shoulder a disproportionate share of responsibility for children and other dependents, which places a burden on women faculty members that their male colleagues ordinarily do not bear.

WHY CHANGE IS NECESSARY

This nation can no longer afford the underperformance of our academic institutions in attracting the best and brightest minds to the science and engineering enterprise. Nor can it afford to underappreciate or devalue the contributions of that workforce through gender inequities and discrimination. There are four compelling reasons for taking action to eliminate gender disparities and bias in science and engineering careers in academe and elsewhere.

1. **Global competitiveness.** America's technological advances, its standard of living, and ultimately its prosperity and security depend on global pre-eminence in science and engineering. Other countries are making strong

---

[6]RK Merton (1968). The Matthew effect in science. *Science* 158:56-63; P Allison and JS Long (1990). Departmental effects on scientific productivity. *American Sociological Review* 55:469-478; B Keith, JS Layne, N Babchuk, and K Johnson (2002). The context of scientific achievement: Sex status, organizational environments, and the timing of publication on scholarship outcomes. *Social Forces* 80(4):1253-1282; Y Xie and KA Shauman (1998). Sex differences in research productivity: New evidence about an old puzzle. *American Sociological Review* 63:847-870.

[7]National Science Foundation (2003). *Survey of Doctorate Recipients*. Data provided by Joan Burrelli, Division of Science Resource Statistics.

[8]The National Science Foundation has compiled a table on marital status and spousal employment for men and women scientists and engineers in 2001, see *http://www.nsf.gov/statistics/wmpd/employ.htm*, Table H-31.

gains emulating the successes of the United States by investing heavily in science and technology.[9] To remain competitive in a fast-changing global economy, the United States needs to make optimal use of its scientific and engineering talent.

2. **Law.** Our nation has strong anti-discrimination laws. Title VII of the Civil Rights Act of 1964[10] prohibits employment discrimination based on race, color, religion, sex, and national origin. Title IX, passed in 1972,[11] prohibits discrimination or exclusion on the basis of sex from any education program or activity receiving federal financial assistance. The Science and Engineering Equal Opportunities Act of 1980 made "equal opportunity [for men and women] in education, training and employment in scientific and technical fields" the official policy of the United States.

3. **Economics.** States, the federal government, and the private sector invest heavily in training scientists and engineers. The average annual support provided for a full-time doctoral student is about $50,000, not including research and training expenses.[12] The average doctoral student takes about 7 years to complete the PhD,[13] bringing the investment to $350,000 per PhD. That is a substantial cost. It makes no sense economically to have highly educated, expensive PhDs leave science and engineering because they perceive a lack of opportunity to excel.

4. **Ethics.** Men and women should have an equal opportunity to serve society, work in rewarding jobs, and earn a living.

> Until women can feel as much at home in math, science, and engineering as men, our nation will be considerably less than the sum of its parts. If we do not draw on the entire talent pool that is capable of making a contribution to science, the enterprise will inevitably be underperforming its potential.
>
> —The Presidents of the Massachusetts Institute of Technology, Stanford University, and Princeton University[14]

---

[9]See NAS/NAE/IOM (2007). *Rising above the Gathering Storm: Energizing and Employing America for a Brighter Economic Future.* Washington, DC: The National Academies Press.

[10]Pub. L. 88-352. For a full description, see *http://www.eeoc.gov/policy/vii.html.*

[11]Title 20 U.S.C. Sections 1681-1688. See *http://www.dol.gov/oasam/regs/statutes/titleix.htm.*

[12]In 2001, the average annual stipend support was $37,234, and tuition and fees were $8,070. Overheads on federal grants help to support health benefits. The numbers do not include the amount invested in research or teaching. Data from National Center for Education Statistics (2002). *Digest of Education Statistics, 2002* (NCES 2003060). Washington, DC: US Department of Education Statistics.

[13]National Science Board (2006). *Science and Engineering Indicators, 2006* (NSB 06-01). Arlington, VA: National Science Foundation, Figure 2-27 and Appendix Table 2-34.

[14]J Hennessey, S Hockfield, and S Tilghman (2005). Women and science: The real issue. *The Boston Globe,* Feb. 12, *http://www.boston.com/news/education/higher/articles/2005/02/12/women_and_science_the_real_issue/.*

WHAT MUST BE DONE: A BLUEPRINT FOR ACTION

Career impediments for women deprive the nation of an important source of talented and accomplished scientists and engineers. Transforming institutional structures and processes to eliminate gender bias requires a major national effort, incorporating strong leadership and continuous attention, evaluation, and accountability. It will require persistent diligence and abiding patience.[15] The committee's recommendations are rooted in strategies shown to be successful. They are large-scale and interdependent, and require the combined efforts of university leaders and faculties, professional societies and higher education organizations, funding agencies, federal agencies, and Congress.

> Attaining gender equity is a deep cultural problem, one that most scientists would like to see overcome, but one that is likely to persist unless active steps are taken to change the culture in which we live.
>
> —Richard Zare, Chair, Chemistry Department, Stanford University[16]

Change Institutional Processes to Combat Bias

Faculty members and administrators at all levels need to correct or eliminate the policies and practices that lead to or permit gender bias. How should faculty interact with students? How should young women faculty deal with unwelcome social or sexual advances? How should faculty members work with staff? How should institutions and individuals interview and hire? What are effective, unbiased strategies for evaluating performance? A recent Harvard Task Force developed a comprehensive list of policy actions for improving the retention and advancement of women in science and engineering, across the educational and career path (Box 6-2).

Many women faculty cite workplace climate as an important factor in career satisfaction and decisions about whether to pursue a career in academe.[17] All too often, newly minted scientists begin their faculty positions

---

[15]JH Franklin (2005). *Mirror to America*. New York: Farrar, Straus, and Giroux.

[16]R Zare (2006). Sex, lies, and Title IX. *Chemical and Engineering News* 84(2):46-49, *http://pubs.acs.org/cen/education/84/8420education.html*.

[17]For example, see LLB Barnes, MO Agago, and WT Coombs (1998). Effects of job-related stress on faculty intention to leave academia. *Research in Higher Education* 39(4):457-469; P Bronstein and L Farnsworth (1998). Gender differences in faculty experiences of interpersonal climate and processes for advancement. *Research in Higher Education* 39(5):557-585;

DEFINING THE ISSUES

BOX 6-2 The Harvard University Task Force on Women in Science and Engineering[a]

"A diverse faculty is a strong faculty because it emerges from the broadest possible consideration of available talent."

On February 3, 2005, Harvard University announced the formation of two Task Forces—the Task Force on Women Faculty (WF-TF) and the Task Force on Women in Science and Engineering (WISE-TF)—to "develop concrete proposals to reduce barriers to the advancement of women faculty at Harvard." WISE-TF was charged to analyze and make recommendations concerning effective ways to build and sustain the pipeline of women pursuing academic careers in science, from undergraduate studies to graduate and postdoctoral work to advancement through faculty ranks. The task force made recommendations across several broad topics: sustaining commitment, mentoring and advising, enabling academic careers in the context of family obligations, and faculty development and diversity.

Sustaining commitment

- For undergraduates, create study centers in the science concentration courses and enhance summer science research programs.
- Improve the environment in science departments.
- Create, enhance, and sustain departmental activities that promote the success of all doctoral students and appoint a graduate school advisory council member to oversee these activities.
- Create an office for postdoctoral affairs.

---

with little or no training in effective strategies for running a laboratory, lacking even basic training and skills in writing and managing a budget, hiring and evaluating personnel, and conflict management. The dearth of training contributes in turn to some of the observed climate problems in the academic science workplace.[18] In recent years, training strategies and pro-

---

LS Hagedorn (2000). Conceptualizing faculty job satisfaction: Components, theories, and outcomes. *New Directions for Institutional Research* 105:5-20; MF Fox and P Stephan (2001). Careers of young scientists: Preferences, prospects and realities by gender and field. *Social Studies of Science* 31(1):109-122; CA Trower and RP Chait (2002). Faculty diversity. *Harvard Magazine*, *http://www.harvard-magazine.com/on-line/030218.html*; L August and J Waltman (2004). Culture, climate, and contribution: Career satisfaction among female faculty. *Research in Higher Education* 45(2):177-192.

[18]ER Rice and AE Austin (1988). Faculty morale: What exemplary colleges do right. *Change* 20(3):51-58; WM Plater (1995). Future work: Faculty time in the 21st century. *Change* 27(3):22-33; VJ Rosser (2004). Faculty members' intentions to leave: A national study on their worklife and satisfaction. *Research in Higher Education* 45(3):285-309.

Mentoring and advising

- Require pedagogical training with a gender bias component for doctoral students.
- Improve freshman advising.
- Track the progress of graduate students and postdoctoral fellows, and provide mentoring and professional development.
- Limit the length of appointment and set a base salary for postdoctoral fellows.
- Provide mentors for junior faculty in the science departments.

Enabling academic science careers in the context of family obligations

- Explore options to provide paid maternity leave and increase child-care scholarships for doctoral students and postdoctoral fellows.
- Expand the dependent care fund for short-term professional travel.
- Establish research-enabling grants for primary caregivers in the sciences.

Faculty development and diversity

- Design programs on diversity.
- Revise and expand search processes to increase the recruitment of women and underrepresented minority faculty in the sciences.
- Establish programs to provide funding and relief for key transition points in academic careers.

[a]*Executive Summary from Task Force Report on Women in Science and Engineering* (2005). Cambridge, MA: Harvard University, *http://www.faculty.harvard.edu/01/pdf/WISE_Final_ Report.pdf.*

grams have emerged to fill the void. Box 6-3 details an existing program that has proven effective at increasing the retention of women and men junior faculty.

Tenured faculty with management responsibilities—including department chairs, deans, and search committee chairs—would benefit from periodic workshops in which they examine ground rules and work to correct gender bias. Efforts should focus on providing mandatory workshops for deans, department heads, search committee chairs, grant reviewers, and other faculty with personnel evaluation and management responsibilities. The workshops should include an integrated component on diversity and the strategies needed to overcome bias and gender schemas. For example, the WISELI program at the University of Wisconsin-Madison convenes department heads for workshops on department climate (Box 6-4). Such forums provide an opportunity for general discussion of how to manage

EXPERIMENTS AND STRATEGIES

BOX 6-3 Improving the Retention of Junior Faculty Case Study: Johns Hopkins Department of Medicine Task Force

The Task Force on Women's Academic Careers in Medicine at the Johns Hopkins Department of Medicine is a model for academic departments to reduce gender bias and foster career development for women faculty.[a]

This case study begins in 1989 with a report from the Provost's Committee on the Status of Women that showed lower salaries for women faculty compared with men and substantially slower rates of promotion. In 1990, the chair of the Department of Medicine appointed a Task Force on Women's Academic Careers in Medicine to evaluate and characterize career pathways for men and women medical faculty. They found women faculty were less likely than men to be nominated for promotion, to have mentors who actively fostered their careers, to have comparable salaries, and to participate in decision making. Women faculty were more likely than male faculty to have mentors who used the women faculty's work for the mentor's own benefit, to feel isolated, and to experience conflict between work and personal responsibilities.

The Task Force set out to evaluate the basis of the obstacles to career advancement, hypothesizing that they were due to a combination of institutional policy, structure, and culture. The Task Force collected baseline data using individual interviews and a survey administered to all full-time faculty. Based on these data, they implemented interventions and evaluated the impact of these interventions by tracking such factors as faculty turnover, tenure rate, and proportion of men and women faculty at various ranks along the tenure-track, and by re-administering the same survey 3 and 5 years later. They found a substantial improvement in the proportion of junior women retained and promoted—without any change in evaluation criteria—as well as improvement for both men and women in timeliness of promotions, manifestations of gender bias, access to information needed for faculty development, isolation, and salary equity.

What did they do? The Task Force outlined six intervention areas and associated tasks to eliminate the gender-based obstacles to women's careers.

1. Leadership

• The department chair and task-force members committed to a long-term 15-year intervention.

• The Task Force on Women's Academic Careers in Medicine was formalized and provided an operating budget that included funds for members to attend faculty development conferences.

• A faculty/organization development specialist was hired to evaluate department structure and decision-making processes, and to assist individual faculty members.

2. Education

• Lectures, workshops and focus groups educated all members of the faculty on gender discrimination and bias.

• Female faculty members participated in a monthly department-level professional development colloquium.

3. Decrease Isolation

• Weekend and after-hours meetings were rescheduled to weekday working hours.

• Two or more women were included in every departmental search committee.

4. Faculty Development

• Each faculty member's curriculum vita was reviewed annually by the promotions committee.

• Based on the professional development colloquia, the Task Force produced a document defining the essential characteristics of mentorship; this was used to educate fellows and faculty members.

5. Academic Rewards

• Faculty salaries were reviewed by department chair; those below scale are increased.

• Department chair and division heads identified faculty ready for promotion in annual review process.

• The faculty/organization development specialist worked with the department chair and division directors to evaluate processes and to recommend changes that would make processes more explicit and equitable.

• The length of time at each pay scale rank is increased to ensure promotion possibility for faculty needing time to meet personal demands.

6. Monitoring and Evaluation

• Task force presented an annual written evaluation to the department and divisions.

A follow-up survey 3 years later indicated that this multifaceted strategy significantly decreased gender bias and improved the retention and promotion of men and women junior faculty. Isolation decreased. There was a 77% increase in the proportion of women faculty reporting that their division director had informed them of promotion criteria, and a 110% increase in the proportion who had mentors. The women in the department also reported significant improvement in the quality of mentoring. Monitoring of promotion rates from 1990-1995 showed that the number of women and men on the tenure track had increased, and the proportion of women faculty at the associate ranks increased from 4/45 (9%) in 1990 to 26/64 (41%) in 1995, a proportion similar to that of men (57/167 in 1990 and 70/223 in 1995).

Key lessons: (1) implement a long-term strategy that has multiple facets; (2) while interventions can start with a marginalized group, to minimize backlash it is critical that programs be generalized to all faculty;[b] (3) leadership is critical in maintaining focus and expectations; and (4) the quality and effectiveness of the program must be evaluated to determine what works and what does not.

---

[a]LP Fried, CA Francomano, SM MacDonald, EM Wagner, EJ Stokes, KM Carbone, WB Bias, MM Newman, and JD Stobo (1996). Career development for women in academic medicine: Multiple interventions in a department of medicine. *Journal of the American Medical Association* 276(11):898-905.

[b]See also S Mark, H Link, PS Morahan, L Pololi, V Reznik, and S Tropez-Sims (2001). Innovative mentoring programs to promote gender equity in academic medicine. *Academic Medicine* 76:39-42. This article reviews the four National Centers of Leadership in Academic Medicine. It found that a key indicator for failure was whether women were marginalized in gender-isolated programs. In these cases, the institution does not buy in and give full support and there is backlash from male colleagues. Mark et al. show that the Centers of Leadership succeeded because they created a gender neutral environment with gender-specific elements.

EXPERIMENTS AND STRATEGIES

BOX 6-4 Women in Science and Engineering Leadership Institute: Climate Workshops for Department Chairs

Climate (klī¯'mi˘t), *n*. The atmosphere or ambience of an organization as perceived by its members. An organization's climate is reflected in its structures, policies, and practices; the demographics of its membership; the attitudes and values of its members and leaders; and the quality of personal interactions. *Committee on Women, University of Wisconsin-Madison's Working Group on Climate* (2002).

Many women cite workplace climate—hostility from colleagues, exclusion from the department community and its decision-making process, and slights and ridicule—as pervasive in university settings. Men are often unaware of the impact that climate has on women and describe a better climate for women than women report experiencing. Those troubling trends in campus climates have been documented in faculty surveys at the Massachusetts Institute of Technology, Princeton, the University of Wisconsin-Madison, and the University of Michigan. Harsh climates have made it difficult for universities to recruit and retain women faculty members.

At the University of Wisconsin-Madison, the Women in Science and Engineering Leadership Institute (WISELI)[a] has developed a series of workshops, the WISELI Climate Workshops for Department Chairs, that engage small groups of department chairs in discussions of climate in their own departments and give participants a chance to learn from each others' experiences and ideas. The WISELI Climate Workshops for Department Chairs also provide information about various resources and people on campus that can assist department chairs in their efforts.

The goals of these workshops are

• To increase awareness of climate and its influence on the research and teaching missions of a department.

bias, and a vehicle for department leaders to exchange strategies and best practices.

A recent national meeting of chemistry department chairs in collaboration with the major federal funders of academic chemistry research—the Department of Energy, the National Science Foundation, and the National Institutes of Health—is an example of an effective cross-institutional strategy (Box 6-5).

- To identify various issues that can influence climate in a department.
- To present research on unexamined assumptions and biases and how they may influence climate.
- To enable chairs to assess climate in their own departments.
- To provide chairs with advice and resources, including a network of department chairs, they can use to improve climate in their departments.

Workshops are conducted over three sessions and structured around a Web-based department climate survey. The survey is administered between the first and second workshops. The survey enables chairs to identify specific concerns of their departments. During the course of the workshop, participants develop an action plan to address the issues raised in the survey. The third workshop is an opportunity for the chairs to discuss the impact of the changes they have implemented and to identify the key challenges they still face.

WISELI conducted a survey of the chairs within a year of completing the workshop. Of the 19 chairs surveyed, all but one said that the five goals stated above were met. Fourteen said that the climate in their department had improved and five said the climate was unchanged. Perhaps the most telling results were derived from a campus-wide survey of faculty, which was conducted in 2003 (before the climate workshops were instituted) and again in 2006 (after the workshops were instituted). An analysis of perceptions of climate in departments in which the chair had participated in WISELI training indicated that both men and women in those departments gave the climate for women a higher rating in 2006 than they had in 2003, whereas those in departments whose chairs had not participated rated it less favorable in 2006. The chairs who had participated in workshops were more aligned with the ratings given by their faculty than in 2003, suggesting that the workshops shifted their perception of the climate to be closer to the actual climate.

---

[a]Women in Science and Engineering Leadership Institute, *http://wiseli.engr.wisc.edu/*.

Create New Institutional Structures

Changing the "culture" of departments and institutions will not suffice to eliminate bias and institutional constraints on women's careers unless institutions frankly confront and resolve the issues raised by child and family responsibilities. The traditional career model clearly does not take into account the life course of women scientists who wish to become parents, because it requires unbroken concentration on work during their peak reproductive years; indeed, the career interruption associated with motherhood has been identified as the most likely factor that keeps a woman with science or engineering training from pursuing or advancing in a scientific or

EXPERIMENTS AND STRATEGIES

BOX 6-5 Building Strong Academic Chemistry Departments through Gender Equity[a]

In January 2006, 60 chemistry department chairs or senior leaders from the most active research universities convened with funding agency representatives and academic, government, and national chemistry leaders to identify specific strategies that chemistry departments, universities, and federal agencies could implement to encourage and enable broader participation of women in academic chemistry careers. The program for the workshop was developed by a steering committee of chemistry department chairs and several Committee on the Advancement of Women Chemists (COACh) (Box 4-3) board members, and was sponsored by the National Science Foundation, the Department of Energy, and the National Institutes of Health. Presentations by university leaders, social scientists, and funding agency representatives were intermixed with breakout sessions and panel discussions.

The workshop focused on (1) presentation of demographic data on the top 50 chemistry departments; (2) research on discriminatory biases and practices that negatively impact the recruitment, hiring, and advancement of women faculty; (3) identification of challenges and opportunities for chemistry departments, academic institutions, and federal funding agencies as they strive for gender equity in the sciences; and (4) development of action items for adoption by departments, institutions, and federal funding agencies. These action items included doubling the pool of women chemists considered for faculty positions in chemistry departments, creating sufficient child-care facilities, and strategies to advance the careers of young faculty such as modifying tenure rules, developing departmental procedures that mesh with family schedules, educating all faculty members to understand gender and caregiving bias, and providing opportunities for two-career families.

An on-site postworkshop survey was developed and conducted by COACh to determine what parts of the workshop the participants found most informative and useful. Participants attached high priority to gaining a better appreciation of subtle biases and discrimination that can accumulate to become a major career disadvantage for female faculty members. That issue was highlighted in several presentations and was effectively reinforced through both the presentation of the CRLT Players (Box 4-4), who provided an interactive and realistic demonstration of department communication, and by the testimony of women chemistry faculty members and women department chairs present at the meeting. Also identified as ef-

technical career.[19] Nor does the model take into account the needs of unmarried scientists—women and men—who have household, family, and community obligations without spousal support. It is a model that fits the

[19]Y Xie and KA Shauman (2003). *Women in Science: Career Processes and Outcomes.* Cambridge, MA: Harvard University Press; D Ginther (2006). The economics of gender differences in employment outcomes in academia. In *Biological, Social, and Organizational*

fective was a presentation by Senator Ron Wyden, who spoke on the need to diversify the scientific workforce.

COACh also conducted an on-line survey completed by the department chairs and their representatives before and after the workshop to learn their views on what limited their ability to hire women, of factors that could affect women's career progress, and to see whether any of these views changed as a result of the workshop. *Before the conference, chairs generally believed that factors limiting their ability to hire women were largely beyond their control.* Over two-fifths of the respondents indicated that having too few female applicants, losing female candidates to other departments, and not having employment for spouses or partners limited their departments' ability to hire women. Less than 12% indicated that the commitment of department faculty or opposition of department faculty to hiring women were limiting factors. The only barrier to women's advancement that was seen as moderately or very important by a majority of the attendees was the issue of balancing career and family life (cited by 88% of the respondents). At the same time, over half believed that heavier teaching loads, few mentoring opportunities, and discrimination in the peer review process were either "not an issue" or "not important."

After attending the conference, department chairs were significantly more likely to perceive that factors under their control limited their hiring of women or served as barriers to their progress. For instance, attendees were more likely than before the conference to report that their department faculty were not committed to hiring women, that some were actually opposed to doing so, that they didn't have enough financing, and that they did not have enough employment for spouses or partners. In addition, they were more likely to say that women faced career barriers involving heavier teaching loads, an unwelcoming department climate, few mentoring opportunities, and subtle biases against women.

Over the subsequent year, COACh will monitor changes in chemistry departments implemented as a result of this workshop. A chemistry department chair Web site has been established for the chairs to report the action items that they have selected to implement in their departments, to provide periodic progress reports, and to assess the effect of their efforts on their departments. It also provides a forum for department chairs to to share their challenges, progress, and successes.

---

[a]The workshop, *Building Strong Academic Chemistry Departments Through Gender Equity*, took place January 29-31, 2006, in Arlington, VA, *http://www.chem.harvard.edu/groups/friend/GenderEquityWorkshop/*.

Components of Success for Women in Academic Science and Engineering. Washington, DC: The National Academies Press; MA Mason and M Goulden (2004). Marriage and baby blues: Redefining gender equity in the academy. *Annals AAPSS* 596:86-103.

EXPERIMENTS AND STRATEGIES

BOX 6-6 Stanford University's Childbirth Policy for Female Graduate Students

In acknowledgment of the conflict between the academic timeline and the prime childbearing years, and in an effort to increase the number of women pursuing advanced degrees, Stanford University put into place in January 2006 a substantial new childbirth policy for female graduate students.

Stanford's university-wide policy has four main features:[a]

• All female graduate students are eligible for an academic accommodation period of up to two academic quarters before and after the birth of a child. During this time, the student may postpone academic requirements.

• During the accommodation period, the student remains eligible for full-time enrollment status and retains access to university facilities, housing, and benefits.

• Students are automatically given a one-quarter extension of department and university academic milestones (for example, PhD qualifying examinations).

• Students who receive support from university fellowships or research or teaching assistantships will be excused from the duties associated with those positions for a period of 6 weeks, during which time the student will continue to receive support.

Stanford's childbirth policy is not a leave-of-absence policy (although students are free to pursue maternity and medical leave under existing policies), and under this policy students are expected to continue to participate in coursework and required research activities, albeit at a reduced rate. Stanford's university-

---

lifestyle of an ever smaller group of people. It is urgent that academic norms and expectations be transformed so that the academy can continue to attract the very best people.

University faculty and leaders must develop and implement hiring, tenure, and promotion policies that take into account the flexibility that scientists need across the life course and that integrate family, work, and community responsibilities. They should provide central policies and funding for faculty and staff on leave and should visibly and vigorously support campus programs that help graduate students, postdoctoral scholars, and faculty with children or other caregiving responsibilities to maintain productive careers. Programs should include provisions for paid parental leave for faculty, staff, postdoctoral scholars, and graduate students (Box 6-6); facilities (Box 5-10) and subsidies (Box 6-7) for on-site and community-based child care;[20] dissertation defense and tenure clock extensions; modi-

---

[20]This was discussed as early as 1988 by Carl Djerassi. See FM Hechinger (1988). About education. *New York Times* B11(November 9).

wide childbirth policy is intended as a minimum standard; departments are encouraged to establish their own policies.

Stanford's Chemistry Department established its own childbirth policy before the enactment of the university-wide policy. The Chemistry Department's policy has an additional critical feature: it allows a student who is pregnant or is a new mother to reduce coursework and research activities for a period of 12 weeks while receiving the financial support of fellowships and assistantships.[b]

Both policies stress the continued importance of continued communication between students and their advisers. The policies aim "to support—not replace—the open communication and good will that should characterize the relationship between student and advisor."[c] Both the Stanford Chemistry Department's policy and the university-wide policy are among the most generous childbirth policies in the country; recently, Dartmouth University announced a similar policy for its graduate students.[d]

---

[a]M Peña (2006). New childbirth policy for female graduate students. *Stanford Report*, http://news-service.stanford.edu/news/2006/february1/mom-020106.html; Stanford University. *Stanford Graduate Student Handbook*. "Childbirth Policy for Women Graduate Students at Stanford University," http://www.stanford.edu/dept/DoR/GSH/childbirth.html.
[b]Stanford University Chemistry Department. *Letter to Graduate Students*, http://pubs.acs.org/cen/news/pdf/Stanford_Policy.pdf?sessid=1602.
[c]Stanford University. *Stanford Graduate Student Handbook*, ibid.
[d]R Wilson (2006). Dartmouth to provide paid leave to graduate students with new children. *The Chronicle of Higher Education* (May 16), http://chronicle.com/cgi-bin/printable.cgi?article=http://chronicle.com/daily/2006/05/2006051904n.htm.

---

fied duty schedules; lactation rooms; and family-friendly scheduling of critical meetings.

As described in **Chapter 5**, the mere existence of apparently family-friendly policies will not reduce the pressure on women faculty or their fear that family life will damage or even destroy their careers. Rather, to reduce the conflict between work and family that faculty members experience, faculties and their Senates must examine tenure guidelines and ensure that committees appropriately evaluate candidates who have taken parental leave. In addition, university leaders, including top administrators and department chairs, must adopt policies that recognize and mitigate the disadvantages imposed by caregiving.[21]

Create Methods for Evaluation and Accountability

Academic institutions must work jointly with scientific and professional societies and federal agencies for lasting change to occur. All three

---

[21]K Ward and L Wolf-Wendel (2004). Fear factor: How safe is it to make time for family? *Academe* 90(6), http://www.aaup.org/publications/Academe/2004/04nd/04ndward.htm.

EXPERIMENTS AND STRATEGIES

BOX 6-7 Financial Support for Dependent Care

Several successful strategies and programs exist in which students, postdoctoral scholars, and faculty are able to receive financial support to cover expenses related to dependent child care. Programs of this sort are sponsored by universities, professional societies, and research funding agencies.

Universities: A number of universities and research centers have programs that provide partial financial support to eligible students, faculty, and postdoctoral scholars to cover childcare expenses.

- **Harvard University's Dependent Care Fund for Conference Travel** provides dependent care assistance for assistant and associate professors attending professional development events such as academic conferences. Awards from the fund may be used by recipients for dependent care at a conference, or at an alternative location, and may include those expenses incurred in transporting a caregiver.[a]
- **Cornell University's Child Care Grant Subsidy (CCGS) Program** covers faculty and staff dependent care for "work days, school holidays, summer vacations and teacher work days."[b] The program is open to all benefits-eligible Cornell faculty and staff (including postdoctoral scholars) whose total household income is less than $150,000 annually and covers expenses for children up to 12 years old. The university deposits up to $5,000 in a FlexBenefits account for each qualifying employee. The intent of the CCGS program is to ease the burden that the cost of quality child care can present to faculty and staff.
- The **Fred Hutchinson Cancer Research Center** offers a **Postdoc Childcare Subsidy Program**. Through this program, selected center medical fellows and postdoctoral scholars receive a subsidy to cover partial cost of child care for prekindergarten children up to 6 years old. The subsidy covers 25% of the cost of childcare, up to $250 a month, for each child.[c]
- The **University of Washington** offers a **Childcare Voucher Program** through which it subsidizes child-care costs for eligible students. Depending on age of the child, this program will provide a subsidy of up to 60% of monthly child care expenses. The program covers children up to 12 years old, and assistance under this program is limited to lower-income students. The program is funded by the university's Services and Activities Fee which is paid by all students.[d]

Scientific and Professional Societies: The availability of child-care services at scientific and professional meetings can be an important factor in encouraging faculty, graduate students, and postdoctoral scholars with children to attend these

---

[a]Harvard University Dependent Care for Conference Travel Program, *http://www.fas.harvard.edu/home/academic_affairs/dependent_care.pdf*.

[b]Cornell University Child Care Grant Subsidy Program, *http://www.ohr.cornell.edu/benefits/childcareGrant/index.html*.

[c]Fred Hutchinson Cancer Research Center. *Postdoc Childcare Subsidy Program, http://www.fhcrc.org/science/education/grad_postdoc/spac/childcare/index.html*.

meetings. Several strategies have emerged through which societies act to make child care available.

• **On-site child-care at a supplemented rate using a high-quality provider.** In this model professional societies contract with a child-care provider, such as KiddieCorp (as the American Sociological Association, American Economic Association, American Political Science Association, and others have done) or the Nanny Network (as the American Geophysical Union has done) to provide on-site child care to members. The cost is supplemented by the society. This strategy can be expensive. Per-day per-child costs of child-care services to the members can be upwards of $50, and the per-meeting costs to the society can often be several thousand dollars.

• **Grants or reimbursement to members to cover child-care costs.** In this model, societies do not provide child-care services themselves but rather help members cover the costs of services. This model has been used by the London Mathematical Society (the chief professional society for mathematics in the United Kingdom)[e] and was recently adopted as a pilot program by the American Philosophical Association.[f] Under this model, nontenured society members apply for a grant (usually $500) to help to defray the cost of child care while attending selected society meetings or other nonroutine research activities. It is worth noting that universities may adopt a similar approach and include partial coverage of childcare expenses as part of travel allowances made to faculty or students (see Harvard University example above).

Funding Agencies and Organizations: Child-care support may also be available from funders.

• The **David and Lucille Packard Foundation awards the Packard Fellowship for Science and Engineering** with the purpose of supporting the research of young scientists with "few funding restrictions and limited paperwork requirements."[g] The fellowships provide grants of $625,000 over a 5-year period. The foundation received an Internal Revenue Service ruling that approves the use of up to $10,000 per year of fellowship funds for child-care expenses. The ruling is based on the understanding "that child care will be provided to enable [Packard] fellows to pursue their research and not for the personal or family needs of the individual." The fellow's university has the responsibility to provide budgetary oversight for the fellowship grant and ensure that grant funds are dispersed appropriately. The use of funds in this way is intended to allow Packard fellows to work on nonroutine research-related actives or attend related conferences and meetings that would be difficult without child care.

---

[d]University of Washington. Childcare Voucher Program, *http://depts.washington.edu/ovpsa/childcare/voucher.html.*

[e]*http://www.lms.ac.uk/activities/women_maths_com/childcare.html.*

[f]Email communication from Sally Scholz, American Philosophical Association, to Laurel Haak, May 26, 2006.

[g]Packard Foundation. Packard Fellowships for Science and Engineering 2006 Guidelines, *http://www.packard.org/assets/files/conservation%20and%20science/2006_fellows_guidelines.pdf.*

continued

BOX 6-7 Continued

- The **National Institute of Allergy and Infectious Diseases (NIAID)** of the National Institutes of Health operates a pilot program, called **Primary Caregiver Technical Assistance Supplements**, which provide NIAID principal investigators with additional funds to be used to hire middle- to senior-level technicians to fill in for postdoctoral researchers who need to be away from the laboratory to take care of children or sick family members. The program is funded at only $500,000 per year.[h]

---

[h]National Institutes of Allergies and Infectious Diseases, National Institutes of Health, *Primary Caregiver Technical Assistance Supplements* Web page, *http://www.niaid.nih.gov/ncn/training/pctas.htm*.

---

sectors must provide leadership in equity, hold their constituents accountable for change, and provide clear measures and standards. Together, the three sectors can work to promote and ensure equity, increase the pool of talented scientists and engineers, and increase their integration into the nation's economy (Box 6-8).

Coordinating Body

To help coordinate efforts between the actors, the assistance of an **inter-institution monitoring organization** body is crucial. An example of such an organization is the National Collegiate Athletic Association (NCAA), which works with its member institutions to set standards and review Title IX compliance.[22] The NCAA has published an annual gender-equity report since 1992.[23] The NCAA, established in 1906, is a voluntary organization through which the nation's colleges and universities govern their athletic programs. It comprises more than 1,250 institutions, conferences, organizations, and individuals committed to the best interests, education, and athletic participation of student-athletes. The member colleges, universities, and conferences appoint volunteer representatives that serve on committees that introduce and vote on rules called bylaws. The members also establish programs to govern, promote, and further the purposes and goals of intercollegiate athletics.

---

[22]The Office of Civil Rights of the Department of Education is responsible for enforcement.

[23]For example, see the 2002-2003 NCAA gender-equity report at *http://www.ncaa.org/library/research/gender_equity_study/2002-03/2002-03_gender_equity_report.pdf*.

National higher education organizations, including the American Council of Education (ACE), Association of American Universities, and the National Association of State Universities and Land Grant Colleges, through formation of an inter-institution monitoring body, could play a leading role in promoting equal treatment of women and men studying and working in our nation's universities. Such a body could serve to recommend norms and measures, collect data, and track compliance and accountability across institutions. ACE is an umbrella organization encompassing all of higher education: degree-granting colleges, universities, and higher education-related associations, organizations, and corporations.[24] ACE, with its convening power and strong reputation for consensus-building, is the logical organization to take the initial step to convene higher education groups to discuss the creation of such a monitoring organization. A primary focus of the discussion should be on defining the scope and structure of data collection.

In addition, scientific and professional societies could serve in a role similar to that of the national governing bodies for sports[25] and help to set professional and equity standards, collect and disseminate field-wide education and workforce data, and provide professional development training for members that include a component on bias in evaluation.

> While opportunities for male and female athletes are an important issue, the possible implications of Title IX on educational opportunities for male and female college students have the potential of influencing many more students in a much more important manner. Access to high quality educational programs is more important from a policy standard point than whether one gets to play in intercollegiate soccer.
>
> —James Monks, Department of Economics, University of Richmond[26]

---

[24]ACE has over 1,800 member institutions and organizations. Among the over 100 national member organizations that are members of ACE are the American Association of State Colleges and Universities, American Association of University Professors, American Chemical Society, Association of American Colleges and Universities, Association of American Medical Colleges, Association of American Universities, National Association of Independent Colleges and Universities, National Association of College and University Business Officers, National Association of State Universities and Land-Grant Colleges, and the National Collegiate Athletic Association.

[25]See *http://www.ncaa.org/library/general/achieving_gender_equity/resources.pdf*.

[26]J Monks (2005). *Title IX Compliance and Preference for Men in College Admission* (Working Paper 80). Ithaca, NY: Cornell Higher Education Research Institute, *http://www.ilr.cornell.edu/cheri/wp/cheri_wp80.pdf*.

TRACKING AND EVALUATION

BOX 6-8 Scorecard for Evaluating How Well Research Universities Serve Women and Minorities in Science and Engineering

This scorecard should be used as a tool for continuous assessment of institutional efforts to remove the barriers to participation in science and engineering by women. It can be used to identify and publicize institutions that recruit and nurture talented individuals from diverse backgrounds, to create a culture that welcomes and supports all scientists and engineers and helps them realize their potential, and to work to overcome barriers to talented scientists and engineers at all levels.

A. Demographics	Number This year		Number 5 yrs ago		Number 10 yrs ago	
Students/Scholars (report by department)	Men	Women	Men	Women	Men	Women
(A1) S&E undergraduate degrees						
(A2) S&E doctoral degrees (see A1)						
(A3) S&E postdoctoral scholars (see A1)						
Professors (report by department/unit)	Number this year		Number last year		Number 2 yrs ago	
(A4) Assistant tenure track professors						
(A5) Associate professors • Tenure-track • Tenured						
(A6) Full professors						
(A7) Endowed chairs						
(A8) Department chairs						
(A9) Center Directors						
(A10) Academic Deans[a]						
(A11) Provost						
(A12) President						

B. Faculty turnover *(report by department /center/hiring unit)*	Number this year		Number last year		Number 2 yrs ago		Number 3 yrs ago	
	Men	Women	Men	Women	Men	Women	Men	Women
(B1) Number of faculty searches								
(B2) Number of applications								
(B3) Number of interviews								
(B4) Number of faculty hired								
(B5) Number of faculty who left before tenure review								
(B6) Number of faculty who are awarded tenure/ total up for tenure								

[a]This term applies to those faculty leading colleges or schools, and does not include academic advisors in residential colleges.

C. Practices *Access to Resources (report by department/center/unit)*	**Average Salary** __ 9 mo __ 12 mo		**Start-Up Costs** **(Range)**		**Laboratory Space (sq. ft)**	
	Men	Women	Men	Women	Men	Women
(C1) Assistant tenure-track professors						
(C2) Associate professors						
(C3) Full professors						
Committee Appointments						
(C4) Is there a policy for gender equity on all key university committees?	Yes *(provide URL or staff contact)*		No			
(C5) Which are the main university committees with decision-making power over the allocation of resources for faculty?						
(C6) Which are the main university committees with decision-making power over the teaching and advising obligations for faculty?						

	Number this year		**Number last year**		**Number 2 yrs ago**	
	Men	Women	Men	Women	Men	Women
(C7) Number of faculty on committees *(report by committee)*						
(C8) Resource allocation committees						
(C9) Curriculum and advising committees						

D. Policies			
Climate	**Yes** (provide URL or staff contact)	**No**	**Don't Know**
(D1) Does your institution have a formal mentoring program for • Undergraduates • Graduate Students • Postdoctoral Scholars • Pre-tenure Faculty • Tenured Faculty			
(D2) Does your institution provide management training or workshops with an integrated component that addresses gender and ethnic and racial equity for • Undergraduates • Graduate Students • Postdoctoral Scholars • Pre-tenure Faculty • Tenured Faculty • Department chairs • Search committee chairs			
(D3) Is there a university-wide grievance policy?			

continued

BOX 6-8 Continued

(D4) Does it apply to: • Undergraduates • Graduate Students • Postdoctoral Scholars • Pre-tenure Faculty • Tenured Faculty			
(D5) Is there an office or person designated to handle grievances?			
(D6) To whom/what office are sexual harassment cases brought?			
(D7) What percentage of sexual harassment cases were forwarded for action?	**This Year**	**Last Year**	**2 Years Ago**

Flexible work schedules

	Yes (provide URL or staff contact)	No	Don't know
(D8) Does your institution have a central written policy and budget to allow part-time appointments for: • tenure-track faculty • tenured faculty			
(D9) Does your institution have a university-wide written policy and budget to allow temporary relief from teaching or other modifications of duties with <u>no</u> reduction in pay for faculty: • family care • personal disability			
(D10) Does your university have university-wide formal written policies providing full or partial replacement pay • For new biological mothers during leaves for disability related to pregnancy and childbirth during the academic year? • For adoptive mothers? • For biological fathers? • For adoptive fathers? • For unmarried partners?			
(D11) Does your institution have a formal pregnancy leave policy for: • Undergraduates • Graduate Students • Postdoctoral Scholars • Pre-tenure Faculty • Tenured Faculty			

E. Outreach	Yes (provide URLs or staff contact)	No	Don't Know
(E1) Does the university have: • A science and mathematics outreach and mentoring program for high school or middle school students? • Summer internships in labs for high school students?			

F. Public Relations and Benchmarking			
(F1) Have there been, in the past 5 years, publicized statements by the university President and/or other leaders that the university is supportive of the advancement of faculty with caregiving or other personal responsibilities, throughout their careers?			
(F2) Does the university have a committee or commission on the status of women, with a budget, that identifies problems and recommends action?			
(F3) Does the university have a committee or commission on the status of minorities, with a budget, that identifies problems and recommends action?			
(F4) Does the university publicize success in science and engineering—and do they make an effort to feature successful women?			

[a] This term applies to those faculty leading colleges or schools, and does not include academic advisors in residential colleges.

Continuous Evaluation: Scorecard

Monitoring and evaluating progress toward gender equity in access to science and engineering education and academic careers require making appropriate measurements and comparisons. The committee has developed a proposed scorecard for measuring many of the factors relevant to equity, including climate, or "intangible" environment (see Box 6-8). The committee recommends that universities monitor their programs through annual self-audits that collect data on the education and employment of scientists and engineers disaggregated by sex and race or ethnicity. The recommended audits should be part of a larger effort to establish metrics for gender equity in academic science and engineering. Coordinating organizations should act to create uniform standards among their members and provide a central clearinghouse for publication of the results.

Federal Standards and Compliance Issues

Relevant civil rights statutes include Title IX (see Box 6-9), Title VI for students, and Title VII and Executive Order 11246 for faculty and employees. Together those laws bar discrimination on the basis of sex, race, and disability.[27] The federal agencies should work with higher education institutions to establish clear guidelines and measures for compliance with all civil rights statutes.

Civil rights statutes cover every aspect of student education and faculty employment. For students, these statutes cover recruitment, admission to undergraduate programs (at a minimum at public institutions), admission to graduate programs, housing arrangements, scholarships and fellowships, internships and work-study opportunities, assignment to classes, assignment of advisers, selection for teaching assistantships, and "intangible" environment.

For faculty and employees the statutes bar discrimination based on sex, race, and national origin in all aspects of employment in educational institutions and programs, including recruitment; hiring; selection of graduate fellowships or teaching assistantships if these create an employer-employee

---

[27]There are distinct enforcement agencies for each statute. Title VI and Title VII are enforced by the Equal Employment Opportunity Commission, which investigates and resolves discrimination complaints and can bring lawsuits on behalf of claimants. Individual commissioners may also file charges to initiate investigations of discrimination even absent a specific complaint. Executive Order 11246 is enforced by the Office of Federal Contract Compliance Programs at the Department of Labor, which has the authority to resolve complaints and undertake compliance reviews of federal contractors. Overall, the Department of Justice acts in a coordinating role to enforce the statutes.

DEFINING THE ISSUES
BOX 6-9 Title IX

Title IX bans sex discrimination in education and covers (a) students, faculty, and employees at institutions of higher education that receive federal funds and (b) students and employees of educational programs that are offered by other institutions that receive federal funds. When it was passed, however, the law did not specify how institutions would be measured to be in compliance. The Office of Civil Rights (OCR) of the Department of Education was charged with establishing these details. After years of review and extensive public feedback, the OCR issued standards in 1979.

The Three-Prong Title IX Compliance Test

To show compliance with Title IX of the Education Amendments of 1972, institutions must meet at least one of the following tests:

1. provide participation opportunities substantially proportional to the ratio of males to females in the student body;
2. show a history and continuing practice of upgrading girls' and women's programs;
3. meet the interests and abilities of women on campus.

That policy provides flexibility in meeting compliance, but many universities and most courts have focused on the proportionality standard in Title IX compliance and litigation.[a]

Every federal agency that gives funds to institutions of higher education or to other institutions that run educational programs—including all cabinet agencies (such as the Department of Education and the Department of Defense), and such agencies as the National Science Foundation, the National Institutes of Health, and the National Aeronautics and Space Administration—is obliged to enforce Title IX. Each federal agency has issued regulations delineating its enforcement responsibilities under the law, and each has the authority to investigate and resolve discrimination complaints and to initiate compliance reviews of recipients of federal aid. The Department of Justice is charged with coordination of agency efforts under Title IX and is obliged to ensure overall enforcement of the statute.

_____

[a]*Cohen v. Brown University; Horner v. Kentucky High School Athletic Association; Kelley v. Board of Trustees; Neal v. Board of Trustees of the California State Universities;* and *Roberts v. Colorado State Board of Agriculture.*

relationship; promotion; tenure; termination; allocation of resources, such as laboratory space, research assistants, and research funding; receipt of awards and opportunities for public recognition; terms and conditions of employment, including leave, benefits, teaching load, availability of sabbaticals, appointments as department chairs, selection for research projects, committee assignments, and office location; and "intangible" environment.

Sanctions

The current stated sanction for noncompliance with federal statutes is retraction of federal funds or cancellation of federal contracts. What the NCAA has done with regard to Title IX compliance is create an intermediate sanction to precede such action: withdrawal from competition of a member organization found to be in noncompliance. There are no analogous science and engineering "teams," however, an option that could be considered by the NCAA-like organization is withdrawal of an institution's ability to compete for federal funds for a given period. The pressure of civil rights enforcement tends to be indirect: institutions change behavior not because of the threat of sanctions, but rather because the law cultivates a normative environment that legitimates and motivates compliance.[28]

Possible Unintended Consequences

Some have argued that Title IX as applied to athletics has led to the elimination of men's sports teams in favor of women's teams. However, it appears that institutions are more likely to add female teams and female athletes than to cut male teams and reduce the number of male athletes in response to a finding of noncompliance.[29] A more common strategy used by institutions that are out of compliance with the proportionality standard is to provide preference to men in college admissions, and thereby establish a lower proportion of female students.[30] That has the obvious effect of

---

[28]WT Bielby (2000). Minimizing workplace gender and racial bias. *Contemporary Sociology* 29:120-129; B Reskin (2000). The proximate causes of employment discrimination. *Contemporary Sociology* 29(2):319-328; S Strum (2001). Second generation employment discrimination: A structural approach. *Columbia Law Review* 101(3):458-568; E Hirsh (2006.) *Enforcing Equal Opportunity: The Impact of Discrimination Charges on Sex and Race Segregation in the Workplace* (Working Paper). Department of Sociology, University of Washington.

[29]DJ Anderson and JJ Cheslock (2004). Institutional strategies to achieve gender equity in intercollegiate athletics: Does Title IX harm male athletes? *American Economic Review Papers and Proceedings* 94(2):307-311.

[30]J Monks (2005). Title IX Compliance and Preference for Men in College Admission (Working Paper 80). Ithaca, NY: Cornell Higher Education Research Institute, *http:// www.ilr.cornell.edu/cheri/wp/cheri_wp80.pdf.*

exacerbating imbalances between men and women and should be carefully considered in the crafting of standards for evaluation and compliance in science and engineering.

CALL TO ACTION

> "Institutions of higher education have an obligation, both for themselves and for the nation, to develop and utilize fully all the creative talent available."
>
> —Nine-University Statement on Gender Equity, 2005[31]

America's competitiveness in today's global economy depends on fully developing and using all the nation's scientific and engineering talent. However, substantial barriers still exist to the full participation of women, not only in science and engineering, but also in other academic fields throughout higher education.

That women are capable of contributing to the nation's scientific and engineering enterprise but are impeded in doing so because of gender and racial or ethnic bias and outmoded "rules" governing academic success is a *call to action.* Creating environments that promote the professional success of all people, regardless of their sex, race, or ethnicity, must be a top priority for all institutions and individuals concerned with maintaining and advancing the nation's scientific and engineering enterprise.

Transforming academic institutions so that they will foster the career advancement of women scientists and engineers at all levels of their faculties is a complex task of identifying and eliminating institutional barriers. Individual institutional efforts have had dramatic effects but sustained change across higher education is unlikely unless there is a transformation of the process by which students and faculty are educated, trained, recruited, evaluated, tenured, and retained.

Our analysis shows that policy changes are sustainable only if they create a "new normal," a new way of doing things. Increasing the number of women and underrepresented minority-group faculty substantially will require leadership from faculty, individual departments, and schools; rigorous oversight from provosts and presidents; and sustained normative pressure from external sources. The first step is to understand that women are

---

[31]Nine-University Statement on Gender Equity (2006), *http://www.berkeley.edu/news/media/releases/2005/12/06_geneq.shtml.*

DEFINING THE ISSUES

BOX 6-10 Elephants in the Room[a]

I'm going to offer you a set of recommendations that will cost you nothing but courage. They can also be used more broadly well beyond the hallowed halls, and thus impact the "cross-institutional interlock," or as I would say as an electrical engineer, "the system."

- First of all, we should have zero tolerance for bullying behavior. It should not be acceptable in the workplace or anywhere else. If you are an academic leader, you should confront faculty and others who are abusive to students, staff, and other faculty, particularly senior faculty.
- Tenure is not a license to kill. How many of you have seen on an academic campus, senior people with tenure over and over abuse people who are lower than them in the power structure, and nobody ever does anything? Why does that happen? Why do we let that happen? It's unacceptable.
- If you have issues with dealing with conflict and you are an academic leader, take a class. Get help. Seek support. It's not so difficult. We are conflict avoiders in the academy. People don't want to confront each other, but we have to. *It's our job.* It's in the position description. We can learn from conflict. We do learn from conflict.
- Confront people's biases.
- Support your local senior feminist colleagues, male and female. It's lonely at the top. Support them in their endeavors for social justice.

We must confront and act on these "elephants in the room"[b] as much as we must also change recruitment processes, become more family-friendly, ensure presence of role models, create new models for evaluation and promotion, and revamp the academic salary structure for staff and faculty.

---

[a]Closing comments by Denice Denton, *National Academies' Convocation on Biological, Social, and Organizational Components of Success*, December 9, 2005, Washington, DC.

[b] *"Elephants in the room"* is an English idiom for an obvious truth that is being ignored, for various reasons. It is based on the ironic fact that an elephant in a small room would be impossible to ignore. It sometimes is used to refer to a question or problem that very obviously stands to reason, but which is ignored for the convenience of one or more involved parties. The idiom also implies a value judgment that the issue *should* be discussed openly. See *http://en.wikipedia.org/wiki/Elephant_in_the_room*.

as capable as men of contributing to the science and engineering enterprise. Second, the science and engineering community needs to come to terms with the biases and structures that impede women in realizing their potential. Finally, the community needs to work together, across departments, through professional societies, and with funders and federal agencies to bring about gender equity.

The current situation is untenable and unacceptable. We must unite to ensure that all of our nation's people are welcomed and encouraged to excel in science and engineering at our colleges and universities.

Our nation's future depends on it.

Appendix A

Biographical Information

DONNA E. SHALALA (CHAIR) became professor of political science and president of the University of Miami on June 1, 2001. Born in Cleveland, Ohio, she received her AB in history from Western College for Women and her PhD from the Maxwell School of Citizenship and Public Affairs at Syracuse University. A leading scholar on the political economy of state and local governments, she has held tenured professorships at Columbia University, the City University of New York (CUNY), and the University of Wisconsin-Madison. She served in the Carter administration as assistant secretary for policy development and research at the US Department of Housing and Urban Development. From 1980 to 1987, she served as president of Hunter College of CUNY; from 1987 to 1993, she was chancellor of the University of Wisconsin-Madison. In 1992, *Business Week* named her one of the top five managers in higher education. In 1993, President Clinton appointed her secretary of health and human services; she served for 8 years, becoming the long-serving health and human services secretary. At the beginning of her tenure, the Department of Health and Human Services had a budget of nearly $600 billion and included a wide variety of programs, such as Social Security, Medicare, Medicaid, child care and Head Start, welfare, the Public Health Service, the National Institutes of Health, the Centers for Disease Control and Prevention, and the Food and Drug Administration. Dr. Shalala has more than three dozen honorary degrees and a host of other honors, including the 1992 National Public Service Award, and the 1994 *Glamour* magazine Woman of the Year Award. In 2005, she was named one of America's Best Leaders by *US News and*

World Report and the Center for Public Leadership at Harvard University's Kennedy School of Government. She has been elected to the Council on Foreign Relations, the National Academy of Education, the National Academy of Public Administration, the American Academy of Arts and Sciences, the National Academy of Social Insurance, the American Academy of Political and Social Science, and the Institute of Medicine.

ALICE M. AGOGINO is the Roscoe and Elizabeth Hughes Professor of Mechanical Engineering and affiliated faculty at the University of California, Berkeley (UCB) Haas School of Business in its Operations and Information Technology Management Group. She directs the Berkeley Expert Systems Technology Laboratory and the Berkeley Instructional Technology Studio. She is vice chair of the UCB Division of the Academic Senate and served as chair during the 2005-2006 academic year. She has served in a number of administrative positions at UCB including associate dean of engineering and faculty assistant to the executive vice chancellor and provost in educational development and technology. She also served as director for Synthesis, a National Science Foundation (NSF)-sponsored coalition of eight universities with the goal of reforming undergraduate engineering education, and she continues as principal investigator for the National Engineering Education Delivery System and the digital libraries of courseware in science, mathematics, engineering, and technology. She has supervised 65 MS projects and theses, 26 doctoral dissertations, and numerous undergraduate researchers. Dr. Agogino is a registered Professional Mechanical Engineer in California and is engaged in a number of collaborative projects with industry. Before joining the UCB faculty, she worked in industry for Dow Chemical, General Electric, and SRI International. Her research interests include intelligent learning systems; information retrieval and data-mining; multiobjective and strategic-product design; nonlinear optimization; probabilistic modeling; intelligent control and manufacturing; sensor validation, fusion, and diagnostics; wireless sensor networks; multimedia and computer-aided design; design databases; design theory and methods; microelectromechanical systems (MEMS) synthesis and computer-aided design; artificial intelligence and decision and expert systems; and gender equity. She serves on the editorial boards of three professional journals and has provided service on a number of government, professional, and industry advisory committees. Dr. Agogino received a BS in mechanical engineering from the University of New Mexico (1975), an MS in mechanical engineering (1978) from the UCB, and a PhD from the Department of Engineering-Economic Systems at Stanford University (1984). She received an NSF Presidential Young Investigator Award in 1985. She is a member of the National Academy of Engineering and the European Academy of Science; is a Fellow of the American Association for the Advancement of Science, the American Society for Mechanical Engineers, and of the Association of Women in Science; and was awarded the NSF Director's Award for Distinguished Teaching Scholars in 2004.

LOTTE BAILYN is a professor of management (in the Organization Studies Group) at the Massachusetts Institute of Technology (MIT) Sloan School of Management and Co-director of the MIT Workplace Center. In her work, she has set out the hypothesis that by challenging the assumptions in which current work practices are embedded, it is possible to meet the goals of both business productivity and employees' family and community concerns and to do so in ways that are equitable for men and women. Her most recent book—*Beyond Work-Family Balance: Advancing Gender Equity and Workplace Performance* (Jossey Bass, 2002) with Rhona Rapoport, Joyce K. Fletcher, and Bettye H. Pruitt—chronicles a decade of experience working with organizations that supports this hypothesis while showing how difficult it is to challenge workplace assumptions. She serves on the National Academies Committee on Women in Science and Engineering.

ROBERT J. BIRGENEAU became the ninth chancellor of UCB on September 22, 2004. An internationally distinguished physicist, he is a leader in higher education and is well known for his commitment to diversity and equity in the academic community. Before coming to UCB, he served 4 years as president of the University of Toronto. He previously was dean of the School of Science at MIT, where he spent 25 years on the faculty. He is a foreign associate of the National Academy of Sciences, has received many awards for teaching and research, and is one of the most cited physicists in the world for his work on the fundamental properties of materials. A Toronto native, Dr. Birgeneau received his BSc in mathematics from the University of Toronto in 1963 and his PhD in physics from Yale University in 1966. He served on the Yale faculty for 1 year, spent 1 year at Oxford University, and was a member of the technical staff at Bell Laboratories from 1968 to 1975. He joined the MIT physics faculty in 1975 and was named chair of the Physics Department in 1988 and dean of science in 1991. At UCB, Dr. Birgeneau holds a faculty appointment in the Department of Physics in addition to serving as chancellor.

ANA MARI CAUCE is the executive vice provost and Earl R. Carlson Professor of Psychology at the University of Washington. She graduated from Yale University, earning a PhD in psychology in 1984. She began teaching at the University of Washington in 1986 in the Department of Psychology. She also has a joint appointment in the Department of American Ethnic Studies and an adjunct appointment in women's studies, and served as chair of the Department of Psychology. Since she began her graduate work, she has been particularly interested in normative and nonnormative development in ethnic-minority youth and in at-risk youth more generally. She has published almost 100 articles and chapters and has been recipient of grants from the W.T. Grant Foundation, the National Institute of Mental Health, the National Institute of Child Health and Human Development, and the National Institute of Alcoholism and Alcohol Abuse. She is the recipient of numerous awards, including recognition by the American Psychological Association for excellence in research on minority issues; Distinguished Contribution Awards from the Society for Community Research and Action; and membership in the American Psychological Association Minority Fellowship program. She has also received the University of Washington's Distinguished Teaching Award. Dr. Cauce is currently president-elect of the Society for Community Research and Action.

CATHERINE D. DEANGELIS is editor-in-chief of the *Journal of the American Medical Association (JAMA)*, editor-in-chief of *Scientific Publications and Multimedia Applications*, and professor of pediatrics at Johns Hopkins University School of Medicine. She received her MD from the University of Pittsburgh's School of Medicine, her MPH from the Harvard Graduate School of Public Health (Health Services Administration), and pediatric specialty training at the Johns Hopkins Hospital. Dr. DeAngelis oversees *JAMA*, nine *Archives* publications, and *JAMA*-related Web-site content. Before her appointment with *JAMA*, she was vice dean for academic affairs and faculty at Johns Hopkins University School of Medicine; from 1994 to 2000, she was editor of *Archives of Pediatrics and Adolescent Medicine*. She has been a member of numerous journal editorial boards. She has written or edited 11 books on pediatrics and medical education and has published more than 200 original articles, chapters, editorials, and abstracts. Most of her recent publications have focused on conflicts of interest in medicine, on women in medicine, and on medical education. Dr. DeAngelis is a member of the Institute of Medicine, a Fellow of the American Association for the Advancement of Science, and she has served as an officer of numerous national academic societies, including being chairman of the American Board of Pediatrics and chair of the Pediatric Accreditation Council for Residency Review Committee of the American Council on Graduate Medical Education.

DENICE DEE DENTON was the chancellor of the University of California, Santa Cruz. She had been dean of and a professor in the University of Washington's College of Engineering. Earlier, she was a faculty member in electrical engineering and chemistry at the University of Wisconsin-Madison. While at the University of Washington, Dr. Denton led the development of the Faculty Recruitment Toolkit, a resource for attracting a top-notch and diverse faculty. In a single year (2001), nine faculty members received the prestigious NSF Career Award. In addition, federal research funding more than doubled in 3 years (1998-2001), from $33.1 million in grants and contract awards to more than $75 million. She emphasized implementing effective ways to teach a diverse engineering student body using a more project-oriented, experiential approach. Her work was facilitated by the Center for Engineering Learning and Teaching, the first center of its kind when it was established in 1998. Dr. Denton directed the University of Washington's NSF ADVANCE program for advancing women faculty in science and engineering. In 2004, Dr. Denton was honored by the White House with the Presidential Award for Excellence in Science, Mathematics, and Engineering Mentoring, recognizing her role as a national leader in engineering education. Dr. Denton chaired the National Academy of Engineering's Board on Engineering Education from 1996 to 1999. She was a Fellow of the American Association for the Advancement of Science, the Association of Women in Science, and the Institute of Electrical and Electronics Engineers (IEEE). Her awards for research and teaching included the NSF Presidential Young Investigator Award (1987), the Kiekhofer Distinguished Teaching Award (University of Wisconsin, 1990), the American Society of Engineering Education AT&T Foundation Teaching Award (1991), the Eta Kappa Nu C. Holmes MacDonald Distinguished Young Electrical Engineering Teaching Award (1993), the Benjamin Smith Reynolds Teaching Award (University of Wisconsin, 1994), the W.M. Keck Foundation Engineering Teaching Excellence Award (1994), the ASEE George Westinghouse Award (1995), and the IEEE/HP Harriet B. Rigas Award (1995). Dr. Denton earned her BS, MS (1982), and PhD (1987) in electrical engineering at MIT and conducted research on MEMS as an enabling technology particularly in life-sciences applications.

BARBARA J. GROSZ is Higgins Professor of Natural Sciences in the Division of Engineering and Applied Sciences and dean of science of the Radcliffe Institute for Advanced Study at Harvard University. Dr. Grosz is known for her seminal contributions to the fields of natural-language processing and multiagent systems. She developed some of the earliest and most influential computer-dialogue systems and established the research field of computational modeling of discourse. Her work on models of collaboration helped to establish that field of inquiry and provides the framework for several collaborative multiagent systems and human computer interface systems. She has been elected to the American Philosophical Society and the American Academy of Arts and Sciences. She is a fellow of the American Association for Artificial Intelligence, the American Association for the Advancement of Science, and the Association for Computing Machinery; is a recipient of the UCB Computer Science and Engineering Distinguished Alumna Award, awards for distinguished service from major artificial-intelligence societies, and is widely respected for her contributions to the advancement of women in science. She chaired the Harvard Faculty of Arts and Sciences (FAS) Standing Committee on the Status of Women when it produced the report *Women in Science at Harvard; Part I: Junior Faculty and Graduate Students* in 1991. She was interim associate dean for affirmative action at Harvard in 1993-1994 and served on the FAS Ad Hoc Committee on Faculty Diversity from 1998 to 2001 and the Standing Committee on Women from 1988 to 1995 and again in 1999. Dr. Grosz recently chaired the 2005 Harvard Task Force on Women in Science and Engineering. Before joining the faculty at Harvard, she was director of the natural-language program at SRI International and co-founder of the Center for the Study of Language and Information. She received an AB in mathematics from Cornell University and a PhD in computer science from UCB.

JO HANDELSMAN is a Howard Hughes Medical Institute professor in the Department of Plant Pathology at the University of Wisconsin-Madison (UW-Madison). She received a BS in agronomy from Cornell University and a PhD in molecular biology from UW-Madison. In addition, from 1997 to 1999, she was director of the Institute for Pest and Pathogen Management at UW-Madison. Dr. Handelsman studies the communication networks of microbial communities. She is a coauthor of a book about inquiry-based biology teaching titled *Biology Brought to Life*. In 2002, she was named Clark Lecturer in Soil Biology and received the Chancellor's University Teaching Award at UW-Madison. In addition, she has been active in achieving equity for women and minorities on campus, and her contributions were recognized with the Cabinet 99 Recognition Award. She contributed to the inception of the Women in Science and Engineering residence hall; has chaired the provost's Climate Working Group, an initiative dedicated to improving the campus climate for women and nonwhites; and, through an NSF grant, established, with others, the Women in Science and Engineering Leadership Institute.

NANNERL O. KEOHANE is the Laurance S. Rockefeller Distinguished Visiting Professor of Public Affairs at Princeton University. She was the eighth president of Duke University, serving from 1993 to 2004. Dr. Keohane came to Duke from the presidency of Wellesley College. She was the first woman to serve as Duke's president and among the first women to oversee a leading US research university. Under her leadership, Duke launched major programs in fields ranging from genomics to ethics, raised more than $2 billion through the Campaign for Duke, established the Duke University Health System, and became a much more diverse and international institution. Dr. Keohane is a 1961 graduate of Wellesley and earned advanced degrees at Oxford University and Yale University before beginning a career as a professor of political science at Swarthmore College, the University of Pennsylvania, and Stanford University. She returned to Wellesley in 1981 and served as its president for 12 years before moving to Duke.

SHIRLEY MALCOM is head of the Directorate for Education and Human Resources Programs of the American Association for the Advancement of Science and a fellow of the association. The directorate includes programs in education, activities for underrepresented groups, and public understanding of science and technology. Dr. Malcom serves on several boards—including the Howard Heinz Endowment, the H. John Heinz III Center for Science, Economics and the Environment, and the National Park System Advisory Board—and is an honorary trustee of the American Museum of Natural History. She serves as a regent of Morgan State University and as a trustee of California Institute of Technology. In addition, she has chaired a number of national committees addressing education reform and access to scientific and technical education, careers, and literacy. Dr. Malcom is a former trustee of the Carnegie Corporation of New York. She is a fellow of the American Academy of Arts and Sciences. She served on the National Science Board, the policy-making body of the NSF, from 1994 to 1998 and on the President's Council of Advisors on Science and Technology from 1994 to 2001. Dr. Malcom received her doctorate in ecology from Pennsylvania State University; her master's degree in zoology from the University of California, Los Angeles; and her bachelor's degree with distinction in zoology from the University of Washington. In addition, she holds 13 honorary degrees. In 2003, Dr. Malcom received the Public Welfare Medal of the National Academy of Sciences, the highest award given by the Academy.

GERALDINE RICHMOND is the Richard M. and Patricia H. Noyes Professor in the Department of Chemistry and Materials Science Institute at the University of Oregon. Dr. Richmond received her bachelor's degree in chemistry from Kansas State University and her PhD in chemical physics at the UCB. For the last 25 years, her research has focused on the development and application of state-of-the-art lasers to study surface chemistry and physics. On a national level, Dr. Richmond has served on many science boards and advisory panels overseeing funding for science, technology, and education. She has been honored with numerous national and regional awards for her research, her teaching, and her efforts in encouraging women of all ages to enter and succeed in science careers. In 2001, she was named Oregon Scientist of the Year by the Oregon Academy of Science. Dr. Richmond is a member of the Chemical Sciences Roundtable of the National Academy of Sciences and a governor's appointee to the Oregon State Board of Higher Education for 1999-2006. She is the founder and chair of the Committee on the Advancement of Women Chemists and was the 2005 winner of the American Chemical Society Award for Encouraging Women into Careers in the Chemical Sciences.

ALICE M. RIVLIN is a visiting professor at the Public Policy Institute of Georgetown University and a Senior Fellow in the Economic Studies Program at the Brookings Institution. She is the director of the Greater Washington Research Program at Brookings. Dr. Rivlin served as vice chair of the Federal Reserve Board from 1996 to 1999. She was director of the White House Office of Management and Budget from 1994 to 1996 and deputy director in 1993-1994. She served as chair of the District of Columbia Financial Management Assistance Authority (1998-2001). Dr. Rivlin was the founding director of the Congressional Budget Office (1975-1983). She was director of the Economic Studies Program at Brookings (1983-1987). She also served at the Department of Health, Education, and Welfare as assistant secretary for planning and evaluation (1968-1969). Dr. Rivlin received a MacArthur Foundation Prize Fellowship; taught at Harvard, George Mason, and New School Universities; and has served on the boards of directors of several corporations and as president of the American Economic Association. She is a member of the board of directors of BearingPoint and the Washington Post Company. She is a frequent contributor to newspapers, television, and radio and has written numerous books. Her books include *Systematic Thinking for Social Action* (1971), *Reviving the American Dream* (1992), and *Beyond the Dot.coms* (with Robert Litan, 2001). She is coeditor (with Isabel Sawhill) of *Restoring Fiscal Sanity: How to Balance the Budget* (2004) and (with Litan) of *The Economic Payoff from the Internet Revolution* (2001). Dr. Rivlin received a BA in economics from Bryn Mawr College in 1952 and a PhD in economics from Radcliffe College in 1958.

RUTH SIMMONS became president of Brown University in 2000. She has spent her career advocating for a leadership role for higher education in the arena of national and global affairs. Dr. Simmons has created a set of initiatives designed to expand the faculty; increase financial support and resources for undergraduate, graduate, and medical students; improve facilities; renew a broad commitment to shared governance; and ensure that diversity informs every dimension of the university. Those initiatives have led to a major investment of new resources in Brown's educational mission. A French professor before entering university administration, Dr. Simmons also holds an appointment as a professor of comparative literature and of

African studies at Brown. She graduated from Dillard University in New Orleans before completing her PhD in Romance languages and literatures at Harvard. She served in various administrative roles in the University of Southern California, Princeton University, and Spelman College before becoming president of Smith College, the largest women's college in the United States. At Smith, she launched a number of initiatives, including an engineering program, the first at an American women's college. Dr. Simmons is the recipient of many honors, including a Fulbright Fellowship, the 2001 President's Award from the United Negro College Fund, the 2002 Fulbright Lifetime Achievement Medal, and the 2004 Eleanor Roosevelt Val-Kill Medal. She has been a featured speaker in many public venues, including the White House, the World Economic Forum, the National Press Club, the American Council on Education, and the Phi Beta Kappa Lecture at Harvard University. She has been awarded numerous honorary degrees.

ELIZABETH SPELKE is Berkman Professor of Psychology and co-director of the Mind, Brain, and Behavior Initiative at Harvard University. She studies the origins and nature of knowledge of objects, persons, space, and number by assessing behavior and brain function in human infants, children, and adults, and nonhuman animals. A member of the National Academy of Sciences and the American Academy of Arts and Sciences and cited by *Time* magazine as one of America's Best in Science and Medicine, she has received such honors as the Distinguished Scientific Contribution Award of the American Psychological Association and the William James Award of the American Psychological Society.

JOAN STEITZ is Sterling Professor of Molecular Biophysics and Biochemistry at Yale University School of Medicine and an investigator at the Howard Hughes Medical Institute. She earned her BS in chemistry from Antioch College in 1963 and her PhD in biochemistry and molecular biology from Harvard University in 1967. She spent the next 3 years in postdoctoral studies at the MRC Laboratory of Molecular Biology in Cambridge and joined the Yale faculty in 1970, where her teaching focuses on undergraduates. Dr. Steitz is best known for discovering and defining the function of small nuclear ribonucleoproteins, which occur only in higher cells and organisms. These cellular complexes play a key role in the splicing of premessenger RNA, the earliest product of DNA transcription. Dr. Steitz is a member of the National Academy of Sciences, the American Association of Arts and Sciences, the American Philosophical Society, and the Institute of Medicine. She is a recipient of the National Medal of Science, 11 honorary degrees, and a Gairdner Foundation International Award. She serves on numerous review and editorial boards.

ELAINE WEYUKER is a principal technical staff member at AT&T Labs in Florham Park, New Jersey. Dr. Weyuker received a PhD in computer science from Rutgers University and an MSE from the Moore School of Electrical Engineering, University of Pennsylvania. Before moving to AT&T Labs in 1993, she was a professor of computer science at the Courant Institute of Mathematical Sciences of New York University, where she had been on the faculty since 1977. Her research interests are in software engineering, particularly software testing and reliability, and software metrics, and she has published many papers in those fields. She has been elected to the National Academy of Engineering, is a Fellow of the Institute of Electrical and Electronics Engineers, and is a Fellow of the Association of Computing Machinery (ACM). Dr. Weyuker is one of only two female AT&T Fellows. In each of the past 6 years, the *Journal of Systems and Software* has rated her as one of the top five software engineering researchers in the world. In November 2001, the New York City YWCA honored Dr. Weyuker as a Woman Achiever for both her career achievements and her community service. She has made major contributions to the formal foundations of testing and to establishing testing as an empirical discipline and has been a prime mover in making testing a recognized professional specialty. She has been a lecturer, teacher, and mentor; and she has been actively involved in professional activities. She was a founding member of the ACM Committee on the Status of Women and Minorities, which was established to improve the status of underrepresented groups by developing programs to target girls and young minority-group members. During her tenure, the committee established a successful distributed-mentoring program.

MARIA T. ZUBER is the E.A. Griswold Professor of Geophysics at MIT, where she also leads the Department of Earth, Atmospheric, and Planetary Sciences. Dr. Zuber has been involved in more than a half dozen National Aeronautics and Space Administration (NASA) planetary missions aimed at mapping the Moon, Mars, and several asteroids. She received her BA from the University of Pennsylvania and ScM and PhD from Brown University. She was on the faculty at Johns Hopkins University and served as a research scientist at Goddard Space Flight Center in Maryland. She is a member of the National Academy of Sciences and the American Philosophical Society and is a fellow of the American Academy of Arts and Sciences and of the American Geophysical Union, where she served as president of the Planetary Sciences Section. Among her awards are the NASA Distinguished Public Service Medal, the NASA Scientific Achievement Medal, the Brown University Horace Mann Medal, and a Scientific Achievement Award from the American Institute of Aeronautics and Astronautics. Dr. Zuber served on the Mars Program Independent Assessment Team that investigated the

Mars mission losses in 1999 and more recently on the Presidential Commission on the Implementation of the United Space Exploration Policy tasked with conceiving a plan to implement President Bush's Vision for Space Exploration. In 2002, *Discover* magazine named her one of the 50 most important women in science.

Appendix B

Statement of Task

Research in science and engineering has been and remains central to the US role in the world, the culture of the nation, its continuing economic development, and its security. It is imperative that the nation access its entire talent pool. However, it is clear from several recent studies that while women are an increasing proportion of those earning undergraduate and graduate degrees in science and engineering fields, they have not been hired into academic positions commensurate with this increasing representation. Ultimately, this means that the academic research enterprise is missing out on talent, and will underperform relative to its potential.

The study committee will integrate the wealth of data available on gender issues across all fields of science and engineering. The committee will focus on academe, but will examine other research sectors to determine if there are effective practices in place relevant to recruiting, hiring, promotion, and retention of women science and engineering researchers. Throughout the report, profiles of effective practices, scenarios, and summary boxes will be used to reinforce the key concepts.

The committee is charged to:

1. Review and assess the research on gender issues in science and engineering, including innate differences in cognition, implicit bias, and faculty diversity.

2. Examine the institutional culture and practices in academic institutions that contribute to and discourage talented individuals from realizing their full potential as scientists and engineers.

3. Determine effective practices to ensure women doctorates have access to a wide range of career opportunities, in academe and in other research settings.

4. Determine effective practices on recruiting and retention of women scientists and engineers in faculty positions.

5. Develop findings and provide recommendations based on these data and other information the committee gathers to guide the following groups on how to maximize the potential of women science and engineering researchers:

(a) Faculty: roles in hiring, promotion, retention, and mentoring.

(b) Deans and Department Chairs: roles in hiring and promotion and equitable provision of resources.

(c) Academic Leadership: roles in hiring, promotion, resource allocation, tracking, and setting the tone for institutional culture.

(d) Funding Organizations: roles in education and training, compensation levels, review, and tracking of grant applicant and recipient data.

(e) Government: roles in enhancing and diversifying access to education, training, and research funding, and in ensuring that data about program users are collected and available for assessment purposes.

Appendix C

Chapter 4 of
Measuring Racial Discrimination (2004),
National Research Council,
Washington, DC,
The National Academies Press

Theories of Discrimination

In Chapter 3, we developed a two-part definition of racial discrimination: differential treatment on the basis of race that disadvantages a racial group and treatment on the basis of inadequately justified factors other than race that disadvantages a racial group (differential effect). We focus our discussion on discrimination against disadvantaged racial minorities. Our definition encompasses both individual behaviors and institutional practices.

To be able to measure the existence and extent of racial discrimination of a particular kind in a particular social or economic domain, it is necessary to have a theory (or concept or model) of how such discrimination might occur and what its effects might be. The theory or model, in turn, specifies the data that are needed to test the theory, appropriate methods for analyzing the data, and the assumptions that the data and analysis must satisfy in order to support a finding of discrimination. Without such a theory, analysts may conduct studies that do not have interpretable results and do not stand up to rigorous scrutiny.

The purpose of this chapter is to help researchers think through appropriate models of discrimination to guide their choice of data and analytic methods for measurement. We begin by discussing four types of discrimination and the various mechanisms that may lead to such discrimination. The first three types involve behaviors of individuals and organizations: intentional discrimination, subtle discrimination, and statistical profiling. The fourth type involves discriminatory practices embedded in an organizational culture. Next, we compare these discriminatory behaviors and institutional practices with existing legal standards defining discrimination in the courts (as delineated in Chapter 3). We then discuss how these discriminatory behaviors and practices might operate within the domains of education, employment, housing, criminal justice, and health. Finally, we discuss concepts of how cumulative discrimination might operate across domains and over time to produce lasting consequences for disadvantaged racial groups. This chapter is not concerned with identifying the relative importance of the various types of discrimination; rather, it is designed to present a set of conceptual possibilities that can motivate and shape appropriate research study designs.

TYPES OF DISCRIMINATION

Most people's concept of racial discrimination involves explicit, direct hostility expressed by whites toward members of a disadvantaged racial group. Yet discrimination can include more than just direct behavior (such as the denial of employment or rental opportunities); it can also be subtle and unconscious (such as nonverbal hostility in posture or tone of voice). Furthermore, discrimination against an individual may be based on overall assumptions about members of a disadvantaged racial group that are assumed to apply to that individual (i.e., statistical discrimination or profiling). Discrimination may also occur as the result of institutional procedures rather than individual behaviors.

Intentional, Explicit Discrimination

In 1954, Gordon Allport, an early leader in comprehensive social science analysis of prejudice and discrimination, articulated the sequential steps by which an individual behaves negatively toward members of another racial group: verbal antagonism, avoidance, segregation, physical attack, and extermination (Allport, 1954). Each step enables the next, as people learn by doing. In most cases, people do not get to the later steps without receiving support for their behavior in the earlier ones. In this section, we describe these forms of explicit prejudice.

Verbal antagonism includes casual racial slurs and disparaging racial comments, either in or out of the target's presence. By themselves such comments may not be regarded as serious enough to be unlawful (balanced against concerns about freedom of speech), but they constitute a clear form of hostility. Together with nonverbal expressions of antagonism, they can create a hostile environment in schools, workplaces, and neighborhoods (Essed, 1997; Feagin, 1991).

Verbal and nonverbal hostility are first steps on a continuum of interracial harm-doing. In laboratory experiments (see Chapter 6 for detailed discussion), verbal abuse and nonverbal rejection are reliable indicators of discriminatory effects, in that they disadvantage the targets of such behavior, creating a hostile environment. They also precede and vary with more overtly damaging forms of treatment, such as denial of employment (Dovidio et al., 2002; Fiske, 1998; Talaska et al., 2003). For example, an interviewer's initial bias on the basis of race will likely be communicated nonverbally to the interviewee by such behaviors as cutting the interview short or sitting so far away from the interviewee as to communicate immediate dislike (Darley and Fazio, 1980; Word et al., 1974). Such nonverbal hostility reliably undermines the performance of otherwise equivalent interviewees. In legal settings, verbal and nonverbal treatment are often presented as evidence of a discriminator's biased state of mind; they may also constitute unlawful discriminatory behavior when they rise to the level of creating a hostile work environment.

Avoidance entails choosing the comfort of one's own racial group (the "ingroup" in social psychological terms) over interaction with another racial group (the "outgroup"). In settings of discretionary contact—that is, in which people may choose to associate or not—members of disadvantaged racial groups may be isolated. In social situations, people may self-segregate along racial lines. In work settings, discretionary contact may force outgroup members into lower-status occupations (Johnson and Stafford, 1998) or undermine the careers of those excluded from informal networks.

Becker (1971) describes a classic theory about how aversion to interracial contact—referred to as a "taste for discrimination"—can affect wages and labor markets (more complex versions of this model are provided by Black, 1995; Borjas and Bronars, 1989; and Bowlus and Eckstein, 2002). Laboratory experiments have measured avoidance by assessing people's willingness to volunteer time together with an outgroup individual in a given setting (Talaska et al., 2003). Sociological studies have measured avoidance in discretionary social contact situations by report or observation (Pettigrew, 1998b; Pettigrew and Tropp, 2000). In legal settings, avoidance of casual contact can appear as evidence indicating hostile intent.

Avoidance may appear harmless in any given situation but, when cumulated across situations, can lead to long-term exclusion and segregation. It may be particularly problematic in situations in which social networking matters, such as employment hiring and promotion, educational opportunities, and access to health care. Avoiding another person because of race can be just as damaging as more active and direct abuse.

Segregation occurs when people actively exclude members of a disadvantaged racial group from the allocation of resources and from access to institutions. The most common examples include denial of equal education, housing, employment, and health care on the basis of race. The majority of Americans (about 90 percent in most current surveys; Bobo, 2001) support laws enforcing fair and equal opportunity in these areas. But the remaining

10 percent who do not support civil rights for all racial groups are likely to exhibit intentional, explicit discrimination by any measure. The data indicate that these hardcore discriminators view their own group as threatened by racial outgroups (Duckitt, 2001). They view that threat as both economic, in a zero-sum game, and as value based, in a contest of "traditional" values against nonconformist deviants. Moreover, even the 90 percent who report support for equal opportunity laws show less support when specific remedies are mentioned (see Chapter 8).

Physical attacks on racial outgroups have frequently been perpetrated by proponents of segregation (Green et al., 1999) and are correlated with other overt forms of discrimination (Schneider et al., 2000). Hate crimes are closely linked to the expression of explicit prejudice and result from perceived threats to the ingroup's economic standing and values (Glaser et al., 2002; Green et al., 1998; for a review of research on hate crimes, see Green et al., 2001).

Extermination or mass killings based on racial or ethnic animus do occur. These are complex phenomena; in addition to the sorts of individual hostility and prejudice described above, they typically encompass histories of institutionalized prejudice and discrimination, difficult life conditions, strong (and prejudiced) leadership, social support for hostile acts, and socialization that accepts explicit discrimination (Allport, 1954; Newman and Erber, 2002; Staub, 1989).

Our report focuses more on the levels of discrimination most often addressed by social scientists. In most cases involving complaints about racial discrimination in the United States, explicit discrimination is expressed through verbal and nonverbal antagonism and through racial avoidance and denial of certain opportunities because of race. Racial segregation is, of course, no longer legally sanctioned in the United States, although instances of de facto segregation continue to occur.

Subtle, Unconscious, Automatic Discrimination

Even as a national consensus has developed that explicit racial hostility is abhorrent, people may still hold prejudicial attitudes, stemming in part from past U.S. history of overt prejudice. Although prejudicial attitudes do not necessarily result in discriminatory behavior with adverse effects, the persistence of such attitudes can result in unconscious and subtle forms of racial discrimination in place of more explicit, direct hostility. Such *subtle prejudice* is often abetted by differential media portrayals of nonwhites versus whites, as well as de facto segregation in housing, education, and occupations.

The psychological literature on subtle prejudice describes this phenomenon as a set of often unconscious beliefs and associations that affect the attitudes and behaviors of members of the ingroup (e.g., non-Hispanic whites) toward members of the outgroup (e.g., blacks or other disadvantaged racial groups). Members of the ingroup face an internal conflict, resulting from the disconnect between the societal rejection of racist behaviors and the societal persistence of racist attitudes (Dovidio and Gaertner, 1986; Katz and Hass, 1988; McConahay, 1986). People's intentions may be good, but their racially biased cognitive categories and associations may persist. The result is a modern, subtle form of prejudice that goes underground so as not to conflict with antiracist norms while it continues to shape people's cognitive, affective, and behavioral responses. Subtle forms of racism are indirect, automatic, ambiguous, and ambivalent. We discuss each of these manifestations of subtle prejudice in turn (Fiske, 1998, 2002) and then examine their implications for discriminatory behavior.

Indirect prejudice leads ingroup members to blame the outgroup—the disadvantaged racial group—for their disadvantage (Hewstone et al., 2002; Pettigrew, 1998a). The blame takes a Catch-22 form: The outgroup members should try harder and not be lazy, but at the same time they should not impose themselves where they are not wanted. Such attitudes on the part of ingroup members are a manifestation of indirect prejudice. Differences between the ingroup and outgroup (linguistic, cultural, religious, sexual) are often exaggerated, so that outgroup members are portrayed as outsiders worthy of avoidance and exclusion. Indirect prejudice can also lead to support for policies that disadvantage nonwhites.

Subtle prejudice can also be unconscious and *automatic*, as ingroup members unconsciously categorize outgroup members on the basis of race, gender, and age (Fiske, 1998). People's millisecond reactions to outgroups can include primitive fear and anxiety responses in the brain (Hart et al., 2000; Phelps et al., 2000), negative stereotypic associations (Fazio and Olson, 2003), and discriminatory behavioral impulses (Bargh and Chartrand, 1999). People have been shown to respond to even subliminal exposure to outgroups in these automatic, uncontrollable ways (Dovidio et al., 1997; Greenwald and Banaji, 1995; Greenwald et al., 1998; Kawakami et al., 1998; for a review, see Fazio and Olson, 2003; for a demonstration of this effect, see https://implicit.harvard.edu/implicit/ [accessed December 5, 2003]). However, the social context in which people encounter an outgroup member can shape such instantaneous responses. Outgroup members who are familiar, subordinate, or unique do not elicit the same reactions as those who are unfamiliar, dominant, or undifferentiated (Devine, 2001; Fiske, 2002). Nevertheless, people's default automatic reactions to outgroup members represent unconscious prejudice that may be expressed nonverbally or lead to racial avoidance, which, in turn, may create a hostile, discriminatory environment. Such automatic reactions have also been shown to lead to automatic forms of stereotype-confirming behavior (Bargh et al., 1996; Chen and Bargh, 1997).

The main effect of subtle prejudice seems to be to favor the ingroup rather than to directly disadvantage the outgroup; in this sense, such prejudice is *ambiguous* rather than unambiguous. That is, the prejudice could indicate greater liking for the majority rather than greater disliking for the minority. As a practical matter, in a zero-sum setting, ingroup advantage often results in the same outcome as outgroup disadvantage but not always. Empirically, ingroup members spontaneously reward the ingroup, allocating discretionary resources to their own kind and thereby relatively disadvantaging the outgroup (Brewer and Brown, 1998). People spontaneously view their own ingroups (but not the outgroup) in a positive light, attributing its strengths to the essence of what makes a person part of the ingroup (genes being a major example). The outgroup's alleged defects are used to justify these behaviors. These ambiguous allocations and attributions constitute another subtle form of discrimination.

According to theories of ambivalent prejudice (e.g., for race, Katz and Hass, 1988; for gender, Glick and Fiske, 1996), the *ambivalence* of subtle prejudice means that outgroups are not necessarily subjected to uniform antipathy (Fiske et al., 2002). Outgroups may be disrespected but liked in a condescending manner. Versions of the "Uncle Tom" stereotype are a racial example. At other times, outgroups may be respected but disliked. White reactions to black professionals can exemplify this behavior. Some racial outgroups elicit both disrespect and dislike. Poor people, welfare recipients, and homeless people (all erroneously perceived to be black more often than white) frequently elicit an unambivalent and hostile response.

The important point is that reactions need not be entirely negative to foster discrimination. One might, for example, fail to promote someone on the basis of race, perceiving the person to be deferential, cooperative, and nice but essentially incompetent, whereas a comparable ingroup member might receive additional training or support to develop greater competence. Conversely, one might acknowledge an outgroup member's exceptional competence but fail to see the person as sociable and comfortable—therefore not fitting in, not "one of us"—and fail to promote the person as rapidly on that account.

All manifestations of subtle prejudice—indirect, automatic, ambiguous, and ambivalent—constitute barriers to full equality of treatment. Subtle prejudice is much more difficult to document than more overt forms, and its effects on discriminatory behavior are more difficult to capture. However, "subtle" does not mean trivial or inconsequential; subtle prejudice can result in major adverse effects.

For example, Bargh and colleagues (1996) demonstrated how categorization by race can activate stereotypes and lead to discriminatory behavior. In their study, the experimenter first showed white participants either black or white young male faces, presented at a subliminal level. The experimenter then either did or did not provoke the participant by requiring that the experiment be started over because of an apparent computer error. Compared with other participants, those who saw the black faces and were also provoked by the experimenter behaved with more hostility as revealed in a videotape of their immediate facial expressions and in their subsequent behavior, as rated by the experimenter.

Generally, an emerging pattern of results from laboratory research (see, e.g., Dovidio et al., 2002) suggests that explicit measures of prejudice (e.g., from responses to attitudinal questionnaires) predict explicit discrimination (verbal behavior), whereas implicit measures of prejudice (e.g., speed of stereotypic associations) predict subtle discrimination (such as nonverbal friendliness). In any event, the implicit measures have been shown to be statistically reliable (Cunningham et al., 2001; Kawakami and Dovidio, 2001).

Some of these laboratory findings have been generalized to the real world—for example, in contrasting subtle and explicit forms of prejudice (Pettigrew, 1998b) and in research on specific phenomena, such as ingroup favoritism (Brewer and Brown, 1998). The discussion of experimental methods in Chapter 6 elaborates on this point.

Statistical Discrimination and Profiling

Another process that may result in adverse discriminatory consequences for members of a disadvantaged racial group is known as *statistical discrimination* or *profiling*. In this situation, an individual or firm uses overall beliefs about a group to make decisions about an individual from that group (Arrow, 1973; Coate and Loury, 1993; Lundberg and Startz, 1983; Phelps, 1972). The perceived group characteristics are assumed to apply to the individual. Thus, if an employer believes people with criminal records will make unsatisfactory employees, believes that blacks, on average, are more likely to have criminal records compared with whites, and cannot directly verify an applicant's criminal history, the employer may judge a black job applicant on the basis of group averages rather than solely on the basis of his or her own qualifications.

When beliefs about a group are based on racial stereotypes resulting from explicit prejudice or on some of the more subtle forms of ingroup-versus-outgroup perceptual biases, then discrimination on the basis of such beliefs is indistinguishable from the explicit prejudice discussed above. Statistical discrimination or profiling, properly defined, refers to situations of discrimination on the basis of beliefs that reflect the actual distributions of characteristics of different groups. Even though such discrimination could be viewed as economically rational, it is illegal in such situations as hiring because it uses group characteristics to make decisions about individuals.

Why might employers or other decision makers employ statistical discrimination? There are incentives to statistically discriminate in situations in which information is limited, which is often the case. For example, graduate school applicants provide only a few pages of written information about themselves, job applicants are judged on the basis of a one-page resume or a brief interview, and airport security officers see only external appearance. In such situations, the decision maker must make assessments about a host of unknown factors, such as effort, intelligence, or intentions, based on highly limited observation.

Why is information limited in such cases? The decision maker typically views an individual's own statements about himself or herself as untrustworthy (e.g., "I will work hard on this job" or "I am not a terrorist") because they can be made as easily by those for whom they are not true as by those for whom they are true. Instead, decision makers look for signals that cannot easily be faked and are correlated with the attributes a decision maker is seeking. Education is a prime example. If an employer checks a job applicant's education credentials and finds that he or she has a degree from a top-rated college and a 4.0 grade point average, that individual likely has a proven track record of intellectual ability and effort. It is difficult to "fake" this information (short of outright lying about one's education credentials) because it really does take effort to accumulate such a record.

Only so much information can be transmitted, however, and many aspects of a person's record and qualifications are difficult to document even if the individual should be committed to doing so truthfully. Hence, decision makers must regularly make judgments about people based on the things they do know and decide whether to invest in acquiring further information (Lundberg, 1991). In the face of incomplete information, they may factor in knowledge about differences in average group characteristics that relate to the individual characteristics being sought. The result is statistical discrimination: An individual is treated differently because of information associated with his or her racial group membership.

Faced with the possibility of statistical discrimination, members of disadvantaged racial groups may adopt behaviors to signal their differences from group averages. For example, nonwhite business people who want to signal their trustworthiness and belonging to the world of business may dress impeccably in expensive business suits. Nonwhite parents who want their children to get into a first-rate college may signal their middle-class background by sending their children to an expensive private school. An implication of statistical discrimination is that members of a disadvantaged racial group for whom group averages regarding qualifications are lower than white averages may need to become better qualified than non-Hispanic whites in order to succeed (Biernat and Kobrynowicz, 1997). Thus, the practice of statistical discrimination can impose costs on members of the targeted group even when those individuals are not themselves the victims of explicitly discriminatory treatment.

Moreover, statistical discrimination may be self-perpetuating, since today's outcomes may affect the incentives for tomorrow's behavior (Coate and Loury, 1993; Loury, 1977; Lundberg and Startz, 1998). If admissions officers at top-ranked colleges believe, on the basis of group averages to date, that certain groups are less likely to succeed and admit few members of those groups as a result, incentives for the next generation to work hard and acquire the skills necessary to gain admittance may be lessened (see Loury, 2002:32–33, for a more extensive discussion of this example). Similarly, if black Americans are barred from top corporate jobs, the incentives for younger black men and women to pursue the educational credentials and career experience that lead to top corporate jobs may be reduced. Thus, statistical discrimination may result in an individual member of the disadvantaged group being treated in a way that does not focus on his or her own capabilities. It can affect both short-term outcomes and long-term behavior if individuals in the disadvantaged group expect such discrimination will occur.

Organizational Processes

The above three types of racial discrimination focus on individual behaviors that lead to adverse outcomes and perpetuate differences in outcomes for members of disadvantaged racial groups. These behaviors are also the focus of much of the current discrimination law. However, they do not constitute a fully adequate description of all forms of racial discrimination. As discussed in Chapter 2, the United States has a long history as a racially biased society. This history has done more than change individual cognitive responses; it has also deeply affected institutional processes. Organizations tend to reflect many of the same biases as the people who operate within them. Organizational rules sometime evolve out of past histories (including past histories of racism) that are not easily reconstructed, and such rules may appear quite neutral on the surface. But if these processes function in a way that leads to differential racial treatment or produces differential racial outcomes, the results can be discriminatory. Such an embedded institutional process—which can occur formally and informally within society—is sometimes referred to as *structural discrimination* (e.g., Lieberman, 1998; Sidanius and Pratto, 1999). In Chapter 11, we discuss the interactions among these processes that occur within and across domains.

One clear example of this phenomenon occurs in the arena of housing.

In the past, overt racism and explicit exclusionary laws promoted residential segregation. Even though these laws have been struck down, the process by which housing is advertised and housing choices are made may continue to perpetuate racial segregation in some instances. Thus, real estate agents may engage in subtle forms of racial steering (i.e., housing seekers being shown units in certain neighborhoods and not in others), believing that they are best serving the interests of both their white and their nonwhite clients and not intending to do racial harm. Likewise, banks and other lending institutions have a variety of apparently neutral rules regarding mortgage approvals that too often result in a higher level of loan refusals for persons in lower-income black neighborhoods than for equivalent white applicants. Research also suggests that ostensibly neutral criteria are often applied selectively. Credit history irregularities that are overlooked as atypical in the case of white mortgage applicants, for example, are often used to disqualify blacks and Latinos (Squires, 1994; Squires and O'Connor, 2001).

Another example of this sort of biased institutional process that has been debated in the courts is the operation of hiring and promotion networks within firms. Many firms hire more through word-of-mouth recommendations from their existing employees than through external advertising (Waldinger and Lichter, 2003). By itself such a practice is racially neutral, but if existing (white) employees recommend their friends and neighbors, new hires will replicate the racial patterns in the firm, systematically excluding nonwhites. Such practices do not necessarily entail intentional discrimination, but they provide a basis for legal action when the outcome is the exclusion of certain groups. Seniority systems that give preference to a long-established group of employees can produce similar racially biased effects through promotion or layoff decisions, even though the Supreme Court has ruled that seniority systems are generally not subject to challenge under Title VII on this basis.[1]

Institutional processes that result in consistent racial biases in terms of who is included or excluded can be difficult to disentangle. In many cases, the individuals involved in making decisions within these institutions will honestly deny any intent to discriminate. In dealing with such cases in the courts (disparate impact cases; see Chapter 3), weighing the benefits to an organization of a long-established set of procedures against the harm such procedures might induce through their differential racial outcomes is a complex and difficult process. Thus the panel does not wish to condemn any specific organizational process. In most cases, each situation needs to be

---

[1]International Brotherhood of Teamsters v. United States, 431 U.S. 324 (1977) (the "routine application of a bona fide seniority system" is not unlawful under Title VII).

analyzed with regard to the particular history and reasonable organizational needs of a specific institution. But we do want to emphasize that facially neutral organizational processes may function in ways that can be viewed as discriminatory, particularly if differential racial outcomes are insufficiently justified by the benefits to the organization. We noted above that large and persistent racial differentials, although not direct evidence of discrimination, may provide insight on where problems are likely to exist. In this way, persistent racial differences in access to or outcomes within institutions (e.g., hiring or promotions) can be used to provide information on which processes and which institutions may deserve greater scrutiny.

COMPARISON OF LEGAL STANDARDS WITH THE FOUR TYPES OF DISCRIMINATION

As discussed in Chapter 3, the legal definition of discrimination includes two standards: disparate treatment discrimination, whereby an individual is treated less favorably because of race, and disparate impact discrimination, whereby treatment on the basis of nonracial factors that lack sufficiently compelling justification has an adverse impact on members of a disadvantaged racial group. The quintessential case of disparate treatment discrimination involves intentional behavior motivated by explicit racial animus. However, disparate treatment applies in other types of discrimination as well. For instance, a black cab driver who refuses to pick up blacks may be acting without racial animus but may be engaging in statistical discrimination by making probabilistic predictions about the risk of being victimized by crime, of receiving a lower tip, or of ending up in a distant neighborhood from which the prospect of receiving a return fare is small. Employers and police officers who profile job candidates or security risks can be motivated by similar beliefs or concerns, and their probabilistic assessments may be correct or completely inaccurate. In any event, as noted above, this type of statistical discrimination is considered intentional differentiation on the basis of race and falls squarely in the category of unlawful disparate treatment discrimination. In evaluating a job applicant, for example, it is unlawful to consider what the "average" black worker would be like and then to treat individual blacks in conformity with this stereotypical prediction.

In short, although vexing issues of proof complicate real-world cases, the law has clearly identified the theoretically prohibited discriminatory actions that emanate from either racial animus or the rational calculation of risk using race as a proxy. More subtle types of discrimination, however, are more difficult to deal with legally. As discussed above, there may be no conscious bias or rational calculation that prompts someone to treat whites differently from nonwhites. Such precognitive patterns of conduct have been well documented and are in practice treated as cases of unlawful disparate treatment discrimination if they are found to generate differential treatment of blacks. Note, however, that issues of proof make it more difficult to establish these unconscious forms of discriminatory behavior, although statistical approaches are commonly used to ferret out just such unconscious bias. Indeed, the legal requirement that unlawful disparate treatment discrimination must involve intentional discrimination may result in many indirect, subtle, and ambiguous types of discrimination being overlooked. In some cases, nonetheless, an organization has been found guilty of intentional discrimination for failing to compensate for the unconscious, automatic discrimination of its employees.

DOMAINS IN WHICH DISCRIMINATION OPERATES

As discussed in Chapter 1, this report focuses on the measurement of discrimination in specific domains: labor markets and employment, education, housing and mortgage lending, criminal justice, and health care. The focus on these areas reflects the expertise of the members of this panel. There are a variety of other domains, such as civic participation, in which racial differences in outcomes are large, and discrimination is a valid social concern. We believe that our comments about assessing discrimination, although directed at the domains and examples with which we are most familiar, may be useful and applicable in other arenas as well. In this section, we briefly review some of the key points at which the forms of discrimination delineated above may operate within the domains on which we focus.

Table 4-1 shows how discrimination might operate across the five domains of labor markets, education, housing, criminal justice, and health care at three broadly defined points. The first point is discrimination in access to the institutions within a domain; examples are racial differentials in hiring in the labor market, racial steering in housing, financial aid for schooling, arrest rates or policing activity within communities, and access to certain medical institutions or procedures. The second point is discrimination while functioning within a domain; examples are racial differentials in wages, mortgage loan pricing, placement into special education programs, assignment of pro bono legal counsel, and quality of health care. Closely related is discrimination in movement or while progressing within a domain from one activity to another; examples are racial differentials in job promotions, home resale value, grade promotion in schools, sentencing or parole rates, and medical referrals or follow-up health care. Of course, such discrimination often follows discriminatory behavior at an earlier point in time. Finally, the table lists possible actors within each domain who may discriminate on the basis of race. These actors include employers, customers, and coworkers in the labor market; teachers, administrators, and students

TABLE 4-1 A Map of the Potential Points of Discrimination Within Five Domains

Source Points for Discrimination	Labor Markets	Education	Housing/ Mortgage Lending	Criminal Justice	Health Care
Access to institutions or procedures	• Hiring • Interviewing • Unemployment	• Acceptance —Into college —Into special education programs • Financial aid	• Steering • Mortgage redlining	• Policing behaviors • Arrests	• Access to care • Insurance
While functioning within a domain	• Wages • Evaluation • Work environment	• Track placement • Ability grouping • Grades and evaluations • Learning environment • Per-pupil expenditure • Special education placement	• Loan pricing	• Police treatment • Quality of legal representation	• Quality of care • Price
Movement through a domain	• Promotion • Layoffs • Rehiring	• Promotion and graduation • Retention	• Resale value • Wealth accumulation	• Parole • Sentencing	• Referrals
Key actors	• Employers • Customers • Coworkers	• Teachers • Administrators • Fellow students	• Landlords • Sellers • Lenders • Neighbors	• Police • Prosecutors • Judges • Juries • Parole boards	• Health care workers • Administrators • Insurance companies

NOTE: We provide a selected bibliography of research on discrimination within the domains listed above at the end of this report.

in schools; landlords, sellers, lenders, and neighbors in housing; police officers, judges, and juries in criminal justice; and health care professionals, insurance companies, and administrators in the health care system.

At any of the points shown in the table, one might observe direct adverse behavior or aversion to contact with racial minorities, unconscious or subtle biases, statistical discrimination, or institutional processes that result in adverse outcomes. The remainder of this report addresses the methods that are used to investigate possibly discriminatory behavior within the various cells of this matrix.

We do not attempt to provide a comprehensive review of the literature on racial discrimination within each of the categories and domains listed in Table 4-1. Several extensive articles and reports review the literature within specific domains. We provide a selected bibliography of major papers from the theoretical and empirical literature at the end of this report. This bibliography includes research that demonstrates the methods used to assess discrimination within particular domains. Although in Part II of our report we do not discuss specific methods applied in each domain in turn, we do examine the broad approaches used to measure the types of discrimination outlined above. We also discuss where alternative approaches may be implemented more easily within one domain than another. In some cases, we suggest that specific methods should be applied in domains where they have not yet been used.

MOVING FROM EPISODIC TO DYNAMIC DEFINITIONS OF DISCRIMINATION: THE ROLE OF CUMULATIVE DISADVANTAGE

Much of the discussion of the presence of discrimination and the effects of antidiscrimination policies assumes discrimination is a phenomenon that occurs at a specific point in time within a particular domain. For instance, discrimination can occur in entry-level hiring in the labor market or in loan applications in mortgage lending. But this episodic view of discrimination occurring may be inadequate. Here we explore the idea, noted in Chapter 3, that discrimination should be seen as a dynamic process that functions over time in several different ways.

First, the effects of discrimination may cumulate across generations and through history. For instance, impoverishment in previous generations can prevent the accumulation of wealth in future generations. Similarly, learned behavior and expectations about opportunities and life possibilities can shape the behaviors and preferences of future generations for members of different racial groups.

Second, effects of discrimination may cumulate over time through the course of an individual's life across different domains. Outcomes in labor markets, education, housing, criminal justice, and health care all interact with each other; discrimination in any one domain can limit opportunities and cumulatively worsen life chances in another. For instance, children who are less healthy and more impoverished may do worse in school, and in turn, poor education may affect labor market opportunities. The possibility that the effects of discrimination cumulate over an individual's lifetime is rarely discussed in the literature on the measurement of discrimination. Yet even small initial disadvantages, experienced at key points in an individual's life, could well have long-term cumulative effects.

Third, effects of discrimination may cumulate over time through the course of an individual's life sequentially within any one domain. Again, small levels of discrimination at multiple points in a process may result in large cumulative disadvantage. For instance, children who do not learn basic educational skills in elementary school because of discrimination may face future discrimination in the way they are tracked or the way their test scores are interpreted in secondary school. Small effects of discrimination in job search (e.g., application or interviewing stages), job retention, job promotion, and wage setting may result in large differences in labor market outcomes when these effects cumulate over time, even if no further discrimination occurs.

There are many instances in which the application of neutral rules harms a member of a disadvantaged racial group because of discrimination at some other time or place in the social system. However, there is presently no case law that addresses these broad social effects; the law frequently will not deem the challenged conduct to be unlawful if it merely transmits, rather than expands, the extent of racial discrimination. Similarly, the law does not hold any agents or institutions responsible for problems outside their legitimate purview. Discrimination occurring in other domains or in society generally need not be remedied; hence, cumulative discrimination is not a legal issue. An employer who needs highly educated workers can hire them as he or she finds them, even if doing so means that only a small percentage of black or Hispanic workers will be hired because prior discrimination in educational opportunities limited the number of members of these groups with the requisite skills.

Whether cumulative discrimination is important across generations, across a lifetime in different domains, and over time within a specific domain are empirical questions. However, these questions have not been addressed to any great extent by empirical social scientists. In Chapter 11, we return to the issue of the importance of developing methods focused not just on measuring discriminatory behavior at a particular point in time in a specific process but also on understanding the cumulative and dynamic effects of discrimination over time and across processes.

SUMMARY

Discrimination manifests itself in multiple ways that range in form from overt and intentional to subtle and ambiguous, as well as from personal to institutional, whether through statistical discrimination and profiling or organizational processes. Discrimination also operates differently in different domains and may cumulate over time within and across domains. Regardless of which form it takes, discrimination can create barriers to equal treatment and opportunity and can have adverse effects on various outcomes. Clear theories about how discriminatory behavior may occur are important in order to develop models that help identify and measure discrimination's effects.

Although discrimination is sometimes still practiced openly, it has become increasingly socially undesirable to do so. Consequently, such discrimination as exists today is more likely to take more subtle and complex forms. Subtler forms of discrimination can occur spontaneously and ambiguously and go undetected, particularly at the institutional level. Although legal standards address specific forms of unlawful intentional or statistical discrimination, subtler forms are more difficult to address within the law. Thus, shifts in kinds of discriminatory behavior have implications for the measurement of discrimination. As we discuss in the next chapter, some types of discrimination may be more difficult to identify and may require collecting new and different data and the further development of new methods of analysis.

Appendix D

References

Aberson CL, M Healy, and V Romero (2000). Ingroup bias and self-esteem: A meta-analysis. *Personality and Social Psychology Review* 4:157-173.

Adelman C (1999). Answers in the toolbox: Academic intensity, attendance patterns, and bachelor's degree attainment (PLLI 1999-8021). Washington, DC: US Department of Education.

Adelman CL (2006). *The Toolbox Revisited: Paths to Degree Completion from High School through College.* Washington, DC: US Department of Education, *http://www.ed.gov/ rschstat/research/pubs/toolboxrevisit/toolbox.pdf.*

Akerlind I, K Alexanderson, G Hensing, M Liejon, and P Bjurulf (1996). Sex differences in absence in relation to parental status. *Scandinavian Journal of Social Medicine* 24(1): 27-35.

Alderfer CP (1992). Changing race relations embedded in organizations: Report on a long-term project with the XYZ corporation. In ed. SE Jackson, *Diversity in the Workplace: Human Resources Initiatives.* New York: Guilford Press.

Alessio JC and J Andrzejski (2000). Unveiling the hidden glass ceiling. *American Sociological Review* 26(2):311-315.

Allison P and S Long (1990). Departmental effects on scientific productivity. *American Sociological Review* 55:119-125.

Altonji JG and RM Blank (1999). Race and gender in the labor market. In eds. O Ashenfelter and D Card, *Handbook of Labor Economics, Volume 3,* Amsterdam: Elsevier Science.

American Association of University Professors (2001). *Statement on Principles of Family Responsibilities and Work, http://www.aaup.org/statements/REPORTS/re01fam.htm.*

American Association of University Women (2004). *Tenure Denied. Cases of Sex Discrimination in Academia.* Washington, DC: American Association of University Women Educational Foundation and Legal Advocacy Fund.

American Chemical Society (2006). *Directory of Graduate Research.* Washington, DC: American Chemical Society.

American Council on Education (2005). *An Agenda for Excellence: Creating Flexibility in Tenure-Track Faculty Careers, Executive Summary, http://www.acenet.edu/bookstore/pdf/2005_tenure_flex_summary.pdf.*

American Physical Society. *Improving the Climate for Women Site Visits, http://www.aps.org/educ/cswp/visits/index.cfm.*

American Psychological Association (2000). *Women in Academe: Two Steps Forward, One Step Back, http://www.apa.org/pi/wpo/academe/report.html.*

American Society for Cell Biology Web page, *http://www.ascb.org/.*

Anderson DJ and JJ Cheslock (2004). Institutional strategies to achieve gender equity in intercollegiate athletics: Does Title IX harm male athletes? *American Economic Review Papers and Proceedings* 94(2):307-311.

Antonio A (2003). Diverse student bodies, diverse faculties. *Academe* 89(6):14-18.

Antonio A (2002). Faculty of color reconsidered: Reassessing contributions to scholarship. *Journal of Higher Education* 73:582-602.

Ash A, P Carr, R Goldstein, and RH Friedman (2004). Compensation and advancement of women in academic medicine: Is there equity. *Annals of Internal Medicine* 141(3):205-212.

Association of American Law Schools (1996). Retaining faculty of color. *AALS Newsletter, http://www.aals.org/mlt3.html.*

Association of American Medical Colleges (2005). *Analysis in Brief: The Changing Representation of Men and Women in Academic Medicine.* Washington, DC: AAMC.

Association of American Medical Colleges. *Faculty Roster, http://www.aamc.org/data/facultyroster/start.htm.*

Association of American Medical Colleges. *FAMOUS User's Guide, http://www.aamc.org/data/facultyroster/famous.pdf.*

Association of American Medical Colleges. *Reports Available Through Faculty Roster, http://www.aamc.org/data/facultyroster/reports.htm.*

Astin, HS (2005). *Annual Survey of the American Freshman, National Norms.* Los Angeles, CA: High Education Research Institute.

Astin HS and LJ Sax (1996). Developing scientific talent in undergraduate women In eds. CS Davis, AB Ginorio, BB Hollenshead, and PM Rayman. *The Equity Equation: Fostering the Advancement of Women in the Sciences, Mathematics and Engineering.* San Francisco, CA: Jossey-Bass Publishers.

August L and J Waltman (2004). Culture, climate, and contribution: Career satisfaction among female faculty. *Research in Higher Education* 45(2):177-192.

Baginole B (1993). How to keep a good woman down: An investigation of the role of institutional factors in the process of discrimination against women academics. *British Journal of Sociology of Education* 14(3):261-274.

Baillargeon R, L Kotovksy, and A Needham (1995). The acquisition of physical knowledge in infancy. In eds. D Sperber and D Premack, *Causal Cognition: A Multidisciplinary Debate* (pp 79-116), New York: Clarendon Press/Oxford University Press.

Ball P (2006). Prestige is factored into journal ratings. *Nature* 439(16):770-771. *http://www.nature.com/nature/journal/v439/n7078/pdf/439770a.pdf.*

Banaji MR and AG Greenwald (1995). Implicit gender stereotyping in judgments of fame. *Journal of Personality and Social Psychology* 68:181-198.

Barbezat D (1992). The market for new PhD economists. *Journal of Economic Education* 23:262-276.

Barnes LLB, MO Agago, and WT Coombs (1998). Effects of job-related stress on faculty intention to leave academia. *Research in Higher Education* 39(4):457-469.

Barnett R and C Rivers (2004). *Same Difference: How Gender Myths Are Hurting Our Relationships, Our Children, and Our Jobs.* New York: Basic Books.

Baron-Cohen S (2002). *The Essential Difference: The Truth about the Male and the Female Brain.* New York: Basic Books.

Belenkey MF, BM Clincy, NR Goldberger, and JM Tarule (1986). *Women's Ways of Knowing: The Development of Self, Voice, and Mind.* New York: Basic Books.

Bellas M (1997) Disciplinary differences in faculty salaries: Does gender play a role? *Journal of Higher Education* 68(3):299-321.

Benbow CP (1988). Sex differences in mathematical reasoning ability in intellectually talented preadolescents: Their nature, effects, and possible causes. *Behavioral and Brain Sciences* 11:169-232.

Benbow C and O Arjmand (1990). Predictors of high academic achievement in mathematically talented students: A longitudinal study. *Journal of Educational Psychology* 82: 430-441.

Benbow CP, D Lubinski, DL Shea, and H Eftekhari-Sanjani (2000). Sex differences in mathematical reasoning ability at age 13: Their status 20 years later. *Psychological Science* 11(6):474-480.

Benbow CP and JC Stanley (1980). Sex differences in mathematical ability: fact or artifact? *Science* 210:1262-1264.

Benbow CP and JC Stanley (1988). Sex differences in mathematical reasoning ability: more facts. *Science* 222:1029-1031.

Bendick M, ML Egan, and SM Lofhjelm (1998). *The Documentation and Evaluation of Anti-Discrimination Training in the United States.* Geneva: International Labor Organization.

Berryman SE (1983). *Who Will Do Science? Minority and Female Attainment of Science and Mathematics Degrees: Trends and Causes.* New York: Rockefeller Foundation.

Bertrand M and S Mullianathan (2004). Are Emily and Greg more employable than Lakisha and Jamal? *American Economic Review* 94(4):991-1013.

The Best Initiative (2004), *The Talent Imperative: Diversifying America's Science and Engineering Workforce,* http://www.bestworkforce.org/PDFdocs/BESTTalentImperative FINAL.pdf.

Bickel J (2000). Encouraging the advancement of women. *JAMA* 283(5):671.

Bickel J, D Wara, BF Atkinson, LS Cohen, M Dunn, S Hostler, TRB Johnson, AH Rubenstein, GF Sheldon, and E Stokes (2002). Increasing women's leadership in academic medicine: Report of the AAMC project implementation committee. *Academic Medicine* 77(10):1043-1061.

Bielby WT (2000). Minimizing workplace gender and racial bias. *Contemporary Sociology* (29)12-129.

Biernat M and ER Thompson (2002). Shifting standards and contextual variation in stereotyping. *European Review of Social Psychology* 12:103-137.

Blalock HM (1957). Precent non-white and discrimination in the South. *American Sociological Review* 22:677-682.

Blank RM (1991). The effects of double-blind versus single-blind reviewing: Experimental evidence from the *American Economic Review. American Economic Review* 81:1041-1067.

Blau PM (1977). *Inequality and Heterogeneity.* New York: Free Press.

Bobo LD (2001). Racial attitudes and relations at the close of the twentieth century. In eds. NJ Smelser, *America Becoming: Racial Trends and their Consequences,* Vol. 1. WJ Wilson, and F Mitchell, Washington, DC: National Academy Press.

Boyer E (1990). *Scholarship Reconsidered: Priorities of a Professoriate.* Princeton, NJ: Princeton University Press.

Brainard SG and L Carlin (1997). *A Longitudinal Study of Undergraduate Women in Engineering and Science,* http://fie.engrng.pitt.edu/fie97/papers/1252.pdf.

Brewer MB (1999). The psychology of prejudice: Ingroup love of outgroup hate? *Journal of Social Issues* 55:429-444.

Brewer MB and R Brown (1998). Intergroup relations. In eds. D Gilbert, ST Fiske, and G Lindzy, *The Handbook of Social Psychology*, 4th Edition. New York: McGraw-Hill.

Brewster KL and RR Rindfuss (2000). Fertility and women's employment in industrialized nations. *Annual Review of Sociology* 26: 271-296.

Bridgeman B and C Wendler (1991). Gender differences in predictors of college mathematics performance and in college mathematics course grades. *Journal of Educational Psychology* 83(2):275-284.

Broder I (1993). Review of NSF economics proposals: Gender and institutional patterns. *American Economic Review* 83:964-970.

Brody LE and CJ Mills (2005). Talent search research: What have we learned? *High Ability Studies* 16(1):97-111.

Bronstein P and L Farnsworth (1998). Gender differences in faculty experiences of interpersonal climate and processes for advancement. *Research in Higher Education* 39(5):557-585.

Brown A, W Swinyard, and J Ogle (2003). Women in academic medicine: A report of focus groups and questionnaires, with conjoint analysis. *Journal of Women's Health* 12(10):999-1008.

Brown KH and D Gillespie (1999). Responding to moral distress in the university: Augusto Boal's theater of the oppressed. *Change* (September-October):34-39.

Browne KR (2002). *Biology at Work*. New Brunswick, NJ: Rutgers University Press.

Bullers S (1999). Selection effects in the relationship between women's work/family status and perceived control. *Family Relations: Interdisciplinary Journal of Applied Family Studies* 48(2):181-188.

Burke D (1988). *A New Academic Marketplace*. New York: Greenwood Press.

Burroughs Wellcome Fund and Howard Hughes Medical Institute (2004). *Making the Right Moves: A Practical Guide to Scientific Management for Postdocs and New Faculty*, http://www.hhmi.org/labmanagement.

Byrnes JP, H Li, and X Xhaoging (1997). Gender differences on the math subset of the scholastic aptitutde test may be culture specific. *Educational Studies in Mathematics* 34:49-66.

Calas M and L Smircich (1993). Dangerous liaisons: The feminine-in-management meets globalization. *Business Horizons* 36(2):71-81.

Callister RR (2006). The impact of gender and department climate on job satisfaction and intentions to quit for faculty in science and engineering fields. *Journal of Technology Transfer* 31:367-375.

Campbell G, R Denes, and C Morrison (2000). *Access denied: Race, ethnicity, and the scientific enterprise*. New York: Oxford University Press.

Campbell JR, CM Hombo, and J Mazzeo (2000). *NAEP 1999 Trends in Academic Progress: Three Decades of Student Performance*. (NCES 2000-469). Washington, DC: US Department of Education, National Center for Education Statistics.

Carnes M (2006). Gender: Macho language and other deterrents. *Nature* 442:868.

Carnes M, S Geller, E. Fine, J Sheridan, and J. Handelsman (2005). NIH Director's Pioneer Awards: Could the selection process be biased against women? *Journal of Women's Health* 14(8):684-691.

Case A and C Paxson (2005). Sex differences in morbidity and mortality. *Demography* 42(2):189-214.

Casey MB, RL Nuttall, and E Pezaris (1997). Mediators of gender differences in mathematics college entrance test scores: A comparison of spatial skills with internalized beliefs and anxieties. *Developmental Psychology* 33(4):669-680.

Casey MB, R Nuttall, E Pezaris, and CP Benbow (1995). The influence of spatial ability differences in mathematics college entrance scores across diverse samples. *Developmental Psychology* 31(4):697-705.

Cheng K (2005). Reflections on geometry and navigation. *Connection Science* 17(1-2):5-21.

Chesler N and M Chesler (2005). Theater as a community-building strategy for women in engineering: Theory and practice. *Journal of Women and Minorities in Science and Engineering* 11(1):83-96.

Chliwniak L (1997). *Higher Education Leadership: Analyzing the Gender Gap.* ASHE-ERIC Higher Education Report ED 410 847. Washington, DC: George Washington University.

The Clare Boothe Luce Program. *Proposal Guidelines for Invited Colleges/Universities, http://www.hluce.org/4cbldefm.html.*

Clegg R (2006). Faculty hiring preferences and the law. *Chronicle of Higher Education* 52(37):B13.

Cohen J (1988). *Statistical Power Analysis for the Behavioral Science,* 2nd ed. Hillsdale, NJ: Erlbaum.

Cohen GL, J Garcia, N Apfel, and A Master. (2006) Reducing the racial achievement gap: A social-psychological intervention. *Science* 313:1307-1310.

Cohen-Bendahan CCC, C van de Beek, and SA Berenbaum (2005). Prenatal sex hormone effects on child and adult sex-typed behavior: Methods and findings. *Neuroscience and Biobehavioral Reviews* 29:353-384.

Cole JR and H Zuckerman (1984). The productivity puzzle: Persistence and change in patterns of publication of men and women scientists. *Advances in Motivation and Achievement* 2:217-258.

Collins DW and D Kimura (1997). A large sex difference on a two-dimensional mental rotation task. *Behavioral Neuroscience* 111(4):845-849.

Columbia University (2005). Columbia University College of Physicians and Surgeons Task Force on Women Faculty Report February 2005. *http://www/cumc.columbia.edu/dept/ps/facultycouncil/docs/TaskForceonWomen Faculty Final Report 02_24_05.doc.*

Colwell R (2002). *Rethinking the Rules to Promote Diversity.* NSF Director Rita R. Colwell's Remarks to the American Chemical Society, *http://www.nsf.gov/od/lpa/forum/colwell/rc02081acsdiversity.htm.*

Commission on Professionals in Science and Technology (2002). *Professional Women and Minorities: A Total Human Resources Data Compendium,* 14th ed. Washington, DC: Commission on Professionals in Science and Technology.

Committee on Women in Science and Engineering. *Gender Faculty Studies at Research 1 Institutions, http://www7.nationalacademies.org/cwse/gender_faculty_links.html.*

Condry SM and JC Condry (1976). Sex differences: A study of the eye of the beholder. *Child Development* 47:812-819.

Condry SM, JC Condry, and LW Pogatshnik (1983). Sex differences: A study of the ear of the beholder. *Sex Roles* 9(6):697-705.

Congressional Commission on the Advancement of Women and Minorities in Science, Engineering, and Technology Development (CAWMSET) (2004). *Land of Plenty: Diversity as America's Competitive Edge in Science, Engineering, and Technology, http://www.nsf.gov/pubs/2000/cawmset0409/cawmset_0409.pdf.*

Connellan J, S Baron-Cohen, S Wheelwright, A Batki, and J Ahluwalia (2000). Sex differences in human neonatal social perception. *Infant Behavior and Development* 23:113-118.

Corley E and M Gaughan (2005). Scientists' participation in university research centers: What are the gender differences? *Journal of Technology Transfer* 30:371-381.

Cornell University Child Care Grant Subsidy Program, *http://www.ohr.cornell.edu/benefits/childcareGrant/index.html.*

Correll SJ and S Benard (2005). *Getting a Job: Is There a Motherhood Penalty?* Presentation at American Sociological Association Annual Meeting, August 15, 2005, Philadelphia, PA, *http://sociology.princeton.edu/programs/workshops/Correll_Benard_manuscript.pdf.*

Couzin J (2006). US rules on accounting for grants amount to more than a hill of beans. *Science* 311:168-169.

Cox TH (1993). *Cultural Diversity in Organizations: Theory, Research, and Practice.* San Francisco: Berrett-Keohler.

Creamer EG (1998). *Assessing faculty publication productivity: Issues of equity* (ASHE-ERIC Higher Education Report 26(2)). Washington, DC: George Washington University.

Crocker J and KM McGraw (1984). What's good for the goose is not good for the gander: Solo status as an obstacle to occupational achievement for males and females. *American Behavioral Scientist* 27(3):357-369.

Crowley K, MA Callanan, HR Tenenbaum, and E Allen (2001). Parents explain more often to boys than to girls during shared scientific thinking. *Psychological Science* 12(3):258-261.

Curtis JW (2004). Balancing work and family for faculty: Why it's important. *Academe* 90(6), *http://www.aaup.org/publications/Academe/2004/04nd/04ndtoc.htm.*

Custred G and T Wood (1996). California's Proposition 209, *http://www.acri.org/209/209text.html.*

Davenport DS and JM Yurich (1991). Multicultural gender issues. *Journal of Counseling and Development* 70(1):64-71.

Davies PG, SJ Spencer, and CM Steele (2005). Clearing the air: Identity safety moderates the effects of stereotype threat on women's leadership aspirations. *Journal of Personality and Social Psychology* 88:276-287.

Davies PG, SJ Spencer, DM Quinn, and R Gerhardstein (2002). Consuming images: How television commercials that elicit stereotype threat can restrain women academically and professionally. *Personality and Social Psychology Bulletin* 28(12):1615-1628.

Davis G (2005). *Optimizing the Postdoctoral Experience: An Empirical Approach* (Working Paper). Research Triangle Park, NC: Sigma Xi, The Scientific Research Society.

Davison HK and MJ Burke (2000). Sex discrimination in simulated employment contexts: A meta-analytic investigation. *Journal of Vocational Behavior* 56:225-248.

Dawson MRW and DA Medler. *Dictionary of Cognitive Science, http://www.bcp.psych.ualberta.ca/~mike/Pearl_Street/Dictionary/contents/C/cognitive_psychology.html.*

DeAngelis C (2000). Women in academic medicine: New insights, same sad news. *New England Journal of Medicine* 342(6):426-427.

Delazer M (2003). Sex differences in cognitive functions. *Personality and Individual Differences* 35(4):863-875.

Deloitte and Touche (2005). *Why Flexible Work Arrangements Are Not the Answer: The Case for Career Customization* (internal document).

Desai S and LJ Waite (1991). Women's employment during pregnancy and after the first birth: Occupational characteristics and work commitment. *American Sociological Review* 56(4):551-566.

Devine PG and AJ Elliott (1995). Are racial stereotypes really fading? The Princeton Trilogy revisited. *Personality and Social Psychology Bulletin* 21:1139-1150.

Didion CJ, MA Fox, and ME Jones (1998). Cultivating Academic Careers: AWIS project on academic climate. *AWIS Magazine* 27(1):23-27, *http://www.awis.org/pubs/mentoring/98winter.pdf.*

Di Stefano C (1990). Dilemmas of difference: Feminism, modernity, and postmodernism. In *Feminism/Postmodernism.* New York: Routledge.

Dobbin F and A Kalev (2006). *Diversity Management and Managerial Diversity: Addendum to "Best Practices or Best Guesses."* Special Report to the National Academies Committee on Women in Academic Science and Engineering.

Dooris MJ and M Guidos (2006). Tenure Achievement Rates at Research Universities, *Presentation at the Annual Forum of the Association for Institutional Research, Chicago, IL, May 2006. http://www/psu.edu/president/pia/planning_research/reports/AIR_ Tenure_Flow_Paper_06.pdf.*

Drago R (2006). The value of work-family policies. In *Biological, Social, and Organizational Components of Success for Women in Academic Science and Engineering.* Washington, DC: National Academies Press.

Drago R and C Colbeck (2003). *Final Report from the Mapping Project: Exploring the Terrain of U.S. Colleges and Universities for Faculty and Families. http://lsir.la.psu.edu/ workfam/mappingproject.htm.*

Drago R, C Colbeck, KD Stauffer, A Pirretti, K Burkum, J Fazioli, G Lazarro, and T Habasevich (2005). Bias against caregiving. *Academe* 91(6), *http://www.aaup.org/publications/Academe/2005/05so/05sodrag.htm.*

Dundar H and DR Lewis (1998). Determinants of research productivity in higher education. *Research in Higher Education* 39(6):607-631.

Eagly AH and MC Johannesen-Schmidt MC (2001). The leadership styles of women and men. *Journal of Social Issues* 57(4):781-797.

Eagly AH and SJ Karau (2002). Role congruity theory of prejudice toward female leaders. *Psychological Review* 109:573-598.

Eccles JS (1994). Women's educational and occupational choices. *Psychology of Women Quarterly* 18:585-609.

Edmonson Bell ELJ and SM Nkomo (2001). *Our Separate Ways: Black and White Women and the Struggle for Personal Identity.* Boston, MA: Harvard Business School Press.

Education Sector (2006). *The Truth About Boys and Girls.* Washington, DC: Education Sector.

Educational Studies in Mathematics 34:49-66.

Ehrenberg RG, MJ Rizzo, and GH Jakubson (2003). Who bears the growing cost of science at universities? (Working Paper 9627). Cambridge, MA: National Bureau of Economic Research, *http://www.nber.org/papers/w9627.*

Ely R (2004). A field study of group diversity, participation in diversity education programs and performance. *Journal of Organizational Behavior* 25(6):755-780.

Ely RJ and DE Meyerson (2000). Theories of gender in organizations: A new approach to organizational analysis and change. *Research in Organizational Behavior* 22:105-153.

Ely RJ and DA Thomas (2001). Cultural diversity at work: The effects of diversity perspectives on work group processes and outcomes. *Administrative Science Quarterly* 46: 202-228.

England P (1992). *Comparable Worth: Theories and Evidence.* New York: Aldine de Gruyter.

England P, P Allison, S Li, N Mark, J Thompson, M Budig, and H Sun (2004). *Why Are Some Academic Fields Tipping Toward Female? The Sex Composition of US Fields of Doctoral Degree Receipt, 1971-1998, http://www.stanford.edu/dept/soc/people/faculty/ england/Tipping.pdf.*

Epstein CF (1988). *Deceptive Distinctions.* New Haven, CT: Yale University Press.

Etaugh C and G Gilomen (1989). Perceptions of mothers: Effects of employment status, marital status, and age of child. *Sex Roles: A Journal of Research* 20:59-70.

Etaugh C and C Moss (2001). Attitudes of employed women toward parents who choose full-time or part-time employment following their child's birth. *Sex Roles: A Journal of Research* 44:611-619.

Etzkowitz, C Kemelgor, M Neuschatz, and N Uzzi (1994). Barriers to women in academic science and engineering. In eds. W Pearson Jr. and I Fechter, *Who Will Do Science? Educating the Next Generation,* Baltimore, MD: John Hopkins University Press.

Evans ME, H Schweingruber, and HW Stevenson (2002). Gender differences in interest and knowledge acquisition: The United States, Taiwan, and Japan. *Sex Roles: A Journal of Research* 47(3-4):153-167.

Executive Summary from Task Force Report on Women in Science and Engineering (2005). Cambridge, MA: Harvard University, *http://www.news.harvard.edu/gazette/daily/2005/05/wise_summary.pdf.*

European Science Foundation (2002). Towards a new paradigm of education, training, and career paths in the natural sciences *European Foundation Policy Brief 16, http://www.esf.org/publication/139/ESPB16.pdf#SEARCH=%22Torsten%20Wiesel%20training%20paradigm%22.*

Faculty Diversity Committee, Northwestern University 2004. *http://www.northwestern.edu/provost/committees/diversity/reports.html.*

Flax J (1990). Postmodernism and gender relations in feminist theory. In ed. LJ Nicholson, *Feminism/Postmodernism.* New York: Routledge.

Fell A (2005). New program to improve lab management. *Dateline UC-Davis, http://www.dateline.ucdavis.edu/dl_detail.lasso?id=8404.*

Ferber MA and M Teiman (1980). Are women economists at a disadvantage in publishing journal articles? *Eastern Economic Journal* 6(3-4):189-193.

Fidell L (1970). Empirical verification of sex discrimination in hiring practices in psychology. *American Psychologist* 25:1094-1098.

Fine E and J Sheridan (2006). *Searching for Excellence & Diversity—Training Workshops for Search Committees.* Poster presentation, 5th Annual ADVANCE Institutional Transformation Principal Investigators Meeting. Washington, DC, May 17, *http://wiseli.engr.wisc.edu/initiatives/hiring/UWMadison_Poster2006_2.ppt.*

Fisher M, SB Friedman, and B Strauss (1994). The effects of blinding on acceptance of research papers by peer review. *JAMA* 272:143-146.

Fiske ST, M Linn, and SL Neuberg (1999). The continuum model: Ten years later. In eds. S Chaiken and Y Trope, *Dual Process Theories in Social Psychology.* New York: Guilford Press.

Fletcher J (2001). *Disappearing Acts. Gender, Power, and Relational Practice at Work.* Cambridge, MA: MIT Press.

Forsburg S (2004). Ensuring diversity at the podium. *The ASCB Newsletter* 27(2):13-14.

Fox MF (2005). Gender, family characteristics, and publication productivity among scientists. *Social Studies of Science* 35(1):131-150.

Fox MF (1992). Research, teaching, and publication productivity: Mutuality versus competition in academia. *Sociology of Education* 65(4):293-305.

Fox MF (1985). Publication, performance and reward in science and scholarship. In ed. JC Smart, *Higher Education: Handbook of Theory and Research,* Vol. 1. New York: Agathon.

Fox MF and JS Long (1995). Scientific careers: Universalism and particularism. *Annual Review of Sociology* 21:45-71.

Fox MF and P Stephan (2001). Careers of young scientists: Preferences, prospects and realities by gender and field. *Social Studies of Science* 31(1):109-122.

Frank RH (1978). Family location constraints and the geographic distribution ofd female professionals. *Journal of Political Economy* 86:117-130.

Franke GR, DF Crown, and DF Spake (1997). Gender differences in ethical perceptions of business practice: A social role theory perspective. *Journal of Applied Psychology* 82:920-934; 17.

Franklin JH (2005). *Mirror to America.* New York: Farrar, Straus, and Giroux.

Fred Hutchinson Cancer Research Center. Postdoc Childcare Subsidy Program, *http://www.fhcrc.org/science/education/grad_postdoc/spac/childcare/index.html.*

Freeman R, E Jin, and C-Y Shen (2004). *Where Do New US-Trained Science-Engineering PhDs Come From?* (NBER Working Paper 10554). Cambridge, MA: National Bureau of Economic Research.

Fried LP, CA Francomano, SM MacDonald, EM Wagner, EJ Stokes, KM Carbone, WB Bias, MM Newman, and JD Stobo (1996). Career development for women in academic medicine: Multiple interventions in a department of medicine. *Journal of the American Medical Association* 276(11):898-905.

Frost JA, JR Binder, JA Springer, TA Hammeke, PSF Bellgowan, SM Rao, and RB Cox (1999). Language processing is strongly lateralized in both sexes. *Brain* 122(2):199-208.

Gaertner SL, JF Dovidio, BS Banker, MC Rust, JA Nier, GR Mottola, and CM Ward (2003). The challenge of aversive racism: Combating pro-white bias. In ed. S Plous, *Understanding Prejudice and Discrimination*. New York: McGraw-Hill.

Gallagher A, JY Levin, and C Cahalan (2002). *Cognitive Patterns of Gender Differences on Mathematics Admissions Tests* (GRE Board Professional Report No. 96-17P). Washington, DC: Educational Testing Service.

Gallagher A, R De Lisi, PC Holst, AV McGillicuddy-De Lisi, M Morely, and C Cahalan (2000). Gender differences in advanced mathematical problem solving. *Journal of Experimental Child Psychology* 75:165-190.

Gallagher AM and JC Kaufman (2005). *Gender Differences in Mathematics*. New York: Cambridge University Press.

Gaughan M and S Robin (2004). National science training policy and early scientific careers in France and the United States. *Research Policy* 33:569-581.

Geary DC (2001). Sex differences in spatial abilities among adults from the United States and China: Implications for evolutionary theory. *Evolution and Cognition* 7(2):172-177.

Geary DC (1998). *Male, Female: The Evolution of Human Sex Differences*. Washington, DC: American Psychological Association.

Geary DC (1996). Sexual selection and sex differences in mathematical abilities. *Behavioral and Brain Sciences* 19:229-284.

Geary DC, SJ Saults, F Liu, and MK Hoard (2000). Sex differences in spatial cognition, computational fluency, and arithmetical reasoning. *Journal of Experimental Child Psychology* 77:337-353.

Georgi H (2000). The Back Page: Is there an unconscious discrimination against women in science? *American Physical Society Newsletter, http://schwinger.harvard.edu/~georgi/women/backpage.htm.*

Gerstel N and K McGonagle (1999). Job leaves and the limits of the Family and Medical Leave Act: The effects of gender, race, and family. *Work and Occupations.* 26:510-534.

Gilbert JA, BA Stead, and JM Ivancevich (1999). Diversity management: A new organizational paradigm. *Journal of Business Ethics* 21:61-76.

Gilligan C (1982). *In a Different Voice*. Cambridge, MA: Harvard University Press.

Ginorio A (1995). *Warming the Climate for Women in Academic Science*. Washington, DC: Association of American Colleges and Universities.

Ginther D (2006). The economics of gender differences in employment outcomes in academia. In *Biological, Social, and Organizational Components of Success for Women in Academic Science and Engineering*. Washington, DC: National Academies Press (In Press).

Ginther D (2001). *Does Science Discriminate Against Women? Evidence from Academia* (Working Paper 2001-02). Atlanta, GA: Federal Reserve Bank of Atlanta.

Ginther D and S Kahn (2006). *Does Science Promote Women? Evidence from Academia 1973-2001* (NBER SEWP Working Paper). Cambridge, MA: National Bureau of Economics Research, *http://www.nber.org/~sewp/GintherKahn_Sciences_promo_NBER.pdf.*

Gjesdal S and E Bratburg (2002). The role of gender in long-term sickness absence and transition to permanent disability benefits. *The European Journal of Public Health* 12(3): 180-186.

Gladwell M (2000). *The Tipping Point: How Little Things Can Make a Big Difference.* Boston, MA: Little, Brown.

Glick P and S Fiske (1996). The Ambivalent Sexism Inventory: Differentiation hostile and benevolent sexism. *Journal of Personality and Social Psychology* 70:491-512.

Goldin C (2002). *A pollution theory of discrimination: Male and female differences in occupations and earnings* (Working Paper 8985). Cambridge, MA: National Bureau of Economic Research.

Gmelch WH, PK Wilke, and NP Lovrich (1986). Dimensions of stress among university faculty: Factor-analytic results from a national survey. *Research in Higher Education* 24:266-286.

Goldin C, LF Katz, and I Kuziemko (2006). *The Homecoming of American College Women: The Reversal of the College Gender Gap* (NBER Working Paper 12139). Cambridge, MA: National Bureau of Economic Research.

Gottleib EE and B Keith (1997). The academic research-teaching nexus in eight advanced-industrialized countries. *Higher Education* 34:397-420.

Government Accountability Office (2004). *Gender Issues: Women's Participation in the Sciences Has Increased, but Agencies Need to Do More to Ensure Compliance with Title IX* (GAO-04-639). Washington, DC: US Government Accountability Office.

Gutek B and B Morasch (1982). Sex ratios, sex-role spillover, and sexual harassment of women at work. *Journal of Social Issues* 38:55-74.

Gutek BA (1985). *Sex and the Workplace.* San Francisco, CA: Jossey-Bass.

Guttierez C (2001). Who will do chemistry? *Chemical and Engineering News* 79(21):5.

Guttman JM (1996). Rational actors, tit-for-tat types, and the evolution of cooperation. *Journal of Economic Behavior and Organization* 29:27-56.

Hagedorn LS (2000). Conceptualizing faculty job satisfaction: Components, theories, and outcomes. *New Directions for Institutional Research* 105:5-20.

Hagedorn LS, M Arredondo, and FA Dicrisi (2002). Faculty research productivity: Exploring the role of gender and family-related factors. *Research in Higher Education* 43(4): 423-446.

Halari R, M Hines, V Kumari, R Mehrotra, M Wheeler, V Ng, and T Sharma (2005). Sex differences in individual differences in cognitive performance and their relationship to endogenous gonadal hormones and gonadatropins. *Behavioral Neuroscience* 119(1): 104-117.

Halpern DF (2006). Biopsychosocial contributions to cognitive performance. In *Biological, Social, and Organizational Contributions to Science and Engineering Success.* Washington, DC: The National Academies Press.

Halpern DF (2005). Sex, brains, hands: Gender differences in cognitive abilities. *Limbic Nutrition*: *http://www.limibicnutrition.com/blog/archives/028860.html.*

Halpern DF and U Tan (2001). Stereotypes and steroids: Using a psychobiosocial model to understand cognitive sex differences. *Brain and Cognition* 45:392-414.

Hamilton K (2002). The state of the African American professoriate. *Black Issues in Higher Education* 19(7):30-31.

Handelsman J, N Cantor, M Carnes, D Denton, E Fine, B Grosz, V Hinshaw, C Marrett, S Rosser, D Shalala, and J Sheridan (2005). More women in science. *Science* 309:1190-1191, *http://www.sciencemag.org/cgi/content/full/309/5738/1190.*

Hanson SL (2004). African American women in science: Experiences from high school through the post-secondary years and beyond. *NWSA Journal* 16(1):96.

Harding S (1986). *The Science Question in Feminism.* Ithaca, NY: Cornell University Press.

Harrigan MN (1999). *An Analysis of Faculty Turnover at the University of Wisconsin-Madison.* Univerisity of Wisconsin-Madison, *http://wiscweb3.wisc.edu/obpa/FacultyTurnover/FacultyTurnover2.html.*

Harvard University (2005). *Report of the Task Force on Women Faculty, http://www.news.harvard.edu/gazette/daily/2005/05/women-faculty.pdf.*

Harvard University Dependent Care for Conference Travel Program, *http://www.fas.harvard.edu/home/academic_affairs/dependent_care.pdf.*

Harvey WB (2003). *20th Anniversary Minorities in Higher Education Annual Status Report.* Washington, DC: American Council on Education.

Hausmann M, D Slabbekoorn, SHM Van Goozen, PT Cohen-Kettenis, and O Güntürkün (2000). Sex hormones affect spatial abilities during the menstrual cycle. *Behavioral Neuroscience* 114(6):1245-1250.

Hechinger FM (1988). About Education. *New York Times.* B11 (November 9).

Hedges LV and A Nowell (1995). Sex differences in mental test scores, variability, and numbers of high-scoring individuals. *Science* 269:41-45.

Heilman ME, AS Wallen, D Fuchs, and MM Tamkins (2004). Penalties for success: Reactions to women who succeed at male gender-typed tasks. *Journal of Applied Psychology* 89(3):416-427.

Hemmasi M, LA Graf, and JA Lust (1992). Correlates of pay and benefit satisfaction: The unique case of public university faculty. *Public Personnel Management* 21(4):442-443.

Hennessey J, S Hockfield, and S Tilghman (2005). Women and science: The real issue. *The Boston Globe,* Feb. 12, *http://www.boston.com/news/education/higher/articles/2005/02/12/women_and_science_the_real_issue/.*

Herlitz A, LG Nilsson, and L Baeckman (1997). Gender differences in episodic memory. *Memory and Cognition* 25:801-811.

Hill SA (2002). Teaching and doing gender in African American families. *Sex Roles: A Journal of Research* 47(11-12):493-506.

Hilton TL and VE Lee (1988). Student interest and persistence in science. *Journal of Higher Education* 59(5):510-526.

Hines M (2003). Sex steroids and human behavior: Prenatal androgen exposure and sex-typical play behavior in children. *Annals of the New York Academy of Sciences* 1007:272-282.

Hines M, BA Fane, VL Pasterski, GA Mathews, GS Conway, and C Brook (2003). Spatial abilities following prenatal androgen abnormality: Targeting and mental rotations performance in individuals with congenital adrenal hyperplasia. *Psychoneuroendocrinology* 28:1010-1026.

Hirsh E (2006). Enforcing equal opportunity: The impact of discrimination charges on sex and race segregation in the workplace (Working Paper). Department of Sociology, University of Washington.

Hoffer TB and K Grigorian (2005). *All in a Week's Work: Average Workweeks of Doctoral Scientists and Engineers* (NSF 06-302). Arlington, VA: National Science Foundation, *http://www.nsf.gov/statistics/infobrief/nsf06302/nsf06302.pdf.*

Hofstede G (2001). *Culture's Consequences: Comparing Values, Behaviors, Institutions and Organizations across Nations.* Thousand Oaks, CA: Sage.

Hojat M, JS Gonnella, and AS Caelleigh (2003). Impartial judgment by the "gatekeepers" of science: Fallibility and accountability in the peer review process. *Advances in Health Sciences Education* 8(1):75-96.

Holder JC and A Vaux (1998). African American professionals: Coping with occupational stress in predominantly white environments. *Journal of Vocational Behavior* 53(3):315-333.

Hooks B (2000). Black and female: Reflections on graduate school. In eds. J Glazer-Raymo, EM Bensimon, and BK Townsend, *Women in Higher Education*, 2nd ed. Boston, MA: Pearson Publishing.

Hopkins N (2006). Diversification of a university faculty: Observations on hiring women faculty in the schools of science and engineering at MIT. *MIT Faculty Newsletter* 18(4):1, 16-23.

Horn LJ and L Kojaku (2001). *High School Academic Curriculum and the Persistence Path through College: Persistence and Transfer Behavior of Undergraduates 3 Years After Entering 4-Year Institutions* (NCES 2001-163). Washington, DC: US Department of Education.

Hosek SD, AG Cox, B Ghosh-Dastidar, A Kofner, N Ramphal, J Scott, and SH Berry (2005). *Gender Differences in Major Federal External Grant Programs*. Washington, DC: RAND.

Howard Hughes Medical Institute and Burroughs Wellcome Fund (2004). *A Practical Guide to Scientific Management for Postdocs and New Faculty*. Bethesda, MD: HHMI.

Hrdy S (1997). Raising Darwin's consciousness: Female sexuality and the prehominid origins of patriarchy. *Human Nature* 8(1):1-49.

Hull GT, B Smith, and PB Scott (eds.) (1982). *All the Women are White, All the Blacks are Men, But some of Us Are Brave*. Toronto: Hushion House.

Humphreys LG, D Lubinski, and G Yao (1993). Utility of predicting group membership and the role of spatial visualization in becoming an engineer, physical scientist, or artist. *Journal of Applied Psychology* 78(2):250-261.

Huttenlocher J, S Levine, and J Vevea (1998). Environmental input and cognitive growth: A study using time-period comparisons. *Child Development* 69:1012-1029.

Hyde JS (2005). The gender similarities hypothesis. *American Psychologist* 60:581-592.

Hyde JS and MC Linn (1988). Gender differences in verbal ability: A meta-analysis. *Psychological Bulletin* 104:53-69.

Hyde JS, E Fennema, and JS Lammon (1990). Gender differences in mathematics performance: A meta-analysis. *Psychological Bulletin* 107(2):139-155.

Hyde JS, E Fennema, M Ryan, LA Frost, and C Hopp (1990). Gender comparisons of mathematics attitudes and affect: A meta-analysis. *Psychology of Women Quarterly* 14: 299-324.

Inglehart R and P Norris (2003). *Rising Tide: Gender Equality and Cultural Change*. New York: Cambridge University Press.

InterAcademy Council (2006). Women for Science. Amsterdam: InterAcademy Council, *http: //www. interacademycouncil.net/?id=11228*.

Inzlicht M and T Ben-Zeev (2000). A threatening intellectual environment: Why females are susceptible to experiencing problem-solving deficits in the presence of males. *Psychological Science* 11(5):365-371.

Islam MR and M Hewstone (1993). Dimensions of contact as predictors of intergroup anxiety, perceived out-group variability, and out-group attitude: An integrative model. *Personality and Social Psychology Bulletin* 38:203-210.

Ivie R and KN Ray. (2005). *Women in Physics and Astronomy, 2005*. College Park, MD: American Institute of Physics, *http://www.aip.org/statistics/trends/reports/women05.pdf*.

Ivie R, S Guo, and A Carr (2006). *2004 Physics and Astronomy Academic Workforce Report*. College Park, MD: American Institute of Physics, *http://www.aip.org/statistics/trends/facultytrends.html*.

Izraeli DF (1983). Sex effects or structural effects: An empirical test of Kanter's theory of proportions. *Social Forces* 62:153-165.

Jackson PB, PA Thoits, and HF Taylor (1995). Composition of the workplace and psychological well-being: The effects of tokenism on America's black elite. *Social Forces* 74(2):543-557.

Jackson SE, KE May, and K Whitney (1995). Understanding the dynamics of diversity in decision-making teams. In eds. RA Guzzo and E Salas, *Team Effectiveness and Decision-Making in Organizations.* San Francisco, CA: Jossey-Bass.

Jackson SE, JF Brett, VI Sessa, DM Cooper, JA Julin, and K Peyronnin (1991). Some differences make a difference: Individual dissimilarity and group heterogeneity as correlates of recruitment, promotions, and turnover. *Journal of Applied Psychology* 76:675-689.

Jacobs J and S Winslow (2004). The academic life course: Time pressures and gender inequality. *Community, Work and Family* 7(2):143-161.

Jacobs JE and JS Eccles (1992). The impact of mothers' gender-role stereotypic beliefs on mothers' and children's ability perceptions. *Journal of Personality and Social Psychology* 63(6):932-944.

Jacobs JE, P Davis-Kean, M Bleeker, JS Eccles, and O Malanchuk (2005). "I can, but I don't want to": The impact of parents, interests, and activities on gender differences in math. In eds. AM Gallagher and JC Kaufman, *Gender Differences in Mathematics: An Integrative Psychological Approach.* New York: Cambridge University Press.

Jaffee S and JS Hyde (2000). Gender differences in moral orientation: A meta-analysis. *Psychological Bulletin* 126:703-726.

Jena SPK (1999). Job, life satisfaction, and occupational stress of women. *Social Science International* 15(1):75-80.

Johns M, T Schmader, and A Martens (2005). Knowing is half the battle: Teaching stereotype threat as a means of improving women's math performance. *Psychological Science* 16:175-179.

Johnson NL (2000). *Developmental insights into evolving systems: Roles of diversity, non-selection, self-organization, symbiosis.* Paper presented at Seventh International Conference on Artificial Life. Portland OR, August 1-6.

Johnstone WB and AE Packer (1987). *Workforce 2000: Work and Workers for the Twenty-First Century.* Indianapolis, IN: Hudson Institute.

Joiner KA (2005). A strategy for allocating central funds to support new faculty recruitment. *Academic Medicine* 80(3):218-224.

Jordan D (2005). *Sisters in Science.* Ashland, OH: Purdue University Press.

Kalev A, F Dobbin, and E Kelly (2006). *Best Practices or Best Guesses? Diversity Management and the Remediation of Inequality* (Working Paper). Cambridge, MA: Harvard University, *http://www.wjh.harvard.edu/~dobbin/cv/working_papers/eeopractice1.pdf.*

Kanter RM (1977). *Men and Women of the Corporation.* New York: Basic Books.

Kavathas P, M LaFrance, and S Benhabib (2006). *Task Force on the Retention and Promotion of Junior Faculty.* New Haven, CT: Yale Women Faculty Forum.

Keith B, JS Layne, N Babchuk, and K Johnson (2002). The context of scientific achievement: Sex status, organizational environments, and the timing of publication on scholarship outcomes. *Social Forces* 80(4):1253-1282.

Keller J (2002). Blatant stereotype threat and women's performance: Self-handicapping as a strategic means to cope with obtrusive negative performance expectations. *Sex Roles: A Journal of Research* 47:193-198.

Kempf M (2002). EmPOWREment and ADVANCEment for women: NSF programs for women in science. *Science:* September 20.

Kerber LK (2005). We must make the academic workplace more human and equitable. *Chronicle of Higher Education* 51(28):B6.

Kern S (2002). Fellowship goals for PhDs and MDs: A primer on the molecular biology postdoctoral experience. *Cancer Biology and Therapy* 1:74-85.

Kirkman EE, JW Maxwell, and CA Rose (2005). 2004 Annual Survey of the Mathematical Sciences. *Notices of the American Mathematical Society, http://www.ams.org/employment/2004Survey-Third-Report.pdf.*

Klein A (2004). Affirmative-action opponents suffer setbacks in Colorado and Michigan. *Chronicle of Higher Education* 50(31):A23.

Konrad AM and F Linnehan (1995). Formalized HRM structures: Coordinating Equal Employment Opportunity or concealing organizational practices? *Academy of Management Journal* 38:787-829.

Konrad AM, S Winter, and BA Gutek (1992). Diversity in work group sex composition: Implications for minority or minority members. In eds. PS Tolbert and SB Bacharach, *Research in the Sociology of Organizations.* Greenwich, CT: JAI Press.

Kray LJ, L Thompson, and A Galinsky (2001). Battle of the sexes: Gender stereotype confirmation and reactance in negotiations. *Journal of Personality and Social Psychology* 80(6):942-958.

Krefting LA (2003). Intertwined discourses of merit and gender: Evidence from academic employment in the USA. *Gender, Work, and Organization* 10(2):260-278.

Kuck VJ, CH Marzabadi, SA Nolan, and J Buckner (2004). Analysis by gender of the doctoral and postdoctoral institutions of faculty members at the top-fifty ranked chemistry departments. *Journal of Chemical Education* 81(3): 356-363, *http://www.chem.indiana.edu/academics/ugrad/Courses/G307/documents/Genderanalysis.pdf.*

Kulis S, Y Chong, and H Shaw (1999). Discriminatory organizational contexts and black scientists on postsecondary faculties. *Research in Higher Education* 40(2):115-148.

Laband DN and MJ Piette (1994). A citation analysis of the impact of blinded peer review. *JAMA* 272(2):147-149.

Lach J (1999). Minority women hit a "concrete ceiling". *American Demographics* 21(9): 18-19.

Lagendijk A (2005). Pushing for power. *Nature* 438:429.

Larkey LK (1996). Toward a theory of communicative interactions in culturally diverse workgroups. *Academy of Management Review* 21:463-491.

Laurich-McIntyre S and SG Brainard (1995). Retaining women freshmen in engineering and science: A success sory. *Women in Engineering Conference Proceedings: Is Systemic Change Happening?* Washington, DC.

LaVaque-Manty D, J Steiger, and A Stewart (forthcoming). Interactive theater: Raising issues about the climate with science faculty. In *Transforming Science and Engineering: Advancing Women in Science and Engineering:* Ann Arbor: University of Michigan Press.

Leaper C, KJ Anderson, and P Sanders (1998). Moderators of gender effects on parents' talk to their children: A meta-analysis. *Developmental Psychology* 34(11):3-27.

Leggon CB (2006). Women in science: Racial and ethnic differences and the differences they make. *Journal of Technology Transfer* 31:325-333.

Leggon CB and W Pearson (1997). The baccalaureate origins of African American female PhD scientists. *Journal of Women and Minorities in Science and Engineering* 3:213-224.

Lehrer E and M Nerlove (1986). Female labor force behavior and fertility in the United States. *Annual Review of Sociology* 12:181-204.

Leslie MW (2005). Women learn how to pierce the 'polycarbonate ceiling' in chemistry careers, *http://www. Eurekalert.org/pub_release/2005-09/uoo-wlh092105.php.*

Levy LJ, RS Astur, and KM Frick (2005). Men and women differ in object memory but not performance of a virtual radial maze. *Behavioral Neuroscience* 119:853-862.

Linn MC and AC Petersen (1985). Emergence and characterization of sex differences in spatial ability: A meta-analysis. *Child Development* 56:1479-1498.

Lintner T (1996). *The Forgotten Scholars: American Indian Doctorate Receipt, 1980-1990, http://eric.ed.gov/ERICDocs/data/ericdocs2/content_storage_01/0000000b/80/25/be/36.pdf.*

Linville PW (1988). The heterogeneity of homogeneity. In eds. JM Darley and J Cooper, *Attribution and Social Interaction: The Legacy of Edward E. Jones.* Washington, DC: American Psychological Association.

Linville PW and GW Fischer (1993). Exemplar and abstraction models of perceived group variability and stereotypicality. *Social Cognition* 11:92-125.

Loden M (1995). *Implementing Diversity.* Burr Ridge, IL: McGraw-Hill.

Long J, P Allison, and R McGinnis (1993). Rank advancement in academic careers: Sex differences and the effects of productivity. *American Sociological Review* 58(8): 703-722.

Long JS (1992). Measures of sex differences in scientific productivity. *Social Forces* 71: 159-178.

Lovitts BE (2001). *Leaving the Ivory Tower: The Causes and Consequences of Departure from Doctoral Study.* Lanham, MD: Rowman and Littlefield.

Luchtmaya S, S Baron-Cohen, and P Raggatt (2002). Foetal testosterone and eye contact in 12-month-old human infants. *Infant Behavior and Development* 25:327-335.

Lummis M and HW Stevenson (1990). Gender differences in beliefs and achievement: A cross-cultural study. *Developmental Psychology* 26(2):254-263.

Lynch L, C Duan, and B Glass (1992). Categorization of individuals on the basis of multiple social features. *Journal of Personality and Social Psychology* 62:207-218.

Lytton H and DM Romney (1991). Parents' differential socialization of boys and girls: A meta-analysis. *Psychological Bulletin* 109(2):267-296.

Maccoby EE and CN Jacklin (1974). *Psychology of Sex Differences.* Stanford, CA: Stanford University Press.

Malcom SM, PQ Hall, and JW Brown (1976). *The Double Bind: The Price of Being A Minority Woman in Science* (AAAS Publication 76-R-3). Washington, DC: American Association for the Advancement of Science.

Mark S, H Link, PS Morahan, L Pololi, V Reznik, and S Tropez-Sims (2001). Innovative mentoring programs to promote gender equity in academic medicine. *Academic Medicine* 76:39-42.

Martell RF and AL DeSmet (2001). A diagnostic-ratio approach to measuring beliefs about the leadership abilities of male and female managers. *Journal of Applied Psychology* 86(6):1223-1231.

Martell RF, DM Lane, and C Emrich (1996). Male-female differences: A computer simulation. *American Psychologist* 51:157-158.

Martin J (2006). Gendered organizations. In *Biological, Social, and Organizational Components of Success for Women in Academic Science and Engineering.* Washington, DC: The National Academies Press.

Martin J and D Myerson (1998). Women and power: Conformity, resistance, and disorganized coaction. In eds. RM Kramer and MA Neale, *Power and Influence in Organizations.* San Francisco, CA: Sage Publications.

Marwell G, RA Rosenfeld, and S Spilerman (1979). Geographic constraints on women's careers in academia. *Science* 205:1225-1231.

Mason MA, A Stacy, M Goulden, C Hoffman, and K Frasch (2005). *University of California Faculty Family Friendly Edge. An Initiative for Tenure-Track Faculty at the University of California,* http://ucfamilyedge.berkeley.edu/.

Mason MA and M Goulden (2002). Do babies matter? The effect of family formation on the lifelong careers of academic men and women. *Academe* 88(6):21-27, http://www.aaup.org/publications/Academe/2002/02nd/02ndmas.htm.

Mason MA and M Goulden (2004). Marriage and baby blues: Redefining gender equity in the academy. *Annals AAPSS* 596:86-103.

Mason MA, A Stacy, and M Goulden (2003). *University of California Faculty Work and Family Survey*, *http://ucfamilyedge.berkeley.edu/workfamily.htm*.

Massachusetts Institute of Technology (1999). A study on the status of women faculty in science at MIT. *MIT Faculty Newsletter* 11(4), *http://web.mit.edu/fnl/women/women.html*.

Masters MS and Sanders B (1993). Is the gender difference in mental rotation disappearing? *Behavior Genetics* 23:337-341.

Mathot J (2005). Duke expands child care options. *Duke News*, September 9, *http://www.dukenews.duke.edu/2005/09/childcare.html*.

Maznevski ML (1994). Understanding our differences: Performance in decision-making groups with diverse members. *Human Relations* 47:531-552.

McCain BE, C O'Reilly, and J Pfeffer (1983). The effects of departmental demography on turnover: The case of a university. *Academy of Management Journal* 26:626-641.

McCracken DM (2000). Winning the talent war for women. *Harvard Business Review* Nov/Dec (Reprint R00611).

McDowell JM, LD Singell, and M Stater (2006). Two to tango? Gender differences in the decisions to publish and coauthor. *Economic Inquiry* 44(1):153-168.

McGlone MS and J Aronson (2006). Stereotype threat, identity salience, and spatial reasoning. *Journal of Applied Developmental Psychology* (in press).

McGrath JE, JL Berdahl, and H Arrow (1995). Traits, expectations, culture and clout: The dynamics of diversity in workgroups. In eds. SE Jackson and MD Ruderman, *Diversity in Work Teams*. Washington, DC: American Psychological Association.

McLeod PL, SA Lobel, and TH Cox (1996). Ethnic diversity and creativity in small groups. *Small Group Research* 27:248-265.

McNutt RA, AT Evans, RH Fletcher, and SW Fletcher (1990). The effects of blinding on the quality of peer review: A randomized trial. *JAMA* 263(10):1371-1376.

Mednick MT (1989). On the politics of psychological constructs: Stop the bandwagon, I want to get off. *American Psychologist* 44:1118-1123.

Merton RK (1973). *The Sociology of Science: Theoretical and Empirical Investigations*. Chicago, IL: University of Chicago Press.

Merton RK (1968). The Matthew effect in Science. *Science* 158:56-63.

Meyerson DE and JK Fletcher (2005). A modest manifesto for shattering the glass ceiling. In *Harvard Business Review on Women in Business*. Boston, MA: Harvard Business School.

Milem JF (2003). The educational benefits of diversity: Evidence from multiple sectors. In eds. M Chang et al., *Compelling Interest: Examining the Evidence on Racial Dynamics in Higher Education*. Stanford, CA: Stanford Education.

Miller F (1992). *Discussant commentary. Leadership Diversity Conference: Beyond Awareness into Action*. Center for Creative Leadership, Greensboro, NC.

Mincer J (1978). Family migration decisions. *Journal of Political Economy* 86:749-773.

Moguerou P (2002). *Job Satisfaction among US PhDs: The Effects of Gender and Employment Sectors* (Working Paper), *http://www.rennes.inra.fr/jma2002/pdf/moguerou.pdf*.

Monks J (2005). Title IX Compliance and Preference for Men in College Admission (Working Paper 80). Ithaca, NY: Cornell Higher Education Research Institute, *http://www.ilr.cornell.edu/cheri/wp/cheri_wp80.pdf*.

Morgan C, JD Isaac, and C Sansone (2001). The role of interest in understanding the career choices of female and male college students. *Sex Roles* 44(5-6):295-320.

Morrison A (1996). *The New Leaders: Leadership Diversity in America*. San Francisco, CA: Jossey-Bass.

Morrison AM (1992). New solutions to the same old glass ceiling. *Women in Management Review* 7(4):15-19.

Moses Y (1989). *Black Women in Academe: Issues and Strategies.* Washington, DC: Association of American Colleges.

Myers SL and CS Turner (2004). The effects of PhD supply on minority faculty representation. *The American Economic Review* 94(2):296-301.

Naff KC and JE Kellough (2003). Ensuring employment equity: Are federal diversity programs making a difference? *International Journal of Public Administration* 26(12):1307-1336.

NAS/NAE/IOM (2007). *Rising Above the Gathering Storm: Energizing and Employing America for a Brighter Economic Future.* Washington, DC: The National Academies Press.

NAS/NAE/IOM (2005). *Policy Implications of International Graduate Students and Postdoctoral Scholars in the United States.* Washington, DC: The National Academies Press.

NAS/NAE/IOM (2004). *Facilitating Interdisciplinary Research.* Washington, DC: The National Academies Press.

NAS/NAE/IOM (1997). *Adviser, Teacher, Role Model, Friend: On Being a Mentor to Students in Science and Engineering.* Washington, DC: National Academy Press.

National Center for Education Statistics (2004). *Trends in Educational Equity of Girls and Women: 2004* (NCES 2005-016). Washington, DC: US Department of Education.

National Center for Education Statistics (2002). *Digest of Education Statistics, 2002* (NCES 2003060) Washington, DC: US Department of Education Statistics

National Center for Education Statistics (2000). *Trends in Educational Equity of Girls and Women: 2000* (NCES 2000-030). Washington, DC: US Department of Education.

National Center for Education Statistics (1997). *The Third International Mathematics and Science Study.* Washington, DC: US Department of Education, *http://www.ed.gov/nces.*

National Institutes of Allergies and Infectious Diseases, National Institutes of Health, *Primary Caregiver Technical Assistance Supplements, http://www.niaid.nih.gov/ncn/training/pctas.htm.*

National Research Council (2004). *Measuring Racial Discrimination.* Washington, DC: The National Academies Press.

National Research Council (2001). *From Scarcity to Visibility: Gender Differences in the Careers of Doctoral Scientists and Engineers.* Washington, DC: National Academy Press.

National Research Council (1996). *The National Scholars Program: Excellence with Diversity for the Future.* Washington, DC: National Academy Press.

National Research Council (1996). *The Path to the PhD.* Washington, DC: National Academy Press.

National Research Council (1995). *Research Doctorate Programs in the United States: Continuity and Change.* Washington, DC: National Academy Press.

National Research Council (1992). *Science and Engineering Programs: On Target for Women?* Washington, DC: National Academy Press.

National Research Council (1991). *Women in Science and Engineering: Increasing Their Numbers the 1990s: A Statement on Policy and Strategy.* Washington, DC: National Academy Press.

National Research Council 1989. *Everybody Counts: A Report to the Nation on the Future of Mathematics Education.* Washington, DC: National Academy Press.

National Science Board (2006). *Science and Engineering Indicators, 2006.* (NSB 06-02) Arlington, VA: National Science Foundation, Appendix Table 1-17.

National Science Board (2004). *Science and Engineering Indicators, 2004* (NSB 04-01). Arlington, VA: National Science Foundation.

National Science Foundation (2006). *Survey of Doctoral Recipients, 2003.* Arlington, VA. National Science Foundation.

National Science Foundation (2004). *Gender Differences in the Careers of Academic Scientists and Engineers* (NSF 04-323). Arlington, VA: National Science Foundation.

National Science Foundation (2004). *Graduate Students and Postdoctorates in Science and Engineering.* Arlington, VA: National Science Foundation.

National Science Foundation (2004). *Women, Minorities and Persons with Disabilities in Science and Engineering, 2004.* Arlington, VA: National Science Foundation.

National Science Foundation (2003). *Survey of Earned Doctorates, 2003.* Arlington, VA: National Science Foundation.

National Science Foundation (1999). *Survey of Doctoral Recipients.* Arlington, VA: National Science Foundation.

Nelson DJ (2005). *A National Analysis of Diversity in Science and Engineering Faculties at Research Universities, http://cheminfo.chem.ou.edu/~djn/diversity/briefings/Diversity%20Report%20Final.pdf.*

Nelson S and G Pellet (1997). *Shattering the Silences [videorecording].* San Francisco: Gail Pellet Productions.

Nemeth CJ (1995). Dissent as driving cognition, attitudes, and judgments. *Social Cognition* 13:273-291.

Nemeth CJ (1985). Dissent, group process, and creativity: The contribution of minority influence. *Advances in Group Processes* 2:57-75.

Nettles MT and CM Millett (2006). *Three Magic Letters: Getting to PhD.* Baltimore, MD: Johns Hopkins University Press.

Newcombe NS and J Huttenlocher (2006). Development of spatial cognition. In eds. D Kuhn and RS Siegler, *Handbook of Child Psychology: Vol. 2. Cognition, Perception, and Language* (6th ed.). New York: Wiley.

Newkirk MM, E Richie, and JK Lunney (2005). Advancing women scientists: The immunology experience. *Nature Immunology* 6(9):855.

Niemann YF and JF Dovidio (1998). Relationship of solo status, academic rank, and perceived distinctiveness to job satisfaction of racial/ethic minorities. *Journal of Applied Psychology* 83(1):55-71.

Nieva V and B Gutek (1980). Sex effects on evaluation. *Academy of Management Review* 5:267-276.

Nieves-Squires S (1991). *Hispanic Women: Making their Presence on Campus Less Tenuous.* Washington, DC: Association of American Colleges.

Nordenström A, A Servin, G Bohlin, A Larsson, and A Wedell (2002). Sex-typed toy play behavior correlates with the degree of prenatal androgen exposure assessed by CYP 21 genotype in girls with congenital adrenal hyperplasia. *Journal of Clinical Endocrinology and Metabolism* 87(11):5119-5124.

Nosek, BA, MR Banaji, and AG Greenwald (2002). Math = Male, Me = Female, Therefore Math ≠ Me. *Journal of Personality and Social Psychology* 83:44-59.

Nowell A and LV Hedges (1998). Trends in gender differences in academic achievement from 1960 to 1994: An analysis of differences in mean, variance and extreme scores, *Sex Roles: A Journal of Research*:21-43.

Oakes J (1990). Opportunities, achievement, and choice: Women and minority students in science and mathematics. *Review of Research in Education* 16:153-222.

O'Boyle MW, EJ Hoff, and HS Gill (1995). The influence of mirror reversals on male and female performance in spatial tasks: A componential look. *Personality and Individual Differences* 18:693-699.

Office of Extramural Research (2005). *Sex/Gender in the Biomedical Science Workforce.* National Institutes of Health, *http://grants2.nih.gov/grants/policy/sex_gender/q_a.htm#q5.*

Oldenziel R (2000). Multiple entry visas: Gender and engineering in the US, 1870-1945. In eds. A Canal, R Oldenziel, and K Zachmann, *Crossing Boundaries, Building Bridges: Comparing the History of Women Engineers 1870s-1990s*, Amsterdam: Overseas Publishers Association.

Olsen D, SA Maple, and FK Stage (1995). Women and minority faculty job satisfaction: Professional role interests, professional satisfactions, and institutional fit. *The Journal of Higher Education* 66(3):267-293.

Opinion of the court. Grutter v. Bollinger 539 US 306, 2003, *http://www.law.cornell.edu/supct/pdf/02-241P.ZO.*

O'Reilly C, DF Caldwell, and WP Barnett (1989). Work group demography, social integration, and turnover. *Administrative Science Quarterly* 34:21-37.

Orfield G. (2005) *Dropouts in America: Confronting the Graduation Rate Crisis*. Cambridge, MA: Harvard Education Press.

Ostrom TM, SL Carpenter, C Sedikeides, and F Li (1993). Differential processing of in-group and out-group information. *Journal of Personality and Social Psychology* 64:21-34.

Ostrow E (2002). The backlash against academic parents. *Chronicle of Higher Education* (February 22), *http://chronicle.com/jobs/2002/02/2002022202c.htm.*

Packard Foundation. Packard Fellowships for Science and Engineering 2006 Guidelines. *http://www.packard.org/assets/files/conservation%20and%20science/2006_fellows__guidelines.pdf.*

Paglin M and AM Rufolo (1990). Heterogeneous human capital, occupational choice, and male-female earnings differences. *Journal of Labor Economics* 8(1):123-144.

Palepu A, PL Carr, RH Friedman, H Amos, AS Ash, and MA Moskowitz (1998). Minority faculty in academic medicine. *JAMA* 280(9):767-771.

Palfrey TR and H Rosenthal (1994). Repeated play, cooperation and coordination: An experimental study. *Review of Economic Studies* 61:545-565.

Park B and CM Judd (1990). Measures and models of perceived group variability. *Journal of Personality and Social Psychology* 59:173-191.

Park SM (1996). Research, teaching and service: Why shouldn't women's work count? *Journal of Higher Education* 67:46-84.

Pasterski VL, ME Geffner, C Brain, P Hindmarsh, B Charles, and M Hines (2005). Prenatal hormones and postnatal socialization by parents as determinants of male-typical toy-play in girls with congenital adrenal hyperplasia. *Child Development* 76:264-278.

Pearson W (1985). *Black Scientists, White Society, and Colorless Science: A Study of Universalism in American Science*. Millwood, NY: Associated Faculty.

Pelled LH (1996). Demographic diversity, conflict, and work group outcomes: An intervening process theory. *Organization Science* 7:615-631.

Peña M (2006). New childbirth policy for female graduate students. Stanford Report, *http://news-service.stanford.edu/news/2006/february1/mom-020106.html.*

Pettigrew TF and J Martin (1987). Shaping the organizational context for Black American inclusion. *Journal of Social Issues* 43(1):41-78.

Pinker S (2005). The science of gender and science. In Pinker and Spelke: A debate. *Edge: The Third Culture, http://www.edge.org/3rd_culture/debate05/debate05_index.html.*

Pinker S (2005). The science of difference: Sex ed. *The New Republic*, February 14.

Pinker S (2002). *The Blank Slate: The Modern Denial of Human Nature*. New York: Viking.

Pion G and M Ionescu-Pioggia (2003). Bridging postdoctoral training and a faculty position: Initial outcomes of the Burroughs Wellcome Fund Career Awards in the Biomedical Sciences. *Academic Medicine* 78(2):177-186.

Plater WM (1995). Future work: Faculty time in the 21st century. *Change* 27(3):22-33.

Plous S (2003). The psychology of prejudice, stereotyping and discrimination: An overview. In ed. S Plous, *Understanding Prejudice and Discrimination*. New York: McGraw-Hill.

Polyani M (1962). The Republic of Science: Its political and economic theory. *Minerva* 1: 54-74.

Pratto F and JA Bargh (1991). Stereotyping based on apparently individuating information: Trait and global components of sex stereotypes under attention overload. *Journal of Experimental Social Psychology* 27:26-47.

Preston AE (2004). *Leaving Science: Occupational Exit from Scientific Careers*. New York: Russell Sage Foundation.

Pribbenow C, C Maidl, and J Winchell (2005). *WISELI's Workshops for Search Chairs: Evaluation Report*. Madison: University of Wisconsin.

Quinn DM and SJ Spencer (2001). The interference of stereotype threat with women's generation of mathematical problem-solving strategies. *Journal of Social Issues* 57(1):55-71.

Rapoport R, L Bailyn, JK Fletcher, and BH Pruitt (2002). *Beyond Work-Family Balance: Advancing Gender Equity and Workplace Performance*. San Francisco, CA: Jossey-Bass.

Rennie DJ (1998) Peer review in Prague. *JAMA* 280(3):214-215.

Reskin B (2000). The proximate causes of employment discrimination. *Contemporary Sociology* 29(2):319-328.

Reskin B and P Roos (1990). *Job Queues, Gender Queues: Explaining Women's Inroads into Male Occupations*. Philadelphia, PA: Temple University Press.

Resnick SM, SA Berenbaum, II Gottesman, and TJ Bouchard (1986). Early hormonal influences on cognitive functioning in congenital adrenal hyperplasia. *Developmental Psychology* 22(2):191-198.

Rice ER and AE Austin (1988). Faculty morale: What exemplary colleges do right. *Change* 20(3):51-58.

Roach R (2005). Ford diversity fellows urged to defend affirmative action. *Diverse Issues in Higher Education*, *http://www.diverseeducation.com/artman/publish/article_4898.shtml*.

Rolison DR (2003). Can title IX do for women in science and engineering what it has done for women in sports? *American Physical Society News Online* 12(5):8.

Rosenfeld RA and JA Jones (1987). Patterns and effects of geographic mobility for academic women and men. *Journal of Higher Education* 58(5):493-515.

Rosenthal R, RL Rosnow, and DB Rubin (2000). *Contrasts and Effect Sizes in Behavioral Research: A Correlational Approach*. Cambridge, UK: Cambridge University Press.

Ross JS, CP Gross, MM Desai, Y Hong, AO Grant, SR Daniels, VC Hachinski, RJ Gibbons, TJ Gardner, and HM Krumholz (2006). Effect of blinded peer review on abstract acceptance. *JAMA* 295:1675-1680.

Rosser S and JL Chameau (2006). Institutionalization, sustainability, and repeatability of ADVANCE for institutional transformation. *Journal of Technology Transfer* 31: 335-344.

Rosser SV (2006). Creating an inclusive work environment. In *Biological, Social, and Organizational Components of Success for Women in Science and Engineering*. Washington, DC: The National Academies Press.

Rosser SV (2004). *The Science Glass Ceiling*. New York: Routledge.

Rosser VJ (2004). Faculty members' intentions to leave: A national study on their worklife and satisfaction. *Research in Higher Education* 45(3):285-309.

Roth S (2003). *The Steering Committee's Report on the Women's Initiative*. Durham, NC: Duke University, *http://www.duke.edu/womens_initiative/exec.htm*.

Rouse C and C Goldin (2000). Orchestrating impartiality: The impact of "blind" auditions on female musicians. *American Economics Review* 90:715-741.

Rudman LA and P Glick (2001). Gender effects on social influence and hireability: Prescriptive gender stereotypes and backlash towards agentic women. *Journal of Social Issues* 57(4):743-762.

Rudman LA and SE Kilianski SE (2000). Implicit and explicit attitudes toward female authority. *Personality and Social Psychology Bulletin* 26(11):315-1328.

Rutgers University (2001). *A Study of Gender Equity in the Faculty of Arts and Sciences, http://fas.rutgers.edu/onlineforms/gender_report.pdf.*

Sandler BR (1991). *The Campus Climate Revisited: Chilly Climate for Women Faculty, Administrators, and Graduate Students.* Washington, DC: Association of American Colleges.

Saults SJ, F Liu, and MK Hoard (2000). Sex differences in spatial cognition, computational fluency, and arithmetical reasoning. *Journal of Experimental Child Psychology* 77: 337-353.

Sax LJ, S Hagedorn, M Arredondo, and FA Dicrisi (2002). Faculty research productivity: Exploring the role of gender and family-related factors. *Research in Higher Education* 43(4):423-446.

Schmader T (2002). Gender identification moderates stereotype threat effects on women's math performance. *Journal of Experimental Social Psychology* 38:194-201.

Schmader T, M Johns, and M Barquissau (2004). The costs of accepting gender differences: The role of stereotype endorsement in women's experience in the math domain. *Sex Roles: A Journal of Research* 50:835-850.

Schmidt P (2006). From "Minority" to "Diversity". The transformation of formerly race-exclusive programs may be leaving some students out in the cold. *Chronicle of Higher Education* 52(22):A24.

Schmidt P (2006). Southern Illinois U. and Justice Dept. near accord on minority fellowships. *Chronicle of Higher Education* 52(22):A26.

Schneider A (2000). Support for a rare breed: Tenured women scientists. *Chronicle of Higher Education*, November 10.

Schneider B (1987). The people make the place. *Personnel Psychology* 40:437-453.

Sears ALW (2003). Image problems deplete the number of women in academic applicant pools. *Journal of Women and Minorities in Science and Engineering* 9:169-181.

Serbin LA, D Poulin-Dubois, KA Colburne, MG Sen, and JA Y Eichstedt (2001). Gender stereotyping in infancy: Visual preferences for and knowledge of gender stereotyped toys in the second year. *International Journal of Behavioral Development* 25:7-15.

Seymour E and NM Hewitt (1997). *Talking About Leaving.* Boulder, CO: Westview Press.

Sharpe NR and CH Fuller (1995). Baccalaureate origins of women physical science doctorates: Relationship to institutional gender and science discipline. *Journal of Women and Minorities in Science and Engineering* 2(1):1-15.

Shauman KA and Y Xie (1996). Geographic mobility of scientists: Sex differences and family constraints. *Demography* 33(4):455-468.

Shaywitz BA, SE Shaywitz, KR Pugh, RT Constable, P Skudlarski, RK Fulbright, RA Bronen, JM Fletcher, DP Shankweler, L Katz, and JC Gore (1995). Sex differences in the functional organization of the brain for language. *Nature* 373:607-609.

Shepard RN and J Metzler (1971). Mental rotation of three-dimensional objects. *Science* 171(972):701-703.

Sheridan J, PF Brennan, M Carnes, and J Handelsman (2006). Discovering directions for change in higher education through the experiences of senior women faculty. *Journal of Technology Transfer* 31:387-396.

Shih M, TL Pittinsky, and N Ambady (1999). Stereotype susceptibility: Identity salience and shifts in quantitative performance. *Psychological Science* 10(1):80-83.

Simpson R and C Cohen (2004). Dangerous work: The gendered nature of bullying in the context of higher education. *Gender, Work and Organization* 11(2):163-186.

Sinclair L and Z Kunda (2000). Motivated stereotyping of women: She's fine if she praised me but incompetent if she criticized me. *Personality and Social Psychology Bulletin* 26(11):1329-1342.

Singer JM and JE Stake (1986). Mathematics and self-esteem: Implications for women's career choice. *Psychology of Women Quarterly* 10:339-352.

Skolnik M (2000). Does counting publications provide any useful information about academic performance? *Teacher Education Quarterly* 27(2):15-25.

Smith DG, S Parker, AR Clayton-Pedersen, JF Moreno, and DH Teraguchi (2006). *Building Capacity: The Study of Impact of The James Irvine Foundation Campus Diversity Initiative.* Irvine, CA: The James Irvine Foundation.

Solomon BM (1985). *In the Company of Educated Women: A History of Women and Higher Education in America.* New Haven, CT: Yale University Press.

Solorzano DG (1994). The baccalaureate origins of Chicana and Chicano doctorates in the physical, life, and engineering sciences: 1980-1990. *Journal of Women and Minorities in Science and Engineering* 1(4):253-272.

Sommer IEC, A Aleman, A Bouma, and RS Kahn (2004). Do women really have more bilateral language representation than men? A meta-analysis of functional imaging studies. *Brain* 127(8):1845-1852.

Sonnert G and G Holton (1996). Career patterns of women and men in the sciences. *American Scientist* 84:63-71.

South SJ, CM Bonjean, WT Markham, and J Corder (1982). Social structure and intergroup interaction: Men and women of the federal bureaucracy. *American Sociological Review* 47:587-599.

Spelke ES (2005). Sex differences in intrinsic aptitude for mathematics and science? A critical review. *American Psychologist* 60(9):950-958.

Spencer SJ, CM Steele, and DM Quinn (1999). Stereotype threat and women's math performance. *Journal of Experimental and Social Psychology* 35:4-28.

Stacy A (2006). Recruitment practices. In *Biological, Social, and Organizational Components of Success for Women in Science and Engineering.* Washington, DC: The National Academies Press.

Stanford University Chemistry Department. *Letter to Graduate Students, http://pubs.acs.org/cen/news/pdf/Stanford_Policy.pdf?sessid=1602.*

Stanford University. Stanford Graduate Student Handbook. "Childbirth Policy for Women Graduate Students at Stanford University," *http://www.stanford.edu/dept/DoR/GSH/childbirth.html.*

Steele CM (1997). A threat in the air: How stereotypes shape intellectual identity and performance. *American Psychologist* 52:613-629.

Steele CM and J Aronson (1995). Stereotype threat and the intellectual test performance of African Americans. *Journal of Personality and Social Psychology* 69:797-811.

Steinpreis R, K Sanders, and D Ritzke (1999). The impact of gender on the review of the curriculum vitae of job applicants and tenure candidates: A national empirical study. *Sex Roles: A Journal of Research* 41:509-528.

Stewart AJ, D LaVaque-Manty, and JE Malley (2004). Recruiting women faculty in science and engineering: Preliminary evaluation of one intervention model. *Journal of Women and Minorities in Science and Engineering* 10(4):361-375.

Strangor C, L Lynch, C Duan, and B Glass (1992). Categorization of individuals on the basis of multiple social features. *Journal of Personality and Social Psychology* 62:207-218.

Strum S (2001). Second generation employment discrimination: A structural approach. *Columbia Law Review* 101(3):458-568.

Sullivan B, C Hollenshead, and G Smith (2004). Developing and implementing work-family policies for faculty. *Academe* 90(6), *http://www.aaup.org/publications/ Academe/2004/ 04nd/04ndsull.htm.*

Taylor SE and ST Fiske (1976). The token in the small group: Research findings and research implications. In ed. J Sweeney, *Psychology and Politics: Collected Papers.* New Haven, CT: Yale University Press.

Tetlock PE (1985). Accountability: A social check on the fundamental attribution error. *Social Psychology Quarterly* 48:227-236.

Tenenbaum HR and C Leaper (2003a). Are parents' gender schemas related to their children's gender-related cognitions? A meta-analysis. *Developmental Psychology* 38(4):615-630.

Tenenbaum HR and C Leaper (2003b). Parent-child conversations about science: The socialization of gender inequities. *Developmental Psychology* 39(1):34-47.

Teodorescu D (2002). *Faculty Gender Equity at Emory: PCSW Study Finds Both Fairness and Imbalances, http://www.emory.edu/ACAD_EXCHANGE/2002/octnov/pcsw.html.*

Thomas DA (2004). Diversity as strategy. *Harvard Business Review* 82(9):98-108.

Thornton S (2003). Maternity and childrearing leave policies for faculty: The legal and practical challenges of complying with Title VII. *University of Southern California Review of Law and Women's Studies* 12(2):161-190.

Tomasello M and J Call (1997). *Primate Cognition.* New York: Oxford University Press.

Tomaskoviv-Devey D, M Thomas, and K Johnson (2005). Race and the accumulation of human capital across the career: A theoretical model of fixed-effects application. *American Journal of Sociology* 111:58-89.

Toren N and V Kraus (1987). The effects of minority size on women's position in academia. *Social Forces* 65:1090-1100.

Tregenza T (2002). Gender bias in the refereeing process? *TRENDS in Ecology and Evolution* 17(8):349-350.

Trix F and C Psenka (2003). Exploring the color of glass: Letters of recommendation for female and male medical faculty. *Discourse and Society* 14(2):191-220.

Trower C and R Chait (2002). Faculty diversity: Too little for too long. *Harvard Magazine* (March-April).

Trower CA and JL Bleak (2004). *Study of New Scholars. Gender: Statistical Report* [Universities]. Cambridge, MA: Harvard Graduate School of Education, *http://www.gse.harvard. edu/~newscholars/newscholars/downloads/genderreport.pdf.*

Turner CSV (2002). Women of color in academe: Living with multiple marginality. *The Journal of Higher Education* 73(1):74-93.

Turner CSV (2000). New faces, new knowledge. *Academe* 86:34-37.

Turner CSV and SL Myers (2000). *Faculty of Color in Academe: Bittersweet Success.* New York: Allyn and Bacon.

Tyre P (2006). The trouble with boys. *Newsweek* 147(5):44-52 (Jan 30).

Umbach PD (2006). *Gender Equity in the Academic Labor Market: An Analysis of Academic Disciplines.* Paper presented at the 2006 annual meeting of the American Educational Research Association, San Francisco, CA, April 7-11, *http://myweb.uiowa.edu/pumbach/ AERA2006_equitypaper.pdf.*

University of California-Davis Lab Management Institute Web page, *http://www.research. ucdavis.edu/home.cfm?id=OVC,14,1488.*

University of California-Santa Cruz Chancellor's Inaugural Symposium, November 3, 2006, *http://celebration2005.ucsc.edu/symposium.asp.*

University of Colorado at Boulder (2001). *Faculty Recruitment and Retention Task Force Report, http://www.colorado.edu/AcademicAffairs/fac_recruit/fac_recruit.doc.*

University of Michigan STRIDE Web Page, *http://sitemaker.umich.edu/advance/stride.*

University of Washington ADVANCE Web Page, *http://www.engr.washington.edu/advance/ workshops/index.html*.

University of Washington (2003). *ADVANCE Center for Institutional Change Faculty Retention Toolkit*, *http://www.engr.washington.edu/advance/resources/Retention/index.html*.

University of Washington. Childcare Voucher Program, *http://depts.washington.edu/ovpsa/ childcare/voucher.html*.

US Department of Education (2004). *International Outcomes of Learning in Mathematics Literacy and Problem Solving: PISA 2003 Results From the US Perspective: Highlights* (NCES 2005–003). Washington, DC: US Department of Education.

Valian V (1998). *Why So Slow? The Advancement of Women*. Cambridge, MA: MIT Press.

van Marle K (2004). *Infants' Understanding of Number: The Relationship Between Discrete and Continuous Quantity*. Doctoral dissertation, Yale University.

van Rooyen S, F Godlee, S Evans, R Smith, and N Black (1998). Effect of blinding and unmasking on the quality of peer review: A randomized trial. *JAMA* 280(3):234-237.

Vistnes JP (1997). Gender differences in days lost from work due to illness. *Industrial and Labor Relations Review* 50(2):304-323.

Vogt C (2006). Women's participation in ICT careers in industrialized nations. In eds. J Eccles and H Watt, *Explaining Gendered Occupational Outcomes*. Washington, DC: American Psychological Association.

Voyer D, S Voyer, and MP Bryden (1995). Magnitude of sex differences in spatial abilities: A meta-analysis and consideration of critical variables. *Psychological Bulletin* 117(2): 250-270.

Waldfogel, J, Y Higuchi, and M Abe (1999). Family leave policies and women's retention after childbirth: Evidence from the United States, Britain, and Japan. *Journal of Population Economics* 12:523-545.

Ward K and L Wolf-Wendel (2004). Fear factor: How safe is it to make time for family? *Academe* 90(6), *http://www.aaup.org/publications/Academe/2004/04nd/04ndward.htm*.

Weinberger CJ (2005). *Is the Science and Engineering Workforce Drawn from the Far Upper Tail of the Math Ability Distribution?* (Working Paper). Institute for Social, Behavioral and Economic Research and Department of Economics, University of California at Santa Barbara.

Weiss EM, G Kemmler, EA Deisenhammer, W Fleischhacker, and M Delazer (2003). Sex differences in cognitive functions. *Personality and Individual Differences* 35(4):863-875.

Wennerås C and A Wold (1997). Nepotism and sexism in peer-review. *Nature* 387:341-343.

Wenzel SA and C Hollenshead (1998). *Former Women Faculty: Reasons for Leaving One Research University*. (ED 465 327). Washington, DC: ERIC Document Service.

Williams J (2005). Are your parental leave policies legal? *The Chronicle of Higher Education*, *http://chronicle.com/jobs/2005/02/2005020701c.htm*.

Williams JC (2006). Long time no see: Why are there still so few women in academic science and engineering. In *Biological, Social, and Organizational Components of Success for Women in Academic Science and Engineering*. Washington, DC: The National Academies Press.

Williams JC (2006). Moving beyond the "Chilly Climate" to a new model for spurring organizational change. In *Biological, Social, and Organizational Components of Success for Women in Science and Engineering*. Washington, DC: The National Academies Press.

Williams JC (2004). Hitting the maternal wall. *Academe* 12(6), *http://www.aaup.org/publications/Academe/2004/04nd/04ndwill.htm*.

Williams JC and HC Cooper (2004). The public policy of motherhood. *Journal of Social Issues* 60(4):849-865.

Williams JC (2000). *Unbending Gender: Why Work and Family Conflict and What to Do About It*. New York, NY: Oxford University Press.

Wilson G, I Sakura-Lemessy, and JP West (1999). Reaching for the top: Racial differences in mobility paths to upper-tier occupations. *Work and Occupations* 26:165-186.

Wilson R (2006). Dartmouth to provide paid leave to graduate students with new children. *The Chronicle of Higher Education* (May 16), *http://chronicle.com/cgi-bin/printable. cgi?article=http://chronicle.com/daily/2006/05/2006051904n.htm.*

Wilson R (2003). Duke and Princeton will spend more to make female professors happy. *The Chronicle of Higher Education* (October 10).

Witelson SF (1991). Neural sexual mosaicism: Sexual differentiation of the human temporo-parietal region for function asymmetry. *Psychoneuroendocrinology* 16(1-3):131-153.

Witelson SF, II Glezer, and DL Kigaar (1995). Women have greater density of neurons in the posterior temporal cortex. *The Journal of Neuroscience* 15(5):3418-3428.

Wolf-Wendel LE, SB Twombly and S Rice (2003) *The Two-body Problem: Dual-Career Couple Hiring Practices in Higher Education.* Baltimore, MD: Johns Hopkins University Press.

Wolf-Wendel LE, SB Twombly, and S Rice (2000). Dual-career couples: Keeping them together. *Journal of Higher Education* 71(3):291-321.

Women in Science and Engineering Leadership Institute. *Advice to the Top: Top 10 Tips for Academic Leaders to Accelerate the Advancement of Women in Science and Engineering.* University of Wisconsin: WISELI, *http://wiseli.engr.wisc.edu/Products/Sex_and_Science.pdf.*

Women in Science and Engineering Leadership Institute. *Training for hiring committees.* University of Wisconsin: WISELI, *http://wiseli.engr.wisc.edu/initiatives/hiring/training_hiring.html#Workshops.*

Xie Y (1996). A demographic approach to studying the process of becoming a scientist/engineer. In *Careers in Science and Technology: An International Perspective.* Washington, DC: National Academy Press.

Xie Y and KA Shaumann (2003). *Women in Science: Career Processes and Outcomes.* Cambridge, MA: Harvard University Press.

Xie Y and KA Shauman (1998). Sex differences in research productivity: New evidence about an old puzzle. *American Sociological Review* 63(6):847-870.

Yoder J (1991). Rethinking tokenism: Looking beyond numbers. *Gender and Society* 5(2): 178-192.

Young R and H Sweeting (2004). Adolescent bullying, relationships, psychological well-being, and gender-atypical behavior: A gender diagnosticity approach. *Sex Roles: A Journal of Research* 50(7/8):525-537.

Zare R (2006). Sex, lies, and Title IX. *Chemical and Engineering News* 84(2):46-49, *http://pubs.acs.org/cen/education/84/8420education.html.*

Zhang L (2004). *Crowd Out or Opt Out: The Changing Landscape of Doctorate Production in American Universities* (Working Paper 63). Ithaca, NY: Cornell Higher Education Research Institute, *http://www.ilr.cornell.edu/cheri/wp/cheri_wp63.pdf.*

Zhou Y and JF Volkwein (2004). Examining the influences on faculty departure intentions: A comparison of tenured versus nontenured faculty at research universities using NSOPF-99. *Research in Higher Education* 45(2):139-176.

Zimmer L (1998). Tokenism and women in the workplace: The limits of gender-neutral theory. *Social Problems* 35(1):64-77.

Index